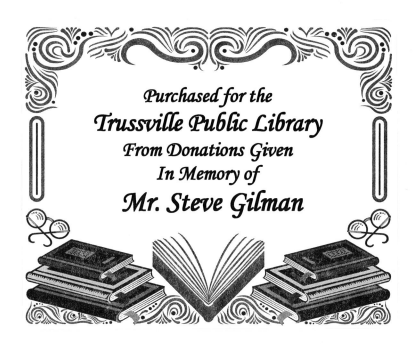

FREEDOM'S
FORGE

FREEDOM'S FORGE

How American Business Produced
Victory in World War II

Arthur Herman

RANDOM HOUSE
NEW YORK

Copyright © 2012 by Arthur Herman

Published in the United States by Random House,
an imprint of The Random House Publishing Group,
a division of Random House, Inc., New York.

RANDOM HOUSE and colophon are registered trademarks
of Random House, Inc.

LIBRARY OF CONGRESS CATALOGING-IN-PUBLICATION DATA
Herman, Arthur
Freedom's forge: how American business produced victory in
World War II / Arthur Herman.
p. cm.
Includes bibliographical references and index.
ISBN 978-1-4000-6964-4
eISBN 978-0-679-60463-1
1. World War, 1939–1945—Economic aspects—United
States.   2. Industrial mobilization—United States—History—
20th century.   3. Industrial management—United States—History—
20th century.   4. Manufacturing industries—Military aspects—United
States—History—20th century.   5. United States—Economic
policy—1933–1945.   I. Title.
HC106.4.H467 2012 940.53'1—dc23 2011040661

Printed in the United States of America on acid-free paper

www.atrandom.com

6 8 9 7

Book design by Christopher M. Zucker

For Beth,
my arsenal of love and strength

PREFACE

THIS IS THE story of America's forgotten heroes of World War II. They didn't wear uniforms, at least not at first. They wore business suits, dungarees and flannel shirts, spectacles and Stetsons, Homburg hats and hard hats, lab coats and welding leathers and patterned head scarves.

They were the American businessmen, engineers, production managers, and workers both male and female who built the most awesome military machine in history: the arsenal of democracy that armed the Allies and defeated the Axis. Together they produced two-thirds of all Allied military equipment used in World War II. That included 86,000 tanks, 2.5 million trucks and a half million jeeps, 286,000 warplanes, 8,800 naval vessels, 5,600 merchant ships, 434 million tons of steel, 2.6 million machine guns, and 41 *billion* rounds of ammunition—not to mention the greatest superbomber of the war, the B-29, and the atomic bomb.

How this remarkable mobilization of American industry, technology, and material production happened remains the great untold story of World War II. This book builds that story around two central figures, William Signius Knudsen and Henry Kaiser. One was a Danish immigrant who worked his way up from the shop floor to become president of General Motors. The other grew up as a problem child in upstate New York before going west to head the most titanic construction cartel in America, the Six Companies, who built Hoover Dam.

Almost forgotten today, their names and faces were emblazoned across the news in wartime America.

At Roosevelt's call, Knudsen left GM in 1940 to spearhead America's rearmament, first as director of the Office of Production Management and then to accept a lieutenant general's commission (the first and only civilian in American history to receive this honor) as head of industrial production for the U.S. Army.

Henry Kaiser became America's most famous shipbuilder and the living symbol of the productive power of the arsenal of democracy with his launching of the Liberty ships. A 1945 Roper poll named Kaiser as the civilian most responsible for winning the war, right after Franklin Roosevelt himself.

Knudsen knew how to make things, especially out of metal. Kaiser knew how to build. They each gathered around them a few chosen businessmen who joined them in starting America's mobilization effort. Many of these men had never been to college; some were school dropouts. None had heard of an MBA. But eventually hundreds, then hundreds of *thousands* of other businesses and companies joined in. Their foes weren't German or Japanese soldiers but Washington politicians and bureaucrats, shrill journalists, military martinets, the denizens of Big Labor as well as Big Government—and sometimes the forces of blind fate.

Many paid a terrible price. American workers in war-related industries in 1942–43 died or were injured in numbers twenty times greater than the American servicemen killed or wounded during those same years. At General Motors alone 189 senior executives died on the job during the war, trying to ensure final American victory.

Most accounts of America in World War II center on the great climactic battles from Midway and Tarawa to D-day and Iwo Jima. The battles American business fought and won came earlier—some a year before the country went to war. Yet they enabled the United States to win those battles to come, and crush the forces of Fascism. In so doing, they transformed America's military into the biggest and most powerful in the world. They also laid the foundations for a postwar prosperity that would extend across three decades until the 1970s and fuel the economic growth of the rest of the planet.

Japanese admiral Yamamoto famously said he feared the attack on America at Pearl Harbor had "awakened a sleeping giant." In fact, it had been aroused to life more than a year before by other events—events that led a man in a wheelchair to pick up the phone and dial a number in Detroit.

CONTENTS

FREEDOM'S FORGE

PROLOGUE

U.S. Army, mid–1930s. *Courtesy National Archives*

> Our opponents are miserable worms. I saw them
> at Munich.
>
> —*Adolf Hitler*

IT WASN'T A DAY to expect catastrophe.

Across Western Europe, May 10, 1940, dawned bright and clear. Then, with a whine accelerating to a scream, swarms of German Stuka dive-bombers swooped out of the skies over Holland and Belgium and unloaded their bombs. The skies turned from blue to white as thousands of parachutes opened and German paratroopers descended to earth to seize key bridges and installations. The supposedly impregnable Fort Eben Emael fell in a matter of hours. Dutch and Belgian troops, stunned into impotence, dropped their rifles and surrendered—beaten by an enemy they barely had time to see, let alone fight.

After seven months of what the French called *la drôle de guerre* and the British the Phony War, the war declared back in September 1939 between Germany and the Allies had finally turned real.

With drill-like precision, German shock troops crossed the Meuse River and grabbed key bridges for a thrust deep into French territory. On May 14 hundreds of German tanks began pouring through the gap at Sedan and into the open countryside. Entire divisions of the French army were cut off. Back at headquarters, generals ordered their troops to hold positions, only to learn that German panzers had already bypassed them.[1]

That same afternoon, French and British Royal Air Force bombers set out to blow up the crucial bridges across the Meuse. German antiaircraft fire and fighters shot down more than half in what was the bloodiest single day in RAF history. Yet the Meuse bridges remained unscathed. That same afternoon, German bombers devastated the ancient Dutch city of Rotterdam, killing a thousand civilians and rendering thousands more homeless. It was the world's first taste of what massed modern bombers could do to a helpless civilian population.

German tank columns, meanwhile, were pressing on toward Paris. Hitler's Blitzkrieg, a mechanized tidal wave of planes, tanks, and armored cars, was sweeping aside everything in its path.

Winston Churchill had been prime minister less than five days when he was awakened at 7 A.M. by a phone call from his French counterpart. "We have been defeated," Paul Reynaud said in English. Churchill rubbed his eyes, but said nothing. Reynaud then repeated, "We are beaten; we have lost the battle."[2] Churchill flew to Paris that day to see what could be salvaged from imminent defeat. But he paused to send a telegram across the Atlantic to the White House and President Franklin D. Roosevelt. It read in part:

> As you are no doubt aware, the scene has darkened swiftly. If necessary, we shall continue the war alone and we are not afraid of that. But I trust you realize, Mr. President, that the voice and the force of the United States may count for nothing if they are withheld too long.[3]

Sitting four thousand miles away, Roosevelt could read the headlines in the *Washington Post:* DOZEN FRENCH CITIES BOMBED. He was also getting private reports from his ambassadors in Paris and London, reports of Allied consternation and confusion, and imminent collapse.

Churchill's telegram seemed to burn a hole in his desk in the Oval Office. "You may have a completely subjugated, Nazified Europe established with astonishing swiftness," it went on, "and the weight may be more than we can bear."[4] If France fell, and then possibly Britain, the entire balance of power in the world would change. The United States would face a hostile continent across the ocean—with a once-mighty British Empire rendered impotent almost everywhere else.

Roosevelt drummed his fingers and thought. For years his political instincts had told him to stay away from what was happening in Europe. He had come into office in 1933 to deal with a domestic crisis, the economic depression left unsolved by Herbert Hoover. Unemployment had stood at 25 percent. Industrial production had fallen by a third; one-half of the nation's wealth had been wiped out. His job had been tackling breadlines, closed factories, and a budget out of balance by $2.5 billion. Dabbling in foreign affairs had seemed a distraction.

In addition, the Democratic Party he headed had been badly burned by European entanglements under Woodrow Wilson. It was led by men disillusioned by the failure of Wilson's promises regarding the First World War, "the war to end all wars," and what had seemed then to be a Carthaginian peace imposed on Germany at Versailles. Having once been determined to save the world, American progressives were now just as determined to turn their backs on it.

Contrary to later myth, the Republican years of the twenties were not the heyday of isolationism. Presidents Harding, Coolidge, and Hoover had remained actively engaged in European affairs. Their representatives attended disarmament conferences, mediated disputes over war reparations, helped to rebuild a broken Germany, and provided famine relief to a starving Soviet Union.

Roosevelt and New Deal Democrats rejected this legacy of engagement. It was a Democratic Congress that passed two Neutrality Acts in 1935 and 1936, prohibiting American companies from selling any war equipment to any belligerent in an armed conflict, and a Democratic president—Franklin Roosevelt—who signed them both.[5]

Roosevelt had also encouraged Senator Gerald Nye (a Republican) and his young legal counsel Alger Hiss in their sensational investigations into the conduct of American armaments manufacturers in the First World War. The Nye Committee blasted companies like DuPont, General Electric, General Motors, Colt Arms, Electric Boat (makers of submarines), Curtiss, Boeing, and Sperry Gyroscope as "merchants of death." It even blamed their "lies, deceit, hypocrisy, greed, and graft" for getting the United States into the war in the first place.[6]

Nye's proposed solution was nationalizing the armaments industry. That didn't happen, but companies like DuPont got the message. The Wilmington, Delaware, firm had supplied America's armed forces with gunpowder since the American Revolution. Now it slashed its munitions-making division to less than 2 percent of operations.[7] Other companies drew the same lesson: Supplying America with arms was business you did *not* want.*

That didn't matter much, because the defense budget was moribund. Cuts President Hoover had imposed on the War and Navy departments with the onset of the Depression became self-sustaining. "Niggardly appropriations for the operation and maintenance of the Navy put naval operations in a veritable straitjacket," one historian would write of those bleak years.[8] Ships were scrapped or mothballed; fleet exercises were curtailed by a lack of fuel and support vessels. Building and fortifying facilities ceased, especially in the western Pacific. The naval base at Pearl Harbor, which was supposed to anchor a chain of fortified

---

* Airplane makers like Curtiss and Boeing and Glenn Martin had little choice. Military contracts were the only way they could survive during the Great Depression. Boeing, however, felt the full force of the government's revenge. In 1934 its leading executives, including Pratt & Whitney founder Fred Rentschler, found themselves banned from the industry for five years—unprecedented for an act of Congress. A disgusted Bill Boeing quit the company he had founded back in 1917 from a barn on the shore of Lake Union. His partner Phil Johnson had to find work manufacturing trucks in Seattle, then moved to Canada to operate the airline that would become Air Canada.

Pacific naval stations stretching from Midway to Guam and the Philippines, became a lonely outpost in a vast and empty sea.

From the fourth-biggest military force in the world in 1918, the United States Army shrank to number eighteen, just ahead of tiny Holland. By 1939 the Army Air Corps, forerunner of the U.S. Air Force, consisted of some seventeen hundred planes, all fighters and trainers, and fewer than 20,000 officers and enlisted men.[9]

In the late thirties, as tensions grew in Europe between the totalitarian powers and the liberal democracies, the United States remained reluctant to break its neutrality and take sides. Roosevelt and his special White House aide Harry Hopkins did not admire men like Hitler and Mussolini; quite the opposite. But their overriding goal was peace in Europe, in order to keep America out of war. If that meant appeasement of Hitler's incessant demands, then so be it. When Roosevelt learned in October 1938 that Neville Chamberlain had handed over a large chunk of Czechoslovakia to the Third Reich, he sent a congratulatory telegram: "Good man."[10]

But soon after the surrender at Munich, Roosevelt's mood began to change. He realized Hitler's thirst for power was not going to be assuaged, ever. This would inevitably mean war, and once again America would find itself one ocean away from a Europe in flames. "If the Rhine frontiers are threatened," he told friends in January 1939, "the rest of the world is too"—including the United States.[11]

So after years of avoiding foreign affairs, Roosevelt began taking small, cautious steps, like a man feeling his way along in the dark.

In 1936 the Washington Naval Treaty, which had sharply limited the future growth of the U.S. Navy in the name of arms control, expired. Roosevelt let it lapse. He then ordered the Navy to launch its first major shipbuilding program in more than twelve years (one of the ships to come out of it was the aircraft carrier USS *Enterprise*). In 1938 the Army Air Corps got the biggest authorization for buying planes in its history.[12] Roosevelt began talking about an American air force on a par with those of Britain, France, and Germany.

The Army and Navy Munitions Board, which decided what kinds of weaponry America would make, became an executive office of the president—a bureaucratic consolidation that showed the commander-in-chief's new interest in military matters. He also authorized the transfer of American capital ships from the Pacific to the Atlantic, the first significant shift in the country's naval dispositions since the close of World War I.

Then when Europe went to war in September 1939, Roosevelt joined forces with Nevada senator Key Pittman to call for a bill modifying the Neutrality Act. Starting in November, the United Kingdom and France were free to purchase munitions from American companies on a "cash-and-carry" basis.

All well and good for Britain and France. But what about munitions for *America*? Reports that summer had it that Hitler's Luftwaffe had reached a combined strength of nearly 8,500 fighters and bombers—most of them advanced types less than three years old. The Army Air Corps had barely a fifth of that number, and most were out of date. When it came to the other ingredients of modern mechanized warfare—tanks, armored cars, antiaircraft guns, and troop-carrying trucks—Americans were even more hopelessly behind.

Brigadier General George Patton learned this when he took charge of the Army's Second Armored Brigade at Fort Benning, Georgia, the summer of 1939. Patton had 325 tanks—at a time when the Germans had more than 2,000—but no reliable nuts and bolts to hold them together. Patton asked the quartermaster for the necessary nuts and bolts; they never reached him. In desperation he ordered them at his own expense from the Sears and Roebuck catalogue.[13]

All of this is hardly surprising, considering that the Army had just six working arsenals for manufacturing weapons. Eighty-five percent of the machinery in those arsenals was over ten years old, and much of it predated the start of the century. Some went back all the way to Gettysburg and Antietam.

Then in August 1939, on the eve of war in Europe, the Army held major war games at Plattsburgh, New York, to find out what it could do. Fifty thousand men were put on the field—but more than two-thirds were part-time National Guardsmen. They quickly lost their direction as units haplessly bumped into each other. Without radios to issue orders, soldiers began wandering in search of officers to give them. Some stumbled on lines of Good Humor trucks parked in a field: The Army had been forced to hire them to serve as decoy tanks because there weren't enough real tanks or armored cars to go around. "The U.S. Army," *Time* magazine said, summing up, "looked like a few nice boys with BB guns."[14]

No wonder, then, that on September 1, when Ambassador to Russia William Bullitt called the White House to say that Germany had invaded Poland, Roosevelt's response was, "God help us all."

Neither the collapse of Poland nineteen days later nor Germany's unleashing of its U-boats to prowl the Atlantic nor the fall of Norway and Denmark in April 1940 had roused the rest of the country to thinking about its own defense. After Poland fell, Roosevelt dared to appoint a War Resources Board of industrial leaders to consider what might be needed if America did have to prepare for a modern war. The board sat for six weeks before public outrage forced him to disband it.[15]

Right up to May 13, 1940, Roosevelt was still unwilling to challenge a Congress, and a vast majority of Americans, who were deeply opposed to getting involved in another shooting war, anywhere and under any circumstances. He began thinking about retirement. Two terms as president were enough, he was telling friends; time to retire to Hyde Park and write his memoirs. In January he told Treasury Secretary Henry Morgenthau he didn't want to run again, "unless things get very, very much worse in Europe."[16]

On May 14 they very much did. Roosevelt realized he had to act.

Less than twenty-four hours after getting Churchill's telegram, Roosevelt summoned Morgenthau and Army Chief of Staff General George Catlett Marshall to his office. For the past months, the pair had been locked in a brutal battle over the Army budget. In 1939 defense spending topped $1 billion for the first time since 1918. The armed forces had grown to 334,000 men from 291,000. Still, Marshall knew that was barely a quarter of the 1.2 million the British and French had mobilized to stop the German invasion—and *they* were losing the war.

All the same, the Treasury secretary wanted another $6 million cut

out of the Army's appropriations for 1940. He was worried about the
United States reaching its debt limit. Marshall was worried about the
United States' survival. He had pleaded and begged to have the money
restored.

Now Roosevelt wanted some answers. What were they finally going
to do about the 1940 Army appropriation?

Morgenthau weighed in again with his arguments about fiscal pru-
dence, hammering again and again on the point of the debt limit. Then
Marshall stood up and said, "Mr. President, can I have three minutes?"

Roosevelt nodded yes.[17]

From Virginia Military Institute to West Point to General Pershing's
staff during the Great War, George Marshall had dedicated his life to
the Army. He was a soft-spoken, taciturn man, known to be smart and
serious but hardly eloquent. Now he gave the speech of his life. France
was about to collapse. Then it might be Britain's turn. The United
States would be facing the Nazi empire alone.

America simply didn't have enough planes, enough soldiers, enough
tanks or artillery or machine guns, he said, to fight a war with Germany.

"If five German divisions landed anywhere on the coast," Marshall
told the president, "they could go anywhere they wished."[18] If, meanwhile, trouble heated up in the Pacific over Japan's ambitions there, the
situation would be even more hopeless.

It was time, Marshall concluded, for the president to get serious
about arming America for war. He had to get together a group of industrialists to draw up a plan for defense preparation and production.
There was not a day to spare. They should be brought to Washington
that same week.

"If you don't do something," Marshall concluded, "and do it right
away, I don't know what's going to happen to the country."[19]

Roosevelt was convinced. Within hours he sent an urgent message
to Congress, asking that the $24 million appropriation for the Army be
expanded to $700 million. He said, "This nation should plan at this
time a program that will provide us with 50,000 military and naval
planes.... I should like to see this nation geared up to the ability to turn
out at least 50,000 planes a year."

The country was stunned. Charles Lindbergh, a key figure in the opposition to getting entangled in Europe and self-appointed guru on all things relating to aviation, dismissed the numbers as "hysterical chatter." Republican leader Senator Vandenberg of Michigan warned that "it would take more than appropriations to make a national defense." The president of the Air Transport Association of America said it was "fooling the people" to raise unrealistic hopes about how many planes could be made and when they could be delivered.[20]

Meanwhile, Secretary Morgenthau called a meeting of American airplane executives at the White House for May 18. He wanted to know what *they* thought they could produce in terms of warplanes, and how many.

Morgenthau's visitors included executives from Glenn Martin of Baltimore and Lockheed of California, as well as Douglas, North American, and Consolidated. They had taken one kick after another from Roosevelt's administration, from stripping away their airmail contracts to divesting them of their civilian airline routes, the so-called big breakup of 1934. With the Depression in full swing, they had only a thin trickle of military orders, fifty or sixty planes at a time; it was all that kept them alive. In 1938 they had barely supplied the Army Air Corps with ninety planes a month.[21] Now the White House was telling them they wanted planes by the thousands.

What kind of planes do you want? they asked. Morgenthau could not tell them. They wanted to know exactly how many were needed and when the delivery date would be. Again the Treasury secretary drew a blank. The executives went home, more confused than ever.[22]

Meanwhile, news from Europe grew steadily worse. On May 20 the Germans reached the Channel. The British army in France was cut off. Unless they were able to retreat to the closest port still not in German hands, Dunkirk, they would have to surrender. Churchill began to plan for a German invasion. Britain's odds of surviving, which Roosevelt had privately set at fifty-fifty, now looked like running to zero.

On the seventeenth, Churchill had drafted one last telegram to Roosevelt. In it he warned the president that if Britain lost the war, it might mean that Germany would seize the Royal Navy, the single greatest armed force in the world. "I could not answer for my successors," he wrote, "who in utter despair and helplessness would have to accommodate themselves to the German will." In other words, Churchill was saying, if Britain lost, Roosevelt would find himself facing a German fleet large enough to patrol in force right off America's Atlantic shore.[23]

A man of many gifts and strengths, on policy matters FDR was a procrastinator. He preferred to put off decisions—or at least to keep news about them from going public—as long as possible, especially the big ones. But on May 23 he sensed his options had run out. He called the one person whose advice in this hour he trusted, the person he believed could figure out a way to get America ready for a war it didn't want and hadn't yet been declared, but which now seemed inevitable.

Bernard Baruch was a wealthy financier and longtime Democratic fund-raiser, and Roosevelt's point man in dealing with Wall Street and big business since the beginning of the New Deal. More relevantly, Baruch had been head of the War Industries Board that had coordinated the effort to arm America during World War I—for which the Nye Committee had ruthlessly raked him over the congressional coals.

But as assistant secretary of the Navy, the young Franklin Roosevelt had watched Baruch pull that war production effort back from the brink of chaos in the summer of 1917 and impose some rational order on a process that had baffled and frustrated both the American military and American business alike. Now Roosevelt wanted Baruch to do it again.

Baruch turned him down. He knew no modesty, and he had anticipated this moment for a long time. Back in March 1939, his friend Winston Churchill had warned him, "War is coming very soon."[24] Baruch had briefed the short-lived War Resources Board on what it had to do to get America's major corporations involved in war production. He had drawn on his experience of securing the right raw materials, organizing the multitude of contracts needed to produce ships, trucks, guns, uniforms, and ammunition, and getting them shipped from points around the country to America's armed forces.

But the sixty-nine-year-old financier sensed that putting it together this time was a task too complicated even for him. In the previous war, Baruch's War Industries Board had managed to build mountains of war materiel. The problem was, almost none of it was ready in time to fight the war. Three million American soldiers had had to fly French air-planes, carry British rifles, and crouch behind British machine guns. Of the 10,000 75mm artillery pieces the War Department ordered, only 143 ever reached the front—and not one American-made tank.[25]

The pressures of time, materials, and distribution had been immense then, when America's economy was strong and growing. They would be far worse now for an American industrial base that had deteriorated for a full decade. In addition, the country needed to build a modern air force as well as a two-ocean navy—and fleets of transport ships to bring it all into action.

Someone else, Baruch told Roosevelt, would have to take charge.

The president wanted to know whom he should call. "Who are the three top industrial production men in the United States right now?" he asked.

"First, Bill Knudsen," Baruch replied. "Second, Bill Knudsen. Third, Bill Knudsen."[26]

When Roosevelt announced his plans for 50,000 planes a year, Hitler branded the number a fantasy. He scoffed, "What is America but beauty queens, millionaires, stupid records, and Hollywood?"[27]

He was about to find out.

CHAPTER ONE

THE GENTLE GIANT

KNUDSEN William S.

GM

1879 – 1948

USA

William S. Knudsen, as he appeared as head of Chevrolet, 1921–22.

My business is making things.
—*William S. Knudsen, May 28, 1940*

ON A FREEZING cold day in early February 1900, the steamer SS *Norge* pulled into New York Harbor.* It was carrying five hundred Norwegian, Swedish, and Danish passengers looking for a new beginning in a new world. One of them stood eagerly on deck. Twenty-year-old Sig-

---

* On June 28, 1904, sailing again from Copenhagen, the *Norge* struck rocks off the coast of Scotland and sank, killing 635 passengers.

nius Wilhelm Poul Knudsen braced his Scotch-plaid scarf tight against the cold and yanked a gray woolen cap more firmly on his head.[1]

William McKinley was president. Theodore Roosevelt, fresh from his triumph at San Juan Hill in the Spanish-American War, was governor of New York. The United States had just signed a treaty for building a canal from the Atlantic to the Pacific—in Nicaragua.

New York City was about to break ground for a subway system. And six cities—Boston, Detroit, Milwaukee, Baltimore, Chicago, and St. Louis—had agreed to form baseball's American League.

Young Knudsen's first sight after passing the Verrazano Narrows was the Statue of Liberty, holding her barely discernible torch high in the fog. Then, as the ship swung past Governors Island, objects loomed out of the icy mist like giants from Norse legend.

They were the office buildings of Lower Manhattan, the first skyscrapers—the nerve centers of America's mightiest companies. Almost half a century later, Knudsen could recall each one.[2]

There was the twenty-nine-story Park Row Building, topped by twin copper-tipped domes and deemed the tallest building in the world. There was the St. Paul Building, completed in 1898, twenty-six stories, or 312 feet from ground floor to roof. There was the New York World Building with its gleaming golden dome. In a couple of years, they would be joined by the Singer Building, rising forty-seven stories; the Woolworth Building at fifty-seven stories; and then, looming above them all, the Standard Oil Building, its 591-foot tower topped by a flaming torch that could be seen for miles at sea—a torch to match that of Lady Liberty herself.

"When you go to Europe," Knudsen liked to say, "they show you something that belonged to King Canute. When you go to America they show you something they are going to build."[3] No king or emperor had built these mighty edifices, the twenty-year-old Danish immigrant told himself. No king or emperor had built this country of America. It was ordinary men like himself, men who worked hard, who built with their minds and hands, and became rich doing it. Signius Wilhelm Poul Knudsen was determined to be one of them.

He was one of ten children, the son of a Copenhagen customs in-spector who had made his meager salary stretch by putting his off-spring to work. Work for Knudsen had begun at age six, pushing a cart of window glass for a glazier around Copenhagen's cobblestone streets. In between jobs, he had squeezed in time for school, and then night courses at the Danish Government Technical School. Bill Knudsen was still a teenager when he became a junior clerk in the firm of Christian Achen, which was in the bicycle import business.[4]

Knudsen's first love was bicycles. With one of Achen's salesmen, he built the very first tandem bicycle in Denmark. In a country with more bicycles than people, he and his friend became minor celebrities. Soon they were doing stints as professional pacers for long-distance bicycle races across Denmark, Sweden, and northern Germany.

But Knudsen had bigger horizons. He knew America was the place where someone skilled with his hands and with a head for things me-chanical could flourish. So he had set off for New York, with his suit-case and thirty dollars stuffed in his pocket. Years later, when newspaper articles described him as arriving as "a penniless immigrant," he would archly protest. "I wasn't penniless," he would proudly say. "I had saved enough to come with thirty dollars."

The *Norge* disgorged its passengers at Castle Garden, the southern tip of Manhattan. Before putting his foot on American soil for the first time, he paused for a moment on the gangplank to gawp at the new world around him.

A voice barked out from behind, "Hurry up, you square-headed Swede!"[5]

From that moment, Bill Knudsen used to tell people, he never stopped hurrying. That is, until he became a living legend of the auto-motive industry—bigger in some ways than Henry Ford.

Knudsen landed a job not very far from where he had disembarked, in the Seabury shipyards in the Bronx's Morris Heights. Ironically per-haps, his first job in America was in the armaments industry. Knudsen found work reaming holes in steel plate for Navy torpedo boats for seventeen and a half cents a day, then graduated to join a gang of Irish riveters as the "bucker-up," the man who held the chunk of steel be-hind the hole as the red-hot rivet was hammered into place.

After a long day at the yards, he would go home by a steam-driven train on the Seventh Avenue Elevated to 152nd Street, where he had a shabby room in a boardinghouse run by a Norwegian immigrant named Harry Hansen. There he would wash away the soot and sweat, then head downtown to the beer gardens along the Bowery or to the saloons on Christopher Street in Greenwich Village, which was still a village. There a nickel bought him a dinner of roast beef, smoked fish, pickles, bread, and sliced onions.[6]

"If I had to start over again," he said many years later, "I would start exactly where I started the last time." But it was sweaty, brutally tough work with brutally tough men. Bill Knudsen was big, almost six foot four. So his landlord was amazed when he came home after his second day in the yards with welts across his face, and an eye that was nearly swollen shut.

"What happened to you?" Hansen wanted to know.

"I got into a fight—with a little fellow," Knudsen muttered. "If I could have got my hands on him, I would have broken his neck. But I couldn't. He just danced around and did this—" He waved his arms around like a boxer, and then pointed to his wounds. "And then did *this*! Where can I learn to do it?"[7]

So Hansen handed him over to a fellow Norwegian named Carlson, who taught boxing at the Manhattan Athletic Club at 125th Street and Eleventh Avenue. There Knudsen strapped on a pair of boxing gloves for the first time. Soon he became so adept at the pugilistic art that he was presiding champ of the shipyards—no small feat—and did amateur bouts at the Manhattan Club and all around New York.

From building ships he graduated to repairing locomotives for the Erie Railroad, and then in 1902 he got the opportunity he had been waiting for. It was a job building bicycles for a firm in Buffalo called Keim Mills. Buffalo was already New York State's fastest growing industrial town, and John R. Keim was a Buffalo jeweler who had bought himself a bicycle factory. Knowing nothing about bicycles, he left the running of it to his shop superintendent, a Connecticut Yankee named William H. Smith.[8]

Knudsen packed his suitcase and boxing gloves and took the train to Buffalo. If he imagined working in a bicycle plant meant making bicycles, however, he was disappointed. With the new century, the business had fallen on hard times and Keim was turning his machines over to other work. Some of it was for an inventor of a steam-powered horseless carriage called the Foster Wagon. Since Knudsen knew about steam engines, he found himself making engines for Foster.[9] In the process, he also learned about machine tools, the machines that made machines, and about toolmaking—and how diagramming out tool-work problems on paper could speed up the manufacturing process.

After his work with machine tools, Knudsen took a course on steel-making at the Lackawanna Steel Company plant, and later he and Smith developed their own steel alloy. Soon he was supervising the making of brake drums for a Lansing, Michigan–based company called Reo Motor Company, run by Ransom E. Olds. Olds had been making his version of the horseless carriage since 1896, but by 1904 he was finding plenty of competition from an upstart entrepreneur operating out of Detroit named Henry Ford.

Smith and Knudsen learned that Ford, who had been in business barely a year, was looking for someone who could make steel axle housings for his cars. They immediately bought train tickets out to Detroit and met Ford himself at his plant on Piquette Avenue. They spoke amid the placid and rhythmic clop of horses' hoofs and carriage wheels from the street outside, and came back with an order worth $75,000—the biggest in Keim's history.[10]

The partnership would grow and prosper at both ends as the infant automobile industry grew. By 1908—the year the first Model T chugged out of the Piquette Avenue factory and entrepreneur Billy Durant founded General Motors—the twenty-nine-year-old Knudsen was general superintendent at Keim and employing fifteen hundred people. Three years later he proudly took a bride, a girl of German descent named Clara Elizabeth Euler. That same year, 1911, Ford was impressed enough with the Keim operation that he bought the whole company outright. Knudsen suggested Ford think about assembling Model T's right there in the Buffalo plant, as well as in Ford's brand-new setup in Highland Park off Detroit's Michigan Avenue.

Knudsen spent weeks arranging the tools and machines on the Keim floor in order to put together the Model T components. He taught his mechanics how to assemble the car in separate stages, from bolting to-

gether the chassis to trimming the body and varnishing. Then one morning Knudsen was stunned to come in and find all the machines idle.

The Keim workers told him they were on strike. They had decided
they didn't like the piecework rates they were being paid on some of
the outside contracts. Knudsen couldn't believe they were so short-
sighted as to break off building the country's fastest-selling automobile
over a minor contract dispute. But the men wouldn't budge. He decided this was a crisis requiring the advice of the owner himself. At
great trouble and expense, Bill Knudsen managed to reach Ford on the
primitive telephone in the Keim office.

Ford listened and said, "That suits me. If the men don't want to
work, get some flatcars and move the machinery to Highland Park."[11]

Three days later it was done. Then Ford ordered Knudsen himself,
William H. Smith, and other key Keim managers out to Michigan.

They were now part of the team running the most famous factory
in the world.

Nineteen hundred and twelve was a crucial moment in the evolution
of Ford's business. His Model T* consisted of nearly four thousand
separate parts. Eight years earlier Walter Flanders, a veteran machinist
who had dropped out of grade school and gone to work at Singer
Sewing Machine, had shown Ford the value of making as many parts
as possible interchangeable. These eliminated the need for custom or
form fitting, which slowed production to a crawl. Flanders also
showed him and his young engineers—Carl Emde, Peter Martin, and
another Danish immigrant named Charlie Sorensen—how to ar-
range their machines in a priority sequence so that tools and parts
were easily accessible.[12]

Flanders had just taught them the rudiments of assembly line production. Ford was lucky to have on hand young engineers like Martin
and Sorensen, men whose idea of fun was breaking the assembly of a
Model T down into eighty-four discrete stages—from forging the

---

* Success did not come easy. The Model T was Ford's *ninth* attempt at producing a
profitable automobile, after Models A, B, C, F, N, R, S, and K all proved relative failures.

crankshaft and drilling out the engine block to stuffing the seat upholstery—then lining them up to form a single process.[13] Highland Park
became the first mass-production assembly line in automotive history.
When Knudsen arrived, they were making a Model T every hour and
a half, at a rate of five hundred a day.

Outsiders treated Highland Park as a manufacturing miracle. People
toured the factory and snapped pictures (Ford sensed that inviting visitors, even other automakers, to see his assembly line would only en-
hance its mystique).[14] Others tried to reproduce its elements, without
success. But when Bill Knudsen arrived, he found the surroundings
looked rather familiar. He realized he and Smith had used the same
techniques at Keim for stamping steel parts for fenders and doors and
for Ransom Olds's brake drum assemblies. Instead of being mystified or
dazzled by Ford's accomplishment, Knudsen set about finding ways to
make it work at a whole new level.

He had learned other things at Keim, especially from its manager
William Smith. He had learned he had a special gift for making something with his hands while visualizing its outcome in his mind—and he
learned the value of practical experience. When Knudsen was trying to
save enough money to get an engineering degree at Cornell University, Smith had told him, "You're a better engineer right now than any
college graduate I have ever seen," and he was right.[15]

When Keim was first contracted to assemble Ford cars, Smith had a
Model T delivered and then he and Knudsen spent the day taking it
apart and putting it back together again. Then Knudsen drove it around
the plant floor—it was the first car he had ever driven—and out the
door. He took Smith home and then drove to his lodging, where he
stayed up half the night studying the transmission and gear system. "By
the time I went to bed," Knudsen later remembered, "I had a good
working knowledge of the Model T."[16]

From Smith he also learned certain economic lessons. Smith made
Knudsen think about a factory as something more than a place for
making things. A factory is a place for wealth creation, his mentor
would tell him, and a place for practicing the dignity of work. There is
something sacred about work, about an honest productive effort that
earns the wages that are the foundation of home and health, education

and security—and the foundation of the America the Danish immigrant had fallen in love with.

Knudsen took to Ford for the same reason. Its owner paid his men a standard five-dollar-a-day wage and looked out for their welfare. But above all, the factory floor at Highland Park offered a fascinating array of problems and challenges, into which he jumped with the same enthusiasm as a conductor with a new orchestra.

"It takes us too long to make cars," Ford told him the first day. "We are beginning to get good materials, but we are not moving ahead as fast as we should. . . . That's what I want you for."[17] Ford and his engineers had figured how the assembly line worked. Knudsen's ultimate feat was to figure out *why* it worked, and how to make it a continuous process.

He started with materials.

"Don't lay anything down if you can help it," Bill Smith used to tell him. "Whatever you put on the floor you have to pick up again. Try to keep things moving until you get them to the shipping room."

Knudsen realized that the key to mass production was not uniformity or even speed. It was creating a continuous linear sequence that allowed every part to be fitted where and when it was needed, while keeping costs down by growing the volume instead of skimping on materials. Knudsen had found the key to the economy of scale underlying all industrial manufacturing. "In other words," as Knudsen liked to explain it, "the less complex parts were, the easier they were to make; the easier to make, the less the cost; the less the cost, the greater the demand." It was a guaranteed formula for success and profit.[18]

Ford had developed his assembly line to make a single product. Knudsen would show him how it could be used to make *any* product, anywhere. He was happy to explain the process in his gruff Danish accent to anyone willing to listen—including later the president of the United States.

"First determine what machinery should be used," he would say. "Next decide where every machine tool is going to be placed."

Then he would spread out a blueprint with the floor layout. "Be sure the flow of materials coincides with the sequence of operations," so there was no wasted motion or unnecessary steps. Finally, once you have your machines and operations and materials all in a row, "be certain all noses are pointed in the right direction," he warned—so there were no bottlenecks and no need to back and fill in order to complete the job.[19]

What other Ford engineers had made seem complicated and mysterious, Knudsen revealed as simplicity itself. Henry Ford caught on at once. He sent Knudsen out to set up Ford production assembly lines around the country, from Buffalo to Los Angeles. By 1916 Ford was operating twenty-eight branch factories, most of them developed by Knudsen.[20] Knudsen also found just the architect he needed for his factory plans in Albert Kahn, a poor immigrant like himself with a positive genius for industrial architecture. Kahn had revealed that gift in 1907 in his factory building for Packard—the nation's first modern factory with great cathedral-like windows that flooded the shop floors with sunlight—and then with Ford's Highland Park plant.

Kahn understood the core elements of the Knudsen formula. "If you wanted to build a factory," Knudsen explained, "the thing to do was to make a layout of your machinery, and the flow of material, and then build a building around it"—instead of the other way around.[21] In all, Kahn would erect more than one thousand plants for Ford. Ford factories sprang up in Chicago, Boston, Indianapolis, St. Louis, Memphis, Atlanta, Portland, Seattle, San Francisco, and Los Angeles. Knudsen would go on to do the same in Europe, while Kahn would even lay out the plans for a plant in the Soviet Union, based on Highland Park.[22]

Together Knudsen and Kahn made the Ford emblem a universal symbol of America's industrial might. When on a chilly January morning in 1941 engineers set to survey the land on the far edge of San Francisco for what would become Henry Kaiser's Richmond shipyards, their one glimpse of civilization was the Ford Motor Company sign rising high above the marshes.

Knudsen was grateful for his opportunities at Ford. They enabled him to build his own home on Moss Avenue in Highland Park and to buy a car for his wife, an all-white Model T with black-rimmed wheels.[23] He enjoyed the constant challenge of new assignments, including building Eagle boats for the Navy during World War I—Knudsen's first experience of contract work for the federal government. In fact, Ford made him head of all the company's wartime production. When the big Dane scrounged up hard-to-find steel for Ford plants during the wartime steel shortage and devised a way to mass-produce Ford's Liberty aircraft engine cylinders, Ford made him his corporate production manager. He raised Knudsen's salary to a robust twenty-five thousand dollars, with a 15 percent annual bonus.[24]

An industry that had produced fewer than 90,000 automobiles in 1910 was now making ten times that number. Two in three were made by Ford.[25] He and Knudsen had triggered a second industrial revolution based on mass production, one that lowered costs by making more, not fewer, of a product—and one that ruthlessly weeded out the old and obsolete to make way for the new.

But there were also problems at Ford. The old man ran his company like a Renaissance court, with partner James Couzens, Henry's son Edsel, production chief Pete Martin, labor relations head Harry Bennett, and Martin's assistant Charles "Cast-Iron Charlie" Sorensen jockeying to be the current favorite. Then there was the paternalism that sometimes chafed. Any employee who wanted to buy his own Model T had to get permission from a Ford company officer. Even getting Ford's famous five-dollar-a-day wage, an employee had to prove he was married and taking good care of his family, or, if single, that he was either the sole support of next of kin or able to "prove his thrifty habits." At one point Ford hired a team of investigators to check up and report on the home life of his employees. Knudsen talked him out of it, and the files were burned.[26]

The fifty-seven-year-old patriarch didn't just believe he knew better than his workers (one reason he later resisted unions so long and so fiercely). He also believed he knew better than his customers. This was the issue that first drove the wedge between Knudsen and Ford.

Nearly a million Model T's were on American roads, and there were more in Ford's lots and showrooms. In 1915 every second car in America was a Model T. Knudsen sensed that with the war's end and the return to peace, Americans' demand for automobiles would soar—as would their demand for a more advanced car than the old Tin Lizzie.

Knudsen had some sketches made for a new car design and showed them to Ford. They could begin production at the River Rouge plant where they had built the Eagle boats, he explained, while finishing up the Model T line at Highland Park before converting over to the new car there.

Ford looked over the drawings. He noted that it was heavier than the Model T and had a gearshift like the more expensive models of his competitors. What color? he asked. The customer would choose, Knudsen said.

Ford digested this. Model T's, after all, came in only one color: black. He asked, "How long will it take you to get into production on this new model?"

"A few months, maybe six."

"How long will it take you to get into production on the Model T?" Meaning at River Rouge.

"Sixty days," Knudsen said.

Ford handed back the sketches. "There's your answer," he said, and walked away.[27]

Ford never mentioned the subject again. Neither did Knudsen. But after he helped Ford through an economic downdraft in 1920, when every division of General Motors except Buick and Cadillac had to lock its gates and Ford had to cut prices from $575 to $440 per car, he began to sense Ford's trust slipping away. Ford saw in Knudsen less of an employee than a rival. Then one day he learned Ford had told some employees to ignore one of Knudsen's directives. Knudsen drafted a simple letter of resignation and dropped it on the desk of Henry's son Edsel.

Early the next morning, Henry Ford marched down to the River Rouge plant. There, amid the sounds of rivet guns and grinders and lathes and the hum and click of conveyor belts,* Ford and Knudsen had their final confrontation.

"Edsel tells me he has a letter from you, saying you are resigning."

---

* Knudsen introduced them to the Ford assembly line, getting the idea from the overhead trolley system used in meatpacking plants—hence the myth that Ford's assembly line was inspired by observing slaughterhouses.

"Yes, Mr. Ford," said the ever courteous Knudsen.

"What's the matter, William?" Ford demanded.

"Well, Mr. Ford, I've thought it over very carefully, and I've made up my mind to quit."

"Now, William, you can't do that," Ford protested. "You're tired, so go away and take a rest. Take two or three months."[28]

But Knudsen didn't want a rest. He wanted out of Ford. The old man stormed out, and although he sent Knudsen's mentor William Smith back to try to dissuade him, Knudsen could not be moved. On April 1, 1921, Knudsen left the Ford Motor Company and his salary of fifty thousand dollars a year—plus the 21 percent bonus. He had almost no savings. Most of his money went to various Detroit charities or to his family back in Denmark. His wife knew their situation was precarious but also knew that tensions with Ford had been steadily mounting. She simply hugged him and said, "Now we can have some peace around this place."[29]

The auto industry was stunned. Knudsen never told Ford why he had decided to leave, but Ford told friends at a dinner party why he had finally decided to accept the resignation of his wizard of production— the man who had propelled Ford sales from $90 million to more than $680 million.

"I woke up one morning to the realization that I was exhausting my energy fighting Mr. Knudsen," he said, "instead of fighting the opposition. Now I can concentrate my energies."[30]

What was Ford's loss, however, was about to become General Motors' opportunity.

News of Knudsen's resignation came as a surprise to everyone. But one man took particular notice. He was Alfred P. Sloan, the new executive vice president of General Motors. Sloan had a hell of a mess on his hands, and wondered if Knudsen might be the man to help out.

Sloan was something of an anomaly in the rough-and-tough world of self-made automobile men. He came from a bookish and genteel family, with a father who owned a successful coffee-roasting company on Hudson Street in New York and a brother who was a professor. But early on, young Alfred became fascinated with machinery. Like Knudsen, he started with bicycles (his one childhood photograph shows him astride a high-wheel 1886 Columbia Light Roadster). He ended with the noisy, oil-smeared but reliably rhythmic workings of the automobile.[31]

His company, Hyatt Roller Bearings, had been bought up by Billy Durant in one of his last great waves of acquisitions for General Motors (another was Dayton Engineering Laboratories, better known later as Delco). Sloan's twin devotion to superior engineering and the bottom line had turned it into one of the smoothest-running companies in the Northeast, and a major supplier of roller bearings to Ford. When Durant asked him in the spring of 1916, "Is Hyatt for sale?" Sloan had been shocked. He had always imagined if anyone made a bid, it would be Ford.[32]

Sloan liked Billy Durant. As Walter Chrysler said, "Billy could charm the birds off the trees." There was no doubt the man also had a gift for the automobile business. It was Durant, not Henry Ford, who first asked himself the crucial question, What if everyone in America wanted an automobile? It was Durant who set himself the task of making that possible. "I look forward to the day when we'll make and sell a million cars a year," he would tell his friends, and meant it.[33]

To make his dream come true, Durant bought up every company connected with making automobiles he could and made them part of General Motors. They ranged from those of Ransom Olds and David Dunbar Buick to Cadillac of Detroit, which Durant bought from founder Henry M. Leland for $4.75 million in cash. He bought Chevrolet, a company founded by strapping, handlebar-mustached Swiss immigrant Louis Chevrolet, who learned to build cars in France and loved to race his own machines, beating the famed Barney Oldfield three times.[34]

Then there was a car-body-making plant in Flint owned by the four Fisher brothers, and another called Pontiac Body, which Durant merged with Oakland Motors. There was also former bicycle enthusiast Albert Champion's company, which made a spark plug that suited Buick's high-speed, high-compression valve-in-head engine so well Durant bought the entire operation and moved it to Flint, where it became AC Spark Plugs. There was a company in Saginaw that made steering wheel mechanisms, called Saginaw Steering Gear. There was even a refrigerator company called Frigidaire.[35]

But while Billy Durant could create, he could not administer. Although GM had a financial department, the boss never paid attention to the numbers it generated. Sitting on GM's Executive Committee, Sloan watched as Durant's foibles and mercurial temper drove out first Walter Chrysler as president ("He banged the door on the way out," Sloan wrote in his autobiography, "and out of that bang came the Chrysler Corporation"), and then William Nash, who, like Chrysler, set up his own company in direct competition with GM.[36]

Twice powerful outside investors had to save General Motors from going under. Then the 1920 economic downdraft that almost swept away Ford, the best-selling automobile company in the world, toppled Durant's awkward conglomerate like a cardboard garage.

In 1919 GM had been selling at one hundred dollars a share. By November 10, 1920, it hit fourteen dollars.[37] In a brutal all-night session, Durant's key investors—bankers from J. P. Morgan and Pierre S. du Pont, scion of the famous munitions firm—negotiated a buyout of Durant, who agreed to quit as president of GM. Du Pont agreed to take his place, and brought Sloan in as his assistant.

The situation was dire. Du Pont and Sloan had to turn the company around in a down market. They did have an inventory they could write off as a tax loss, and enough remaining cash to stay solvent for at least a year. Still, the livelihood of 85,000 workers was at stake—not to mention the portfolios of investors large and small. Alfred Sloan's entire personal fortune was wrapped up in GM stock.[38]

The solution they came up with revolutionized American business. At its heart was a paradox. The best way to make General Motors a single integrated company, they decided, was to give each separate division, from Buick and Chevrolet to Pontiac and Oakland Trucks, as much freedom as possible. Let each division's chief executive produce the products he saw as best suited to his share of the market, and best suited to his factories and engineers and workers. Then keep overall control strictly limited to coordinating the different divisions and making sure everyone was staying profitable.

In effect, Thomas Jefferson had been as right about business as he had been about political constitutions. The best corporate government was the one that governed least. "Decentralization [is] analogous to free enterprise," Sloan later wrote, "Centralization, to regimentation."[39] The best way to run a complex corporation was to have the boss at the top providing only an overall direction and oversight, while turning the entrepreneurial instincts of his top executives loose on the problem of how to produce cars and bring them to market. Meanwhile, the chief executive's job was not to give orders but gather information, in order evaluate the company's overall progress, anticipate problems, smooth out bottlenecks, and, as Bill Knudsen might have said, keep all noses pointed in the right direction.[40]

On New Year's Day, 1922, Sloan presented his plan to the board of GM, which enthusiastically endorsed it.[41] There was only one question. Would it work?

That depended on getting the right man to put the new GM corporate culture to the test. Sloan decided that was Big Bill Knudsen.

Almost as soon as he had finished sorting out the final details of the General Motors reorganization, he picked up the phone. A few days later, Knudsen was in his office. Sloan explained that he had no particular job at GM in mind for Knudsen, but that he needed someone good on his staff—"someone who can help the operating units do a better job. If you would like that job, we would like to have you here."

"All right," Knudsen said.

"How much shall we pay you, Mr. Knudsen?"

"Anything you like," Knudsen replied with a shrug. "I'm not here to set a figure."

"What were you getting at Ford?"

"Fifty thousand dollars a year," came the answer.[42]

So Sloan started him on February 23, 1922, at six thousand dollars a year.

Knudsen didn't care. It wasn't where he started, but where he'd finish, that mattered.

As Sloan soon discovered, Knudsen could make almost anything out of metal. Since leaving Ford, he had already developed his own design of muffler that could be assembled from its simple parts in less than two minutes. He had taken it to the parts department at Chevrolet, where the purchasing agent, Donald O'Keefe, asked him what made it different. Knudsen picked it up and said, "It's strong!" Then he smashed it bodily against the shop floor with a resounding clang. Chevrolet still turned him down.[43] But a more enduring link between the Dane and the company was about to be forged.

Chevrolet was Sloan's problem child. It was GM's lowest-priced, but also least profitable, division. In 1921 Chevrolet had lost more than $8 million—the equivalent of almost $140 million today. Many doubted it would ever turn a profit again. Expert consultants Sloan had brought in argued that the line should simply be shut down. Sloan argued forcefully to Du Pont that this would be a mistake. With better engineering and a new head, Sloan believed Chevrolet could ultimately replace Ford as America's choice for a low-cost, high-quality car. "Forget the reports," Du Pont finally said. "See what we can do."[44] So in March 1922, Sloan turned the troubled company over to Knudsen.

A couple of weeks later, the same Donald O'Keefe was passing through the GM building hall when he spied the familiar figure of Knudsen. "Say," O'Keefe said, "are you still trying to find someone at Chevrolet to buy your muffler?"

Knudsen smiled. "No," he said in a husky half whisper, "I'm now the company vice president."[45]

For some, the twenties were the era of Jazz Age parties, flappers, gangsters, and bathtub gin. For Sloan and Knudsen, it was an era of nine-to ten-hour workdays six days a week, of pouring over piles of balance sheets and inventory lists, long phone calls with suppliers and distributors and short memos to subordinates, as well as painstaking inspections of assembly lines.

Sloan knew if Knudsen could turn Chevrolet around, it would prove his new business philosophy was right. He and Du Pont were now paying the big Dane $50,000 a year on that bet.[46] Knudsen, meanwhile, was determined to show that the continuous assembly line was not a Ford fluke but a way to turn any manufacturing company into a profit winner. "If we work hard," he told Du Pont, "then we'll get some business."[47] He became famous for wearing his hat in his Flint office because he never sat down long enough to take it off. He was always on his feet, throwing on a coat, and hurrying down to the various plants along Chevrolet Avenue to see what was happening—and to make sure his instructions were followed to the last screw, bolt, and casting.

Everyone who dealt with him noted Knudsen was a driven man, but a soft-spoken one. It went back to his days at Keim, where he had earned a reputation for a ferocious temper that, combined with his commanding figure and his skills as a boxer, made him a dangerous man to cross. One day an angry worker tried to do just that. Knudsen came back to the office after leaving the man flat on his face on the shop floor.

His mentor Bill Smith shook his head. "If you're going to fight one," he finally said, "are you going to be ready to fight them all?" Knudsen didn't answer. Then Smith said something that Knudsen never forgot. He said, "From now on you've got to lead, not drive."[48]

It was the last lesson Smith left him, and one of the most important. From that day Knudsen learned to bottle up his rage and lock it away, and deal with his employees, even the most menial, patiently as equals. "I learned when you shout at someone," he once said, "you make him afraid. And when he's afraid, he won't tell you his troubles"—or tell a manager the truth about what on the assembly line wasn't working, or what had gone wrong. An old Ford employee later put it this way. "Mr. Sorensen," he said, meaning Knudsen's rival Cast-Iron Charlie, "was a wild man, Mr. Knudsen a mild man."[49]

Many years later, in wartime Washington, some people would mistake Knudsen's gentle manner for meekness or a lack of conviction. It wasn't, as employees and colleagues at Chevrolet had learned. It was the manner of a man who had learned that the price of being a true leader was self-mastery.

Knudsen kicked things off by breaking the production of Chevrolet into three stages. First came the castings, forgings, and stampings of steel and other materials, he explained to O'Keefe and his other managers. Then came the machining and assembly divided between five principal plants, with engines and major axle subassemblies being completed at Plants No. 2 and 4 and the chassis after 1923 being formed at Fisher Body's new plant across the street. Finally came the finishing, including painting and undercoating.[50] /

To deal with the first stage, Knudsen put all the ordering of Chevy's primary materials—steel, iron, zinc, rubber, copper, and the rest—into O'Keefe's hands, with all orders to be placed six to nine months ahead. At the same time, he left the actual purchasing of those materials to the five principal plant managers, on the theory that they would know best where to buy, and find the best price. To deal with the second stage, Knudsen worked closely with machine tool manufacturers, converting the Chevrolet production line into using as many multipurpose tools as possible, in order to speed up tool ordering but also use floor space more efficiently.[51]

As for the final stage, when Knudsen had first come back to Buffalo to make Model T's, he had taken away every file and hammer in the factory. He now did something similar in the Chevy plants, in order to train his workers to depend upon the machining process to make every part fit. The goal of mass production, as he never tired of explaining, was not to make things faster or to make them all look alike. It was to make them all *work* alike, so that every Chevrolet engine or transmission performed exactly like the previous one. That in turn required an *accuracy* measured down to the hundredth of an inch, which must elude even the most experienced craftsmen—and which only machines could provide.

"Speed produces nothing in manufacturing," Knudsen liked to say—which was one reason he eschewed the complicated time-and-motion studies of production gurus like William Taylor. "Accuracy is the only straight line to great production."[52] Knudsen was moving automobile production out of the workshop mentality and into modern manufacturing.

With Knudsen in charge, Chevrolet made a sharp U-turn. Sales jumped from 72,000 to almost a quarter million cars and trucks in

1922, and the company that had lost $8.6 million when Knudsen stepped in showed a net income of $11.2 million.[53] Pierre S. du Pont smiled, announced to Sloan that he would now be president of GM, and retired to his enormous home in Longwood Gardens to tend his orchids and figs.

The next year, Chevy sales and income jumped again. But there was more to come. In January 1924 two thousand of the company's dealers met at the Palmer House in Chicago. Knudsen was there, and as he walked through the lobby into the ballroom, dealers came up to shake his hand and slap the back of the man who had saved their livelihoods and given their cars a future.

Knudsen made to sit at the head table, but his sales manager, Dick Grant, caught him by the arm.

"Mr. Knudsen," he said, "you just can't sit there and expect me to do all the talking. You're the boss, so you have to say something to these people."

Knudsen had never given a public speech in English in his life. He struggled to his feet before the cheering throng, his mind a complete blank. In desperation he glanced back at Grant. "What do I say to them?" he whispered.

"Whatever you've got in your head," Grant hissed back encouragingly, his hand cupped against the side of his mouth.

Knudsen stared out across the sea of humanity, studded with waiters clearing dishes and the steady updrift of cigar smoke.

Then suddenly he raised both hands over his head, his index fingers extended.

"I vant vun for vun!!" he shouted in his thick Danish accent, and then abruptly sat down.[54]

At first there was a stunned silence. Then those who understood the message whispered it to others, and soon the entire room knew what Knudsen had meant. He wanted one Chevrolet to sell for every Ford Model T. It was the first open challenge by a car company to Ford's sales supremacy, and the dealers loved it. Pandemonium broke loose. They cheered, they stamped their feet, they pounded the tables. Some stood on their chairs as they roared their approval. "Vun for vun" spread through the company and became the new battle cry for Chevrolet.

Dealers, managers, and even workers were sensing that Knudsen was about to push them toward another major breakthrough.

And they were right.

The experts call it "flexible mass production": a manufacturing process that allows for constant modification and change. This was the *second* revolution William Knudsen introduced to the auto industry, after the continuous assembly line he developed at Ford. Flexible mass production was embodied in the idea of the annual model. Billy Durant's consumer-driven car culture was about to become reality.[55]

At first Sloan resisted it. The notion of having to redesign a perfectly fine car every year seemed wildly extravagant, and expensive. "We are all against yearly models," Sloan confessed at the end of July 1925. But he added, "I don't see just what can be done about it."[56]

This was because Knudsen had already started the process with that year's coming model. Even more important, by bringing in the dealers to tell him what customers wanted and how Chevrolet could make a better car, Knudsen had thrust the consumer deep into the production equation. The presumption was that by gratifying consumer preferences, as well as constantly improving engineering performance, GM could sell a new Chevy even to someone who already owned one— and who in turn would come to expect better and bigger changes the next year. The consumer culture's "cult of the newer" was about to spread into the industrial economy—and Sloan wasn't about to stand in the way if the idea also pulled the rest of his General Motors into the black.

Sloan gave the nod. The new Chevrolet would be launched in September 1925, to be available the following year. It's the pattern all auto companies have followed, from that day to this. The 1926 Chevrolet was so much a hit that it slashed the Chevy-to-Model-T sales ratio from thirteen to one to two to one. The goal of "vun for vun" didn't seem so far-fetched after all.[57]

Yet all this would have been moot if Knudsen didn't know how to deliver the goods, by a rapid systematic retooling of the assembly line. "All old machines were discarded," as Knudsen later described, "new heavy type standard machines (not single purpose) were installed, and fixtures strengthened as to withstand the spring, which is the greater factor [in causing inaccuracies] than wear."[58] Now Knudsen could set lower limits on the precision done by his grinders and borers and other tools, which meant less waste and more savings in raw materials.

It also meant his workers and managers could meet changes faster, because their tools were ready to adapt to new engineering demands. Knudsen focused Chevy's satellite plants in Toledo, Detroit, and Bay City, Michigan, on specialty subassemblies and pushed final assembly out to places like St. Louis and Oakland, California, with a branch of Fisher Body at each. In effect, he had turned Sloan's decentralization principle into a way to mobilize the entire division more efficiently.[59]

Knudsen's next car, the 1927 Chevrolet, was an even bigger hit. More than a million cars were sold, and the impact was felt all the way to Dearborn. It was the '27 Chevy that finally forced Henry Ford to abandon the Model T for a new car, the Model A.[60] Eight years earlier Knudsen had told the old man he could make the changeover in under six months. Without Knudsen, Ford was compelled to shut down production for almost a year—a year that gave Knudsen room to spring his next big surprise.

It came when General Motors announced that the new 1929 Chevrolet would sport the first six-cylinder engine for a low-priced car, instead of the usual four. Knudsen and his engineers had been planning out the change almost two years earlier. They had even lengthened the wheel base of the 1928 model by six inches in order to accommodate the future bigger motor. A pilot plant was set up in Saginaw, while Flint continued to make the four-cylinder job. Over September and October, they made almost two hundred of the new engines, before moving every machine tool, jig, and fixture out to Flint—and ordering enough extra to produce six thousand engines a day.[61]

By December Flint was making two thousand a day, and Knudsen could sit back at last, knowing they would be up to speed with the new year. The result was that a couple of weeks after the inauguration of President Herbert Hoover, as customers across the country crowded into showrooms to look at the revolutionary six-cylinder Chevrolet, not one had to wait for the model or the color they wanted.[62]

Few new cars ever quite produced the sensation that the '29 Chevy did, then or afterward. It came in no less than eight different models (from the two-door coupe to the four-door Cabriolet with a rumble seat in the back) and could drive at seventy miles per hour all day—the first low-priced American car to do so. Best of all, thanks to Knudsen's careful economies, it cost no more than the four-cylinder '28 model: $495 for the coupe, and $695 for the standard four-door version.

Knudsen's 1929 Chevrolet was the direct ancestor of the modern automobile. It was also the last to be introduced before the Depression. Its success enabled GM to weather the next several years of economic storms, as the slogan "Vun for vun" became a reality. In 1929 Knudsen could look at sales of an unprecedented 1.3 million cars and trucks; only Ford with his new Model A did better. Ford still held a lead in 1930, the year the Depression first began to bite. But Knudsen's former boss then fell to number two in 1931, and Chevrolet would outsell Ford every year—except for 1935 and 1945—until Ronald Reagan's second term, in 1986.[63]

Knudsen had won. There's a picture of him and a trio of Chevrolet engineers admiring their new model for 1932. For once Knudsen isn't wearing his hat. Instead, he is smiling a smile of quiet satisfaction. He had ample reason to be pleased, not just because the '32 Chevy, except for its lack of automatic transmission and air-conditioning and a V-8 engine, was pretty much the same automobile Americans would be making and driving for the next forty years, but also because Knudsen had built product improvement into the manufacturing process in a way that could go on ad infinitum. It was the bedrock of customer loyalty.

Sloan was blunt about why. "We want to make you dissatisfied with your current car," he told Chevy customers, "so you will buy a new one." But there was a more profound truth underlying flexible mass production. Companies could now change how a product was made—or even introduce a new product—in rapid response to either changing market demands or to new technology, without breaking a single stride. This was true whether they were making cars or radios— or later, tanks, planes, and radar sets.

In 1936 Sloan's GM was selling more cars than it had before the

Depression. In 1937 it was selling more. By giving Knudsen and Chevrolet their lead, he had made General Motors the largest industrial corporation in the world.

Sloan knew he had received another gift. This was Knudsen himself, the quiet gentle giant who had spawned one manufacturing revolution and replaced it with another. Sloan had gotten him cheap for six thousand dollars a year, arguably the best bargain since the original sale of Manhattan Island.

On May 3, 1937, Sloan became chairman of GM and made Bill Knudsen his successor as president. The ceremony described by *The Detroit News* was simple and understated. Knudsen and Sloan shook hands in the directors' room as the cameras flashed. In the background was the president's leather-bound chair, high backed, specially upholstered, austere, and commanding. Then Knudsen sat down—in a regular chair at the foot of the table.[64]

Centralization equals regimentation. Decentralization equals free enterprise. By 1937 the Sloan-Knudsen formula had saved GM. In three years it would have to save the world.

CHAPTER TWO

THE MASTER BUILDER

The Six Companies partners at Hoover Dam, 1935. Henry Kaiser is third from left. Steve Bechtel stands on the extreme left; Harry Morrison is third from right.

> I've been dreaming about what lies ahead for us.
> —*Henry Kaiser, 1930*

BEFORE AMERICANS COULD buy cars, they had to have roads to drive them on. That was where Henry Kaiser came into the picture.

"Picture" is the appropriate word in talking about Henry Kaiser. Born deep in upstate New York in 1882, he grew up with the dream of becoming the Thomas Edison of photography. The image of Edison for most Americans is the one left over from newsreels in the twenties: the white-haired deaf old man who invented the electric lightbulb and the phonograph.

For American boys of an earlier generation, however, there was a different and more daring Edison. This was Edison the lonely child his parents and neighbors had treated as a hopeless dummy. He was the misunderstood boy genius who had risen up, Horatio Alger–like, from his small-town background to create a thousand and one miraculous inventions with nothing more than his own talent, a pencil, and a few bent wires—and grew up to humble every adult who had once dismissed him as a dull problem child.

If being a problem child was proof of genius, Henry Kaiser filled the formula to overflowing.

He was the youngest child of a German immigrant shoemaker, a hardworking precise man who appreciated the virtues of the quiet, orderly life he had made for himself in the village of Whitesboro, New York. Franz Kaiser's exuberant little boy embodied the opposite. When he was hardly more than a toddler, Henry would spend the day hiding under the house and then, when his parents' fears about their missing boy had reached near panic, burst through the front door with whoops of laughter.[1]

At school he was worse. Henry was geared to drive his teachers crazy: restless, hilarious, relentlessly curious, always looking for ways to evade or bend the rules. Today he would be a candidate for Ritalin. Back then thirteen-year-old Henry Kaiser took destiny into his own hands. Many years later, when he was the most widely recognized industrialist in the world and stories circulated about his family being too poor to keep him in school, Kaiser was abruptly frank about what happened. "I thought I was ready to lick the world single-handed," he told an interviewer in 1946, "so I dropped out."[2]

His family wanted him to have an education. Henry Kaiser decided he wanted to make money. He borrowed five dollars from his sister Lizzie and lit out for nearby Utica, where he tramped the streets for three weeks trying to find work, to no avail. When he came back hungry and dirty, Lizzie found him a job as cash boy in the D. R. Wells Dry Goods store.[3] To everyone's surprise the unbridled schoolboy turned out to be a hardworking, reliable employee, and at sixteen Henry volunteered to be Wells's traveling salesman. It was on one of his traveling ventures that Henry Kaiser saw an advertisement from a photography studio looking for an assistant.

He had been fascinated by cameras ever since his parents had given him a pocket Kodak, the very first of George Eastman's low-priced products—the photographic equivalent of the Model T. Soon Henry was dividing his time between his job with Wells and developing photos for a couple of Utica studios, and the Kaiser family saw less and less of their precocious son. When his beloved mother died in 1899, he became still more distant.[4] When he heard that a photographer in Lake Placid named Brownell was looking for someone to take on a share of his studio, Henry Kaiser headed north. In Stephen Brownell he found his first of many business partners, for whom he would make almost as much money as he did for himself. He was all of seventeen.

At the end of a year, Kaiser had done so well he was able to buy out his former boss and refurbish his studio, hanging out a sign that read: "Henry J. Kaiser: the Man with the Smile."[5] When the tourists went south for the winter, Kaiser and his winning grin followed them to Florida, selling tourists rolls of film and then offering to develop their snapshots. At one point he sold a chunk of his Lake Placid studio and used the five thousand dollars to try to establish his own chain of retail camera stores. He spent long, tedious days dashing between one Florida town and another, then snatching sleep on the train, stretched out on the sticky rattan seats while smoke from the engine wafted in through the open windows. "I haven't liked railroads since," Kaiser later said.[6]

The chain never worked. Kaiser became a tour guide at Daytona Beach to make ends meet before heading back to Lake Placid for the last time. At age twenty-three the talented young Mr. Kaiser was a business failure with a dwindling stake in a seasonal photography studio. But he was as charming and popular as ever, and had fallen in love.

Nineteen-year-old Bess Fosburgh was the product of a Boston finishing school and daughter of a wealthy Virginia lumberman. Mr. Fosburgh was wary when the brash young man with little education and fewer prospects asked for his daughter's hand in marriage, but he agreed on three conditions. The first was that Henry Kaiser provide his daughter with a home; the second, that he save $1,000; and the third, that he prove he was earning a minimum of $125 a month.[7]

The astonished Kaiser wanted to know how he was going to do that.

By going out west, Mr. Fosburgh replied. Kaiser was wasting his talents in upstate New York. The Pacific Northwest, he urged, was where a young man could still make his fortune. It was just a matter of figuring out how. Fosburgh offered him the price of a train ticket. Whatever suspicions he may have felt that Fosburgh was simply trying to get rid of him, Henry Kaiser took it.

It was the end of July 1906. Standard Oil was just coming under fire as an illegal monopoly. Congress had passed the Pure Food and Drug Act, and not that far away from Kaiser in Buffalo, Bill Knudsen was setting up America's first acetylene welding plant.[8] Henry Kaiser sold what was left of his photography business and boarded a train headed for the West Coast. Bess returned to West Newton, Massachusetts, to await the fortunes of her fiancé.

As the train rolled along from the hills of Pennsylvania and Ohio across the prairies and Great Plains and up through the snowcapped Rockies, Henry Kaiser must have felt like his previous life was slipping away, as well. At twenty-four he was as much a foreign immigrant as William Knudsen had been when he stood on the deck of the SS *Norge*. Except that instead of stepping into the industrializing Northeast as Knudsen had, with its landscape of smokestacks and mills and machine shops, Kaiser was about to enter the still-trackless wilderness of the American West.

Spokane in those days was a rollicking boom town that had tripled its population in less than a decade to 100,000 people. Silver miners, lumberjacks, apple and wheat farmers, prostitutes, and gamblers mingled and quarreled in the streets—along with every kind of businessman and real estate speculator in between. Yet there was also something about Spokane that would inspire resident Mrs. John Bruce Dodd to launch the movement that would create Father's Day: a yearning for permanence and a hope for improvement, a sense that out of these rough streets a better, more settled life was coming.[9]

Kaiser knew as many people in Spokane as he knew on the face of the moon. His prospective father-in-law knew several owners of saw-mills nearby, but had refused to lift a pen to help. Instead, Henry Kaiser spent fruitless weeks prowling the streets talking to some one hundred local businesses about a job, *any* job, only to have every door slam shut behind him.

Then one day as he stood on the street corner feeling desperate and desolate, he decided to change his tactics. "I decided to pick one fellow I most wanted to work for," he remembered many years later, "and concentrate on him."[10]

The man he chose was James C. McGowan, owner of McGowan Brothers Hardware in the heart of downtown Spokane. McGowan must have wondered what he had done to be so lucky as Henry Kaiser pestered him again and again about work, and each time McGowan said no. A fire had swept through McGowan Brothers, and thousands of dollars of hardware had been ruined. As McGowan bleakly surveyed his insurance documents and wondered what it would cost to get back in business, Kaiser again appeared at his elbow, with that look on his face. Now McGowan was really annoyed. "Don't you see I'm almost ru-ined?" he shouted at the young man with the big smile. "How am I going to hire anyone new?"

"Let me see if I can salvage something from the mess," Kaiser assured him. So McGowan did, and Henry hired a couple dozen local women to clean and polish the fire-damaged goods until they seemed almost new, then sold them. McGowan was impressed enough to hire him as a clerk at seven dollars a week—although, as McGowan remembered later, "he speedily showed at that time that he was not a $7 a week man."[11]

Kaiser was at the store every day before opening, and stayed long past closing. Soon the older, more experienced clerks were asking him the location and prices of goods, and when Kaiser proposed becoming McGowan's outside salesman, the owner was happy to agree. Kaiser turned the warehouse full of rakes, shovels, hammers, screwdrivers, hoses, saws, and barrels of nails and screws into a fountainhead of wealth. He secured major wholesale deals with construction businesses across the Spokane region, including companies in western Montana and southern Idaho. Working twelve- to fifteen-hour days on and off the road began to pay off. He purchased a house on 418 Fourth Avenue, and with a bank account of $1,000 and a salary as McGowan Brothers city sales manager far in excess of what Bess Fosburgh's father had demanded, Henry Kaiser triumphantly took a train back to New York to claim his bride.[12]

It had taken him just ten months to transform his fortunes in Spokane. A year later he and Bess purchased three lots to build an even larger house, with spectacular views of downtown and the Spokane River, at 1115 South Grand Avenue. Henry Kaiser was earning $250 a month—almost $30,000 in today's money—and on the eve of the birth of his first child, Edgar Fosburgh Kaiser, he bought himself a Model T, which he proudly drove around the freshly paved streets of Spokane—little imagining that one day he would be laying down hundreds of miles of roads just like them all across the West.

One day in 1910, a McGowan wholesale customer, Hawkeye Fuel Company, complained that a shaker screen they'd bought for sorting pieces of Sheetrock into different sizes was not working properly. James McGowan loaned them his star salesman to get the screens operating. Henry Kaiser never came back. Instead, he became the star salesman for Hawkeye, whose biggest client, a paving and road contractor, then hired him away at nearly eight thousand dollars a year—more than double what McGowan had been paying him.

Then Kaiser's string ran out. In 1913 he got into a fight with his new employers—he would later claim that they asked him to doctor his sales records, which he refused to do—and a few weeks later he was fired.[13] Henry Kaiser insisted on staying on to finish out four months' worth of unfinished contracts for which he received no pay, but as Christmas came he faced financial ruin. He had a house to pay for, a five-year-old child to feed, very short savings, and no prospects—and just days before Christmas, Bess entered the hospital after giving birth to a stillborn daughter.

To Kaiser the only option was obvious: start his own business. Never again would he submit himself to the vicissitudes of working for some-

one else. Instead, he started his own company in the field that was becoming wildly popular with other would-be entrepreneurs in the West.
He would build highways for motorcars.

The decision was not as strange as it might sound. His last employer
had done road construction, and Henry Kaiser with his quick mind
had mastered the essentials. As more and more Americans were buying Model T's and Packards and cars from Billy Durant's General
Motors, the demand for roads safe enough to drive was becoming
overwhelming, even out West.[14] Municipalities like Spokane and Seattle and Vancouver were desperate for contractors who could give
them suitable highways at the lowest cost.

Kaiser also knew road contracting demanded very little capital out-
lay—one reason it was so popular—and lots of cheap labor. A few
dozen workers, some shovels and wheelbarrows and a couple of horse-
drawn scrapers, and a man could find himself in business as a contractor. But competition was fierce and the profits meager. "Contractors
are all alike," Kaiser used to say, remembering his early days. "They start
out broke, with a wheelbarrow and a piece of hose. Then, suddenly,
they find themselves in the money. Everything's fine. Ten years later
they are back where they started—with one wheelbarrow, a piece of
hose, and broke."[15] Henry J. Kaiser was determined that this would
never happen to him.

Still, he would need some money to get started. He had one key
contact from his earlier job, a Canadian one as it happened. Sir William
McKenzie was a Vancouver banker and a director of the Canadian Bank
of Commerce, and Sir William had let Kaiser know he had been impressed by Kaiser's willingness to complete his outstanding contracts
without pay. Kaiser took the train up to Vancouver and explained to the
banker that the city was looking for a contractor to pave Victoria Avenue. Kaiser had already submitted a bid, and won by being the lowest.
McKenzie nodded his approval.

Now, Kaiser said, all he needed was $25,000 to pay the 10 percent
performance bond (standard in all government road contracts) and to
hire the equipment and men he needed to do the work.

The banker was stunned. "You mean to sit there and inform me, young man, you want me to loan you $25,000 and you don't even have a company?"

Kaiser said yes, that was about the size of it.

"All you have is a contract," McKenzie went on, "and an idea you think might work . . . and you want me, on that sort of basis, to loan you this sum of money?"

Kaiser looked him in the eye and said, "Yes, sir, that's what I'm here for."

McKenzie sat for a moment, grabbed a pad, then wrote out a brief note. "Go down and hand this to the head cashier," was all McKenzie said as he passed it to Kaiser. For a wild moment, Kaiser thought it might be an order to throw the bum out. Instead, it was an authorization for a $25,000 loan—the most important loan Kaiser ever got, he later said. He was now in the road construction business.[16]

Vancouver fell in love with him. Soon he had paved not only Victoria Avenue but other streets and roads. He would take local politicians on tours of earlier jobs in order to persuade them to give him the next one—even when he was not the lowest bidder.

Then Kaiser began chasing the biggest road builder in British Columbia, Warren Brothers of Massachusetts, who had pioneered all-weather bitulithic road paving at the turn of the century—the ancestor of today's asphalt highways. When Kaiser and Robert Warren weren't competing, they were partnering on some of the biggest jobs thrown their way, a strategy Kaiser would use with great skill when he brought his company back to the United States.

Because fate suddenly intervened. The same year the thirty-two-year-old Kaiser set up his construction company, World War I broke out. Thousands of Canadians donned khaki uniforms and sailed for the battlefields of Europe. Suddenly the name "Kaiser" was no longer a business draw, but a positive liability. Reluctantly Henry shifted his business back across the border to his home state of Washington, where virgin tracts of forest and marshland were waiting for someone to punch a road through and open them up to civilization.

There was also another reason for getting back to the States. In 1916 the U.S. Congress passed a landmark highway bill, starting the spread of a national highway system.* Now money would be available in record amounts—not just at the federal but at the state and local levels, to provide thoroughfares for cars and trucks. America was about to become an enormous grid of asphalt and gravel, and Kaiser was poised to lead the way.

Between 1916 and 1921, Kaiser Paving laid some eighty miles of highway roads in Washington State, and almost the same in Oregon. He would go on to build inland canals and tunnels, set up gravel and sand facilities, and transform the face of Washington State and the Pacific Northwest. One job involved cutting no less than one hundred miles of canals across a 44,000-acre tract in northern Oregon, which became the Paradise Irrigation Project.[17]

Photos of Henry Kaiser in those years come from places like Snohomish, Washington, and are usually taken in front of rakes, scrapers, and other machinery, with members of his crew, some in slouch hats and others in bowlers. The famous smile is still there but the chin underneath it is harder, more set and determined. They are portraits of a man who now knows what he wants to do, and how to do it. A man on the move and on the rise, with plans and visions as yet still unfolding.

And his employees sensed it. They had a habit of sticking around, in spite of the hard work and Kaiser's sometimes explosive temper. Alonzo Ordway had been the very first man he hired when he started the company in 1914. Ordway would still be working with him forty years later. Another precious find was Joaquin "Joe" Reis, who started as a timekeeper on a road job in Vancouver and went on to become one of Kaiser's key men in shipbuilding during the Second World War.

Kaiser's restless energy and obsessive commitment to perfection could rankle. Then and later, subordinates would hear doctors warning them to slow down, and watch their family life fall apart under the burden of late night phone calls from the boss and the endless amount of work. They'd quit—then months later they would be back. Life

---

* The very first, U.S. Highway 1, would start in Fort Kent, Maine, and reach all the way down to Florida. Despite the vast growth of the federal interstate highway system since, it's still there.

turned out to be pretty dull when you weren't working for Henry Kaiser.

Yet the biggest bonanza was still waiting for Kaiser and his men, in California.

After the San Francisco earthquake of 1906, the state population grew like a second gold rush. The demand for road construction was desperate. Kaiser got his break—one that would change his life and also the state of California—by luck and accident. Alonzo Ordway had decided, after seven years of nonstop fourteen-hour days, he needed a vacation. He and his wife set out for San Francisco, enjoyed a brief but refreshing holiday, and on their return stopped at a hotel outside Redding, California.

That morning at breakfast, Ordway heard two men in the next booth talking about plans for building a new U.S. Highway connecting Redding and Red Bluff. Ordway casually struck up a conversation, learned the details, and then rushed out of the hotel. In minutes he had a telegram off to Kaiser in Seattle, where he was supervising one of his road contracts. Kaiser phoned him immediately at his hotel. Bess Kaiser remembered they spoke for barely five minutes before her husband ordered "Ord" to meet him in Portland. That contract was going to be his.[18]

In Portland, Ordway gave the rest of the details he had gleaned to his boss, who was more impatient than ever to win that job, no matter what. They looked at the train schedule and then caught the Shasta Limited south for San Francisco, planning to get off at Redding.

As they chugged through the mountain scenery, Ordway asked when the train stopped in Redding. "It doesn't," the conductor told him; "we don't make any stops on that part of the line." The Shasta Limited just slowed enough at Cottonwood, three miles outside Redding, for the engineer to pick up his orders on a mail pole, then set off again for points south.

Ordway broke the news to his boss. Kaiser was unfazed. "Then we'll jump," he said. Ordway stared unbelieving as the portly Kaiser grabbed his briefcase and headed for the end of the car.

Sure enough, the train began to slow as they drew near Cottonwood. "He let go near the little Cottonwood station house and tumbled head over heels," Ordway later remembered, "and skidded headfirst into a pile of railroad ties. When I jumped I rolled over my suitcase and came to a stop right in front of the station door."

Ordway dashed over to his boss, who was still lying on the ground. "I had to find out if he had broken his neck," he said. But Kaiser was all right, only a little bruised and scraped. Ordway helped him to his feet as the Shasta Limited vanished out of sight.

"I've ruined my brand-new suit," Ordway exclaimed with disgust. Kaiser laughed as the pair brushed themselves off.

The station door opened and the stationmaster stepped out. He gazed at the pair and shook his head. "You damned fools," he said.

But Kaiser and Ordway made their meeting in Redding. Although they looked a sight with their torn, dirt-covered suits and bleeding palms, they landed the job—$527,000 worth, the biggest in Kaiser's history up to that time. From that point on, Kaiser and California would be joined at the hip. Neither would ever be the same again.[19]

The California years consolidated Kaiser's pattern of success, so much so that by 1923 he had moved his entire operation down to Oakland. In two years he built more roads than in his five years in Washington put together. Those were also the years that he perfected the business practices and strategies that would become the hallmark of the Kaiser way of doing things.

Kaiser had learned to examine a bid from every conceivable angle before committing his company, and once a contract was drawn up, he insisted on checking out the construction site in person. From his earliest days in Vancouver, Kaiser had a general's gift for assessing and judging terrain. He could tell almost at a glance how long it would take to cut a road along a deer track or through a forest, and how many men it would require.

That number turned out to be fewer than other contractors, because Kaiser got everything he could get out of his team, and not just in terms of work. Employees dubbed him "the suction pump," one of them would remember, "because he would extract every bit of information anyone had." That information had to be accurate, because Kaiser was constantly checking and double-checking figures and estimates and inventories. "He wouldn't get angry if he found you in error, but he would sure correct you." And if he ever found an employee trying to deceive him or lie to him, "he would really raise holy hell."[20]

Kaiser felt free to drive his men hard because they knew he drove himself almost as hard. A twelve- to fifteen-hour day was usual: examining plans, surveying maps and the terrain itself to find the best and quickest route, and then spending his evening planning and assigning teams of workers for the morning. Very often all four Kaisers—father, mother, and the two boys, Edgar and Henry Jr., born in 1917—spent nights on the job sleeping in their automobile, while workers pitched tents and cooked supper around them.[21]

When Kaiser won a major $19 million contract for highway building on the island of Cuba in 1927, he found an even more valuable employee. Fresh from engineering school, he was a medium-sized, rather jowly young man named Clay Bedford, whose father had worked for Kaiser in California and who came with Kaiser to find ways to cut major roads through miles of untracked, undrainable jungle.[22] Kaiser liked the boy's attitude and aptitude, and although Bedford was only twenty-five and there were plenty of more senior engineers on the project, Kaiser put him in charge of the entire operation. Bedford learned fast and brought everything to completion a full year ahead of schedule. He would become one of the inner circle of young men who, as the saying went, "keep the promises Kaiser makes."

Kaiser also taught his inner circle his surprisingly oblique management style. You learned never to say "do this" and "do that," Bedford recalled. "What you do is to ask the kind of questions that will draw the response you want," he told an interviewer, "and once you get that response you say, 'That's a great idea,' never indicating that you planted the idea" in the first place.[23]

Kaiser's other secret was his willingness to look for any technical advance that might make his work easier and cheaper. He was the first contractor to attach rubber tires to the wheels of his company's wheelbarrows—grateful workmen called it the greatest invention since the paycheck. He was one of the first to use tractors that the Caterpillar Company fitted specially for road work by putting a plow blade on the front end. Kaiser would make the name "Caterpillar" synonymous with heavy construction, as he would diesel trucks, which he preferred to gasoline ones because the fuel was cheaper: a dollar a day compared to a dollar an hour for gasoline. Kaiser tried for years to get Caterpillar to install diesel engines on their tractors, but they held out. So Kaiser told Ord Ordway, "All right, I'll buy 'em, but I won't use their damn engines." Instead, as each new Caterpillar was delivered, Henry Kaiser ordered the old engine ripped out and a new diesel one put in its place.[24]

Kaiser was also taken with a contraption made by an inventor named Le Tourneau, which could scoop almost ten cubic yards of earth in a minute. Le Tourneau dubbed it his "earth mover." Kaiser saw at once how it could transform road construction, and ordered a dozen. The earthmover, like the Caterpillar tractor, became another signature piece of equipment at Kaiser sites, along with dump trucks from Kaiser's favorite truck maker: Mack of Cleveland, Ohio.

The last and most essential secret of Kaiser's business was his immense skill in building close relations with local, state, and eventually federal officials. As government dollars poured into road construction, Kaiser was quick to move as close as he could get to the stream's headwaters. His bustling, rotund figure became a familiar sight in the state capitol buildings in Portland and Sacramento. It was Kaiser who lobbied the California legislature to pass a tax on gasoline to help pay for new roads—the first such tax in the nation.[25]

Then and later, Kaiser never could understand businessmen who shunned dealing with the government. He quickly discovered that government contracts were often also the longest running. Later, as the Depression took hold, they offered a security for him and his employees that private contracts no longer could—and state governments wouldn't default on their obligations in the middle of a project. He also grasped that government officials—local, state, or federal—all needed to get certain things done in order to please their constituents, whether it was building a road or a bridge (to complete his highway through swamp-infested Cuba, Kaiser and Clay Bedford built no fewer than five hundred bridges) or, later, dams and ships and planes.

"You've got to help them get these things," he told an audience of business executives at the National Press Club during the war, "you've got to come to Washington and say, 'Here is a way. Now I know this [will work], see if I'm right,' and if he thinks you're right he's tickled to death you came."[26]

One of those happy clients was the government of Cuba. When Bedford and the rest of the Kaiser team returned to the United States in 1930, they had finished their road work a year ahead of schedule—and with a net profit of $2.1 million. Meanwhile, Kaiser Construction had been building roads and dams in California, levees along the Mississippi, and pipeline operations throughout the Far West. At age forty-seven, and even as the Depression was beginning to bite, Henry Kaiser was becoming one of the legends of modern construction.

Yet his biggest success was still to come: Hoover Dam.

Since the time of William McKinley's presidency, engineers and federal officials had thought about building a dam on the Colorado River. It took, however, almost thirty years of political wrangling with the legislatures of seven states before they had finally narrowed its location down to a site in Black Canyon, thirty miles south of what was then the tiny town of Las Vegas, Nevada.

The potential of such a dam was tremendous: not only for controlling and directing the floodwaters of the Colorado, one of the most violent and unpredictable rivers in the world, but for generating what engineers estimated would be more than twice the hydroelectricity of Niagara.[27]

Construction requirements of a dam this size rose to the unimaginable. It would take 4.5 million cubic yards of concrete and 19 million pounds of reinforcing steel—enough to build 575 USS *Arizona*-class battleships—in order to hold back a reservoir of water with a 550-mile shoreline. Thousands of tons of loose rock would have to be scraped from the canyon's surface before massive tunnels could be dug to divert the Colorado's waters into the great reservoir. The federal government was so wary about the costs—including the human cost of risking the lives of the thousands of workers in such a hazardous process in the middle of nowhere—that it demanded up front a $5 million performance bond (the equivalent of $48 million in today's money) for any company that wanted to submit a bid.

Kaiser first got wind of what was up when he was in Cuba. "I lay awake nights in a sweltering tent thinking about it over and over," he later said.[28] Still, $5 million was more money than Kaiser had. If he partnered with a couple of other western construction firms, he realized, it might be a different story.

So began one of the most important partnerships in the history of business, and one of the most vital of the Second World War. The first man Kaiser approached was Warren Bechtel, a Kansas farmer's son and former railway hand who had been putting up buildings and roads around San Francisco since before the great earthquake. Kaiser had first met the tall, beefy man in a slouch hat and a battered three-piece on the Redding–Red Bluff highway contract in 1921. The advantage of working with "Dad" Bechtel was not only that you got a man of vast experience whose word was his bond (Bechtel hated signing papers; if you couldn't trust a man on a handshake, he argued, you shouldn't be doing business with him in the first place) but his three capable and hard-as-iron sons, as well: Steve, Kenneth, and Warren Jr.[29]

Kaiser went to see "Dad" with his idea for pooling a bid, and Bechtel enthusiastically signed on. He spoke to his old partners the Warren brothers, who agreed to put up half a million dollars. Then Kaiser and Bechtel learned two other veteran Bay Area construction contractors, Harry Morrison and his partner Morris Knudsen (no relation to General Motors' William Knudsen), were planning the same thing.[30] Morrison had already approached Edmund and Bill Wattis, brothers who had come out west as teenagers to work on laying tracks for the Great Northern railroad, and who owned the biggest construction firm in Utah. Another outfit, run by a tough Irishman named Charlie Shea, who smoked foul-smelling stogies and dressed like one of his workmen, had already signed on with Morrison. Now he became partners with Kaiser, Bechtel, and the rest.

Then they approached San Francisco's most distinguished building firm, MacDonald and Kahn. Felix Kahn was a shrewd, urbane German Jewish immigrant who also happened to be the brother of Big Bill Knudsen's good friend Albert Kahn, the world's most famous industrial architect. Together with his brilliant, mercurial partner, Alan MacDonald, Kahn had made a fortune constructing some of the city's most famous landmarks, such as the Mark Hopkins Hotel on Telegraph Hill, as well as $75 million worth of buildings, storm drains, sewers, and industrial plants.[31]

Felix Kahn had already been thinking of making a bid on the big dam when Harry Morrison walked into his office with their proposition. Kahn offered to put up $1 million. Years later someone wondered if some of the roughneck group didn't want him there because he was a Jew.

Kahn laughed. "Why, once I put up a million dollars," he said, "it's amazing how fast I became one of the family."[32]

So Henry Kaiser had his bond and his merry band. They would call themselves the Six Companies, although over time that number would fluctuate as new opportunities arose and new partners stepped in and old ones bowed out. The men who led it formed a personal as well as a professional bond. All of them had come west as young men in search of adventure as well as money. Most had left school early to do manual labor. Only Kahn and MacDonald had ever been to college, and MacDonald had been such a misfit that he was fired from fifteen different jobs before finding a man like Kahn, who recognized the genius behind the eccentricity.

The men's talents also complemented one another perfectly. Shea had spent years doing water and tunnel work, and understood the challenge of big-scale hydraulics. Felix Kahn's fine suits and elegant manners made him the king of the boardroom, while Dad Bechtel could ride herd on a construction site like an Oregon Trail wagon master. Morry Knudsen knew mules and horses: They were going to need those to get first men, then equipment and supplies, out to remote Black Canyon.[33] Utah Construction's Marriner Eccles had a keen grasp of the numbers side of the equation. And Morrison-Knudsen had the best engineer in the business, Frank Crowe, who would go on to design not only Hoover but Shasta Dam, as well.

As for Henry Kaiser, he understood the political players and forces involved in a big government contract, so it was not surprising that once the Interior Department accepted the Six Companies' bid, the others immediately chose Kaiser as their point man in dealing with Washington, DC.

It was an inspired decision. Not only would the Six Companies end up having to combat all the forces of nature in order to build their dam, they also had to fight the leading lights of the New Deal.

The Six Companies won their bid on March 4, 1931, and immediately set out to survey the site in person. They found a barren wilderness on the edge of the desert, where daytime temperatures soared to 120 degrees in summer, which lasted from May to late September, and plunged to 20 degrees in winter. Laborers would spend nearly a year living in tents and fighting heatstroke, dust storms, falling rocks (so much a problem that the Six Companies ordered thousands of steel helmets for safety, making Hoover Dam the nation's first big "hard hat" construction job), poisonous snakes and Gila monsters, and a constant lack of clean water, until Kaiser and his colleagues managed to build a permanent site to house their workers (which became Boulder City).

When work was done, they squandered their hard-won paychecks in the flyblown bars, brothels, and gambling dens that soon sprang up in nearby Las Vegas.* Radical union organizers from the International Workers of the World, or IWW, turned up to agitate and generate strikes. The worst broke out in the high-summer heat of August 1931, leading to violent clashes with Kaiser-Bechtel security men.

The men who worked seven days a week, ten hours a day on Hoover Dam, however, proved union-resistant. The Great Depression was in full tide, with national income nearly half what it was in 1929 and unemployment at 24 percent. Although ninety-six men would die in accidents and cave-ins, the thousands who worked on the dam were grateful for a job at a competitive wage when tens of thousands of others were on relief. Later one of them expressed their feelings in a poem:

> *Abe Lincoln freed the Negroes,*
> *And old Nero he burned Rome,*

---

* Urban legend has it that the Mafia and George "Bugsy" Siegel were the creators of Las Vegas. They weren't. It was Henry Kaiser and the workers of Boulder Dam.

But the Big Six helped depression
When they gave the stiff a home.[34]

Kaiser missed most of the physical drama of Hoover Dam, although one of the times he went out in the full blast of summer, Dad Bechtel caught him in his arms when he keeled over from heatstroke. Instead, Henry spent much of those three years in Washington, venturing out from his suite at the Shoreham Hotel to flatter and ease tensions with the man overseeing the entire Boulder Dam operation, Secretary of the Interior Harold Ickes—"the Old Curmudgeon," as he was known.

Ickes was a true believer in Franklin Roosevelt's New Deal, a rock-ribbed progressive who wanted Boulder Dam (as it was soon renamed) to be a showcase of enlightened labor relations. In the middle of the Depression, Ickes wanted the Six Companies to hire as many unemployed men as possible. Kaiser had to point out they needed men with genuine skills, not just people willing to turn up for a paycheck. Ickes wanted the door open to union organizing; Kaiser persuaded him the best route to happy workers was paying them well, not giving them a union card. In addition, Ickes wanted every federal safety regulation to be rigorously enforced; Kaiser patiently showed him that doing so would mean the dam would never be finished on time, let alone on budget.[35] The progressive Interior secretary was also deeply suspicious of all capitalist enterprise, and he constantly accused the Six Companies and their subcontractors of trying to cheat the government. At one point Ickes drew up a list of no fewer than 70,000 separate violations of the letter of the contract, and considered imposing a $300,000 fine.

Kaiser struck back—not by confronting Ickes directly but by having a pamphlet with color illustrations drawn up, called "So Hoover Was Built," celebrating the heroic achievements of the Six Companies and its engineers and employees, which Kaiser intended to mail en masse to congressmen and members of the media.

A week before the pamphlet was supposed to go out, Kaiser dropped a copy off on Ickes's desk. The prickly Interior secretary saw he was about to lose a massive public relations battle, and backed down. The fine was reduced to $100,000, and when the dam was finally finished

Ickes wrote Kaiser a grudgingly conciliatory letter. "Your company has made a remarkable engineering record," it read. "I have been very impressed with the fair attitude of you and other officials, which resulted in a satisfactory working relationship."[36] The two men remained friends until Ickes's death, and Henry Kaiser had learned another valuable lesson. It paid to stay close to government officials, even the hostile ones. In exchange for loyalty, he had discovered, they would offer loyalty in return. /

On July 26, 1935, the dam was all but done. The last of the racks for catching trash as it flowed through the intake towers was in place, and the water began rushing in, lapping at the dam's concrete foundations. On September 30 came the ribbon-cutting ceremony, with President Roosevelt himself presiding while Harry Morrison, Charlie Shea, Felix Kahn, Steve Bechtel, and others of the Six Companies team sat with senators, congressmen, Secretary Ickes, and Roosevelt aide Harry Hopkins. Behind the reviewing stand rose a dam more than 700 feet high and 660 feet wide at its base—with a reservoir 110 miles long and the foundations for a 1.2-million-horsepower plant that would generate enough electricity to illuminate seven states. The epic work had all been done ahead of schedule and under budget by some $4 million.[37]

"This morning I came, I saw, and I was conquered as everyone will be who sees for the first time this great feat of mankind," Roosevelt said as the sunlight glinted off the mammoth lake where once there had been only cactus and desert. "This is an engineering victory of the first order," he concluded, "another great achievement of American resourcefulness, skill, and determination." Roosevelt then looked into the face of his audience. "That is why I have the right once more to congratulate you who have created Boulder Dam and on behalf of the nation to say to you, 'Well done.'"[38]

"Before you work yourself out of the last job," Henry Kaiser used to say, "line up a bigger one to pull yourself out." Kaiser had skipped the ceremony out in Nevada. He was back in Oakland, already working on the next big project for the Six Companies, a dam on the Columbia River at Bonneville in Oregon. He and his partners had already submitted their bids. When his son Edgar and thirty-year-old Clay Bedford had finished supervising the work at Bonneville in the spring of

1937, they would be ready to move on to Grand Coulee, which would become the biggest concrete structure in the world.

The building of Boulder Dam had changed Kaiser's company, and changed Kaiser. He had honed his management team to a level of perfection unknown anywhere else in the industry. The sense that they could do anything anywhere was now a given. He had also added another twist. As his workers swarmed to work on the high dam at Grand Coulee, Kaiser had Edgar and Clay Bedford's sections divided into two competitive teams, to see who could complete the work faster and more under budget. Late in life Bedford would claim they first tried out this technique in Cuba. Either way, it would become a hallmark of the Kaiser way of doing things. Bedford and Edgar would use it to raise production to stunning heights in America's dark days after Pearl Harbor.[39]

Kaiser also learned that taking care of business meant taking care of employees. Higher pay and good working conditions, including housing, kept not only the unions but federal government inspectors at bay. At Grand Coulee, Kaiser added one more element. It came at the suggestion of Dr. Sidney Garfield, the on-site physician Kaiser hired to oversee the health of his workers. Garfield suggested setting aside part of the employees' paychecks to provide health insurance in case of injury or illness, which would also extend to their families. Kaiser enthusiastically agreed, and the result was the creation of the Kaiser Health Plan—the biggest and most successful private health insurance plan ever established by a private business, which is still up and running today.

"If you spent as much time on your labor as your sales," he once advised an audience at a business meeting in Washington, "you wouldn't have any problems"—not just with getting the best workers and raising productivity, he might have added, but also in cultivating a good public image. The man who had started developing photographs knew the importance of public image, especially in dealing with the federal government.[40]

As for Kaiser himself, Boulder made him more than just a regional titan, the symbol of a growing California and Pacific West. He was now a national figure, and a committed Roosevelt Democrat. While other businessmen turned their backs on the New Deal, hoping it would go away, Kaiser guessed that Roosevelt and his colleagues were going to be in charge for a very long time. He saw no reason why his opportunities should suffer—indeed, why they should not prosper working with a Washington that wanted a key role in the American economy.

He already had his key contacts and players in place. One was Secretary Ickes. Another was Roosevelt himself, who liked Kaiser's drive and energy and, in Frank Friedel's phrase, "dearly loved a semblance of insubordination."[41] Meanwhile, MacDonald and Kahn's top lawyer, Charles "Chad" Calhoun, had become Kaiser's point man in the capital, as letters, memos, and invitations flowed out from his Washington law office in all directions. Nor did it hurt when Utah Construction's former president and bean counter Marriner Eccles moved to Washington to take a job at Treasury, and rose to become chairman of the Federal Reserve.

That was in 1934. Three years later Kaiser was finishing Bonneville Dam and moving on to Grand Coulee. Yet he was already thinking about what would be his next big adventure.

He could not guess that it would be the biggest in the history of the world.

CHAPTER THREE

THE WORLD OF TOMORROW

Futurama. © *Bettmann/CORBIS*

We can do anything if we do it together.
—William S. Knudsen, 1938

ON APRIL 30, 1939, the World's Fair opened in New York. The General Motors pavilion would be its centerpiece and house its most talked-about exhibit.

The New York World's Fair would be the biggest fair of all time. More than 44 million visitors would eventually come to the 1,262-acre site at Flushing Meadows. They would tour exhibits from across the country and from more than thirty countries—including several that would soon be at war.

The king and queen of England paid a visit to the British pavilion, which had on display a rare copy of Magna Carta. There was a pavilion for the League of Nations, although the unbridled aggression of Germany, Japan, and Italy had reduced that organization to an international joke. The world's biggest pariah, Joseph Stalin, got what everyone agreed was one of the fair's prime spots for the Soviet Union's pavilion, just across from the so-called Court of Peace.

As for Italy, Benito Mussolini spent $5 million on its exhibit, which turned out to be one of the gaudiest. It trumpeted the virtues of Fascism underneath a two-hundred-foot tower that was topped by an enormous statue of the goddess Roma. Imperial Japan was also there, with a pavilion in the shape of a giant Shinto shrine. It harbored a pearl-and-diamond-framed replica of the Liberty Bell, as Japan's ambassador spoke of "the cordial relations existing between the United States and Japan." Despite Japan's unprovoked attack on China just a year earlier, the fair organizers declared June 2 to be official Japan Day.[1]

One important country was missing, however: Nazi Germany. The Führer, a German spokesman explained, had other priorities.

The 1939 World's Fair was supposed to give Americans a window on the world, and epitomize the belief common across the country in the thirties that America's hand of friendship extended to everyone, even Japan and Germany. But it was also a robust exercise in commercial boosterism. After a decade of economic depression and gloom, its organizers hoped the fair would help to revive America's seven million or so businesses. They were still reeling from the second depression in 1937–38, when GNP slid 4.5 percent and unemployment bounced back up to 19 percent. The fair's slogan was "The Dawn of a New Day." If Americans really were ready for a bright new start, all assumed American business would point the way.

Virtually every major corporation had a pavilion to display its wares and coming commercial attractions. There was U.S. Steel and American Tobacco, Borden and American Radiator, Westinghouse and Carrier and Eastman Kodak and American Telephone and Telegraph. DuPont Corporation, once reviled as the "merchant of death," offered the Wonder World of Chemistry. General Electric revealed to the public the first fluorescent lightbulb. Radio Corporation of America offered a television in a monstrous wooden case, with a seven-inch picture tube.[2] In the Aviation Building, shaped like an enormous airplane hangar, Douglas, Boeing, and other companies displayed their latest flying marvels.

There was not a single warplane among them.

At the far end of Flushing Meadows Park, farthest from the Court of Peace and across the Grand Central Parkway, stood the pavilions belonging to America's largest industry and the Big Three automobile companies. Chrysler's, the smallest, was wedged behind the sprawling Ford pavilion designed by Albert Kahn. And looming over both was a long sleek red and silver Art Deco building topped by silver-on-silver letters: GENERAL MOTORS.[3]

The fair's opening day was a blazing hot Sunday, and Bill Knudsen was there. He stood tall and white-haired in the sunshine, a little heavier than when he was running Chevrolet but still strong and erect for a busy executive of sixty. After speeches by President Roosevelt and by Albert Einstein, who explained to the somewhat baffled crowd the concept of cosmic rays, visitors fanned out in all directions to stare at the immense spectacle of the World of Tomorrow, as the organizers dubbed it.

It had been an eventful two years since the Danish immigrant had taken over the company. General Motors now manufactured 45 percent of all cars sold in the United States, with Chevrolet alone outselling all the divisions of Chrysler—Plymouth, Dodge, and DeSoto plus Chrysler itself—and ranking number one in both passenger and commercial for two years in a row. Since 1931 Chevy had ranked number one every year except one.[4] In less than a year he and Alfred Sloan would meet to watch GM's twenty-five millionth car roll off the assembly line.

The year Knudsen had taken over, 1937, had also been the year of a punishing and ugly labor dispute with the United Auto Workers. For four months GM's plants in Flint were shut as police battled strikers while demonstrators threw rocks and bricks at tear-gas-firing cops. Knudsen had handled the day-to-day negotiations with the UAW himself, finally persuading his colleagues to yield to the union's key demands in order to get the men back to work. What struck UAW attorney Lee Pressman most, however, was not Knudsen's understated negotiating manner, or the fact that he was the one GM executive who seemed anxious to end the strike.

It was how the sight of his beloved machines sitting idle and silent gave Knudsen almost physical pain.[5]

Then, in March 1939, Detroit hosted a huge civic celebration for Knudsen's sixtieth birthday, with a banquet at the Detroit Club attended by politicians and businessmen, including his old boss Henry Ford. "Whatever I've done," Knudsen told the crowd, "whatever I've got, is due to the men who helped me. I don't know how I can ever repay for the happiness I have had." Ford expressed his regret he had ever let Knudsen go. "He was too big a man for me," he confessed to friends. "There wasn't room for both him and me at the company."[6] They shook hands, the old bitterness forgotten. For the first time in years, Knudsen knew peace in the industry and on the shop floor.

Yet in his heart Knudsen was troubled. He had been on an inspection tour of GM's European plants in the fall of 1938, and heard on the radio how Neville Chamberlain announced peace for our time. He had met the heads of Germany's air force, Hermann Goering and Ernst Udet, and sensed that in the event of war Germany would unleash a military machine unlike any in history—and that GM's plants there would, willy-nilly, be commandeered into the war effort. He could see a shadow fall across his native Denmark and the rest of Europe as bomb shelters and trenches were being dug in London's Hyde Park and children were evacuated from the city—even as Americans were listening to *Amos 'n' Andy* on the radio and ignoring what was happening to the world beyond their borders.

Knudsen brought home a gas mask as a souvenir. "Thank God we don't have to be quite so scared here," he told an interviewer, "but I think one good way [to avoid trouble] is to be prepared for trouble." Privately he worried Americans were not.[7]

Knudsen slowly walked through the passageway leading into the GM building like a cleft carved from a cliff, then up the gentle slope of one of the two serpentine ramps and past two enormous letters in red and silver: *G* and *M*. "The conception," wrote *Architectural Record*, describing the building, "was one of immense power."[8]

Waiting inside for him was his old boss and now chairman of General Motors Alfred Sloan, looking more anorexic than ever but with a smile of anticipation. He had assembled more than a thousand special guests for the unveiling of GM's pièce de résistance, what would become the most famous exhibit of the entire fair: Futurama.[9]

Of course, there were other things to see in the cavernous GM pavilion. There were displays of the company's latest developments in automobile technology, and exhibits showing the wonders of assembly-line mass production. There was even a section where a visitor could order and purchase a new Chevrolet, watch it being assembled in a mock-up of the factory floor, and drive it home that night.[10]

Ford and Chrysler had similar displays. But the Futurama was unique. It was the brainchild of Norman Bel Geddes, America's foremost industrial architect and a former Broadway set designer. He had come up with the idea after working with J. Walter Thompson on an ad campaign featuring a futuristic city built around the automobile. Bel Geddes presented it to GM as the core for its World's Fair exhibit. Knudsen's right-hand man, Dick Grant, turned him down flat. Too expensive, Grant said, shaking his head. The company was planning instead to replicate the assembly line it used in the 1933 Century of Progress exhibition in Chicago, which would cost only $2 million.

"Can General Motors afford to spend two million dollars to admit it hasn't had a new idea in five years?" Bel Geddes blurted back.[11] That convinced Bill Knudsen. He only agreed to Bel Geddes's futuristic city display on condition that it cost no more than the original $2 million they had slated. It was a promise Bel Geddes was never born to keep.

Sloan and Knudsen, like their guests, walked side by side into a sixty-foot-high chamber where Bel Geddes had assembled a vast diorama of more than half a million miniature buildings, one million miniature trees, and some 50,000 toy-sized cars, along with other accessories to give the series of tableaux a sense of visual realism—right down to miniature cow patties. A moving platform gently dropped each visitor into tall, cushioned seats arranged on a conveyor belt one-third of a mile long, while everything went dark.[12]

Knudsen looked up as an enormous map of the United States flashed across the entire wall. A narrator said, "General Motors invites you on a tour of future America. The moving chairs below the map will transport you to 1960."

Then one by one the chairs were whisked along past the series of dioramas as music and narration were piped through the chairs thanks to a system devised by an engineer named James Dunlop and a team from Westinghouse. Called the Polyrhetor, it used seven photoelectric beams to pull out some 147 units of sound from twenty-one separate film sequences, which it then transmitted to two cars at a time in a continuous synchronized audio loop. Nothing like it had ever been created, and nothing like it would appear again until the advent of digital technology in the nineties. Millions of visitors would pass through Futurama, without the sound track ever once falling out of sync.[13]

What those visitors saw was stunning. Bel Geddes had carefully lit his dioramas to appear almost larger than life size, with cities topped by brightly lit skyscrapers (powered, the narrator said, by something called atomic energy), rural landscapes of rich greens and browns with abundant grain and fruit trees stretching to the horizon. Visitors saw sweeping green meadows and amusement parks with endless Ferris wheels and dancing children, and they saw cars.

They saw cars everywhere. The lanes and streets and highways of every scene of the future were full of them, with moving sidewalks in the cities set above the roadway to protect pedestrians, while out in the hinterland great four-lane thoroughfares called "Super-highways" (a term the Futurama would make famous) allowed you to work, shop, and play miles from the city or your neighborhood, the narrator explained, while workers would leave their cramped tenements to live in the lush countryside, each with his snug little house set behind a green lawn.[14]

Finally the train stopped, and the lights came up. The audience sat in stunned silence for a moment. Now they could see the diorama as it really was, with the enormous "skyscrapers" not much taller than a five-year-old child. As they filed out, each was handed a button to wear. It read, "I have seen the future."

And for tens of millions of them and their children, it *was* the future—not just in 1960 but for decades after. It was an American future. It was not as perfect as the one socialists and other utopians were promising, with an end to every human problem from hunger to housing—and not as regimented or disciplined as Fascists and Communists prescribed. There was no room here for the Aryan Superman or the New Soviet Man. It was simply better than they had now; a future built to human needs and comforts, not mighty ideals. To millions of Americans in 1939, that mattered more than some rational radiant order.

In 1940 the Depression would enter its eleventh year. Average per capita income was two-thirds what it had been in 1929. Unemployment hovered just above 16 percent. The future presented by the GM men seemed dazzling, almost unrealizable. Even Knudsen and Sloan were impressed. Afterward they sat alone together in the pavilion's press room. Knudsen murmured something about hoping people realized the dreams they had just seen *were* realizable through mass production and the spirit of free enterprise; "better methods, good wages, low prices, better tools, and plenty of hard work from everybody."

Then Sloan added, "But who knows what the world of 1960 will be like? The real world of tomorrow will outstrip anything we can imagine today."[15]

Later, Knudsen made a broadcast from the World's Fair to his native land: "May God give continued peace to [Denmark] and her children, and may He also continue to give our beloved United States the progressive, go-ahead spirit, the democratic way."[16]

But his hopes for Denmark, at least, were misplaced. The last sentence uttered by the Futurama narrator was, "All eyes on the future." On September 1 the future arrived.

German tanks and planes roared across the Polish border. The next day France declared war on Germany, and on September 3 Great Britain followed suit. The Polish pavilion was declared closed until further notice. Italy's and Japan's, however, remained open, since although both were Germany's Axis allies, both were still officially neutral. The priceless copy of Magna Carta on display in the British pavilion was supposed to go home when the fair closed on October 1. After high-level discussion, however, officials thought it would be safer to let it stay in the United States.*

When the fair reopened on April 30, 1940, the mood was very different. The slogan of "Building the World of Tomorrow" was replaced by a more somber "For Peace and Freedom." The Soviet, Czech, and Polish pavilions were gone. Newspapers were filled with news of French and British troops poised on the Belgian frontier in the event of a German attack. A pipe bomb set at the gate of the British pavilion went off, killing two New York City policemen.

On April 9, German troops had invaded and occupied Denmark. Bill Knudsen would not hear a word from his four sisters for almost six years.[17]

That spring the number of visitor was down, too. The public face of American industry had changed. The Aviation Building sported its first warplanes and pursuit fighters. The GM Futurama now included churches (their absence in 1939 had inspired some trenchant criticism) as well as a university. An exhibit at the Westinghouse pavilion showed the sterilizing effect of an intense flash of light on water drops. Westinghouse dubbed the show "Microblitzkrieg."[18]

For all its expectations, the fair didn't revive American industry. Two weeks after its reopening, other events would do that. They forced Franklin D. Roosevelt to pick up the phone and thrust Bill Knudsen, to his huge surprise, into the national limelight.

* It would be returned after the war, in 1947.

CHAPTER FOUR

GETTING STARTED

Bill Knudsen meets President Roosevelt in the Oval Office, May 30, 1940. © *AP Photo/ George R. Skadding*

> You cannot just order a Navy as you would a
> pound of coffee, or vegetables or meat, and say,
> we'll have that for dinner. It takes time. It takes
> organization.
>
> —*Bernard Baruch*

ON TUESDAY, MAY 28, Knudsen sat in his office in the General Motors Building. The *Detroit Free Press* headline blared, BELGIANS SURRENDER ON KING'S ORDER. Knudsen, however, was looking over long rows of automobile production numbers. The phone rang.

"Mr. Knudsen," said a voice on the other end, "the president of the United States wants to talk to you—here he is."

The resonant voice with its mid-Atlantic drawl, familiar from radio and newsreels, came on the line. "Knudsen? I want to see you in Washington. I want you to work on some production matters. When can you come down?"

Bill already had some idea what was coming. Bernard Baruch had called to give him a heads-up on what he had told Roosevelt. "I think you will be getting a phone call," the elderly financier had said.[1]

Knudsen told Roosevelt he could be in Washington the day after tomorrow. He had to see Alfred Sloan and the GM board in New York first, but they agreed that Knudsen would come to the White House at ten o'clock on Thursday, May 30. The president rang off.

Knudsen sensed that his life was never going to be quite the same again. He had heard the president on the radio on Sunday night, announcing to the country his plans for national defense—what the president termed "readiness." Roosevelt explained how in the past seven years the government had spent almost $1.3 billion on new armaments for the Navy, Army, and Air Corps, including some 5,640 new planes and 1,700 antiaircraft guns. With the worsening international situation, Roosevelt said, there would be need for more—and the government could not do it alone. He told the American people that he was going to ask private industry to help, and intended to call on key men in American business "to help us in carrying out this program."[2]

When Bill Knudsen told his wife and children he was going to be leaving General Motors to help the president with the defense effort, they were stunned. Why? they protested. America wasn't in any war; why would he give up his life at home in order to move to Washington? Besides, they pointed out, Roosevelt was a Democrat and Knudsen a lifelong Republican. His twenty-year-old daughter, Martha, a coed at the University of Michigan, asked the final question. "Why are you leaving to work for this man now?"

Knudsen's answer was simple and direct. "This country has been good to me, and I want to pay it back."[3]

The Dane flew to New York that afternoon, where he had an acri-

monious meeting with General Motors' chairman and his mentor, Alfred Sloan. "War's not coming anytime soon," Sloan predicted. "Your
duty is here with GM."

Knudsen shrugged. "The president of the United States called me,"
he said quietly, "and asked me to come."

"They'll make a monkey out of you down there," Sloan predicted,
who was no fan of Roosevelt or the New Deal. During the punishing
United Auto Workers strike, he had had Labor Secretary Frances Perkins calling him up in the middle of the night screaming that he was a
scoundrel and a skunk for not giving in to the union's demands. "You
don't deserve to be counted among decent men," she had ranted.
"You'll go to hell when you die."[4]

More recently Sloan had watched another GM executive of his,
John Pratt, get called to Washington for service on Roosevelt's ill-fated
War Resources Board. Pratt had done his level best to give advice on
how to coordinate industry with military needs for war materiel. His
reward was being vilified in the left-wing press as a corporate shill,
while New Dealers attacked the entire WRB as a haven of fascistic
"Wall Streeters and economic royalists." Interior Secretary Harold
Ickes denounced the idea of giving business a major role in organizing
for war, calling it an affront to democracy itself.[5] When Roosevelt
rejected the WRB's final report and dismissed the panel, Pratt wrote
Sloan a long account of the ill-starred affair. Sloan sensed that all a
businessman would get in New Deal Washington was a swift kick in
the pants.

"What do they want you to do?" Sloan finally asked.

"I don't know, exactly, what the president has in mind," Knudsen
admitted.

"And still you go?" Sloan asked, incredulous.

Knudsen said yes. There was a full minute of silence. Then a
tight-lipped Sloan said, "Very well," shook Knudsen's extended hand,
and did not look up as Knudsen walked out.[6]

William Knudsen was taken off the General Motors payroll that
same day. His life in the automobile industry, where he had spent the
past thirty years, was over.

Yet the fact remained he *didn't* know what Roosevelt was expecting of him. When he arrived by train at Union Station on Wednesday, May 29, it began to dawn on him that Roosevelt didn't know, either.

He reached the White House shortly before ten o'clock on the thirtieth. That day, across the ocean, French troops were joining the British in the evacuations from Dunkirk.

Knudsen was greeted by a tall, gaunt man with a twisted smile and pointed chin. It was Harry Hopkins, the president's most trusted advisor. One of the original architects of the New Deal, Hopkins had just left his post as commerce secretary to help Roosevelt organize the defense effort. He and Roosevelt had drawn even closer and he was now living in the White House, down the hall from the presidential bedroom. When Hopkins became engaged to be married, FDR had her move in, too.[7] Roosevelt trusted no man more, and no one in 1940 understood the urgency of the task ahead more than Hopkins.

Hopkins had been a pacifist during World War I. Now with France on the verge of collapse and Britain threatened, he was a pacifist no longer. "We cannot go on sitting here and saying that the war is so many miles away," he had told the *Herald Tribune* a few days before. "We must get realistic. . . . Suppose this war lasts two or three years. What effect is that going to have on the economy of this country? This is not a matter of sitting down at the dinner table and talking about it," he added. "I belong to the school that does not talk about things—you *do* something."[8]

Do something. But what? That is what Hopkins and Roosevelt hoped Knudsen could tell them.

Hopkins shook Knudsen's hand, then whispered, "The president has asked me to tell you that we can't pay you anything, and he wants you to get a leave of absence from your company."

"I don't expect any paycheck," Knudsen replied, "and the other matter has been taken care of." Then he was ushered into the Oval Office.[9]

The president's desk was littered with memoranda and statute books opened to pages describing and debating the president's wartime executive powers. Roosevelt and Hopkins, who had been so decisive in intervening in the domestic economy with the New Deal, were still feeling out what powers they had to protect America from potential adversaries.

Franklin Roosevelt stuck out his hand with his famous grin, his trademark cigarette holder tilting up almost toward the ceiling. Knudsen smiled back, gave a bow as was his custom, and took the president's hand. A photographer was there to capture the moment with the click of a shutter and the flash of a bulb. Roosevelt the genial, gracious host and the master of the New Deal, in a light gray suit; Knudsen the king of Detroit, in a more somber dark suit with a patterned tie, looking all-business. The most extraordinary alliance in modern American history was about to be forged.

Roosevelt thanked him for coming. Knudsen replied he was happy to be called. Happy to help.

Then the truth of what he was really facing hit Knudsen fifteen minutes later when he and the president were ushered into a conference room. Knudsen discovered he was not the only one on FDR's list. There was the silver-haired Edward Stettinius Jr., son of the great J. P. Morgan partner, and president of U.S. Steel, along with Chester Davis of the Federal Reserve Board, and Leon Henderson from the Securities and Exchange Commission. There was a large sloppy man in a nondescript suit: Sidney Hillman, president of the Amalgamated Clothing Workers, along with Ralph Budd of the Chicago Burlington Railroad. Rounding off the group was Harriett Elliott, dean of women from the University of North Carolina, who was there as "advisor on consumer problems."[10] She was as confused as Knudsen about what they were supposed to do as members of the Council of National Defense Advisory Commission, as Roosevelt proudly dubbed them. He explained that they were to be a branch of the Office of Emergency Management, which he had set up to dispense any and all executive powers that the situation in Europe might demand. When they had all met, Knudsen looked around the room and finally asked:

"Who is boss?"

It was a manufacturing term, meaning, Who is the person who will be running the shift and accepting responsibility for getting the job done?

There was a burst of nervous laughter, which the president joined in. "I guess I am," he replied.[11] Then everyone was ushered into the Cabinet Room, where Knudsen found himself shaking hands with Secretary of War Harry Hines Woodring and Navy Secretary Charles Edison, as well as Harold Ickes and Labor Secretary Perkins. Roosevelt explained in vague terms what Knudsen and the others would be doing to help with the defense effort. He also reassured his Cabinet that NDAC's role would be purely advisory. Knudsen, Stettinius, and the rest were not there to replace or supersede normal channels of Cabinet authority. With that, the meeting was over.

Knudsen returned to his hotel that night convinced of two things. The first was that the NDAC had absolutely no legal status; neither the Cabinet nor the War Department nor the Department of the Navy was under obligation to heed their advice—nor was anyone else. No one had even been appointed as chairman. "There was quite a lot of confusion," he wrote in a memorandum for himself. "In true New Deal style, [we have] no authority except what the President delegates piecemeal."[12]

The second realization was that if the council was going to have any real impact on how America would prepare itself for war, then its influence would depend entirely on how it presented the problem of how to convert butter into guns—or more precisely, turn an economy geared around producing consumer goods and services into making more weapons and war materiel than anyone had ever imagined.

Despite a decade of depression and high unemployment, the U.S. economy was still the most productive in the world. Its steel mills had produced an impressive 28 million long tons of steel—although that was less than half of what it produced in 1929. Nonetheless, America still produced more steel, aluminum, oil, and cars than all the world's great powers put together—almost three million cars in 1939 alone.[13]

Yet this industrial output was less than met the eye when it came to getting ready for war. Something would have to be done to raise dramatically that steel output, for instance, which would be the primary sinew of machines of war, as well as to increase the production of iron and coal. In 1939 the American steel industry was at its lowest capacity in twenty years.[14] Likewise a year's production of aluminum, the primary material for making modern warplanes, would have to rise to a minimum of 750 million pounds. The industry's twin giants, Alcoa and Reynolds, were making less than a quarter of that amount.[15]

America's merchant shipbuilding industry on both coasts was producing four ships a month, when it would need to launch hundreds.[16] As for those automobile plants, switching to producing Army trucks and other military vehicles would not so be easy—even for leading truck manufacturers like GM, White, and Mack. Army trucks had dozens of specifications, from minimum speed and fuel standards to being able to drive where there were no roads, which would demand heavy retooling of auto plants.[17] They would also be running on a supply of tire rubber, which would have to double at the very least, when its sources were thousands of miles away in South America and the East Indies.

Great Britain had been mobilizing its factories, plants, and shipyards for war since 1936; Germany, since 1935; and Japan, long before that. Together with the Soviet Union, they were outspending the United States on weaponry at a rate of ten to one—even with the president's expanding defense budget.[18] How could America ever catch up?

Yet Knudsen and his colleagues had no authority whatever to force the changeover or order anyone to make anything. They would have to go from business to business with hat in hand, as Knudsen later put it, to persuade them to prepare for a war two-thirds of the American people opposed—including many businessmen themselves. Everything the NDAC accomplished would depend on the force of ideas and personality. Increasingly, because of his reputation, his rhetorical skill, and his sheer physical bulk, that meant Big Bill Knudsen.

One of those in the room that afternoon who wondered if Knudsen was really the right man for the job was Henry Kaiser's old friend Interior Secretary Harold Ickes. As the meeting went on, he found it "more and more depressing," he confessed in his diary. Knudsen struck him as "hard and cold and dominating," someone too impatient and too hands-on to work well in Washington. "I have heard that Knudsen even makes his own notes in handwriting."[19]

Even worse, Knudsen came from the world of General Motors and mega-capitalist corporations like Ford and DuPont, which "have vast interests in all parts of the world, including munitions," and including

Nazi Germany. That led Ickes to wonder about Knudsen's patriotism and "his desire unselfishly to serve his country."[20] Above all, Ickes worried that Knudsen and his friends would use the rearmament program to get big business's nose "under the Administration tent," as Ickes put it, at the expense of labor (there was already talk about the need for unions to make sacrifices for the war effort, he noted) and the New Deal agenda.

It was a fear shared by many of the ardent liberals in town. The economist Waldo Frank, Vice President Henry Wallace, the First Lady, even the president's chief advisor, Harry Hopkins, watched Knudsen with some misgiving. They were hoping war might offer a chance to *complete* the New Deal agenda—a super New Deal, in fact.[21] Through the regimen of mobilization, the government could finally transform all sectors of American society—business and labor, rich and poor, managers and the unemployed—into a single vast cooperative enterprise. War would force American capitalism to work for the general welfare at last. Businessmen like Sloan, Ford, and Knudsen himself would have to realize "there is no real hope, either for them or for the country," Ickes furiously wrote, "unless they are willing to be satisfied with much less than they have."[22]

In private, Harry Hopkins was even more apocalyptic. "Democracy must wage total war against totalitarian war," he wrote in a secret memo for the president. "It must exceed the Nazi in fury, ruthlessness, and efficiency."[23] How likely was it that a man who had directed one of America's biggest profit-making corporations, and a Republican to boot, would share their collectivist philosophy and goals?

On the other hand, Knudsen did have his supporters. One was Bernard Baruch. He saw the former GM president as "a production genius" but sensed "the formalized rituals of government are not for him."[24] Another was Jesse H. Jones, the former Texas cotton broker who headed the Reconstruction Finance Corporation.

His and Knudsen's paths had crossed back in 1934 when the RFC had put Detroit's failing banks back in business after companies like Ford and Packard had to send executives to New York with empty suitcases to carry back enough cash to pay their workers.[25] A Hoover appointee, Jones had been waging a one-man guerrilla campaign against

the administration's strident New Dealers since they took office. Jones
had liked what he'd seen of Knudsen, and the more Jones got to know
him, the more impressed he became.

"He seemed to carry in his head a picture of the whole manufacturing business in the United States," Jones remembered later, plus the
phone numbers of the corporate heads who ran them. With his ency-
clopedic knowledge of industries from steel and airplane engines to
chemicals and furniture making, Knudsen could tell Jones at once
which plants "would have to be greatly enlarged, which with only a
little retooling were ready to go to work" for the war effort. Knudsen
was a vital resource for what would be Jones's primary job under mobilization: directing RFC loans to those businesses that were getting
their factories ready for wartime use.[26]

For his part, Knudsen found in Jones a kindred spirit: a man who
knew how to get things done in Washington with a simple handshake,
who understood what American business needed to get on board the
war effort—above all, the assurance that wartime conversion wasn't a
prelude to a government takeover—and who had a keen sense of the
bottom line.* When Knudsen got his first office in the Federal Reserve
Building, someone asked him if there was anything special he needed.
Yes, he said. "I want a direct telephone from my desk to Jesse Jones."[27]

Their partnership would be one of the most important in the war
years. One out of every ten dollars spent on the war effort from 1940
to 1945 would flow through one or another of Jones's agencies, especially his Defense Plant Corporation. He would expand airplane plants
and—with the help of former Union Pacific president Bill Jeffers—
create a massive American synthetic rubber industry almost from
scratch.† Abroad, his agents bribed South American officials to keep

---

* Jones was very proud that his Reconstruction Finance Corporation was the one
New Deal agency that actually made the taxpayer money, instead of losing it like the
others.
† Jeffers, Montana-born son of a brakeman who had grown up on the railroad he
would eventually run, decided someone else could run the show when he brought
synthetic rubber output from almost nothing in 1941 to 270,000 tons by 1943, and
resigned. Roosevelt and Jones pleaded with him to stay. But Jeffers refused. He wrote

certain strategic materials such as tungsten out of German hands. Neither America's wartime aircraft industry nor Kaiser's wartime industrial
empire would have been possible without the loans from Jones. Yet
even Jones couldn't help Knudsen with what would be his most daunting task: getting the Army, Navy, and Army Air Corps armed, clothed,
and ready for modern battle.

During his first weeks in Washington, Knudsen learned that the
American military itself had only vague ideas of how to do this. Knudsen was given a copy of their Industrial Mobilization Plan, which was
first drawn up by War and Navy Department experts back in 1922 and
which had gone through multiple revisions since. He was dismayed to
discover it was only eighteen pages long. The IMP did make a good-faith
effort to figure how the U.S. economy could produce enough steel and
rubber for tanks and vehicles and aluminum for airplanes and cotton
for uniforms—something they had failed to do before World War I. It
also identified some 25,000 plants the Army believed could be converted to wartime use.[28] It had also launched a pilot program the year
before called Educational Orders, to revive a moribund American munitions industry. The Army had given contracts to Goodyear to manufacture gas masks, R. Hoe and Company to develop recoil mechanisms
for antiaircraft guns, and General Electric to make sixty-inch searchlights. General Motors had been enlisted to produce military trucks,
and Winchester to make the Springfield Armory's new M1 rifle.[29]

Knudsen himself had signed the 1939 GM order. But the Educational Orders had been tiny, the applications largely theoretical. The
Army and Navy simply did not have the staff to think through problems of this magnitude—or even conceive of war on a scale this big.
Nor had they considered the impact mobilization might have on the
larger economy. They seemed to assume a civilian economy didn't even
exist.[30]

Drawing from their World War I experience, soldiers and sailors—
and many New Dealers—assumed changing to a wartime economy

---

to the president: "I feel I can contribute more to the war effort by getting back to *that*
railroad."

was like throwing a switch. All one had to do was pick a date—the Army even had a term for it, Mobilization Day, or M-Day—and issue the orders. Miraculously, the next day men would be drafted and reserves called up, factories would start making rifles and machines, and trains would steam for ports and depots with their cargoes of men, tires, bullets, shells, and artillery pieces.[31]

Knudsen knew M-Day was a fantasy. It made no allowance for what Knudsen would call "lead time": the time needed for a conversion effort. Based on his own experience at Ford in World War I, he calculated that would be about eighteen months.

Knudsen had been the old man's trusted director of wartime production then. He could remember standing out in hip-deep water in the Rouge River, helping to lay out the pylons for docks where Henry Ford was going to build the Navy subchasers known as Eagle boats (the facility would later become part of the River Rouge plant). What he discovered producing the Eagle boat and the Liberty engine for Glenn Martin and other American aircraft makers was that the process of mass-producing war materiel was no different than mass-producing anything else. Once you broke it down to as many interchangeable parts as possible, and arranged for the parts to come together in a continuous assembly line, you could make as many of what was needed, as quickly as needed, and as fast as anyone demanded—all the while driving the cost down the more you produced.

Designing the mass-assembly process for wartime production had been easy. Knudsen had done it first with cylinders for the Liberty engines and then for the Eagle boat. Before the war was over, he had had seven production lines going at once, each handling seven boats at a time—something unheard of in American shipbuilding—and all using workers who had never built a ship in their lives. By the time of the Armistice, Knudsen was set to produce one 112-foot-long Eagle a day.[32]

Together Knudsen and Ford made the Eagle subchaser famous. "As boats, Eagles were not so hot," remembered one Navy man who piloted one. "But as evidence of Bill Knudsen's production ability they were a magnificent achievement."[33]

The Eagle boats had been one bright spot in the otherwise dismal World War I mobilization picture. When President Woodrow Wilson had declared war in April 1917, the situation had quickly descended into chaos. The Army and Navy had no idea what they needed or how to get it, even as they handed out contracts right and left. In July Wilson appointed the War Industries Board to try to pull things back from the brink. Its first chairman, overwhelmed by the problems, suffered a nervous breakdown. Its second quit in frustration as the Army's insistence on doing everything itself, from handling transportation (it took over the nation's railroads when supplies weren't arriving in time) to supervising industrial plant expansion, did more harm than good.

At last, in January 1918, Wilson appointed Bernard Baruch to restore some sort of order. But it was too late. American companies wound up producing tons of war materiel, but almost all of it arrived in France after the Armistice. British prime minister Lloyd George noted bitterly in his diaries, "It is one of the inexplicable paradoxes of history, that the greatest machine-producing nation on earth failed to turn out the mechanism of war after eighteen months of sweating and toiling and hustling."[34]

Knudsen decided his job was to make sure that never happened again.

On June 2 he sent a letter to President Roosevelt:

"Dear Mr. President," it read, "I trust you will permit me to express my most sincere appreciation of the honor conferred on me by your recent appointment. . . . I will function for any period that may be necessary to demonstrate my fitness, entirely at my own expense and further, I will cheerfully accept for any additional period necessary the duties assigned to me, on the same basis."

In closing, Knudsen penned down at the bottom:

"I am most happy and grateful that you have made it possible for me to show, in small measure, my gratitude to my country for the opportunity it has given me to acquire home, family, and happiness in abundant measure."[35]

Two days later the last British soldier waded out to boats along the shore and left Dunkirk, along with virtually every piece of heavy equipment the British army owned. Only a miracle could save France and Britain now.

The source of that miracle would have to be the United States.

As he headed back to Detroit for one last weekend with his family, Knudsen weighed the heavy obstacles ahead. He did, however, have certain advantages. For one thing, America was not yet at war. Unlike in World War I, there was still lead time for wartime conversion—*if* Britain and France could be kept in the fight. That would have to be one of the priorities of America's conversion to wartime production: finding a way to keep the Allies in Europe from collapsing before America was ready to face Hitler on its own.

Knudsen also had faith in the power of mass production. He knew that in World War I large parts of American industry still had not switched over to the flexible-assembly-line methods that were now common in the automobile industry. Once they did, he reasoned, he could turn America's engineers and managers and workers loose to do what they did best—making things for use, in this case for the United States Army.

Once he got back to Washington, however, he learned that discovering what the Army needed wasn't so easy.

"What do you want?" That would be the first question Knudsen would ask whenever he met the generals in charge of Army procurement. Each time, the answer would be the same. We want an army of 400,000 men equipped and provisioned within three months of M-Day, they would say, and another 800,000 men after one year. Knudsen would then shake his head.

"That's not what *I* need," he would say. "I need to know what kind of equipment you need for these men—and how many . . . Please tell me *how many pieces*."[36]

And increasingly he learned none of them really knew the answer. He had lunch at Fort Myer with General Marshall, who told him his fears of fighting a war when everything from rifles (the Army was still using the '03 Springfield model) and machine guns to telephone

cable and medicine was in chronic short supply, and when trainees
would have to train using wooden guns and fire on wooden boxes
labeled tanks, and fire salvos of artillery from tree stumps labeled artillery.

"Our greatest need is time," Marshall told him. Knudsen could see
that, but he also needed to know exactly what equipment Marshall and
the Army needed and how many, and no one could tell him. The situation in the Navy was much the same.[37] The truth began to dawn on
Knudsen. He couldn't get a straight answer because they were waiting
for *him* to tell *them* what the American economy could produce, and
how much. If the country was going to make itself seriously ready for
war, neither the politicians nor the generals nor the admirals were willing to take the lead. American business and industry would have to
figure it out on their own.

Others besides Harold Ickes had their doubts they could do it without a single person in charge. For them the lesson from the other side
of the Atlantic was clear. America had to mobilize all its resources for
war, and quickly. A comprehensive plan had to be devised, orders had
to be given, and someone needed to take the helm: a Wizard of Oz
figure, with his hands on all the production levers and whose stern
commands carried the moral force of law.

"The nation clearly, almost violently wants a man of action," thundered *Time* magazine the weekend after Dunkirk, "a powerhouse of
strength and sureness." It was worried that America was getting Bill
Knudsen instead, "a ponderous, accented, self-made man, a production
genius," but evidently not *Time* editor Henry Luce's first pick for a war
production czar.[38]

Still, Knudsen believed he and his colleagues could do it without
becoming czars or wizards. "Industry in the United States does more
for the country in direct, or indirect, contributions to the public wealth
than in any other country on earth," he had told an audience in Detroit
three years earlier. "And it will continue to do so if given the opportunity without restrictions."[39] Those restrictions had come in the thirties,
with the Nye investigations that had essentially destroyed America's
munitions industry, and absurd new tax laws that made making arma-

ments almost prohibitive.* Even making as basic a compound as gun-powder, Knudsen was learning, America would have to start virtually from scratch.[40]

The evening after his sobering talk with Marshall, Knudsen sat up all night in his hotel room with a yellow legal pad. He had discovered how primitive the thinking about procurement still was in Army circles, where everything was based on units of one: If one man needed so much cotton for making his uniform at such and such a cost, then two men needed twice as much, and so on.[41] From uniforms to rifles and tanks and airplanes, Knudsen knew mass production would introduce economies of scale and reduce such thinking to nonsense. "The first thing to do," Knudsen told himself, "was to get started on the weapons that required a long cycle in manufacturing." Those would be ships, tanks, airplanes, guns, smokeless powder, and TNT. The second was begin planning for the shorter-cycle items like trucks and vehicles, clothing, food, and smaller arms like rifles and machine guns. The third step was to assemble a team who understood the dynamic power of mass production, but also the technical problems facing a modern economy.

By dawn he had his list. One name he didn't bother to write down. That was his fellow NDAC member Edward Stettinius, chairman of U.S. Steel. Stettinius had been on the short-lived War Resources Board. With Stettinius and his deputy Donald Nelson, the former president of Sears Roebuck, in charge of NDAC's Materials Division, Knudsen knew he had a strong ally on that flank.

The name at the head of his sheet of legal pad paper was that of young, vigorous John D. Biggers, president of Libby-Owens Glass. Knudsen had known him since his Ford days, when Libby-Owens made the glass for Model T windshields, and had worked with him on

---

* His colleague Ed Stettinius could tell him how after World War I Bethlehem Steel had been forced to close down its plant for making large artillery pieces because the federal government demanded the company pay a special tax for the facilities. Bethlehem offered to *give* the government the plant, and its huge forging, boring, and casting machinery, for free. The government had refused. And so, at its own expense, Bethlehem had been forced to break up and tear down every fixture and sell it for scrap.

various charitable causes. Biggers was one of the most principled men Knudsen knew, and an FDR favorite.[42] He decided to make Biggers his personal deputy, as well as head of procurement for trucks, tanks, and other large vehicles.

Then came Harold Vance, chairman of Studebaker, which had one of the smartest engineering divisions in the car business. Knudsen decided he would put Vance to work on machine tools, artillery, and artillery shells, while Earl Johnson, an alumnus of General Motors as well as of DuPont, would be in charge of explosives, small arms, and ammunition. At the end of World War I, America produced more gunpowder and TNT than Britain and France combined. In 1940 it produced almost none. Johnson's skill in mobilizing this most basic side of war mobilization would earn him a nickname in the corridors of the War Department: "Powder Johnson."[43]

There was Bill Harrison, head of construction from American Telephone and Telegraph, whose president had been the first to push for a National Defense Advisory Commission.[44] Knudsen gave Harrison charge of finding communication and radio gear, as well as military construction; while Dr. George Mead, one of the most respected figures in American aviation, co-founder of Pratt and Whitney Aircraft and designer of the original Wasp engine, would deal with airplane production.

The last person on Knudsen's list was a military man, not a business executive. He was Admiral Jerry Land, chairman of the United States Maritime Commission, a man with unparalleled knowledge of America's shipyards, who would supervise what would become one of the biggest projects of the entire war: building up America's merchant shipping fleet. In World War I, lack of an adequate merchant fleet had kept the growing supplies of equipment and munitions stuck on the wrong side of the Atlantic. Knudsen was not going to let that happen this time. Balancing the shipbuilding needs of the Navy and the civilian fleet would remain one of his highest priorities.

Six names, six men. Later there would be others. For now Knudsen would get Bigger, Harrison, and Vance leave of absence from their companies (the others were retired or, in Land's case, already in Washington). He also landed them offices near his own in the Federal Re-

serve Building, the NDAC's temporary home. They were the first of
the so-called dollar-a-year men who would begin to descend on
Washington from scores of other companies and business to take charge
of the war production effort. As a group and as individuals, they would
be scorned and vilified, dismissed as narrow-minded incompetents or,
alternately, denounced as scheming greedy profiteers.

But as a team, Knudsen and his colleagues would guide the country
into facing the greatest and most complex challenge in its history.

And thus far Henry Kaiser was not even a glimmer in anyone's eye.

On June 12, a steamy Wednesday, the National Defense Advisory
Commission held its first official meeting. Far away in Europe, Italy
had declared war on France and Great Britain—a move Roosevelt
denounced in a speech at the University of Virginia as a "stab in the
back"—the most militant speech from the president on foreign policy so far. Meanwhile, a demoralized French government was groping
toward an armistice with Hitler.

The big problem for the commission that day, however, was office
space. William McReynolds, a wiry bespectacled thirty-four-year veteran of nearly every federal department in Washington before becoming FDR's head of the Office of Emergency Management, and whom
Roosevelt had loaned to Knudsen to help him get set up, proposed a
solution. Everyone would move over to the new Social Security
Building, which was nearly finished but had 200,000 square feet of
empty offices.[45] In the meantime, the Federal Reserve Building would
be their temporary home. It also had the advantage of being air-
conditioned, unlike the War or Navy buildings—and during one of
the most torrid summers in Washington memory.

Bill Knudsen's immediate focus was on how a commission that was
entirely advisory, with no powers of its own, was going to proceed.

"First," he told everyone, "we have to find out what the Army and
Navy want, how much, and when." The estimate they had given him of
arming and equipping an additional 280,000 men would be, he believed, totally inadequate to the job that was coming. "I suspect the

Army and Navy can, and will, change their mind pretty fast. . . . So let's not pay attention to that 280,000 figure."[46*]

He then explained to those who weren't engineers how mass production worked. He showed how to take a complete unit like an airplane or a truck or a machine gun, break it down into little individual pieces, then machine the parts back together again so each was uniform and each subassembly functioned exactly like every other subassembly—and then every completed unit functioned exactly like all the rest. This, he said, would be the basic way in which everything necessary for defending the country would have to be made.

"Mass production has never depended on speed and never will," he told his listeners. "Speed, as such, is worthless. The only thing that produces good work is accuracy." Once factories and workers learned how to reproduce that accuracy with new unfamiliar products like tanks and planes, they could go on to make more complex weaponry at the same rate—perhaps weapons more complex than any ever seen.

"I'm not a soldier, and I'm not a sailor," Knudsen concluded. "I am just a plain manufacturer. But I know if we get into war, the winning of it will be purely a question of material and production. If we know how to get out twice as much material as everyone else—know how to get it, how to get our hands on it, and use it—we are going to come out on top—and win."[47]

Knudsen was happy, as well, because in addition to his own team, two more allies had turned up. One was Roosevelt's new secretary of the Navy, Frank Knox, a fellow Republican and Chicago newspaper publisher. The other, even more important, was Henry L. Stimson, the new secretary of war. At age seventy-two, Stimson was a Washington legend. Former secretary of war under President Taft and former secretary of state under Hoover, no man knew more about the ins and outs of American foreign policy—and, as a leading corporate lawyer, the moods and direction of American big business.

He and Knudsen soon discovered they were kindred spirits. "My

---

* He was right. Just three weeks later, the Army would raise that figure to one million men by 1941, and two million by January 1, 1942.

impression of Mr. Knudsen's ability and his tact grows with each time I see him," Stimson would write in his diary.[48] He also agreed with Knudsen that the only way for America to prepare for war was through American private enterprise. "You have got to let business make money out of the process," he would write in his diary, "or business won't work."[49]

Stimson became secretary of war on June 14. That same day the papers carried the news that the Germans had marched into Paris.

Back in New York, Alfred Sloan sat in his office in the General Motors Building and penned a note to his friend John Pratt.

> It looks as if the war in Europe is rapidly moving toward a conclusion. I am probably wrong about this but I can't see how it can be otherwise. It seems clear that the Allies are outclassed in mechanical equipment. . . . They ought to have thought of that five years ago. There is no excuse . . . except for the unintelligent, in fact stupid, narrow-minded and selfish leadership which the democracies of the world are cursed with. . . . [Now] there is nothing for the democracies to do but fold up. And that is about what it looks as if they are going to do.[50]

Bill Knudsen was out to prove his former boss wrong.

"No one can do what we can do if we all get together," he liked to boast. Americans' love of freedom, of individuality, of doing things differently from the other guy—these were sources of strength, he believed, not weakness. He believed in the power of the average American worker—"Progress in the world is accomplished by average people," he would tell audiences—and the power of American business. "American ingenuity has never failed to cope with every specific problem before it," he told a national radio audience, "and if we have your support and confidence, we will surely succeed."[51]

On that count, some American businesses were already giving him a head start.

CHAPTER FIVE

CALL TO ARMS

Lockheed workers build Hudson bombers for the Royal Air Force, mid- to late 1940.
Lockheed Martin Corporation

> America is like a giant boiler. Once the fire is
> lighted under it there is no limit to the power it
> can generate.
>
> —*British foreign secretary Lord Grey*

ONE MORNING LATE in 1939, a woman who had lived in Pittsburgh for the better part of a decade woke up to find smoke pouring up from the hills behind her house. She called the police: Was that a fire across the valley? "No, ma'am," the desk sergeant told her. "That's no fire, lady. Them's the mills."[1] After ten years of economic depression, she had never known there were steel mills in her neighborhood. But now they had roared to life. The first wartime orders from Britain and France had come in.

That the Allies would look to the United States for their war materiel made sense. Even after a decade of depression, America's manufacturing base was still the world's biggest. British and French military planners all assumed American-made planes and other equipment could help to close the gap with the Germans.

In 1938 alone, their orders would total some $350 million—with $84 million in aircraft engines.[2] It was five times what the Army Air Corps was ordering. Britain's war, and France's, resurrected America's aviation industry from the dead. One of the very first orders came in the spring of 1938, when a British team from the RAF flew out to Burbank, California, to tour the factory of Lockheed Aviation, now merged with the struggling Vega company. The British saw nothing they liked, and declared they would move on. The president of Lockheed-Vega, Robert Gross, was desperate. "Give me forty-eight hours," he told the RAF. "Let me see what my engineers can come up with." The RAF waited, and working four times around the clock flat-out, the Lockheed men came up with a "mock-up" of a long-range medium bomber modified from their civilian Super Electra airliner.[3]

The British were impressed. Before flying home, they ordered two hundred. The plane would become the Lockheed-Hudson, the first American-built airplane to fly with the British air forces in World War II. The British would go on to order more than thirteen hundred of them; the Hudson would become the mainstay of RAF Coastal Command. One would guide British destroyers to the Nazi supply ship *Altmark,* freeing three hundred British prisoners and scoring Winston Churchill's first triumph as First Lord of the Admiralty. Another would be the first aircraft to sink a German U-boat, in 1941.

Glenn Martin in Baltimore got his big order from the French in late January 1939, for 115 of what would become his version of a two-engine long-range bomber, the Martin 167 Maryland.[4] The U.S. Army Air Corps showed no interest, but two months later France ordered

700 more, along with extra aircraft engines.* From Pratt and Whitney alone, they ordered 6,000.[5]

The French had also taken a keen interest in a scrappy little fighter plane designed and built by a Long Island plane manufacturer, Roy Grumman. His F4F Wildcat, designed for aircraft carrier use, couldn't raise any interest from his own nation's navy. But the French bought one hundred, and when France surrendered, the British took over the order. Not only was Grumman's balance sheet looking a lot better. The bulldog-like fighter that would spearhead the American war effort in the Pacific at Wake Island, Midway, and Guadalcanal was itself saved from oblivion.[6]

Meanwhile, French and British purchasing agents were ordering machine tools for their own factories, some $100 million worth, while another $138 million was spent providing machine tools for American factories to fill their orders. It was equal to the entire machine tool output of the country the previous year.

Making all these new planes and engines and tools also demanded aluminum and steel, especially steel. In 1929 American mills were annually producing close to 63 million tons. The Depression and failed New Deal years had slashed that number by more than half.[7] Now in 1939 the mills were springing back to life. Ed Stettinius could walk down to a U.S. Steel foundry and watch in the near-darkness as the thin rivulets of glowing molten metal poured into the molds for steel ingots again, while in other plants huge machines spat out long red-hot sheets of rolled steel.

Thanks to Britain and France, America's manufacturing sector showed the first flutterings of activity in a decade. Men returned to work; families gathered to open the first paycheck. Stores in Pittsburgh crammed their windows with refrigerators and radios as crowds gathered in the streets on weekends to gaze and wonder. One clothing store owner remembered a Czech miner coming with his wife, daughter, and two sons. In a thick accent, the miner said, "Fit us out with new

---

* Later the British got their own version, which they dubbed the Baltimore, which the U.S. Army Air Force also adopted and designated as the A-30.

clothes." None of them had seen a new shirt or pair of shoes in ten years.[8]

The one thing that briefly threatened this revival of industrial prosperity was the Neutrality Act. Once hostilities formally began, the delivery to belligerent nations of orders for war goods would have to cease. The British became so spooked after Munich they halted all orders. Then in November 1939, Roosevelt had pushed Congress into modifying the law to allow Britain and France to buy as much as they could pay for in cash. It wasn't just good foreign policy, it was good business. "Cash-and-carry" lifted the last barrier to British and French rearmament from the factories of America. Total orders soared to more than $200 million.[9]

Then when the head of the French purchasing board, Jean Monnet (later architect of the Common Market), suggested the British and French pool their purchases of planes and other equipment, the stream of Anglo-French orders became a torrent.

In the first half of 1940, Britain and France purchased three times more airplanes and engines than they had for all of 1939. American aviation companies found themselves swamped with orders for more than 8,000 planes, and then 13,000—all this at a time when their own Army and Navy could barely scrape together enough money to order 5,000.[10*]

The evacuation of Dunkirk marked the next turning point in America's call to arms—the very week Knudsen arrived in Washington. The British army had left all its tanks, trucks, and field artillery pieces on the beach. Even rifles and machine guns were in desperately short supply. With a German invasion looming, Churchill confessed to one intimate that there might be fewer than seventeen tanks left in the entire British Isles.[11]

---

* One of those would change the course of the war. British representatives went to North American Aviation to see if the California company would agree to build a rival firm's plane, the Curtiss P-40. North American president James "Dutch" Kindelberger said he could design and build a much better fighter if they wanted. The British agreed, but only if he could deliver a flyable prototype in 120 days. What Kindelberger delivered in just 100 days became the best tactical fighter of World War II, the P-51 Mustang.

The most urgent need, however, was rifles. Churchill approached Roosevelt, who in turn approached General Marshall. What from the Army's own current stores could be spared? That was the question Marshall posed to his chief of ordnance. By June 3 he had his answer. There were some 500,000 old Springfield rifles, all made during the last war and then packed away in grease. Since the Army was planning to deploy a new infantry firearm, the M-1 semiautomatic, Ordnance Chief Charles M. Wesson figured he could spare these plus 80,000 World War I–era machine guns, nine hundred 75mm guns, and 130 million rounds of ammunition without setting back the Army's own rearmament plans.[12]

Marshall signed on. That still left the problem of how to get the rifles and other surplus weapons across the Atlantic. Thanks again to the Neutrality Act, the United States still could not directly turn over weapons to a wartime belligerent—not even a democratic one like Britain, with its national existence at stake. Instead, the weapons had to be turned over to an American concern that could then resell the equipment to the British. It would have to be a concern large enough not only to take over and organize the rifles and guns, but also ship them out on a timely basis.

Wesson walked out of the Munitions Building, crossed Constitution Avenue to the Federal Reserve Building, and went to the office of Knudsen's colleague Edward Stettinius, former head of U.S. Steel. He asked Stettinius point-blank if the firm's Export Company, which shipped iron and steel products all over the world, could handle the order. The deal would be good for U.S. Steel, as well, since the British payment for the guns would be down payment for the Army's own order of steel plate for its tanks and new 105mm and 155mm artillery.

Stettinius was delighted to say yes. There was only one hitch. Stettinius had just submitted his resignation from U.S. Steel in order to work on the National Defense Advisory Commission. It would become effective at three o'clock that afternoon. Until then he could make some calls, he told the general, and picked up the phone. In a few minutes, he had Irving Olds, the new chairman of U.S. Steel, on the line and arranged for a meeting the next morning with General Wesson. It was Stettinius's last act as chairman of U.S. Steel, and by far the most important.[13]

By June 11 more than six hundred freight cars were unloading their contents at the Army docks at Raritan, New Jersey, where shifts of one thousand men each worked round the clock piling the rifles, guns, ammunition, and an assortment of TNT and smokeless gunpowder into lighters, which sailed into Gravesend Bay toward the freighter *Eastern Prince*. Back in Washington, British purchase agent Arthur Purvis signed the agreement with U.S. Steel for $36 million, which also turned out to be the price U.S. Steel Export Company paid to the U.S. Army. Two days later the *Eastern Prince* set off for Britain, arriving on June 23—the day after France surrendered. Between July 1 and August 1, another fifteen freighters ferried the remaining supplies across the Atlantic.[14]

Stettinius and U.S. Steel had established a direct lifeline between America and a beleaguered Britain that was only bound to grow larger. Nor did the fall of France halt the orders from that quarter. From the new French government in exile, Jean Monnet put forward his second big idea: pooling Britain's and Free France's gold reserves in order to buy whatever Britain needed to defend its shores—which was now the defense of free government everywhere. Churchill spoke to the House of Commons on June 4, stating that "we will fight on the beaches until, in God's good time, the New World, with all its power and might, steps forth to the rescue and liberation of the Old."

By August, Churchill and Roosevelt had reached a deal to lend the Royal Navy fifty outdated American destroyers. America was committed to the survival of Britain. The rescue Churchill prayed for was under way.

Meanwhile, Knudsen was finally getting through to the Army. The answer to his persistent questions about what it needed and when came in a memo on June 13—the day before Stimson became secretary of war. It called for a one-million-man army by October 1941, and two million by January the following year. It also called for 9,000 and 18,000 new warplanes by those same dates, with a further goal of 36,000 planes by April 1, 1942.[15]

Together with the Navy's appropriations for three new aircraft carriers and 4,050 additional aircraft, Marshall believed this would be just enough to protect America's borders from the Atlantic to the Pacific, as well as the Caribbean. South America would be on its own. As for intervening in Europe, that still belonged to the realm of fantasy, not strategy.[16]

The whole buildup, Marshall estimated, would cost a whopping $11 billion—eleven times the entire defense budget in 1939.[17] This was a raindrop in the Potomac compared to what wartime Washington would later spend, but that summer even the president said it was too much—he could never get an appropriation that size through Congress. Marshall bowed to reality, and the amount shrank to $7.3 billion. How the United States was going to squeeze a fully equipped modern army, navy, and air force out of that amount was anybody's guess.

Even so, Knudsen had some numbers to work with at last. Now American industry could get to work, starting with aircraft engines.

The first meeting came on May 27 with people from Pratt and Whitney and Wright Aeronautical, the nation's leading aircraft engine makers, as Knudsen asked for engines for more than six thousand planes.[18] Allison, a division of GM, was also there. Knudsen saw aircraft engines as crucial to the early stage of industrial mobilization, not just because they were enormously complex machines to manufacture,* but because they were the kind of war machinery he figured other industries might be able to produce with the right machine tools and training. In order for that to happen, however, two big changes in the way the government dealt with business were going to be needed.

Starting in 1933, congressional legislation had placed sharp restrictions on how much war suppliers could make on their government contracts. During the First World War, cost-plus contracts were common, meaning that the government would pay all expenses relating to making an airplane or artillery gun, in addition to a fixed fee or percentage of cost—8 percent was fairly standard. The postwar reaction against "war profiteers" led Congress and the Treasury Department to impose sharp curbs on the profit companies could make on orders larger than $25,000. They also required an advance audit to guarantee

---

* A single Wright Cyclone 14-cylinder 1700-horsepower engine required 8,500 separate parts, 80,000 machine operations, and 50,000 inspections.

that the company's profit would be no more than 8 percent even before the contract was signed.[19]

In addition, every government contract for a new airplane or tank or vehicle required bidding companies to pay for the production of their prototype and the new machine tools to manufacture it. No money was ever advanced, even to the winner of the bid. As one executive from Boeing put it, "There was no sound of coin in Uncle Sam's jeans." An aircraft maker looked at an average of a half-million-dollar investment just to enter a bid—with no guarantee of winning.[20] Even if he did and problems or delays developed, the government was not above pulling the contract, leaving the company high and dry.

Then there were the tax laws. Every American company's investment in new plant construction, tools, and other physical resources necessary to produce a plane or tank or aircraft, even with a contract, took sixteen years in order to be fully deducted as a business expense. Knudsen saw at once that these amortization rules (Knudsen had to get John Biggers to explain to the president and Cabinet what amortization meant) made the short-term investment in plant, property, and equipment necessary for the defense buildup almost impossible.[21]

"Mr. President," Knudsen said, "do you want statistics, or do you want guns?" If the latter, he explained, then amortization should be drastically shortened to five or six years. Hitler's German companies, he pointed out, worked on a seven-year rule. Companies would get their investment back quicker, and be more willing to take risks on manufacturing things that had no commercial value to them but were crucial to the defense effort.

"The government can't do it all," Knudsen told Roosevelt. "The more people we can get into this program"—in other words by offering incentives instead of threats—"the more brains we can get into it, the better chance it will have to succeed."[22]

Knudsen also insisted that a "letter of intent," meaning an official War or Navy Department letter stating the government's intention to do business with a particular firm before a formal contract was drawn up and signed, should be enough to get a company advance funds from their bank—and to protect the company's out-of-pocket expenses in case the contract never went through. It was a practice he borrowed from the British, and critics would hound him for it, decrying the fact that he had abandoned the costly, time-consuming process of competitive bidding. But Knudsen sensed that the time for slow, deliberate action was over. The government had to be willing to work with those companies willing to work with it.[23]

Roosevelt was deeply dubious. He pointed out that never in the history of the United States had such a provision been made for government contractors. Knudsen replied it was time to shatter precedent. Otherwise, he said, they might never get a job of that size done in time. Roosevelt's 50,000 planes a year would remain only a pipe dream, while Hitler's Luftwaffe ruled the skies over Europe.

With Stimson firmly backing Knudsen, the White House at last conceded. In the next weeks and months, people would catch a glimpse of Knudsen cornering some industrialist after an NDAC meeting and saying, "George, in that plant of yours—Plant Number Four, I mean—I'll make sure you get the tools, see?" There would be a grateful handshake, perhaps an appreciative pat on the back.

Then at parting, "I'll see that you get a letter. I won't forget."[24]

At the same time, everyone else's attention was on what was happening in Britain.

On any given day in July 1940, Winston Churchill half expected to see German paratroopers landing on the outskirts of London. On July 12 there was a serious discussion in the War Cabinet about whether the government should encourage the populace to attack German invaders with scythes and stones.[25] Meanwhile, fighting off German air attacks on British shipping in the Channel became a top priority. In Washington the British demands for war materiel, especially planes, came with alarming frequency. Knudsen was forced to confront a new truth. American industry was going to have to satisfy the needs of war on both sides of the Atlantic at once.

Matters came to a head on July 23 at a meeting in the Treasury Building. Knudsen began peppering the British Purchasing Commission's Purvis with questions about how many planes the British would need, and when. Purvis gave his answer: 1,000 planes a month. Britain was putting all its own production into making fighters, Hurricanes and Spitfires, in order to halt what was promising to be a massive German onslaught from the air. It needed every other kind of plane America could provide, from bombers to trainers.[26]

Knudsen swallowed hard. Right now America's aircraft manufacturers were barely producing 550 a month, with 250 a month slated for overseas. He promised that the United States could hit that number for Britain by the end of 1941, by which time the Army Air Corps could count on 2,000 a month for its own force. President Roosevelt's call for 4,000 or more a month still looked a long way away, but this would get things started.

The next morning, however, Purvis stopped by Treasury Secretary Morgenthau's office. The truth was, he said, 1,000 a month might not be enough. By the end of 1941—assuming Britain survived—they would be needing closer to 4,000.

Henry Morgenthau was a dry, precise man who refused to be surprised. In spite of himself, however, he had to smile.

"Pass the ball to Knudsen," he said. "He's the kind of production man who will rise to a challenge like that and meet it."[27]

So Purvis did. Once Knudsen had recovered from his shock, he promised he would see what he could do.

The result was a sharp change in the direction, but not the pace, of aircraft production in the United States. Almost incredibly, the U.S. now agreed to slow its own buildup in order to keep Britain in the air.[28] For all of 1941, one-third of all warplanes produced in the United States—and one-half of all tanks—would be slated to be sent to Great Britain. It was an extraordinary sacrifice of priorities, for the sake of preventing Britain's defeat. Still, figuring out how to achieve production numbers like that meant more late nights at Knudsen's Federal Reserve office huddled with his aviation expert, Dr. Mead.

Knudsen and Stimson were already pushing for radical changes in the work schedules for America's aircraft plants: adding a night shift, for example.[29] Still another question haunted the back of Knudsen's mind. By the end of 1940, British wartime orders in the United States would be almost half of what the federal government itself was spending on armaments.[30] How was Britain going to pay for all this? Already he sensed that a day of reckoning was coming, even supposing Britain survived. And as Stimson's reports were telling him at the end of July, those chances did not look good. The problem of how to supply a customer, in this case Britain, who might suddenly lose the ability to pay arose for the first time on that sweltering morning of July 24. It would not go away until the passage of Lend-Lease eight months later.

At the same time, Knudsen was getting grief from the other direction. The Army was starting to panic. There was real fear that the British demands for planes and tanks and guns would not leave enough for the Army's own revised mobilization plan. On the twenty-fifth Knudsen and Stimson met to discuss the complaints against NDAC from various Army administrative heads who felt the agency was moving too slowly—while Harold Vance, Bill Harrison, and the others felt the men in uniform were shutting them out from major purchasing decisions.[31]

For example, the rising star of Stettinius's team handling materials and supplies was the former president of Sears and Roebuck, Donald T. Nelson. Tall, owlish, and bespectacled, Nelson was a little shocked at the Army's intransigence regarding uniform buttons. It told him that it had to have horn or ivory for its uniform buttons, as in the First World War. Nelson pointed out an American company called Rochester Button was ready to make thousands of perfectly fine celluloid buttons, and that horn and ivory had to be imported from South America or Czechoslovakia—the latter now under Nazi rule. Horn or ivory, the Army said, and for the time being that was where things stuck.[32]

Then there was the problem of what to do about tanks.

Purvis and the British were starved for them. Churchill told Purvis to ask Knudsen and the Americans for help. So on August 6, 1940, Knudsen called a summit meeting with Purvis, British and American officers, and representatives from the truck, railroad, and heavy equipment industry, including American Car and Foundry, the only private company currently making tanks in America besides the Army's own Rock Island Arsenal. Knudsen made them put their heads together and come up with a bulked-up version of the Army's current light tank. It would carry a 75mm gun—equal to the heaviest German tanks at the time—and a 30mm gun mounted on a turret. Purvis announced that this new model, the M3 Medium, would be acceptable to His Majesty's Government. But it would want no fewer than one thousand a month.[33]

The Army officials were stunned. American Car and Foundry was barely making thirteen a month of the old model. How on earth could they ever meet numbers like that—not only for Britain but for the United States? They were discussing possibly asking Baldwin Locomotive, one of the country's leading manufacturers of heavy equipment, when Knudsen cleared his throat.

"How about a car company?" he asked.

As everyone else in the room looked at one another, Knudsen went back to his office. Donald Nelson watched from around the corner as Knudsen picked up his phone. "Give me Detroit," he asked politely, and within minutes he was connected with K. T. Keller at Chrysler.

"We have a problem, K.T.," he said. "We have to make more tanks than any corporation has ever made in the past. Can you do it?"[34]

Kaufman T. Keller was Detroit old school. He knew Knudsen from the automobile's pioneering days and knew the respect his old boss, the ill and retired Walter Chrysler, had for the industrious Dane. Keller replied, "Sure. When do we meet?"

Tomorrow, Knudsen answered. With that he flew off to Detroit and the pair spent the day bent over a desk sketching out plans for a facility that would be able to produce up to five hundred tanks a month.

It was an impossibly formidable task. Chrysler was moving into uncharted territory for an American car company—and neither Keller nor his engineers had ever seen a tank. But two priorities stood out at once. Knudsen and Keller agreed there was only one person who could design the right facility: Albert Kahn. The second was that it would not just have to be a new factory, but a new way of making tanks, as well.[35] It was Chrysler's engineers, not the Army's, who would have to figure out how.

At Knudsen's insistence, on August 9 the other members of NDAC met to approve his and Keller's plan, and the War Department immediately authorized $20 million for construction.[36] It was also agreed that the tank engines would come not from Chrysler but Continental Motors, a nearly defunct automotive company based in Muskegon. Knudsen knew their president, Jack Reese, like he knew everybody. He figured if anyone could come through, it was Jack Reese.

Continental was a dying business when the War Department contract for two hundred engines a month arrived. Reese was a cigar-chomping fireplug of a man who, like Knudsen, worked best in shirtsleeves and a hat. Reese had been made president in 1939, and was Continental's last hope of turning the company around.[37] In addition to firing executives who collected salaries but didn't do any work, one of his plans had been to sell the company's big Detroit plant and transfer everything—machines, workers, tools, the works—to the more efficient operation in Muskegon.

A year had passed, and Reese found no buyers. That proved lucky for the Army, because now Reese had an empty facility in which to start making tank engines. Even better, Reese and his engineer offered to redesign the 440-horsepower aircraft engine they had already starting tooling up for in order to get back in business, to fit into the M3 tank. The Army specified an air-cooled engine, and this was an air-cooled engine, even though it had been designed for the skies, not fighting on the ground. Still, the Army jumped at the chance to get into production months before anyone thought they could. The Continental end of the deal was signed.[38]

Across town at Chrysler, Keller's chief engineer was on the job. Ed Hunt was, like Reese, a physically formidable man, built low to the ground with a natural glower and no-nonsense attitude. Army officers called their visits to Chrysler to see him "going to Fort Hunt." The first time he and Keller showed up at Rock Island Arsenal, outside Davenport, Illinois, the Army showed them several hundred pounds of tank blueprints. Hunt emphatically shook his head.

"I've never seen a tank on the hoof," he said. "If I'm going to build 'em, I'm gonna have to see one. How about it?"[39]

That afternoon, Hunt, Keller, and their Army escorts took one of their prototypes out for a run. When they were done, Hunt stepped out and asked, "Is that what you want?"

"Yes," the general said, "but lots of them."

K. T. Keller glanced at Hunt. "All right, Ed. How about it?"

The Chrysler engineer thought for a moment. "Well," he finally said, "I guess we'd better not get any bright ideas of our own. We'd better let the Army design 'em. We'll just make 'em."

The final design of the M3 came out in early 1941. By March, Chrysler's new facility, dubbed the Detroit Arsenal Tank Plant, was finished—just seven months after Keller broke ground for it driving his own tractor. Hunt and his associates put in fourteen- and eighteen-hour days, making their first tank entirely by hand. Albert Kahn's dream factory took shape overhead and around them, with empty bays where the ordered machine tools would eventually go.

The Chrysler men then discovered the Army-designed M3 had problems. Certain elementary engineering mistakes had crept in, which the Army's Ordnance Board had missed. There were tank treads that worked fine on regular roads but slipped and slid in muddy ditches. There were air-cooled engines, which Continental was contracted to build and Chrysler to install, but which were time-consuming and expensive to machine, and which required cool air to cool. That was going to be in short supply in Egypt's Western Desert, where the M3 would first be deployed.

Then there was the problem of the chassis springs. Hunt and his men scratched their heads over the drawings. They had never seen springs like this: certainly nothing like anything used by the automotive industry, not even for the heaviest trucks. They looked into every manufacturing nook and cranny. Then one of Hunt's assistants came up with the answer, in a railroad manual dating back before World War I. They were so-called volute springs originally designed for freight cars. The railroad industry had abandoned them long ago. Now the Army was using them for its vaunted M3 tank.[40]

Keller and Hunt had to fight to persuade the Army to let the car company, which routinely spent huge sums designing and testing chassis springs, give them a new spring design. In the end, Chrysler would basically redesign the entire vehicle—just as later, Chrysler, Ford, and GM would reengineer the M3's successor, the M4 Sherman. The M3 Grant would finally be ready to fight Rommel in the desert in 1942 with Continental's less-than-ideal engines. But months, and not a few lives, were lost because the Army insisted on pushing ahead on its own design without once asking if the professional experts might do it better.

It would take some time before American companies learned to challenge the War Department on how to design and build the weapons it wanted (aircraft makers of course had known this for years). Meanwhile, Knudsen himself had to step up to deal with the even bigger problem stalking the M3's makers, that of rivets.

Ed Hunt confessed he had never seen anything like it. Trying to get holes bored through the two-inch steel plate took forever. He called in one of American industry's legendary toolmakers, Hank Krueger, to help out. Slowly the problem, and a dilemma, took shape. There were two kinds of steel plate for tanks, cast homogeneous armor, or CHA, and rolled homogeneous armor, or RHA.[41] CHA was easier to work with but hell to cut. RHA was clearly the way to go, but riveting so many separate plates raised manufacturing costs to the roof.

Knudsen proposed a solution. Why not weld the plates instead? Army engineers scoffed. There was no way any welding job, no matter how carefully done, could hold these heavy steel plates together and withstand the kind of rough handling a battle tank had to endure—including shell fire. They had tried it once, they told him. Honestly, rivets were the only way to go.[42]

Knudsen, however, knew people who knew a good deal more about welding than the Army did. There was Bill Smith, for example, whose company, A. O. Smith Corporation of Milwaukee, did welding for car frames and for massive steel piping used by oil companies. Knudsen had already contacted him about using high-efficiency welding techniques instead of rivets for the Maritime Commission's shipbuilding program (which were later adopted across the industry).

Sure, Smith responded, you can weld steel plate of that kind of thickness. Then there were welding people Knudsen knew at General Motors, and so he set off once again for Detroit.[43]

A few days later, Edward Foley Jr., general counsel for the Treasury Department, was passing through the halls of the Federal Reserve Building. Down the hall came Knudsen with something shoved under his arm that to Foley looked like the side of a battleship.

"What have you got there, Bill?" Foley wanted to know.

Knudsen showed him. It was two massive slabs of steel welded together around the outside. "They say welding's not as secure as old-fashioned rivets," Knudsen said, hoisting it up to his shoulder. "So I went to Detroit to get it done. Now I'm going to find those Ordnance people and show them."[44]

It turned out the welding not only sped up production (RHA welded easily, without using the hundreds of costly rivets) but was actually safer, as the Army found out in December 1941 when it ran firing tests at the Aberdeen Proving Ground, north of Baltimore. The Ordnance people discovered that heavy machine gun fire could knock the M3's rivets loose, which then became deadly projectiles flying around inside the tank.[45] A direct hit by an artillery shell was even more lethal. It was too late to change for the Grant, but welding became standard for the next and most famous generation of American battle tanks: the M4 Sherman.

It was a historic turning point, and not just because of the welding. The contract Knudsen, the Army, and Jesse Jones's office drew up on September 9, 1940, for the Reconstruction Finance Corporation to fund Continental's production of Grant tank engines for Great Britain justified the expense as being "essential for the national defense of the United States." It was the first time a government document acknowledged that supporting Great Britain against the Axis had become a national priority—indeed, as vital to America's defense as supplying our own armed forces.[46]

But could Britain hold? That was the question to which no one dared to guess an answer.

Everything depended on the Royal Air Force. It had lost nearly half its airplanes in the battle for France. Fewer than seven hundred Spitfire and Hurricane fighters were ready to face an onslaught of thousands of German bombers and fighters. British factories were working flat-out to produce sixteen hundred planes a month. But those planes also needed engines, especially the twelve-cylinder in-line Merlin engines built by Rolls-Royce, which gave the Spitfire its crucial edge over the Nazis' best fighters. No one in steel-starved Britain knew where they were going to come from in those numbers.

Purvis approached Knudsen. Could the Americans build the Merlins if Rolls-Royce supplied the plans? Knudsen said yes, and made yet another phone call, this time to his old friend Edsel Ford.

Although his name would live on by attachment to the company's biggest marketing flop, Henry Ford's eldest son was a shrewd manager of car production and men—and he trusted Bill Knudsen. Edsel agreed that Ford would produce nine thousand of the Merlin engines under a non-royalty license. Two-thirds of them were to be shipped back to Britain, and one-third would remain in the States to boost American airplane production.

A few days later, Knudsen's phone rang. It was a subdued and chastened Edsel.

"Bill, we can't make those motors for the British."

Knudsen was stunned. "Why?"

"Father won't do it."

"But you're president of the company," Knudsen protested.

"I know," Edsel Ford replied helplessly, "but Father won't do it, and you know how he is."[47]

Knudsen found an Army bomber to fly him to Detroit, and confronted the auto industry's patriarch.

"Those motors for the British," he said when he came into Ford's office. "Edsel telephoned me and said you wouldn't make them."

"Nor will we."

"There will be a hell of a stink about it if you don't."

But the old man was adamant. He was still in the throes of isolationist sentiment and strongly believed that the war in Europe was none of America's business—and that any money used to prop up a tottering British Empire was money wasted. He had initially endorsed the Rolls-Royce Merlin engine contract when Edsel and production chief Charlie Sorensen described the engine's superior performance and what a boon it would be for the Army Air Corps. But he had already told the press and the world that he would never make war supplies for any foreign nation—and when British air minister Lord Beaverbrook announced the Merlin as proof that America and Ford were now standing behind Britain, Henry Ford exploded with fury. The deal was off, he declared. And no amount of persuading or pleading from Knudsen could move him.

Their raised voices carried out into the hall. "You're mixed up with some bad people in Washington," people could hear Ford telling Knudsen, "and you're headed for trouble."[48]

Knudsen came back with, "We have your word you would make them. I told the president your decision, and he was very happy about it."

At the mention of the hated Roosevelt, Ford blew his top. "We won't build the engines at all," he barked. "Withdraw the whole order. Take it to someone else. Let them build the engine; we won't."

The door was flung open and Knudsen headed down the hall. His face, according to one eyewitness, was purple with rage. Henry Ford kept shouting, "They want war, they want war." Men who had known him almost forty years had never heard him more furious.[49]

For Knudsen it was a chilly silent drive to his summerhouse on Grosse Ile. In addition to delays and bottlenecks in airplane production (instead of 50,000 planes, they were looking at 3,750 for the balance of 1940), Knudsen now had one in engine production—not just for helping the British but America's own defense buildup. Yet as he leaned back on his seat while the driver headed for the bridge over the Detroit River, Knudsen knew the flap with Ford was only part of a larger problem. America was not at war, yet Roosevelt, the British, and other policy makers were acting as if it were. They still assumed the nation's industries could produce war materiel more or less on command. If rearmament wasn't going to fall hopelessly and helplessly behind, something would have to be done to entice American business to get in the act, and fast.

The dreary struggle over amortization would drag on until September. Even those American businesses tempted to get into defense contracting for patriotic reasons still held back, fearful of being stuck with having to pay for retooling or hiring new workers in order to meet orders the government would never make.

The only solution was for the government to pay *them*—that is, in the form of advances on contracts for war work. This was something unimaginable in the parsimonious old prewar days—and drawing up contracts in which the government agreed to cover all costs while providing the contractor with a fixed fee set at 7 percent of costs was precisely what had set an outraged Congress in motion against the "merchants of death" after the First World War. But at Knudsen's nod, the practice expanded, and on July 2 Congress gave its reluctant stamp of approval. From then until the end of the war, the War Department would put up more than $7 billion in advance payments to its civilian business contractors, and the Navy Department $2 billion—and the cost-plus contract would become standard.[50]

Many shook their heads over the new arrangements, especially in Congress. Senator Harry Truman, chairman of the Senate's committee to investigate defense production, compared the whole thing to Santa Claus handing out gifts at a church Christmas party. Later, others would see in the new arrangements the ominous outlines of what would come to be called the military-industrial complex.

All the same, Knudsen, like the president himself, was painfully aware of the deadlines everyone faced that fateful summer. America's way of thinking about how to arm for war, and how to pay for it, was about to undergo a radical change. Knudsen's phone calls to his friends in Detroit had marked the first tentative steps in that direction.

That still left Knudsen with the problem of what do about the Rolls-Royce Merlins. When he got to Grosse Ile, he went to his study to make one more phone call. This one was to Alvan Macauley, chairman of Packard Motor Car Company.

"Alvan," he said, "I'm leaving for Washington in a few hours and we need to talk."[51]

For thirty years Macauley had been head of Packard, the maker of high-end luxury cars whose Model B, launched in 1900, introduced the first steering wheel and the first gas pedal. Macauley was a strait-laced irritable man who detested people who had gold-capped teeth or jangled coins in their pockets—or insisted on sporting long names.[52] His real passion, however, was keeping Packard competitive in a market increasingly dominated by Ford, Chrysler, and GM. He did this by making Packard's sleek and powerful multicylindered sedans the gold standard of the luxury market; by being ready to admit mistakes when an ad campaign or new auto line misfired; and by hiring as his chief engineer a man of genuine automotive genius.

Jesse Vincent was an Arkansas farmer's son who quit school after the eighth grade and learned his mechanical engineering through a correspondence school course. As historian James Ward notes, Vincent's technological breakthroughs at Packard read like a history of the modern car: the first four-wheel brakes, the first air-conditioning, the first power booster brakes, and the first independently manufactured automatic transmission, the Ultramatic.[53]

During the First World War, Vincent also worked on the Liberty aircraft engine, and got to know Knudsen well. So it was no surprise when Knudsen's doorbell rang and Vincent and Max Gilman, Packard's president, were standing there at Macauley's request.* Knudsen explained his problem: a great aircraft engine, and no one to build it. Could Packard do the job?

Vincent and Gilman jumped at the chance to work on one of the world's most advanced engines. Here was a chance to show off Packard's engineering expertise, as well as an exciting challenge. Stealing a march on Henry Ford didn't hurt, either.

Gilman told Knudsen he'd consider any deal the government wanted to put in front of him. The big Dane thanked him, and they shook hands as Knudsen headed for the door and his plane back to Washington. Two days later, on June 26, Gilman and Vincent found themselves in the nation's capital, sitting across from Knudsen and his aviation expert, Dr. Mead, as Mead and his assistants explained the technical features of the Merlin XX engine. A day later they were back on the floor of the Packard plant, making plans for an entire new wing where they would be completing nine thousand of the British-designed engines.[54]

They still had no signed contract. All they had was Knudsen's handshake and a box full of Merlin XX engine parts shipped over from Ford. Yet by the twenty-eighth, Vincent had his engineers in the drafting room, laying down schedules for completing each stage of the production process. The company built its own machine tools and dies for parts, built a new factory wing—and still had enough time and workers to bring out their latest car model for 1941, the Clipper.

The Merlin engine blueprints were so secret that the British government arranged for a battleship to carry them across the Atlantic.

* Max Gilman was a Wisconsin boy born to a family so poor he never mentioned them in the rarefied aristocratic atmosphere of Packard. Still, Alvan Macauley knew it took a tough, no-nonsense man to make a profitable luxury automobile, so Gilman was Vincent's first choice as president when he stepped down in 1938.

Morris Wilson was the Montreal banker Purvis arranged to pick them up, and when HMS *Nelson* docked, Wilson arrived armed with a large suitcase. The *Nelson*'s captain asked him what the case was for.

"To carry the plans, of course," Wilson said.

The captain only laughed, then led him down into the hold. He pointed to a crate the size of a railway freight car, marked TOP SECRET.

"There are your plans, Mr. Wilson," the captain said, and walked away.[55]

Back in Detroit, Vincent and his engineers discovered they had to rewrite this vast mass of paper and intricate specifications, from start to finish. They not only had to be translated from English to American measurements, but made exact enough to fit the mathematical tolerance level the auto industry demanded for mass production—one ten-thousandth of an inch.

Nonetheless, by August 1941 Gilman and Vincent had a working prototype for testing. It proved as reliable and resilient as its British counterpart. The difference was that whereas the English Merlin was still made by hand, with workmen still shaping every part to fit each particular motor, Packard's mass-production approach allowed relatively unskilled labor to do the same job three times faster. Indeed, one-third of Packard's new employees were women who had never set foot on a factory floor.[56]

The first nine finished engines came off the assembly line in January 1942. During the war Packard would build more than 55,000 of them. Vincent even developed a maritime version of the Merlin XX. This included a supercharged 1800-horsepower model, four of which could send a 104-foot Navy PT boat hurtling across the water at fifty miles an hour. The aircraft version would be installed not just on the British Spitfire, Hurricane, and the twin-engine Mosquito; it would power to victory the finest fighter plane of World War II, the P-51 Mustang.

It was one of the production triumphs of the war—one of many. Yet while the first nine engines had cost both the government and Packard more than $6.25 million, the company's profit for the entire Merlin deal came to barely $6,000.[57]

Merlin engines weren't the only things coming across the Atlantic that summer.

In August a team of British scientists and engineers arrived in New York on the liner *Duchess of Richmond*. Like the Magi in the Bible, they bore gifts of inestimable value—not frankincense and myrrh this time, but the fruits of British technology and science.

They included proximity fuses, a working model for a power-driven airplane gun turret, and the cavity magnetron, the heart of a device the Brits called RDF but the Americans called radar. The team also brought news of a new aeronautical principle called jet propulsion.[58] All represented new breakthroughs in the science of warfare that might shift the strategic balance—but only if they could be industrially engineered and mass-manufactured. The British knew they couldn't do it, but they sensed Bill Knudsen and his American friends could.

The supply line to Britain was becoming a two-way thoroughfare. British science and American Industrial know-how would become an unbeatable formula—and nowhere more decisively than in the last gift the men on the *Duchess of Richmond* were able to offer.

It was a discovery by a German scientist, of all people, named Otto Frisch. Scientists on both sides of the Atlantic were trying to figure out how to set off a nuclear chain reaction, and Frisch theorized that if you used a peculiar substance called uranium 235, only a few pounds of it would be needed to do the job.

Getting those few pounds was the difficult part. It would require a series of industrial processes no one had conceived of, let alone built. Yet two years after the *Duchess of Richmond* returned to Britain, a clutch of American companies—Allis Chalmers, Houdaille-Hershey, and Du-Pont among them—would gather in the deep Appalachian wilderness of Oak Ridge, Tennessee, to do just that. Under the code name "Manhattan Project," their engineers would turn a formula on a chalkboard into the most decisive weapon of them all.

CHAPTER SIX

ARSENAL OF DEMOCRACY

Meeting of the Automobile Manufacturers Association, October 1940. Bill Knudsen sits fifth from left, beside Packard's Alvan Macauley, on his left. Edsel Ford is second from left. GM's Alfred Sloan stands third from right. *Courtesy of the National Automotive History Collection, Detroit Public Library*

> I shall say it again and again and again: Your boys are not going to be sent into any foreign war.
>
> —*Franklin D. Roosevelt, October 30, 1940*

BY OCTOBER, BILL Knudsen could report that he had overseen some 920 contracts worth nearly $3 billion for the Army and $6 billion for the Navy. More than five hundred companies had been drawn in to make everything from ships and tanks and aircraft engines to eleven new gunpowder and ammonia plants.[1] The joke later would be that anyone with a lathe and a train ticket to Washington was getting a war contract.

Everyone, it seemed, except Henry Kaiser.

He wasn't quite finished with work on the high dam at Grand Coulee when he learned a big buildup of America's military was coming and large sums of federal money would be spent. For the next four months, he collared every administration official who was prepared to listen to what Henry Kaiser could do to help America prepare for war—if only the government would give him a contract.

Kaiser had behind him his team from Grand Coulee and Bonneville: his son Edgar, Clay Bedford, and chief engineer George Havas. The construction of Bonneville, an immense 1,027-foot dam holding back a larger volume of water than Boulder Dam, had taken four backbreaking years. "They said it couldn't be done," Kaiser said proudly, "but my kids went ahead and did it."[2] In his mind they were ready for anything— even breaking into an entirely new industry.*

The first Kaiser looked at was steel. All this war materiel was going to require more steel. Production among the major domestic suppliers was sharply down. Why not bring in a newcomer?

From the start this required a partner who knew something about steelmaking. Kaiser turned to the president of Republic Steel and the king of the Little Steel companies, sixty-three-year-old titan Tom Girdler. He was perfect for Kaiser. Tough and self-made and born in Clark's County, Indiana, Girdler had worked in his uncle's cement factory until graduating from Lehigh University at the turn of the century.[3] Like Kaiser, he knew cement and construction. Like Kaiser, he had fought nonstop to grow his company in the teeth of the Depression (he became chairman of Republic three days before the Great Crash). Like Kaiser, he had a keen eye for new opportunities and talented subordinates.

But the choice of Girdler wound up being a bad one. The president of Republic was an outspoken critic of Big Labor and had told the press he would quit to grow potatoes and apples before he accepted collective bargaining. He had blasted the Congress of Industrial Orga-

---

* He had already done that with cement, building the world's biggest cement plant in the late thirties at Alta Vista, and winning the plaudits of Ickes and the New Dealers for getting around the big cement producers.

nizations, or CIO, as "an irresponsible, racketeering, violent, communistic body." John L. Lewis thundered back that Girdler was "a monomaniac with murderous intentions." The murder charge hung on the Memorial Day massacre in Chicago in 1937, when Chicago police fired on marching Republic Steel strikers, killing ten and wounding thirty.[4]

Since 1940 was a presidential election year, President Roosevelt even devoted his last major campaign speech to a full-blast attack on the Republic Steel executive. "There are certain forces within our national community . . . who would destroy America. They are the forces of dictatorship in our own land—on one hand the Communists, and on the other the Girdlers."[5]

That was the end of any chance of a steel venture for Henry Kaiser.

He also faced another problem. His frenetic ways had raised the ire of the twin gatekeepers in the new high-stakes game of winning federal defense contracts, Jesse Jones and Bill Knudsen.

Jones viewed the smooth-talking, irresistibly affable Kaiser with deep suspicion. It got to the point where he forbade his people from ever meeting with the master salesman alone. "After seeing him they come back to me," Jones used to complain, "and say, 'Mr. Kaiser convinced me to give him my watch. Isn't it wonderful?'"[6] As for Bill Knudsen, he and Kaiser took an immediate dislike to each other. This came as no surprise to anyone who knew them. Both men were blunt and outspoken; both shared a strong conviction that their way was best until proven otherwise. Underneath the frenetic charm of Henry Kaiser ran the hard starch of his German immigrant forebears. Knudsen, the immigrant who had boxed his way to fame in the Bronx shipyards, had drunk the same starch.

He also believed in the value of experience, and that was what turned him off about Kaiser. Describing those early days at NDAC later, he talked about being barraged by would-be defense contractors whose attitude was, "I've never done it before but I can do it again." It was a clear reference to Kaiser.[7]

That summer and fall as Britain's fate hung in the balance, every effort Kaiser made to gain a Washington foothold failed. A lesser man would have packed his bags, checked out of the Shoreham, and headed back to California. But not Henry Kaiser. "So what?" he scribbled on the margin of a letter from his lawyer Calhoun describing Knudsen's skepticism about Kaiser.[8] He figured eventually his luck would turn. So it did, thanks, ironically enough, to his biggest skeptic.

It was October, and outside his office Knudsen could see the leaves on Constitution Avenue starting to turn. Far away in England, the Blitz had begun, as German bombers switched to nighttime raids on London. Japan had formally joined the German-Italian axis, and then occupied French Indochina.[9]

Knudsen knew that the course of war would not wait for more planes, and neither could the Army and Navy. The Navy had already called up almost 28,000 reservists to man ships that were still under construction in yards in Philadelphia and Newport News. It had leased bases in Brazil and Chile in order to supply them. Registration for the draft under the Selective Service Act, passed in the teeth of fierce congressional opposition, would begin in a few days. Knudsen had also had a sobering meeting with the head of the Air Corps, General Hap Arnold. Unless America began making more planes, Arnold told him, Britain was finished.[10]

His success with Chrysler and Packard gave him an idea. Why not turn the whole auto industry loose on the war production problem?

Car companies were already making aircraft engines. In addition to Packard, Knudsen had enticed Ford back into the game by getting him to agree to manufacture nine thousand Pratt and Whitney engines—for American planes this time, not British ones. GM's Allison plant was putting together engines for the Curtiss P-40 Warhawk.[11] While Chrysler was making tanks for the Army, Knudsen and Harold Vance had gotten them involved in manufacturing 40mm antiaircraft guns for the Navy—while Pontiac was getting ready to do the same with the 20mm Oerlikon.

Then on September 15, Knudsen had brought to Washington production men and engineers from Saginaw Steering Gear, AC Spark Plugs, Brown-Lipe-Chapin, and Frigidaire—four companies owned but not operated by GM.

"Can you make guns—a lot of guns—in a hurry?" Knudsen asked. Next to him was his small-arms man, Bill "Powder" Johnson.

A crate was hastily brought in and uniformed men pulled off the cover. Inside, carefully wrapped, were machine guns of various types and two principal calibers, .30 and .50. They came from different plants and arsenals, but all bore the expert mark of their designer, the Browning Company, which had engineered all the basic designs soon after the First World War. They had lain around largely unused and forgotten, until now.

The men gathered around, going over the weapons with their eyes and hands, probing and assessing. "Beautiful workmanship," one of them murmured.

Then: "Do you want them as beautifully finished as these handmade products?"

No, they were told, the Army just wanted lots of guns.

"How many—and when?"

"A hundred a day—two years from today, if possible."

Then they were shown the machine tools used to make these battle-field predators. They were belt-driven contraptions, between twenty and seventy years old, which had been packed in grease and stored in various Army arsenals.

The automobile men were appalled. "We would have junked these a long time ago," one of them explained, shaking his head.[12]

Nonetheless, Saginaw Steering Gear and AC agreed to give shelter to the relics and attempt to make guns out of them, while Frigidaire and Brown-Lipe-Chapin would watch and study the results. America's machine gun production was about to jump ninefold.[13]

Machine guns, tanks, antiaircraft guns: so why not fighters and bombers and artillery of all sizes? What if instead of issuing emergency contracts here and there, the car companies' 1,050 factories and $3 billion worth of manufacturing facilities were put to work systematically on the defense effort? The possibilities might be endless.

The auto industry was the country's biggest single employer, with one out of every twenty Americans employed directly or indirectly by its 850 companies.[14] It had the biggest pool of mechanical and engineering talent—engineers who knew how to make rapid modifications in production and design, including machine tools. It was also an industry of associations, with closely knit ties binding its members together, from the Automobile Manufacturers Association to the National Automotive Parts Association, the Motor and Equipment Manufacturers Association, the Society of Automobile Engineers, and many others—some with members who had less than four employees. Here was a network that could mobilize talent, information, and resources from iron and steel to plate glass, copper, lead, leather, and motor oil, for the defense effort. /

Knudsen also sensed that the auto industry was poised to be a model for the future of the American economy. Everywhere Knudsen looked, he saw an American industrial base woefully unprepared for the scale of demands that would be placed on it. He stunned one audience of politicians and businessmen at the Carleton Hotel by stating that the war effort was going to require a complete retooling of nearly every American factory over the next eighteen months.

America's production plant had become obsolete, run down by depression and a government committed to taxing business and giving more power to labor unions. What Knudsen saw in the defense buildup was more than just rearmament in a time of international danger. He saw a way to revitalize American business and industry.

"If we all work hard enough and keep our noses pointed in that one direction, we can do it," he told his Carleton Hotel audience.[15] But it would never happen until the auto industry itself converted to wartime production.

The biggest priority was to break the burgeoning bottleneck in airplane production. In September, Knudsen went over the figures with Stimson before the secretary of war's meeting with the president on the sixteenth. Of 4,247 planes ordered as part of the Congress's first supplemental appropriation for the Army, 4,151 were now under contract. Of the 14,395 ordered in the second the previous week, 2,681 were under contract—nearly one-fifth the total. Given where they had started, it looked impressive. Roosevelt, however, was disappointed. His 50,000 planes a year still looked very far off.[16]

Knudsen also did a tour with General Hap Arnold of every aircraft plant in the country with whom the government had a contract, from

Dayton and Wichita to the West Coast, as well as the leading airplane engine factories.[17] Their production numbers looked woefully small and their physical plants distressingly primitive.

It was time, Knudsen decided, to get things into high gear.

He took the train to New York. October 15, 1940, for the opening of the annual Automobile Show at Madison Square Garden. The Automobile Manufacturers Association was hosting a dinner in honor of Knudsen, and presented him with a signed edition of Carl Sandburg's biography of Abraham Lincoln. Knudsen, an avid book collector, was touched. As the dinner ended he stood up and asked the attendees to bear with him, as he had a request to make.

Knudsen dumped a load of papers on the table. Sitting at the head table, Edsel Ford could see they were blueprints. Airplane blueprints.

"We must build big bombers," he blurted out. "The British cannot win the war with fighters." It was not just Britain who would suffer, he said, but America's own defense preparations. "We need more bombers than we can hope to get," he said. "We need them sooner than we dare to get them under present circumstances. You've *got* to help!"[18]

The response from the automotive executives was enthusiastic: Tell us where to go and what to do. You're the boss, Bill.

The men gathered again on October 29 in Detroit. The same day, Henry Stimson donned a blindfold and reached into an enormous glass bowl to pull out the first draft registration number. The 250,000-strong U.S. Army was about to expand to over a million. America was getting ready for war.

In Detroit, Knudsen's meeting was at the New Center Building, a former gourmet food market and grocery. None of the attendees from Buick and Chrysler and Fisher Body and the other auto companies had told their secretaries or colleagues where they were going, or why. It was top secret.[19]

Once inside, they met a panel Knudsen had assembled, composed of Air Corps officers and aviation executives, to talk about their problems and issues. For the rest of the day, they explained the challenges of making airplanes using prefabricated parts and castings, the problems with using flexible soft dies for parts instead of the hard-cast dies car men were used to, and the issues involved in an industry where a Navy

Aeronautics Board or Army Ordnance request could change faster than a retail customer's could, and could hold up the entire production line while engineers and mechanics stood and thought of ways to meet the new specifications.

The Air Corps men were led by a short, soft-spoken, dark-eyed major who had been a former staff officer under Billy Mitchell. One or two of the General Motors men who had visited their Allison plant had met him. He had been the Air Corps's point man there. On this day he was an aide to Knudsen, nothing more. But in less than a year and a half, he would be a hero to every American household for his daring raid in revenge for Pearl Harbor—a raid that would change the course of the war. His name was Jimmy Doolittle.

Doolittle laid out a series of engine and equipment parts. There were also complete displays of bomber subassemblies in the nearby Graham-Paige auto plant for the executives to examine. The major stressed that the Army Air Corps needed bombers as well as fighters, and needed them now. "Here are the parts we need," Doolittle said in closing. "Pick out the ones you can build."

First on his feet was William Brown of Briggs Manufacturing, the nation's biggest independent car body maker. Owner Edwin Briggs had quit work as a seventy-five-cents-a-day railway worker to stuff car upholstery for Henry Ford and wound up one of the richest men in Detroit, as well as owner of the Detroit Tigers. Now Brown explained how Briggs engineers were working with Vought-Sikorsky to use their car-body-panel presses to make airplane surfaces. Then others began to chime in with ideas, and finally offers.

Briggs, GM's Fisher Body, and the Murray Corporation agreed to make parts for the B-17 Flying Fortress, an agreement that would require close collaboration between the three body-making rivals. Chrysler and Hudson Motor Car said they would help to make frames for Martin's B-26 Marauder, Fisher Body would help with the North American B-25, and Charlie Sorensen from Ford agreed to pitch in with Consolidated's B-24.[20]

That day the executives also agreed to found the Automotive Committee for Air Defense, with Clarence Carleton of Motor Wheel, a parts manufacturer, as chairman. Its members would all help with manufacturing parts of aircraft as subcontractors for Douglas, Boeing, and the rest. At the same time, they agreed, also at Knudsen's request, to suspend all annual model changes for automobiles, thus freeing up time usually spent retooling to concentrate on plane production. In pure marketing terms, it seemed a suicidal move, particularly with less than one-quarter of Americans thinking the United States should be involved in the war in Europe. But it was a major step in getting American business into wartime production—and all more than a year before Pearl Harbor.[21]

That concession persuaded the aviation people to sign on to Knudsen's plan, as well.[22] In the end it would pay off handsomely. Although Michigan held only 4 percent of the country's population, it would ultimately supply 10 percent of all major war contracts. By D-day almost one out of every five Michigan residents was involved in war work, and 70 percent of that work was confined to the four counties around metro Detroit, the heart of the auto industry. General Motors alone would make 10 percent of everything America produced during World War II, including thousands of aircraft engines, hundreds of different parts for Boeing, Martin, and North American, and entire airplanes for Grumman.[23]

Knudsen coined a phrase to describe the auto industry's commitment to war production: "the arsenal of democracy." It would change the entire nature of the military buildup and spill over into every sector of the American economy that converted to wartime production.

A relieved Knudsen returned to Washington. His plane just had time to touch down before the first serious wave of criticism began to hit.

It started with the War Department. Stimson was delighted with Knudsen's $500 million agreement with the carmakers. "He's going to have dies made and stamped out piece by piece in mass production," Stimson noted in his diary, "large portions of the planes which are now made by hand." It was, he wrote, "the first real stroke of light we've had around here" regarding plane production.[24] The news that Detroit was halting annual model changes pleased him even more.

But union leaders were furious about Knudsen's secret meeting in Detroit. The auto industry had only recently begun to be unionized.

Organizers like Walter Reuther and his CIO boss, Philip Murray, feared this agreement to move car companies into war production would be used to wring concessions from workers. Big Labor was used to having its way in New Deal Washington. The presence of Knudsen and his fellow businessmen made them nervous. If someone has to make concessions to get industry moving again, let companies make the sacrifice in terms of profits, they insisted. Don't expect us to give up our gains for the sake of any defense effort.

Instead, United Auto Workers' president Walter Reuther presented his own plan. His workers could easily produce five hundred planes *a day,* he told government officials. Reuther declared that almost half of the plant capacity at Ford, GM, Chrysler, and the others was underutilized (the automakers themselves said it was far less). By pooling machine tools, the labor leader said, they could convert that space to produce the wings and fuselages for fighters, and convert auto engine plants to make aircraft engines by the thousands. Meanwhile, a national aviation production board would give labor, government, and business equal say in how to do it.[25]

When Reuther unveiled his plan in early December, the press and public were agog. Convert the auto industry to aircraft production! Why hadn't anyone thought of that before? The Reuther Plan, with its picture of P-40s coming down the assembly line at the speed of Chevy convertibles, found many champions in the media, and Congress. If Washington stuck to the pace Knudsen and his fellow businessmen were setting, wrote columnist I. F. Stone, America wouldn't be ready for war until 1947.[26]

Knudsen was less impressed. He was quietly amused that Reuther was getting credit for proposing using car companies to build airplanes, when Knudsen had worked out the actual details more than a month before. He also noted that Reuther's plan focused on building *fighters,* when what both the Air Corps and Britain needed were bombers.[27] He also had serious doubts about the idea of mass-producing entire planes. Knudsen's Detroit deal was about making airplane parts, including engines, and left actual assembly to those who knew the business, the aviation companies themselves.

The auto union leader didn't seem to realize that whereas the average automobile consisted of perhaps 15,000 separate parts, a twin-engined bomber like the B-25 Mitchell demanded 165,000 parts—plus 150,000 rivets. No existing auto plant, no matter how carefully retooled, was ready to produce so complex a piece of machinery, let alone five hundred a day of varying sizes and weights.

Still, Roosevelt was impressed by the Reuther Plan and wanted Knudsen to meet him. Knudsen said yes. Reuther brought with him three men he described as tool designers, "capable of doing whatever was necessary."

Knudsen went over to a drawer and pulled out a set of drawings for the Pratt and Whitney 1830 aircraft engine—the predecessor of the R-2800 Twin Wasp Ford had agreed to build. He put them on the desk and told Reuther, "Here are some drawings. You specify the plant, or plants, that will make five hundred of these motors a day, and I will give you a contract to make them."

Reuther never came back. Instead, a few days later he sent back a message. Reuther's people were having trouble figuring out the specifications from the drawings alone, it said. They needed to get into the aviation shops to measure the machines directly.

Knudsen had to laugh. "If they were real tool designers," he explained to his colleague Sidney Hillman, who had worked in the garment industry and knew nothing about heavy manufacturing, "they could read drawings. As for going into the plants, that's nonsense. Those plants are too busy to permit such interruptions."[28]

So the Reuther Plan died a merciful death, despite its influential support. The Knudsen Plan was less spectacular but more rooted in reality. The Air Corps had figured it would take at least twenty months to convert existing auto plants to large-scale airplane assembly. Getting them ready to stamp out parts and subassemblies would take far less time. The Knudsen Plan let airplane makers make airplanes—even eventually planes they hadn't themselves designed.* Automakers and their subcontractors would concentrate on making whatever would help save time for final assembly. In short, the production chain that

* Including the B-29. See Chapter 18.

Knudsen had worked out for Chevrolet would become the foundation
for building American air power.

In the tense autumn of 1940, however, few saw that coming. Instead,
Knudsen and the commission found themselves under siege for being
at once too weak and too powerful. Criticism was mounting that the
NDAC had no real authority and no single leader—an issue Knudsen
himself addressed in a memo in November, which Roosevelt ignored.[29]
On the other side, Knudsen and his team were blasted as shills for big
business, whose members were scooping up the bulk of the defense
contracts—and doing so with their profits intact.

This would be a major criticism during the war and later. Out of
nearly $100 billion worth of defense contracts, 70 percent went to
America's one hundred largest corporations, from Knudsen's own General Motors, to Dow, DuPont, and General Electric.[30] Senators James
Murray of Montana and Harry Truman of Missouri became obsessed
by the subject. They even insisted on the establishment of a Smaller War
Plants Corporation, as a counterweight to what they saw as NDAC's
bias toward bigness.

Knudsen would not be budged. His strategy of getting the biggest
contracts to the biggest companies was deliberate, because, as he pointed
out, companies like Ford or GE had the biggest and best engineering
staffs. "This is a job calling for quantity and quality," he told colleagues
on the Advisory Commission; "it is absolutely necessary to have an
engineering boss on every job."[31] In fact, Knudsen told Roosevelt
point-blank that only corporations with their own engineering departments should get the most vital defense contracts. Those engineers
would have had years of experience figuring out how to make things
in the greatest number and the fastest possible time—an experience
that was going to get more common as America geared up for war.

The small businessman did have his place in the scheme of things,
Knudsen believed, as subcontractors. A company like GM employed
no less than 18,000; during the war Boeing wound up with more than
1,400 subcontractors for its B-29 project alone.[32] The massive food
chain of mass production would give the subcontractors plenty to
do—and plenty of opportunity to grow. The war eventually would
create more than half a million new businesses, while thousands of

existing businesses boomed supplying orders from defense heavy-weights like Ford and Westinghouse and B.F. Goodrich—and on the West Coast, Kaiser and the Six Companies.

Still, Knudsen's confidence rested on a belief that a free market would generate its own spontaneous order matching supply to demand, even in wartime. In 1940 Washington that belief was itself in short supply. "Decentralization [is] analogous to free enterprise," to quote Alfred Sloan. "Centralization, to regimentation."[33] The New Deal had tried once to mobilize and energize the nation's productive resources through regimentation, and failed. Now with war coming, it was the businessman's turn.

Many were dubious; some were outraged. President Roosevelt, to his lasting credit, suspended judgment. He had built his career on the conviction that government knew best, and on vilifying American business and businessmen, whom he had blamed for the Great Depression. "I welcome their hatred," he told a campaign audience in 1936, and American business had paid him back with interest.[34]

But now he was not so sure. When Knudsen returned to Washington that October, Roosevelt's campaign for a third term was entering the most critical stage. His Republican opponent, Wendell Willkie, a corporate lawyer, was drawing more support than Roosevelt had anticipated. With Hitler dominating Europe from the Pyrenees to the Russian border, and Asia in flames, he and the country were facing unimaginable dangers—and unknown territory.

Despite his affable front—"He calls me Bill!" Knudsen gushed to friends—Roosevelt did not trust the big Dane, although he had discovered to his surprise and pleasure that the former GM executive was a good poker player*—and, more important, had no political agenda. "The way to get power down here is to grab it," Jesse Jones had advised Knudsen, but Knudsen refused.[35] In the long run, it would hurt Knudsen when bombs fell on Pearl Harbor. In the short run, it reassured Roosevelt that the big Dane just wanted to make America safe and strong. So Roosevelt let him stay.

---

* According to daughter Martha, Bill's wife, Clara, was even better, regularly walking away with the winnings at poker sessions at the Balmoral house.

It was not a popular decision. Wendell Willkie accused him of failing to take charge of a growing crisis. The dean of American columnists, Walter Lippmann, warned the president it was time to declare a state of national emergency. "Mobilize the entire manpower, machine power, and money power of this country," he wrote six weeks before the election, and let "everything else take second place."[36]

Yet neither then nor later did Roosevelt ever sign on to the idea of taking full charge of the economy in order to prepare for war—or appointing an all-powerful "war production czar." Perhaps he also instinctively grasped that the war mobilization effort was too big a task for one plan or person—that, in Eliot Janeway's phrase, "a victory small enough to be organized is too small to be decisive."[37] If the American people really did need Washington to tell them what to do, then the war was lost.

In Roosevelt's mind, it didn't matter how confused and disorganized Washington was, as long as mobilization became an irresistible, overwhelming force across the country. And Knudsen was showing him how to do it.

There was one criticism, however, to which Roosevelt could not shut his ears, which he finally brought to Knudsen himself.

This was the call to shut down production of civilian durable goods so that all those resources and labor hours could go directly into war production. It was outrageous, journalists in *The Nation* and *The New Republic* grumbled, that Knudsen was letting Ford, Dodge, Packard, and others continue to make cars for commercial sale as if there were no international crisis. Were Knudsen and his Detroit friends serious about getting itself ready for war, or not?[38]

So Roosevelt asked him, and Knudsen was probably more emphatic than in any other conversation he had with the president. Shutting down civilian car production now, with the winter of 1940 approaching, would mean shutting down the plants for months, to install the new machines and tools.

"If they are shut down," he told Roosevelt, "the toolmakers will scatter"—probably to companies like Boeing and North American and Consolidated on the West Coast. "If the toolmakers scatter, we will have a dickens of a time getting them back again. We will lose far more time if that happens than we will by keeping right on as we are."

Instead, he said, we have to bury the automakers under military orders *now*, far more orders than they can make with their present plants. They'll have to grow their assembly lines and facilities, workers will be hired and trained, and the toolmakers will have to stay on until the time comes when America has no choice but to move to full-time war production. "When the time comes," he assured the president, "and they have more facilities, we can shut down on them and they will still have their toolmakers."[39] American business would be ready to make anything from Army trucks and machine gun belts to merchant ships—and it was merchant ships that suddenly had everyone worried.

It started with a plea for help from the British. That winter German U-boats were sinking their merchant ships three times faster than they could replace them—Stimson was told Britain had lost "four million tons of shipping so far"—even as British shipyards were being pounded by Nazi bombers.[40] Churchill approached Roosevelt. The United Kingdom needed sixty new freighters to replenish her merchant fleet, he said. Otherwise she would be facing starvation, and the war would be lost. Could America help?

Roosevelt wanted to say yes. The problem was that American shipyards had never built that many ships in so short a time. Even the most experienced, like Sun Ship Company in Chester, Pennsylvania, and Todd-Bath Iron Works in Maine, were used to orders less than half that size. Meeting Britain's urgent demand would mean gearing up America's merchant shipbuilding capacity to an entirely new level, after being in the doldrums for almost a decade.

Still, the obvious place to turn was the nation's biggest ship companies, the so-called Big Five. But the Big Five didn't want the contracts. Their yards were filled with Navy orders, and their labor and engineering staffs were going to be stretched to the limit. This was partly due to Bill Knudsen's efficiency in organizing Navy shipbuilding. Starting on June 5, 1940, he and NDAC cleared contracts for no less than 948 navy vessels, including 292 combat ships and twelve 35,000-ton *Essex*-class aircraft carriers. Then when the Navy realized at the end of October they would need 50 more destroyers than the 151 first ordered, Knudsen sat down and figured out the cost of additional facilities (ten slipways in six locations for $25 million) and sent a personal letter to Roosevelt making this a budget priority. Between battleships like the *North Carolina* and *Washington* (finished in July 1941), aircraft carriers, destroyers, cruisers, tankers, and coastal craft, the yards were working around the clock. That left no space for the British order.

So new yards would have to be found. They would have to be modern facilities capable of laying keels, building merchant freighters, and then getting them down the slips faster than ever before. Knudsen's point man on shipbuilding, Admiral Emory Land, started looking at the Gulf and the West Coast. It was a ticklish problem. Land wanted places where business and industry knew something about ships, but were not big or established enough to draw away labor from the vital Navy yards.

There was also the question of what kind of ships to build. At a meeting of the NDAC, Admiral Land told them about having to adapt the original British designs to American capabilities, in order to get the ships built as fast as possible. Bill Knudsen raised a question that seemed obvious to him, and to others in the room. What if Land came up with a design not just for the British, he asked, but as a standard type for expanding the United States' own merchant fleet?

Admiral Emory S. Land sat for a moment and weighed the proposal. "Jerry" Land, born in Canon City, Colorado, had escaped the poverty of the dying mining boomtown with an appointment to the Naval Academy. Blunt, decisive, and outspoken, Land had spent a lifetime slicing through red tape—one reason he got on well with Bill Knudsen. Many a brave proposal for a way to get American goods back on the high seas either went up the food chain or died a merciful death depending on whether Land's large letter *L* was scrawled on its front.

Land thought about Knudsen's idea, and then said no. Shipbuilding wasn't like automaking, he explained. A single standard design might work at a single shipyard, but no one had tried to apply one for them all—let alone on such short notice. Land knew his merchant fleet was in desperate shape after a decade of depression. But he didn't want it rebuilt around a hasty and possibly flawed design. These were "emergency ships." Let the British have them as a temporary stopgap, he concluded, and the NDAC would have to think of something else for the American fleet.

It was a watershed moment. If Land and the NDAC had endorsed Knudsen's idea, it is doubtful whether anyone would have let Henry Kaiser build ships that were headed for America's own merchant fleet. But emergency ships for Britain at British expense was another matter. Knudsen had the authority to veto contracts for more than $500,000. But not even Bill Knudsen felt able to stand in the way of this one.

Because when Kaiser got wind of what was happening, he jumped at it. Just a year earlier, the Six Companies had constructed new shipways for Todd's yards in Seattle, to build five new cargo ships on a different contract for the Maritime Commission. Kaiser and his engineers had learned not just about shipyard construction but also about the shipbuilding business. Kaiser had also forged a good relationship with the head of Todd, John Reilly—who also worked closely with Kaiser's lobbyist in Washington, Tommy Corcoran. Now the British contract offered a chance to enter this lucrative arena, at a time when official Washington couldn't afford to be choosy.

A group of British officials came out to see Kaiser in California. He took them out to a series of forlorn mudflats around Richmond, California, on the eastern side of San Francisco Bay. Shivering in the cold, the Britons looked around in confusion.

"But where are your shipyards?" one of them asked.

"There are the shipyards," Kaiser declared, pointing to the empty mudflats. "It's true you see nothing now, but within months this vast space will have a shipyard on it with thousands of workers building the ships for you."[41]

Phones rang, telegrams were sent, and a contract was drawn up, not just for the ships but for two brand-new shipyards. The British, who were paying for the whole thing, were swayed by the ability of Kaiser and his Todd partners to raise whatever extra capital would be needed. Admiral Land believed that making emergency ships like these would be more an assembly process than traditional shipbuilding, which could take up to ten to eleven months for a single freighter.[42] Land was expecting each of these to be finished in less than three. If anyone could do that, it was Henry Kaiser—even though he didn't know a ship's prow from its stern.

On December 21, the day after the British contract was signed—the largest in U.S. peacetime history—Clay Bedford got a phone call. He was in Corpus Christi, Texas, building a large new air station for the Navy. Bedford had been there since June, supervising eight thousand workers and fighting the heat and flies and isolation.

"Clay?" It was Henry Kaiser on the other line, calling from Washington.

"Yes, sir."

"You're going to build me a shipyard."

Bedford had never seen a shipyard, let alone constructed one. Unfazed, he asked his boss, "Where?"

"Richmond," Kaiser answered.

A week later, Bedford's top foreman, O. H. McCoon, stood in a driving rain and gazed gloomily on the series of mudflats that was to be the home of the Todd California Shipbuilding Corporation. McCoon ordered one of his men to drive a bulldozer into the marsh to clear a service road. The bulldozer immediately sank out of sight.[43]

Such was the beginning of what would become the most famous shipyard in the world, producing the most famous merchant ship in the world—the Liberty ship. Yet even as McCoon and his men pulled out their lost bulldozer, events in Washington were changing the entire tempo of preparation for war.

Bill Knudsen lived in a snug house near Rock Creek while he was in Washington. Two Filipino houseboys took care of his domestic needs, and one of the first things he did when moving in was purchase a piano.

He called the fact that he could play the piano his best-kept secret. It contradicted the image of the tough former Bronx shipyard worker and boxer turned GM executive. Not only could he sight-read tunes from Cole Porter to Chopin, he also played the violin, clarinet, and xylophone.[44] People were also amazed to learn Knudsen was an avid book collector who would stop by a bookstore window and dive in to pick up a rare copy of Edward Gibbon or the philosopher Spinoza.

After breakfast his driver Joe would set off for Constitution Avenue and the office, where Knudsen usually arrived by seven. It was rare to see him home before midnight, although on most Fridays he would catch a plane to Detroit to spend the weekend with Clara and the family.

On Tuesday morning, December 3, he was sitting in his office buried in files and reports when Ed Stettinius leaned in the doorway. There was an emergency lunch called at Stimson's home, he said. They were to be there at one o'clock.

It was an unusually warm day for December, and both men left their overcoats behind as they set out for Woodley, Stimson's stately home on the edge of Rock Creek Park. Donald Nelson joined them, and in the dining room they found Stimson, Navy Secretary Knox, and an elderly man in a dark tweed suit. He was Cordell Hull, the secretary of state, and he was, in Stimson's words, "in a very serious and gloomy state of mind."[45]

As Hull spoke, the gloom spread across the room. German sinkings of merchant ships and the bombing of London and industrial centers were slowly pushing Britain to its knees. The British might have ninety days left, Hull said, to hold out alone—and meanwhile Hitler was threatening the Balkans and Egypt. The only way Britain would make it was with more American aid—far more than they had received so far.

"We need to stir up the country," Stimson explained, "the business people of this country who are still asleep." The trio of executives agreed at once. Stettinius would talk to his fellow steel executives; Nelson promised to fly off to Chicago to talk to people there. Knudsen would start at the National Association of Manufacturers meeting scheduled before Christmas in New York.[46]

Then Stimson and Knudsen drove across town to another meeting at Treasury with Morgenthau, Jesse Jones, and their staffs. The new British aid requests were out, as were estimates on Britain's remaining gold and reserve assets. The numbers covered a large blackboard. They showed that as of June 1, 1941, the British government would owe the United States $3 billion. It was also clear that Britain would be at least a billion short.

"I'm rather shocked at the depth we are getting into," Stimson said. Knox stared at the blackboard and then said what everyone else was thinking. "We are going to pay for the war from now on, aren't we?"

Morgenthau threw up his hands. He said, "Well, what are we going to do, are we going to let them place more orders, or not?" Frank Knox murmured, "Got to. No choice about it." But then someone asked, could American industry meet these incredible numbers—and those for the United States' own military, as well?[47]

Bill Knudsen looked up. "We can make it," he said in his hoarse half whisper, "*if* it can be financed"—that is, by the United States instead of Great Britain. Jesse Jones proposed they bring the whole problem to Congress, and Stimson strongly agreed. No one wanted Britain to starve—but no one dared to suggest loaning Britain the money it needed. They had tried that in the First World War, and it had been a disaster. Something more systematic was needed, something that would allow American factories to fill British orders without the British paying dollars for it. And so the idea of Lend-Lease was born.[48]

The concept was simple. Its contours had been implicit in the fifty-destroyer deal struck back in September. But its underlying rationale was spelled out in the contract Knudsen and Jesse Jones had hammered out for the Continental Motors deal, which stated that making arms for Britain was important to America's national defense.

Starting in December, the federal government would place *all* orders for munitions made in the United States. If the Army and Navy needed them, the United States would keep them. If Washington decided that the defense of the country was better served lending them to Great Britain, then "we could either lease or sell the materials, subject to mortgage, to the people on the other side," as Roosevelt explained in a press conference on the seventeenth. Roosevelt compared the transaction to lending a garden hose to a neighbor whose house was on fire. It's still our hose, he explained. We are just letting the one who needs it most use it first.

Who would have legal title to the goods once they were delivered? a reporter asked. "I don't know, and I don't care," the president said.[49]

Washington's new determination was reflected in two other events. On December 1, Joe Kennedy left as ambassador to Britain. Defeat-

ist, anti–Semite, the prophet of doom and gloom, Kennedy was replaced by John Winant, businessman, liberal Republican, former
governor of New Hampshire, and firm backer of aid to Britain. For the
British it was like lifting the window to let in the fresh air. Winant's
arrival at Windsor Castle, where King George VI personally greeted
him at the train station, signaled that the United States was in this war
to stay.[50]

The other was the creation of the Office of Production Management to replace the NDAC. Advice and encouragement would no longer do the job. A new body was needed that could make decisions and
issue directives, with a single head in charge of mobilizing American
industry for the war effort. Stimson, Knox, and Henry Morgenthau all
agreed on who that person should be: Bill Knudsen.

When they met at the White House on December 20, so did the
president. Roosevelt, however, added one stipulation. There should be
two heads, not one, he said: one to lead American business, the other to
lead labor—which also happened to be a major part of his political
base. Roosevelt named Sidney Hillman of the Amalgamated Garment
Workers, and now on the NDAC. Despite a feeling of foreboding,
Stimson and Knox bowed to the president's wish.[51]

The next day, the secretaries broke the news to Knudsen in Stimson's office. "I told Knudsen that he was to be the chief figure," Stimson
wrote afterward in his diary, and that he "had won his position during
the last six months by his outstanding work here in the Advisory Council [*sic*]." He and Knox affirmed that they would stand behind him and
could be called upon whenever he needed them. He thanked them and
returned to his office across the street.[52]

He was a little stunned—and not a little bemused by the idea of
sharing leadership with a man with whom he had continually crossed
swords over labor shortages and strikes. Hillman, born in Lithuania, was
an immigrant like himself. Rumpled and relaxed, he was, like Knudsen,
deceptively self-deprecating. "Sorry, my best suit has to go to the cleaners," he would say apologetically to the other committee members,
pointing to soup stains on his lapels, "but I wore it anyway." Otherwise
they had little in common. But at least Knudsen could bring his own
team, along with Stettinius and Don Nelson, with him—plus a new

man, Chicago newspaper publisher Merrill Meigs, to head aircraft production. He was also relieved, because at long last preparation for war
would have the force of law behind it.

"When I think of the seriousness of the whole world situation," he
had told the assembled guests at the NAM banquet the week before,
"where the Americas are the only spot where freedom and law still
have a foothold . . . I think that the best and only thing the United
States can do and must do is prepare swiftly and well to protect ourselves." It was time to put the defense buildup on a wartime basis, even
though America was still at peace.

"It is our responsibility to see that this is done in record time," he
said, looking over the representatives of the carmakers, the machine
tool makers, the steel and rubber and copper and chemical industries,
"and now show the world that we can do the things we have been so
wishfully forecasting the last six months."[53]

Four days after Christmas, on the night of December 29, 1940, a
resonant voice familiar to all Americans came onto radios across the
country.

"My friends, this is not a fireside chat on war. It is a talk on national
security."

Like millions of other Americans, Bill Knudsen sat in the living
room of his Rock Creek house and listened to his president.

"Not since Jamestown and Plymouth Rock," Roosevelt said, "has
our American civilization been in such danger as now." The Nazi empire was bent on creating a new global order based on racial superiority
and domination, one with "no liberty, no religion, no hope." Under
such an order, America would survive, if it survived at all, at the point
of a gun.

But by aiding those "in the front line of democracy's battle" and
halting the Axis advance, Roosevelt told the American people, "there is
far less chance of the United States getting into the war. . . . The people
of Europe who are defending themselves do not ask us to do the fighting. They ask us for the implements of war, the planes, the tanks, the
guns, the freighters which will enable them to fight for their liberty and
for our security."

The means to do it are already here, the president said. "American industrial genius, unmatched throughout the world in the solution of production problems, has been called upon to bring its resources and its talents into action." The makers of sewing machines and cash registers and lawn mowers, he said, are now making fuses and telescope mounts and shells and tanks.

"We must be the great arsenal of democracy. For us this is an emergency as serious as war itself."[54]

Knudsen must have smiled. The phrase "arsenal of democracy" was his.[55] It was already happening. Some 50,000 planes, 130,000 engines, 380 Navy ships, 9,200 tanks, and 17,000 heavy guns, plus rifles, helmets, and clothing for an army of 1.4 million men, were being made or under contract to be made. Plant facilities to arm another 2 million, and get a two-ocean navy of 800 ships out to sea, were on their way, as well. Knudsen had calculated all this would require some 18 billion man-hours of mind-bending, back-straining labor—and he sensed that was still a long way from being enough.[56]

"I call upon our people with absolute confidence," the president said in closing, "that our common cause will greatly succeed."

It was three nights before the New Year. Eight days earlier the papers had carried the news that a bankrupt and burned-out F. Scott Fitzgerald, the novelist who had symbolized the Jazz Age and its excesses, had died of a heart attack.

The party really was over. America was about to find a new generation of heroes.

One of them would be Henry Kaiser.

CHAPTER SEVEN

SHIPS, STRIKES, AND
THE BIG BOOK

Richmond shipyards, October 1941. *Courtesy of the Bancroft Library, University of California, Berkeley*

Together we build.

—*Henry Kaiser*

THE EXPERTS PREDICTED it would take Bedford, McCoon, and their teams six months to build up enough solid ground before they could begin work on the shipyard. It took Kaiser's men exactly three weeks.[1]

Truck after truck brought up 300,000 cubic yards of rock and gravel around the clock. In more or less continuous rain, gangs of workmen sank 24,000 iron piles for the shipways and piers, even before Kaiser's architect Morris Wortman had completed the final blueprints. "There was a race," Clay Bedford later remembered, "between the Kaiser draftsmen and the field people as to whether we could build it first or the engineers and architects could draw it first."

Three hundred and thirty-seven thousand cubic yards of silt had to be dredged out of the Santa Fe Canal, and another 300,000 from what was to become the launch basin and canal where completed ships would get their final outfitting. On February 22 the first makeshift office was finished, and Clay Bedford moved in with his team from Corpus Christi: secretary Howard Welch and cost accountant Joe Friedman. And still it rained. The fiberboard ceiling in the building became so waterlogged that it sagged. Bedford had to duck his head every time he went into his office.[2]

Even in fair weather, the construction equipment of the time did not make the job easier. In 1941 there were no hydraulic rigs, only cable scrapers, bulldozers, and cranes on trawlers or trucks. The biggest bulldozers for clearing earth had only 132 horsepower, with the operator constantly hopping off his machine to check the grade against the marked slope numbers. Concrete had to be poured from a crane-hoisted bucket, while water and gas mains required installing time-consuming cast iron or welded steel pipe—at a time when steel was becoming a rare commodity.[3]

Still, the deadline would not wait. "That first keel has to be laid by March 7," Kaiser had told Bedford and, to make his life more complicated, all the work was to be done using union labor. Laborers from sixteen different craft unions applied for work; even union barbers from around the country turned up, expecting that the new yards were going to mean lots of paying customers.[4]

When finished, the yard had seven shipways, each 87½ feet wide and 425 feet long. North of the shipways was a massive steel-framed building housing the plate shop and assembly bay, as well as a large open area where preassembled parts could be moved and stored until hoisted into place. To do the hoisting, each shipway was serviced by cranes that moved along steel tracks set on either side of each slipway, so that the crane could swing from one slipway back to another. Gantry cranes of that size were in short supply in Depression-era America, so Bedford arranged for cranes he had used building Grand Coulee Dam to be dismantled and shipped west.[5] Until now the model for American shipbuilding had been the steel industry. Kaiser and his team would introduce a new model: big-time construction. In so doing, they would revolutionize shipbuilding not just in America but around the world.

All the same, an operation of this size required an experienced superintendent. It was a typical early morning Kaiser phone call that got Edwin W. Hannay, a famed West Coast shipyard manager and troubleshooter for several shipmakers during the First World War, out of bed and out of retirement. Henry's son Edgar was on the line. "Can you come back to work for us?" he asked. Hannay agreed and made some calls of his own. He pulled together sixteen friends and former colleagues, who then brought in *their* friends. In no time a skeleton force was ready to get to work.[6] This was fleshed out with the men who had worked with Kaiser before on every project from Boulder Dam and Grand Coulee to the Oakland–San Francisco Bridge, and who were used to doing the impossible for the boss.

They knew a lot about construction and cement but, as Hannay found out, not a lot about iron or shipbuilding. When Hannay got started on Hull No. 1, he heard someone ask impatiently, "When do we pour the keel?"[7]

Edgar, meanwhile, was on his way up to Portland.

In 1940 Oregon was still the Northwest his father had known and left behind: a world of towering forests, lumber camps, and sawmills, surrounded by thousands of acres of fruit orchards. Oregon was settled, it was said, by Missourians who didn't want to work, and the slow, easy ways of the past still suited the pioneers' grandsons and granddaughters who made up the bulk of the state's population.[8]

When Edgar arrived, he managed with his father's help to pick out eighty acres of barren land outside Portland that were to be the site of the Todd–Six Companies shipyards, otherwise to be known as the Oregon Shipbuilding Corporation. City fathers were unperturbed by the Kaiser hustle and bustle. Shipbuilding activities during the last war had made the town.[9] They also had known Henry Kaiser the road builder for some twenty-five years. They figured (wrongly, as it turned out) that this would be nothing too big or complicated, and that they could keep a handle on the new development.

Edgar had begun work for his father at age twelve, writing out dispatch tickets for truckers supplying equipment for road construction sites. One day a trucker drove off after forgetting his ticket, and Edgar chased after him. The boy slipped, fell under the rumbling vehicle, and had his foot crushed. Ord Ordway and another worker gathered him up and drove him to a hospital. Doctors wanted to amputate, but Ordway warned them they had better wait for the boss to show up. Henry Kaiser arrived, looked at his son's foot, and ordered the doctors to do what they could to save it. They did as they were told, and although Edgar Kaiser walked the rest of his life with a limp, he did it on two feet.[10]

Henry's relationship with Edgar was typical of all his dealings with subordinates, sons or not. "You find your key men by piling work on them," he used to say. "They say, 'I can't do any more,' and you say, 'Sure you can.' So you pile it on and they're doing more and more. Pretty soon you have men you can rely on absolutely."[11] Far from driving a wedge between father and son, Kaiser's demands made them an inseparable team. Henry was devoted to his other son, but Henry Jr. suffered from bad health and would eventually die of multiple sclerosis in 1961. The bond between Henry and his namesake would never be as close, or as vital to the making of the Kaiser corporate empire, as the one between Henry and the bespectacled, hard-driving Edgar.

Edgar had made his bones, as it were, supervising the construction at Grand Coulee—although he had been only thirty-four—and then the Bonneville Dam. Now getting started at Portland, he had learned all he could about shipbuilding from repeated visits to various Todd yards: about the laying of the keel, the fitting of steel plates and support ribbing for decks and holds, and then the installing of engines. He could envision it all in his mind, including finally the electrical and ventilation assemblies, before the main deck was completed and the ship was ready to slide down the slip.[12]

And he knew this particular ship design and the demands it would make on his engineers, foremen, and workers. It required steel plates, each weighing several tons, to be molded and cut into 435 different shapes and an even more bewildering variety of sizes. His Portland operation would be ordering 7,500 components from 600 different suppliers, from condensers and switches to wires, pumps, and the engines themselves.[13]

Even more daunting was the fact that he would have to do all this with men who had never built a ship in their lives, workers from construction jobs, sawmills, and lumber camps, under the supervision of foremen and quartermen who barely knew more.

But like Clay Bedford, Edgar had his own team of trusted engineers and site managers, men he had driven and hounded like his father had hounded him—and who knew how to make anything in a hurry. There was also another goad to action: the desire to beat his rival, the man who was almost Kaiser's other son, Clay Bedford. Over the next thirty-six months, Henry would encourage a less-than-covert competition between the two yards, and the two men in charge. It was another typical Kaiser strategy, and it worked. It never turned ugly, and never became divisive. But Edgar Kaiser and Clay Bedford would work eighteen-hour days for the next three years, each trying to see who could build ships faster and better.

Bedford had a month's head start. In typical Kaiser style, Edgar got to work even before the blueprints were finished. It took him less than two months to get the first set of shipways built.[14] At the end of March, his first buildings and cranes appeared on the Portland horizon, as nine hundred miles away in Richmond, Bedford and Hannay were ready to lay the first keel of the vessels both he and Edgar would be building: the Liberty ships.

Initially the maritime commissioner had rejected Knudsen's idea of making Kaiser's ships the standard for a new generation of American merchant freighters. But as the events of December 1940 grew darker, Land changed his mind. He made secret plans to take over the Kaiser ship contract in case Britain fell—and the growing need to get ships down the slips faster pushed his earlier reservations away. If they didn't take this opportunity, he told Bill Knudsen, it wouldn't just be Britain, but America that wouldn't see a completed ship before 1942.[15]

Knudsen signed on. It would mean that a whole new series of shipyards would have to be acquired or built, in addition to the one Kaiser was building at Richmond and the one Todd and the Six Companies were using in Portland, Maine—and Edgar Kaiser's yards in Oregon.

Baltimore's Sparrow Point, New Orleans, Houston, Jacksonville, Florida, and Mobile, Alabama, were among the places they found.[16] But getting the right sites for shipyards was just one problem. The other was what kind of ship. Land went to New York City to see the man who knew the answer, visiting him at his office on 21 West Twenty-first Street. His name was William Francis Gibbs and the building was the headquarters of Gibbs and Cox, the biggest naval architecture firm in America.

Gibbs was the reigning king of American ship design. When Land contacted him that bleak January of 1941, Gibbs had seen the war clouds gathering for years. He had prepared his firm to be ready for floods of new orders from the United States Navy. Before 1940 was out, his employees had grown from an even dozen to more than a thousand people.[17] In the end, Gibbs and his business partner, William Cox, would design almost three-quarters of U.S. naval vessels during the war. But his most renowned and enduring design would be the one Henry Kaiser and his team would make famous.

When Land approached him about a new merchant vessel, Gibbs already knew about the problem. Kaiser had hired him when he had to adapt the existing British plans to his yards at Richmond. Through Kaiser, Gibbs knew these ships had to be built fast; he knew that meant they had to have a standard plan, especially for a labor and management force like Kaiser's—men who had never been aboard a ship, let alone built one.

He also knew there had to be a standard design, not just for the yards and its engineers, but for the six hundred or so subcontractors, so they would know what parts to make and how many—even while the yards themselves were still being built.

Gibbs showed Land what he had done for the Kaiser-Todd people. Land was impressed and quickly agreed. The Kaiser yard design would be the standard for all.[18]

Working overtime, with Maritime Commission technicians helping out and offering advice, Gibbs turned out acres of blueprints for every part of the ship. When he was done, he had created a vessel that looked rather different from its British predecessor. It had one central deckhouse, instead of the usual two fore and aft. It was oil fired, not coal burning (which made it possible to fuel at sea, if necessary), and on its main deck it had solid steel bulwarks instead of the standard chain rails, so that cargo could be crammed onto every square inch of the ship, including planes and tanks and trucks strapped on deck.

Gibbs's Liberty ship was made with as many straight lines as possible, because it would be made from welding rather than rivets.[19] Also to speed the construction, standard wooden interior decks were replaced with steel, although with wooden hatch covers in between. When someone asked why, they got a bleak answer: That way the hatch covers could be used as life rafts if the ship took a U-boat torpedo and sank.

Because from the beginning, Gibbs and Land assumed the Liberty ship would be an expendable ship. Many would be sunk; many sailors would be lost. Although manned and conned by civilians, they would be directly in the line of fire. No one expected them to have many return voyages.

Partly for that reason, and because speed of construction was key, Gibbs's design made as few concessions as possible to comfort. There was no electricity or running water for the crew; their rooms and bunks were smaller than standard size. There was cement, not tile, in the toilet spaces, and no mechanical ventilation for the engine and boiler rooms and crew's quarters. The galley was lit with oil lamps, and there was no fire detection system.[20] These would not be comfortable trips, even by merchant seaman standards. Gibbs's ship was a seagoing boxcar, able to stow eight thousand tons of material in her hull. She would carry everything from tanks and bombers to copper wire and sugarcane. And she had to be built not only in record time, but in record numbers, in order to keep Britain alive.

The first keel of a Liberty ship was laid at the Bethlehem yard in Baltimore in March, and the first Richmond keel on April 14, 1941. The *Ocean Vanguard* would be the first of 747 that would be built in Richmond yard in the next four years. Even as workmen scrambled that week of the fourteenth, Kaiser found himself under contract for many more.[21] Land gave him the go-ahead to expand the number of slips both at Richmond and Portland, even before the first ship was launched. Under the new regime, some 300 new ships would have to be built, including 72 tankers, and the Six Companies were going to be at the center of it.

That included Kaiser's partner Stephen Bechtel. He had tried to get the British interested in a second West Coast contract for their "Ocean" ships, but they had opted for a more experienced East Coast yard, Todd–Bath of Maine, instead. Now he and his two partners—Ralph Parsons, an engineer specializing in oil refinery designs, and a former Consolidated Steel engineer Steve had known since college days at Berkeley named John McCone—had thrown themselves into a bid for the Liberty ship program in January. Their prospective company, called California Shipbuilding, or Calship, got the contract, and would open with fourteen slipways instead of eight. Richmond would be adding a whole new yard, called Yard No. 2; and Edgar's Portland basin was to add three more shipways even before the first eight were built.[22]

Henry Kaiser, meanwhile, was delighted. This was the kind of massive project he loved, although some in the press, such as *Fortune,* were wondering aloud if perhaps "he had bitten off more than he could chew." They were wrong. As Hannay and the others were laying Hull No. 1 on April 17, Henry Kaiser was already poised to become the living symbol of Knudsen's arsenal of democracy.

April 1941 was important for another reason. On March 11, Roosevelt had signed the first Lend-Lease agreement with Britain. The steady stream of orders for British war materials was about to become a flood. Everything, including the Liberty ship program, was about to get a lot more complicated.

It also meant new headaches for Knudsen and his team. Knudsen estimated it would add 60 percent more to America's war production burden.[23] As the new Office of Production Management, they were now installed in a series of suites in the Social Security Building. OPM was supposed to create a simple division of labor for clearing Army and Navy orders, with Knudsen and his people (Biggers at Production, Nelson at Purchases, and Stacy May doing statistics for everyone) handling management, Hillman dealing with labor problems, and the secretaries of war and Navy speaking as consumers of defense production.

But there was also a fourth guest at the table, namely, Great Britain. Every week, it seemed, the British expected a fresh cornucopia of weapons and materials. Knudsen knew it couldn't be done that quickly, especially since the federal government had no way of ordering anyone to do anything about arming the Americans, let alone the British. In February, Winston Churchill had made the stirring statement "Give us the tools and we will finish the job." But which tools? Thus far it had been pretty much ad hoc guesswork. Knudsen's people had to get ahead of the problem by figuring out what Britain needed and when, and what America could be expected to produce and when—all without derailing America's own effort to arm itself.

This was a problem in statistics as much as production, and the man who figured it out was OPM's numbers man, Stacy May. That summer Knudsen gave him the go-ahead to prepare a comprehensive study of what American industry was making, and could potentially make, by way of war materials. The result was the Big Book, a massive compilation of production figures and forecasts for everything from tanks and gas masks to brass for artillery shells and cotton for uniforms. Knudsen and the others had for the first time a comprehensive picture of what America needed to fight a modern war, what it would take to make it, and how much it would cost—roughly $50 billion.[24]

May lugged his magnum opus off to London to fill the other half of the book with an estimate of what Britain's entire material production potential was and what its stockpiles amounted to. For two months he and his British counterparts conferred, filling in the blank sheets and tabs. When they were done, they had one of the most extraordinary documents of the war: a complete record of American, British, and Canadian military requirements, from tanks and planes to food and uniforms; current and potential production; and current and potential raw material stocks, including steel, aluminum, and copper.

It was in effect a complete balance sheet (the British termed it "the consolidated statement") of the Allied war effort, both present and future—the first ever drawn up. For the Americans, it showed they still had a long way to go. Though the United States had two and a half times the population of Britain and Canada, the country's munitions output still lagged far behind. But at least the people in Washington now knew where they had to go—while Knudsen and the OPM figured out how to get there.[25]

May shook hands with his British counterparts and then boarded a plane in Manchester to begin the long journey back to the States, finally touching down outside Baltimore. "I should have been met at the airport and escorted to Washington by an armed guard," May noted later, "equipped with at least .45's and submachine guns." There was no one. So May simply and quietly caught another cab and then, unobserved and unescorted, brought the single most important book in the Allied war effort to the Munitions Building and set it finally down on Stimson's desk.

A copy also made its way to OPM. The final numbers boggled everyone's mind. Back in March, May had calculated the buildup the Americans and British were looking for could not be done for less than $50 billion. Now Knudsen and Stimson might have to treble that number.[26] As for Congress, its defense authorization for 1942 was stuck at $10.5 billion. That was barely 1 percent of what might be needed.

It didn't matter. For all its impressive bulk and data, the Big Book was a fantasy. The pages of data were a rough guide to what materials would have to come out of the civilian sector to meet Army and Navy orders, but not much more.[27] It gave Washington the illusion of control over war production trends and events when in fact it had none. Even the revised figure of $150 billion wound up being half of what the American economy had to produce to win the war—*less* than half when the value of Lend-Lease aid to Britain and Russia is thrown in.

No one as yet knew what American business could do once it really got started. This was uncharted territory. The fiercest obstacle the war-production effort faced, however, wasn't Washington or the military or even the Axis.

It was the labor unions.

Union membership had surged during the New Deal years, from 6 percent in 1933 to 16 percent of the workforce in 1940. Now labor leaders like Sidney Hillman worried that all-out war production would wipe out past gains and allow employers to break open closed shops.[28] Others saw reviving factories and plants as an opportunity to get new concessions. /

For those associated with the Communist-dominated CIO, there were also political issues involved. The official party line was that the war raging in Europe was still a bourgeois struggle and the working class had nothing to gain by getting involved. The Molotov-Ribbentrop Pact hadn't made the Soviet Union Hitler's ally exactly, but Stalin and his Communist followers had no desire to help Britain or its Dominion allies win. As labor historian Max Kampelman has shown, the Communists' goal was to halt or at least hamper the American war effort, and strikes were one way to do it.[29]

The first was at the Vultee aircraft plant in San Diego. It was easy to see why the CIO targeted Vultee. It was run by the Communist-hating, New Deal–defying Tom Girdler of Republic Steel, who had put the plant under the supervision of an assembly-line whiz named Henry Woodhead. Woodhead had perfected his craft under Felix and Albert Kahn's brother Julius, stamping out factory components for Truscon Steel like steel window sashes and airplane hangar doors, as well as highway guardrails and wire mesh for reinforcing concrete. At Vultee he installed an overhead conveyor line, the first ever in an aviation plant, and used mass-production stamping methods for the airplane parts. In no time he was building trainers for the Army Air Corps and Vengeance dive-bombers for the British.[30]

Then in November the Vultee workers, led by two CIO organizing brothers, struck against having to continue their fifty-cent-an-hour wage in spite of the new work. Woodhead's humming assembly line fell ominously silent. White House pressure forced management to give way, but the Vultee run-in left plenty of bad feelings just as January brought strikes in a radiating wave, closing one factory after another.

In February the CIO pulled workers off the lines at the Allis-Chalmers plant in Milwaukee, which was making turbines for Navy vessels, and at the Cluett and Peabody factory making uniforms. There were strikes at International Harvester, at Ford's major plants, and at the North American plant where B-25s were being built. By March 1941, at a time when airplane production was at a vital premium, there were no fewer than fifteen strikes at aircraft or aircraft-related companies.[31]

Knudsen was furious. "This is criminal," he told the National Press Club, "almost like men fighting about who should hold the hose when the house is on fire"—because he knew most of the strikes weren't over wages or conditions but which union should have jurisdiction over new workers or a new plant.[32]

On March 7, Knudsen sketched out for Stimson and Knox how bad things really were. He was looking at four million labor hours lost at Allis-Chalmers, where the strike was now in its eighth week. He told hair-raising stories of threats of violence against foremen and executives at the Vanadium Steel plant in Pennsylvania.[33] Sidney Hillman, OPM's labor head but also a staunch anti-Communist, agreed to go in person to Milwaukee to hammer out a settlement, but failed. "The unions are so undisciplined, young, and restless," he told Knudsen, "it's hard to do anything with them."

Didn't they understand, Knudsen said, that every week's loss of work to win a nickel or dime raise meant it would take sixteen weeks for the company to get back where they started? Hillman threw up his hands and said nothing.[34] The fact was, Communist-led unions were determined to strike, whatever their wages. Knudsen didn't know that, however, and took the impasse hard. Stimson noted that "poor Knudsen, who is bearing the brunt of it, is getting a little tired and discouraged with it." It was particularly tiresome to have the union's friends in the administration blaming him and big business for moving slowly on war production, when it was the unions who were putting on the brakes— slowing war production before Pearl Harbor, Knudsen later calculated, by as much as 25 percent.[35]

He and Stimson told the president the only solution they could see was a national defense mediation board, and Hillman agreed. The president duly announced its creation on March 19—but the strikes went on as before.

Then, at the start of April, John L. Lewis, the fiery leader of the United Mine Workers, threatened to pull 400,000 of his men out in a nationwide strike. It was not just defense plants but the entire width and breadth of American industry that was looking at a complete shutdown.

America "has got to get over this strike epidemic," thundered Bill Knudsen before an audience of Veterans of Foreign Wars at the Waldorf Astoria on April 5. "The hours lost can never be made up and are precious. . . . I am getting all out of patience with all this talk about money. This is no time to ask for quotations on the defense of the United States." Knudsen said he didn't think there was need for legislation to prevent strikes, but he did say something had to be done to get people to take preparedness seriously. Otherwise, as columnist Stewart Alsop noted in the *New York Herald Tribune,* "every informed person in Washington agrees the result may be tragedy."

March and April saw British reverses in Greece and the Mediterranean. Rommel's Afrika Korps pushed British forces in North Africa almost to the Egyptian border. U-boat sinkings in April reached a new high. For German submarine captains, this was "the happy time." Congress, meanwhile, remained skeptical about spending more on defense, despite passing Lend-Lease.

"This job can't be handled with money," Knudsen had said. But critics could point out that Knudsen and OPM had been very concerned about money when it came to protecting business profits as an incentive to wartime conversion, especially for the auto industry. So in a show of good faith, on April 17 Knudsen negotiated a new round of concessions from Detroit. The entire industry, he told the press, agreed to cut its car production by 20 percent by August, in order to save manpower and materials. Starting August 1, carmakers would be making one million fewer automobiles.

Knudsen had offered a 40 percent cut, but his co-chair, Sidney Hillman, vigorously opposed it. Hillman worried that big production cuts would force Detroit workers to look for jobs elsewhere and decimate the unions, so he pushed for the number to be cut in half. All the same, Knudsen figured this would save 1.4 million tons of steel, 113,000 tons of rubber, almost 125,000 tons of copper, zinc, and lead, 6.5 million square feet of leather, and 41 million yards of hardwood.[36]

But save for what? America's military buildup looked like it was stalling out. The War Department was pushing one way, demanding more production and more materials; labor and strikes were pushing the other way; OPM found itself jammed in the middle. When Donald

Nelson proposed a sweeping reorganization of the Army's procurement system, Knudsen had given it a thumbs-up. Then John Biggers handed Nelson a letter from the War Department, saying no thanks and curtailing his procurement powers. Nelson decided it was time to give his notice, until the president talked him out of it.[37]

This was connected with a larger problem that Nelson and his Priorities Board had to address. How would America prepare for war without starving the rest of the economy? The Big Book offered a sobering picture of war production sucking America's supplies of raw materials dry. The solution Don Nelson had worked out in late 1940 was a system of priorities for purchasing certain critical raw materials, such as wool, cotton, steel, and rubber. This way the military wouldn't run short but civilians wouldn't find store shelves empty, while critical products like tractors and railway cars were still being made and repaired.

The initial system worked out based on the priorities lists drawn up in World War I was soon hopelessly inadequate.[38] Nelson and his hardworking team had to reinvent it again and again, dividing America's raw materials into "strategic," "critical," and "essential" categories, and ultimately creating an A, B, and C priority system for allocating enough of the most critical materials, such as steel and rubber, to defense needs. It was so confusing even the administrators couldn't keep up.

Knudsen and everyone else looked to "the boss," FDR, to break all these impasses, but the president's earlier boldness deserted him. One day when Hillman was out ill, Knudsen and Knox (who was desperate for those Allis-Chalmers turbine engines) issued a joint statement ordering the workers at the Milwaukee plant back to work, but FDR refused to back them up.[39] He also refused to break the logjam over the North American strike, which dragged on into June, even as Communist organizers led 12,000 workers off the job in the sawmills and logging camps around Puget Sound—a major source of construction lumber for shipbuilders in the region.[40]

The president's penchant for putting off big decisions was kicking in. He turned down Churchill's request to help with the convoying of supply ships across the Atlantic, although he did allow British naval vessels to refuel and repair in American ports. Roosevelt also proclaimed a security zone around the United States, warning off Axis warships—but it only extended midway between Brazil and Africa. Inside the zone, U.S. warships could track and warn others of the presence of U-boats, but could not take any further action.

To intimates, Roosevelt that spring seemed "cautious to the point of immobilization."[41] Luckily, Bill Knudsen wasn't.

CHAPTER EIGHT

COUNTDOWN

Interior of Chrysler's Detroit tank arsenal plant, Warren, Michigan. *Courtesy of the National Automotive History Collection, Detroit Public Library*

Mass production takes time to get started.
—William S. Knudsen to FDR, 1941

AT NIGHT KNUDSEN sat with his yellow legal pad and did the numbers.

Despite the strikes, production was going up. A year before, no tanks were being manufactured in the United States except those hand-made in government arsenals. Now, Baldwin Locomotive had a backlog order, Chrysler was coming through with its plant, while American Car Foundry and American Locomotive were ready to turn out tanks on their assembly lines.[1]

"Babe" Meigs (a nickname owing to the fact he was six foot four) had reported that total plane production was up to 1,450 a month; the goal was 2,600 by October. Knudsen estimated they would hit 3,000 to 3,500 a month before 1942 was out.[2] "Powder" Johnson had performed miracles with the help of DuPont as well as companies with names out of Greek mythology—Hercules, Atlas, and Trojan Powder—in getting new American gunpowder and TNT plants up and operating at sites ranging from Radford, Virginia, to Sandusky, Ohio. Meanwhile—the brightest spot on the horizon—small-arms production at places like Saginaw Steering Gear and the Winchester Company was actually running ahead of schedule. Saginaw was supposed to supply the government with 280 machine guns by March 1942. When that date came, they would ship *28,728* guns.[3]

As for raw materials, when Knudsen had come to Washington, the country's aluminum production was barely 25 million tons. Now it was 40 million, and headed to 70 by the end of the year. Steel was showing similar numbers.[4] If imported materials like tungsten, chrome, and rubber were still in critical short supply, once Henry Kaiser's yards began turning out ships ready to go fetch them, that would change.

At the top of the page, however, Knudsen scrawled two large numerals: *1* and *8*. That was the magic number: eighteen months. That's how long Knudsen estimated it would take for American business and industry to make the arsenal of democracy a reality. One year to build new plants and retool the old ones, six months for conversion.

Everywhere he looked, that number held true. A year for tooling for airplane engines, maybe ten months with overtime. A year to tool for tanks of thirty to thirty-one tons. Nine to eleven months for a TNT plant.[5] Then another six months before everyone would see full production—enough guns, tanks, planes, and bombs to sweep Germany and its Axis allies into oblivion.

"Everyone knows that America is the greatest mass producer in the world," Knudsen kept telling Roosevelt. "Not everyone knows that mass production takes time to get started." But "once you get going, the momentum takes you a long way"—all the way to victory.[6]

Why so long to get started? Because American assembly lines could not get moving until they had the machine tools for the job. Machine tools are the heart of the industrial process. They can drill; they can bore; they can turn steel like table legs on a lathe or slice slabs of iron like a wood plane. They take steel, cast iron, brass, and aluminum and mill, grind, shear, and press them into parts for household or industrial goods. Their design depends on the amount of force needed behind the grinding, cutting edge.[7]

This means some machine tools are not much bigger than a bread box; others are the size of a house. In 1940 eighty-seven were necessary to make the average propeller shaft, from lathes to cut the shaft metal to machines to bore it and grinders to finish the job. The men, and later women, who ran the machine tools were the grunts, the unsung but essential foot soldiers of the modern industrial process. The machine tool makers were its elite, its master sergeants—except that they were aloof from the processes they set in motion. One admirer dubbed them the "master builders of the Industrial Revolution"—except that what they brought into being weren't soaring cathedrals of stone but sprawling factories of iron and steel.[8]

In 1940 almost every machine tool in America came from two hundred firms. Most had barely one hundred employees; some, fewer than fifty. Most of the best firms were concentrated in New England, and three of the biggest were in Vermont, in the Black River Valley, where their origins reached back to the American Revolution.[9] Their hands smeared with oil and aprons with grease, generation by generation they labored to create the machines that made every product from cars to refrigerators and industrial fans.

The Depression years had been hard on the machine tool makers. In 1929 total American sales were $185 million; in 1932 they were hardly over $22 million. Companies like Jones and Lamson of Springfield, Vermont, and Cincinnati Milling Machine had filled the gap with foreign orders—ironically, one of their best customers was imperial Japan, whose Mitsubishi and Kawasaki aircraft factories hummed to the tune of American machine tools.* When the war buildup started, Jones and Lamson's president, Ralph Flanders, warned Knudsen and the NDAC that the need for machine tools would be "infinite" and that they were going to find themselves up against the wall in getting enough grinders, borers, and stamping and milling machines.[10] Roosevelt had put a

---

* Another was Stalin's Russia. In 1938 almost one-quarter of all foreign sales were to the Soviet Union, and in 1934 Bryant Chucking Grinder saw more than half of its total sales going to the Workers' Paradise.

halt to exports of machine tools, even to Great Britain. Then machine tool makers could only send new tools to those companies on the defense priorities list. Even so, dealing with the problem had been largely put off until now.

The first part of Knudsen's plan had been under way since the previous June. New plant construction had been booming for almost a year, with Jesse Jones putting up more than $33 million for new facility construction for War Department orders.[11] Some 784 new factories had been started and more than half were finished.[12] Thanks to miracle workers like Albert Kahn, the work went even faster than many thought possible. K. T. Keller came to Kahn on a Wednesday looking to build Chrysler a new machine shop five hundred feet wide and two-thirds of a mile long. Kahn had the plans ready by Friday morning, and ninety days later the building was going up.[13]

April, May, and June 1941 were the next critical months, when retooling around the country would kick in. To make sure that happened, Knudsen went to find Fred Geier.

Geier was president of Cincinnati Milling Machine and president of the Machine Tool Builders' Association. Over time, as America's manufacturing spread over the Old Northwest and across the Mississippi, two firms rose up to challenge the mighty New England machine tool empire. One was Cleveland Machine Tool; the other, Cincinnati Milling Machine. Fred had inherited the latter company from his father, a German immigrant's son who sold Henry Ford his first machine tool before passing the firm over to his extraordinary son.[14]

Fred Geier did not fit the image of the hard-charging American businessman. He was soft-spoken and formally dressed (he often appeared on the golf course in a three-piece suit) and had been educated at exclusive Williams College. He could read Latin and Greek with ease and didn't drink or smoke.[15]

Beginning in 1932–33, he had made several trips to Germany, which was still the Olympus of machine tool makers, and was shocked by what he saw: the persecution of Jews, the dogmatic militarism, the frantic arms buildup. It convinced Fred Geier that war was coming and that his business had better get ready for it. In 1938 he began doubling the size of his plant and put in a new foundry and a new office building—

all out of his own profits (Geier despised debt as much as he hated liquor).[16]

In the spring of 1941, Fred Geier was president of the Machine Tool Builders' Association, and Bill Knudsen caught up with him at the association's annual meeting at the Hotel Cleveland on May 5 and 6. Though Geier's prediction of war had been borne out by events, he was still amazed when Bill Knudsen told him he wanted production of machine tools in America to double, redouble, and redouble again—all inside a year.[17]

"You're crazy," Geier said good-naturedly, "but then so are we. When do you want them?"

"Right away," Knudsen answered with a straight face, "and in the ratio I mentioned." Geier knew Knudsen well enough to know he meant it.[18]

Geier and his colleagues did as the Great Dane asked. Over the next months, they and their factories would labor round the clock to produce a bewildering range of machine tools. In 1940 they had produced some 110,000. In what was left of 1941, they nearly doubled that number, to 185,000.[19] By 1942, Geier's Cincinnati Milling Machine was making a new machine tool every seventeen minutes, seven days a week, around the clock.

One of the biggest and most important was a giant machine for boring giant naval guns. Geier had seen one in action in Germany in the thirties, and secretly bought one in defiance of Nazi export rules. He managed to smuggle it out of the Third Reich, piece by piece, through Switzerland and Italy and then reassembled it in Cincinnati. It was this mammoth machine, the pride of Geier's factories, that would bore the great sixteen-inch guns for battleships like the *Iowa, New Jersey,* and *Missouri.*[20]

Knudsen and Geier did not stop there. In late June they launched a nationwide survey to track down every machine tool made in America in the past ten years, especially twenty-one types that were considered critical to the defense industry. Knudsen put OPM's tool man, Mason Britton, on the scent of "idle" tools, so that used tools could be mobilized as well as new ones.[21]

The amazing machine tool production numbers fell off in 1943 and slid back to normal by 1944. But by then the necessary machines were in the factories and doing their job. The critical fuse for the great explosion of productivity in America's defense industry after Pearl Harbor had been laid, thanks to Knudsen and the tough-minded teetotaler from Cincinnati Milling.

Still, the criticisms did not stop. One of the first, and in many ways the most perceptive, came in the pages of *Fortune* magazine in April. It charged that Washington had underestimated "the size of the effort necessary to build an armament economy without turning the civil economy inside out." The fact is, it read, "national defense is in pretty bad shape, and everyone in and out of Washington has seen the defense program drift and stumble."[22]

Time had been wasted putting Bill Knudsen in charge of policy and contracts, for example, when he should have been put in charge of directing production. *Fortune's* editors blasted Stettinius for accepting the Army's estimates of how much steel would be needed, with shortages now predicted for the rest of 1941 and into 1942. It damned the administration for failing to impose stricter price controls when armaments orders piled on top of a growing civilian demand meant prices would inevitably skyrocket.

Barely 10 percent of the country's factories had converted to war production. America, it seemed, needed a Dunkirk in order to get serious about defense. "The job is plain: tool up now so that we can deliver later"—which was exactly what Knudsen was doing, although no one at *Fortune* took notice.[23]

Instead, many blamed Knudsen for the delays. "Knudsen is simply not delivering the goods," Harold Ickes complained in his diary. "Big business is having too much say." Columnist Walter Lippmann accused Knudsen of organizing the entire war effort "as a kind of annex and superstructure to an immense boom in private business." Stimson himself was getting worried. "I'm afraid that Knudsen is too soft and too slow," he wrote on May 29, "because of his connection with the auto industry."[24] All asked the same question: When would he finally put defense ahead of business as usual?

The person who really needed to answer that question was the president, who had been so passive all spring. Finally something happened to snap Roosevelt out of his lethargy. On May 21 an American freighter, the SS *Robin Moor,* was sunk by a German U-boat inside the security zone. The Germans had allowed the crew and passengers to load into lifeboats before a torpedo sent the *Robin Moor* to the bottom, but it was two weeks before a passing steamer picked up the wretched survivors.

The president decided it was time to act. On May 27 he declared a state of national emergency, saying that "if we were to yield on this, we would inevitably submit to world domination" by Hitler.[25] American naval forces extended the security zone as far as Iceland and occupied that barren island country. On June 9, Roosevelt ordered federal troops in to end the strike at the North American plant. Many predicted a violent backlash. Instead, when troops arrived, workers unveiled an American flag and marched with them back into the factory.[26]

That was the one bright patch on an increasingly dismal labor front. On June 22, Hitler attacked the Soviet Union. Some hoped this would move the Communist Party firmly into the Allies' camp, especially the CIO. Instead, Big Labor came up with another issue to fight about, unionization of all defense contractors. It found a firm new ally in the National Defense Mediation Board, whose members consistently backed every effort to enforce unionization, including walkouts by labor. Overall, 1941 was a near-record year of strikes and disputes, with more than 3,500 of them, costing 23 million man-days of labor— enough to build 124 *Fletcher*-class destroyers.[27]

That second week in August, the strikes came with a dizzying flurry. On August 6, 16,000 CIO shipyard workers walked away from their jobs at Federal Shipbuilding in Kearny, New Jersey. The issue was not pay or conditions, but a contract with the Navy that allowed an open shop. Three tankers, two freighters, six destroyers, and a cruiser sat unfinished and useless as union stewards and management wrangled.

That was Wednesday. On Saturday fifteen hundred workers walked away from the Curtiss-Wright propeller plant in Caldwell, New Jersey, which made propellers for eight types of warplanes. That same day, carpenters struck at the Philadelphia Navy Yard, where they had been building a new dry dock. Their demand was for overtime pay on Saturdays. By the time the strike was settled, almost two weeks of crucial work were gone.[28]

Knudsen watched, helpless to stop the crumbling production effort. Roosevelt was sending conflicting signals on the seriousness of the defense effort, while the American people themselves were sharply divided. Gallup polls showed that almost two-thirds of the country opposed getting involved in the war in Europe, but almost the same number expected the country to be at war in the next year. It was not a formula for boosting morale. *New York Times* reporter Frank Kluckhohn toured the American heartland—Ohio, Minnesota, Illinois, Missouri—and of the hundreds of businessmen and working people he spoke to, only three or four actually supported entering the war. "I would do everything short of going to Leavenworth to sabotage the war if we entered," one young lawyer declared.[29]

A *Time* reporter visited the Army's new training depots to interview eager young draftees, except that few of them were very eager. At one Mississippi camp, soldiers booed newsreel pictures of President Roosevelt and General Marshall, while excerpts from a speech by isolationist Senator Hiram Johnson drew a loud ovation. Certainly it was hard to expect American business to go full out for the war effort when the country itself was so conflicted.[30]

The battle over raw materials bottlenecks brought all the caterwauling in Washington to a fevered pitch. Don Nelson had to report to Knudsen and the rest of OPM that his priorities system for raw materials was breaking down. As many as five thousand factories might have to close because they couldn't get adequate supplies of aluminum, copper, nickel, alloy steels, zinc, tin, and tungsten. Somewhere between one and two million workers might find themselves out of work.[31]

Clearly something had to give. What gave was the Knudsen formula for steadily growing military orders on the backs of civilian production, and letting suppliers find new ways to increase production. Instead on August 28 the president announced the creation of yet another new agency, the Supplies, Priorities, and Allocation Board, to split up available supplies of materials between military and civilian needs. "Don't worry, Bill," Roosevelt said with his engaging grin, "it'll make your job easier."

Knudsen knew better. The New Dealers had won. The membership of the new SPAB told the story. They included Leon Henderson, now head of the Office of Price Administration and Civilian Supply, who wanted deep cuts in civilian production (it puzzled Knudsen and his stalwarts that the man in charge of protecting civilian consumers from the impact of war preparation was always looking for ways Americans could do with less). Harry Hopkins sat at the table in his capacity as head of the Lend-Lease program. So did Roosevelt's vice president, Henry Wallace, the former agriculture secretary and New Deal ideologue who, like Hopkins, saw the defense buildup as a way to deepen and extend the powers of the federal government—in the words of one cynic, "as a version of WPA that Republicans will have to support."

If Knudsen was the big loser, the winner was Donald Nelson as SPAB's executive director. The creation of SPAB involved a larger personnel shake-up. Ed Stettinius was appointed to replace Harry Hopkins in running Lend-Lease. Knudsen's right-hand man, John Biggers, was moved to London to oversee that end of the Lend-Lease knot.[32] At the same time, the first round of curtailment of civilian production had begun.

First came the auto industry, with a drastic cut by more than half. Then in October nonessential construction was ordered halted, to divert materials to defense plant construction. On October 21 manufacturers had to stop using copper in almost all civilian products, followed by sharp cuts in refrigerators, vacuum cleaners, metal office furniture, and similar durable goods.[33]

Yet in the end, SPAB did no better than its predecessors. The Army and Navy would fight it tooth and nail over what it saw as misplaced priorities in the allocation of materials, as they would its successor agency, the War Production Board. Don Nelson's efforts to tell them they could not have everything they wanted, exactly when they wanted it, and that a military buildup without a strong civilian sector (one with enough lumber, for example, to build houses for war plant workers or enough heavy equipment to repair roads and bridges) was impossible, would make him the most-hated man on Constitution Avenue.[34] As for SPAB, it became another lump in Washington's administrative alphabet soup until it was washed away by Pearl Harbor.

Still, Knudsen could look down at his own schedule with some sat-isfaction. Things were on track. The critical period of retooling was almost over. Although the increase in the output of machine tools was not yet visible, by year's end the value of machine tools put out by the industry would be nearly double that of 1940—just as Fred Geier had promised. Likewise, the nation's munitions output would double in the second half of 1941.[35]

No one who read the newspapers knew it yet, but the tap was about to be turned on. In January 1941 defense spending rose to triple what it had been during the previous six months. By July it quintupled, and December it jumped another *twelvefold*. America, the isolationist nation still at peace, was fast approaching Nazi Germany in its defense output. In 1942 it would roar past it.

Every month of the second half of 1941, $2 billion of munitions were being stamped, milled, riveted, punched, or rolled out. While Wal-ter Lippmann and others bayed about unreadiness and the need to move forward, and while agency heads in Washington were panicking, across the country the war production curve was moving steeply up-ward. America was poised to produce arms in quantities no one had ever thought possible. The explosive rate of growth Knudsen and his colleagues triggered from mid-1940 to the end of 1941 eased after 1942, although the numbers of planes, ships, tanks, and weapons would continue to explode (see Appendix A). As historian Geoffrey Perret later put it, "Without the accomplishment of those eighteen months who can doubt that the war would have lasted substantially longer than it did and taken more lives than it did?"[36]

It was all due to Knudsen and his team. They had created, in effect, an almost self-perpetuating mechanism that fed upon its own individual dynamic elements. Theorists of the science of complexity would call it emergence. Economists have another term: "spontaneous order." It was the most powerful and flexible system of wartime production ever de-vised, because in the end no one devised it. It grew out of the underlying productivity of the American economy, dampened by a decade of de-pression but ready to spring to life. Out of what seemed like chaos and disorder to Washington would come an explosion of innovation, adapta-tion, and creativity—not to mention hard work—across the country.[37]

Now it was up to America's military to get ready to use it—and that moment was coming faster than anyone realized.

On a cold blustery Thursday evening in late 1941, Knudsen attended a dinner in the North Lounge of the Carleton Hotel. Vice President Henry Wallace of SPAB was there. So was SPAB's executive director, Donald Nelson, Lend-Lease's Ed Stettinius, and Frank Knox, the secretary of the Navy.

After dinner Knox gave a speech to the assembled distinguished guests.

"I feel I can speak very frankly, within these four walls," Knox said. "We are very close to war. War may begin in the Pacific at any moment."

It was true. In June, Roosevelt had imposed an oil embargo on imperial Japan, and in July he had frozen Japan's assets in America—a virtual *casus belli* if ever there was one for the resource-starved island nation. In October some two thousand Japanese Americans were ordered evacuated from the West Coast. American naval intelligence had discovered that the Japanese were gathering troop transports in their harbors in Indochina—possibly for a strike against British Malaya and Singapore, or the oil-rich Dutch East Indies, or possibly even farther out. On Monday the new Japanese premier, General Hideki Tojo, formally rejected an appeal from Secretary of State Hull for settling America and Japan's differences amicably.

"But I want you to know," Knox continued, striking his fist into his palm, "that no matter what happens, the United States Navy is ready! Every man is at his post, every ship is at its station. The Navy is *ready*. Whatever happens, the Navy is not going to be caught napping."[38]

Knudsen's driver picked him up and took him back to his Rock Creek Park home. It was the evening of Thursday, December 4, 1941.

Three days later, in far-off Hawaii, the roof caved in on Knox's prediction.

America was about to begin the test of total war.

CHAPTER NINE

GOING ALL OUT

Photo courtesy of the Detroit News Archives

America is in production now.
—*William S. Knudsen, January 16, 1942*

A LITTLE BEFORE 2 P.M. on December 7, 1941, the phone rang in the secretary of war's house. It was the president, who said excitedly, "Have you heard the news?"

"Well, I have heard the telegrams which have been coming in about the Japanese advances in the Gulf of Siam," Stimson replied.

"Oh, no, I don't mean that," Roosevelt cried. "They have attacked Hawaii. They are now bombing Hawaii."[1]

The next day, December 8, Adolf Hitler declared war on the United

States. War had come to America without warning, and from both directions.

No one had quite figured out how this was going to work. At the
prompting of Undersecretary Robert Patterson, the Army had finally
worked out its so-called Victory Plan in September 1941, which for the
first time envisaged the United States going full out in a war in the
Atlantic and Europe. It still saw Japan as a problem to be put off until
at least July 1943.[2]

That timetable had suddenly, catastrophically speeded up. Japan's
strike at Pearl Harbor had left eight battleships either sunk or smoldering wrecks, plus two cruisers and four destroyers. On December 10 the
first Japanese troops landed on Luzon in the Philippines, after Japanese
bombers had flattened the U.S. air force there on the ground. When
Knudsen had asked General Marshall back in the summer of 1940
what was the most important thing he needed to get ready for war, he
replied without hesitation, "Time."[3] Time had just run out.

On the Tuesday after Pearl Harbor, a somber Roosevelt summoned
Knudsen to the White House. He had already seen Knudsen's report on
production in 1941. The numbers were impressive: 19,290 planes,
50,684 aircraft engines, 97,000 machine guns, 9,924 40mm Bofors antiaircraft guns, 3,964 tanks, and more.[4] Now the president said he
wanted those numbers accelerated. He needed 30,000 planes in 1942
instead of the 18,000 Knudsen and his team had projected. He wanted
45,000 tanks, and 75,000 in 1943; 20,000 antiaircraft guns; and 8 million tons of merchant shipping instead of the 1.1 million tons produced
in 1941.

"Can we do it?" Roosevelt wanted to know.

"Yes, sir," Knudsen answered at once. He and his team had figured
out that 45,000 planes of all types for 1942 was not out of the question.

"And the other stuff—ships, guns, ammunition, all the other things.
You can step up them, too?"

Knudsen assured him he could.

The next day, Roosevelt told the country in his State of the Union
speech that America would produce 60,000 warplanes in 1942 and
125,000 the following year, and threw a couple of zeroes onto the
other production numbers, as well. "These figures," the president said

with dripping irony, "will give the Japanese and Nazis an idea of what they accomplished in the attack at Pearl Harbor."[5]

If those numbers didn't shock Hitler and Tojo, they certainly shocked Knudsen's assistants. Babe Meigs, his airplane man, was particularly miffed. "I am astounded," he blurted out, "at the scheduling of 60,000 airplanes and 125,000 for next year. I presume this is done for propaganda purposes." Every expert had told him 45,000 "is an all-out, almost impossible, figure to shoot at."[6] How in the world were numbers like that possible?

Knudsen told him what he had reminded the president: that he had promised Roosevelt 18,000 planes in 1941 and exceeded it. They could do this, too, now that the plants, machine tools, and small tools were up and running. "After that's settled," Knudsen added, "the manufacturer himself can do much more for successful production than any number of committees that can be set up"—including OPM itself.

Those numbers were a way for the president to get the maximum effort out of American industry and the rest of the country, to show the rest of the world that America meant business. "Let's go ahead on the basis of what the president wants," Knudsen said, "and adjust our plans" accordingly.[7] America's industrial might would do the rest.

But that wasn't all that was bothering Meigs. Merrill Church Meigs was the ex-publisher of the *Chicago Herald and Examiner,* and just four years younger than Knudsen. He had grown up on a farm in Malcolm, Iowa, and worked as a threshing machine salesman for a company in Racine, Wisconsin, but his true passion was for the internal combustion engine. Racing cars had managed to gratify that urge until one day in 1927, when he learned about Lindbergh's solo flight across the Atlantic. "I had never been on an airplane in my life," he later said. Now he became obsessed by them. He flew on American Airlines' first flight from Chicago to New York, and paid the airlines to fly on their regular airmail routes. Babe Meigs became the country's first great advocate of civilian air travel, running ads in his newspaper and pushing for creating a passenger airport in downtown Chicago, only ten miles from the Loop (known today as Meigs Field).[8]

He passed his exam for a pilot's license in 1929 at the ripe age of forty-six. When rival publisher Colonel McCormick did the same,

Meigs did him one better by getting a commercial pilot's license. He would offer to teach flying to anyone with a passing interest, and often did (one of his students was a senator from Missouri, Harry S. Truman).

When Knudsen's original airplane expert, Dr. George Mead, became too ill to continue, Meigs was probably the best-known amateur aviator in America after Lindbergh himself. Babe Meigs's intimate knowledge of airplanes, his enthusiasm, and his commanding presence and voice made him an unusual but brilliant replacement. "He could make any cloud look bright," said one Ford executive who worked closely with him.[9]*

Meigs didn't just know advertising and aviation. He also understood the ways of Washington, and worried Knudsen didn't. So after the meeting, he went down to Knudsen's office and explained the facts of life.

"You've made enemies here," Meigs told his boss, "even though you don't know it." And now that America was in the war, he said, "if you think the New Dealers are going to let anyone from private industry, and you especially, get credit for this production job—"

"I don't care who gets the credit," Knudsen interrupted, "just so this job gets done."

"Yes," Meigs fired back, "I am sure that is how *you* feel—but they don't feel that way. You're my boss, and I have no business talking to you this way, but I was a publisher before I came here and I know how these New Dealers operate. They have already started to smear you, and they are getting ready to take over this defense program."

Knudsen scoffed at the idea. But Meigs reminded him that the liberals' dislike went further back than just the heat they were applying now.

---

* Meigs, however, was more than just a booster. It was Meigs who proposed forming a Joint Aircraft Committee to standardize the parts and designs of airplanes being ordered by both the British and the Americans, including the Navy. The committee worked out how to supply the fifty-five different types of airplanes in American production with the same screws, parts for landing gears, tires, bombs and bomb releases, and hundreds of other parts—in addition to identifying which were more likely to suffer battle damage and need larger numbers of replacements and which were not. The Joint Committee's work proved a major step forward in keeping both the RAF and the U.S. air force in the air, and a huge step toward bringing mass production to the world of aviation.

The CIO had fought bitterly with Knudsen when he was at General Motors. New Dealers didn't like it when he had dared to criticize the Wagner Act.* They especially didn't like the way he sought to prevent the outright conversion of the auto industry—even though Big Labor's man on OPM, Sidney Hillman, supported his decision.

"Whether you believe it or not," Meigs went on, "they are out to get you—and they are shooting to kill."

"Why should anyone be shooting at me?" Knudsen wanted to know.[10]

Meigs could see he wasn't getting through. But CIO conspiracy or not, the criticism of Knudsen and the OPM's methods reached a crescendo after Pearl Harbor, starting with the unions.

"Why should the agencies of government in Washington today," said CIO chief Philip Murray, "be virtually infested with wealthy men who are supposedly receiving one-dollar-a-year compensation?" Such men were only using war mobilization to pad their old companies' profits and those of their cronies, the critics said. "Patriotism plus 8 percent," they called it, while others argued that the only way to overcome the conflict of interest was to create a British-style Ministry of Supply with complete powers over all wartime production.[11]

Knudsen had a very different take on who posed the main threat to an all-out war effort. He knew that Sunday, December 7, was supposed to mark the start of a nationwide railway strike, until the news from Pearl Harbor intervened.[12] He also knew that on December 16 a strike *was* called at Reuben Fleet's Consolidated plant in San Diego, where engineers were desperately trying to get a new heavy bomber, the B-24, out the door and into the air—anyone who thought the American labor movement was going to forget its grievances in order to go all out against the Axis was about to get a cold dose of reality.

Knudsen, however, had no time to deal with critics. On January 2 the Japanese took Manila. Three days later Knudsen booked a plane to Detroit. That afternoon he assembled every automobile executive he could get hold of, including some who had been there for the dramatic meeting at the New Center back in October 1940.

---

* Passed in 1934, it had legitimated collective bargaining for America's labor unions and also immunized them from court injunctions.

He said he knew many of them were already under contract for war production, from tanks to aircraft engines. The numbers were rising rapidly; they would rise even faster in 1942. Now he was going to ask them to make one more effort.

From his pocket he pulled out a memorandum from Undersecretary Patterson. It was titled "Items of Munitions Appropriate for Production by the Automobile Industry." He produced another from the Navy from the other pocket.

This was about getting the automakers to figure out ways to produce another $5 billion in additional war materiel that had no obvious connection with car production, Knudsen declared.

"We want to know where some of these things will flow from," Knudsen said. "We want to know if you can make them or want to try and make them. If you can't, do you know anyone who can?"

Knudsen put his glasses—an old-fashioned pince-nez with a thick black ribbon—firmly on his nose and began reading.

"We want more machine guns," he said. "Who wants to make machine guns?"

A couple of hands went up hesitantly. Knudsen went down the list.

Who wanted to make turbine engine blades? "Someone ought to be able to forge these things." More hands went up. And so on, until Knudsen had checked off every item on his list.[13]

A secretary recorded each company executive's name as he made his selection. Knudsen's friend Charlie Wilson of GM, for instance, pledged to take on some $2 billion worth of contracts, including building tanks at four different plants. Chrysler and Ford took another $2 billion, while Ford offered to help out others with the machine tool bottleneck by supplying certain simple parts for new tools.[14]

Knudsen was pleased, but when he returned to Washington, the outrage was palpable. Bureaucrats were shocked; commentators were volubly outraged. The director of OPM was accused of putting the nation's defense "up for auction," as *Time* magazine phrased it. The same voices who criticized what he had done wanted to know why all this hadn't been done a year ago, so that every company capable or willing to manufacture important war materiel was already hard at work at it.

Of course Knudsen knew the truth. A year ago, a month ago, America had not been at war. No one had had the authority to compel anyone to do anything, not even participate in surveys of the national inventory of machine tools or available factory space for conversion to defense work.[15] And no one had had the authority to tell industries to go ahead and retool for war work in ways that would have involved a breach of existing union contracts. Indeed, doing that would have invited even more labor trouble.

Indeed, no one had that authority even now. The consequences of Roosevelt's refusal for the past year and a half to cede authority over rearmament to any single person or agency—his insatiable desire to keep his options open—had finally been exposed. Yet it was Knudsen's head on the public chopping block.

Then a new problem arose. Days after Pearl Harbor, Roosevelt had given SPAB some authority to close down unnecessary civilian production. The man in charge was Leon Henderson, who was also the head of Office of Price Administration, and the industry he targeted was everyone's favorite target, the auto industry. Henderson ordered the complete cessation of new car and truck manufacturing as of January 15. The 450,000 civilian vehicles now in the carmakers' inventory and the other quarter million still on the assembly line were not to be sold through dealers, Henderson decreed. Instead, they would be rationed out to high-priority users like doctors, hospitals, fire and police departments, and the like.

This was the kind of bold action critics of Knudsen had been urging for more than a year. The results were exactly what Knudsen would have predicted. More than 400,000 auto workers suddenly found themselves out of work, and 44,000 auto dealers around the country had to lay off employees. Many, if not most, had to shut their doors. Instead of speeding the nation toward readiness, stopping civilian car production had led to chaos.[16]

Still, the blame fell not on Henderson but on Knudsen. Why hadn't he forced Detroit to convert to war production faster, to prevent it hitting it all at once—or at least taken steps to protect these workers thrown out of work and their families, who were facing a future without a paycheck? One of the most vociferous critics was America's best-known protector of the afflicted and downtrodden, the First Lady herself, Eleanor Roosevelt. One day, quivering with indignation, she cornered him at the White House. What was he going to do about this?

Knudsen gave her a look "like a great big benevolent bear," she said later, "as if to say, 'Now, Mrs. Roosevelt, don't let's get excited.' "

"I wonder if you know what hunger is?" she wanted to know. "Has any member of your family ever gone hungry?"[17]

Knudsen could have replied no, because he had been working since the age of eight, including setting rivets in a Bronx shipyard. He also could have told her that those unemployed workers and their families would soon enough have plenty to do, as the war production schedule he and his colleagues had hammered out began to take effect and jobs became plentiful and workers scarce, but he didn't. Yet he would have been right.

Thanks to war work, by D-day total employment in the Detroit area would more than double. The big migraine for Michigan's war contractors was a worker *shortage* as their employees headed for more lucrative jobs in the Kaiser shipyards and elsewhere. Without the migration of thousands of rural newcomers from the South and Appalachia—for whom war work represented a huge economic opportunity—it was hard to see how the big production numbers the automakers eventually made could have ever been achieved.[18*]

At the time, however, Mrs. Roosevelt was not mollified. She described her encounter with Knudsen in a speech to a national meeting of 4H directors, adding this: "The slowness of our officials in seeing ahead . . . is responsible for the whole [defense] mess."

Washington insiders sadly shook their heads. If the First Lady felt free to criticize the director of OPM this openly, his days must be numbered.[19]

Knudsen remained oblivious to what was happening. When a staffer offered him a list of talking points with which to respond to media critics, Knudsen tossed it in the garbage. He was only focused on the growing demands of his job and on January 16 was huddled with the

---

* There were so many migrant workers from the border states that a joke began to circulate around wartime Detroit. "How many states in the Union? Forty-six, because Tennessee and Kentucky are now in Michigan."

SPAB people going over the new production numbers. At four o'clock the door popped open and a messenger handed a note to Vice President Wallace. He read it and passed it along to Don Nelson. Then both men rose and announced that they had an urgent call at the White House, but urged everyone to continue the meeting.

The remaining men talked for another hour or so, then Knudsen headed for his office. John Lord O'Brian, former federal judge and general counsel for OPM, was working down the hall. Like Meigs, O'Brian had been urging Knudsen for months to publicly defend OPM's record and himself from the flurry of attacks in the press. O'Brian had finally gotten Knudsen to agree to go on the radio and give the American people a concise report on what OPM had achieved in the ten months of its existence, and what it was planning to do next. The live broadcast was scheduled for that evening, on CBS radio.

Suddenly O'Brian looked up to see Knudsen standing in his door with a torn piece of news ticker paper in his hand and a dazed look on his face.

"Look here, Judge, I've been fired!"[20]

It was true. The ticker paper said that President Roosevelt had announced the creation of a new defense production agency, called the War Production Board, and the abolition of both its predecessors, OPM and SPAB. The chairman of the new agency, the news report said, would be none other than Donald M. Nelson.

As O'Brian read the news, Knudsen asked him, "Let me use your telephone, will you, Judge?"

"What are you going to do?"

"Call the president."

"I wouldn't do that," O'Brian warned. "Sit down, and let's talk this thing over."

But Knudsen had the receiver in his hand. "I'm going to call the president. I tried to get him before I came in here, and Hopkins said he had left his office and he was not to be disturbed. I'm going to call him anyway."

O'Brian finally dissuaded him from making the call, sensing Knudsen would never get through. The only other thing left to do was to

cancel the CBS broadcast. Knudsen said he had already had his secretary, Bill Collins, make the call.[21]

O'Brian sat with the disconsolate Knudsen until the former head of
America's defense effort went home. What hurt most was that the president hadn't had the stomach to fire him to his face. Just a month ago,
two days after Pearl Harbor, FDR had declared, "This country now has
an organization in Washington built around men and women who are
recognized experts in their own fields . . . and are pulling together with
a teamwork that has never before been excelled."[22] Too late, Knudsen
realized Roosevelt's promises, both public and private, always carried
an expiration date.

One of the first to get word of what had happened was Jesse Jones.
He went straight to Knudsen's Rock Creek house. When one of the
Filipino houseboys opened the door, Jones found Knudsen sitting at
the piano, disconsolately picking out a tune.

Earlier Jones had been on the phone with Harry Hopkins, who told
him about the firing. "It was done in a brutal way," Hopkins said. "I
know it must have hurt Knudsen deeply. Get hold of him at once and
ask him not to make any statement."[23] Hopkins thought they might be
able to get Knudsen a brigadier general's commission to go to the War
Department to help out Patterson and Stimson with their production
problems.

That was poor recompense for a man like Knudsen, Jones retorted.

"I have heard Knudsen make two-minute speeches and I have heard
him speak for an hour," Jones said, "and he is one of the most inspiring
speakers I have ever heard."[24] There had to be someplace where he
could be useful, not only to businessmen but to "the fellow in overalls."

Jones stayed for dinner and tried to get Knudsen to think about the
future, but the big Dane was "a brokenhearted man. I think he would
rather have died than to have been ejected at so desperate a stage in the
war." Jones coaxed him into a game of cards, but Knudsen's mind wasn't
in the game, so they stopped. At midnight Jones said he was going
home. But first he found himself impulsively picking up the phone.
"Give me the White House."

With Knudsen listening, Jones got Harry Hopkins on the line.

"Knudsen will accept a three-star generalship in the Army and report to Bob Patterson to help in promoting production for wartime
production."

Hopkins was incredulous. No one could give away a military commission bigger than a one-star brigadier.

"I repeated that it would have to be lieutenant general," Jones wrote
later in a memorandum.[25] Jones was used to getting his way at the
White House, but it is doubtful his ultimatum would have worked—
except that exactly the same idea had occurred to Stimson and Patterson. Both were less than thrilled when they heard the news about
Nelson heading the new war production agency; and both agreed that
Knudsen had been shabbily treated. It was Patterson who thought there
should be a place for him in the War Department's procurement system
as a mobilization troubleshooter. "He's just the man we need," Patterson firmly said.[26]

So with Jones pushing and the War Department pulling, Knudsen
got his appointment—the only civilian in history to be made a
three-star general. "If you want me to stand sentry downstairs, or anywhere else, I will do that," the big man told Roosevelt in their final
interview at the White House. They shook hands and parted satisfied,
Roosevelt because Knudsen hadn't made a major stink about his dis-
missal; Knudsen because he still had a job to do, one that would take
him back where he always wanted to be: on the factory floors of America. /

"American ingenuity is at work day and night finding new methods
of production. . . . American industry was raised on a free land, and the
spirit of competition that built our machines, which we are now gearing up to a world-record effort, will respond if we all cooperate and
keep our thoughts focused on one object—to preserve our American
way of life and beat the invaders."

The words were from Knudsen's CBS speech to the nation, the one
he never got to give.

"We build things in America—that is why most of the world is
looking toward us, hoping and praying that we will come through.
When we think of our boys in the Arctic or in the jungle standing up
to overwhelming odds; when we think of our allies, the British, the

Russians, the Dutch, and the Chinese, bravely bearing the brunt of the totalitarians; then we know the tide will turn. . . . America is in production now."[27]

Knudsen was gone. The New Dealers thought they had won. They were too late. America was indeed in production now, with 25,000 prime contractors and 120,000 subcontractors making products they had never dreamed of making, and thousands more to come. And nothing the people in Washington or the Axis could do now would stem the tide. A new "Rule of Three" would take root in the American munitions business. In the first year after a production order, output was bound to triple; in the second, it would jump by a factor of seven; at the end of the third year, the only limits on output were material and labor—whether it was trucks or artillery pieces or bombs or planes.[28]

Indeed, for the Axis the issue from now until the end of the war would be trying to catch up. Too late, Hitler realized the industrial monster he faced. In May 1941 he had berated generals and industry leaders alike for their failure to coordinate their wartime needs. Germany was already spending one-quarter of its national product on munitions, and two-thirds of all industrial investment, but Hitler sensed they were falling behind in the race to the production finish line.

Four days before Pearl Harbor, he had issued a Führer decree ordering German industry to start a program of "mass production on modern principles," which meant Knudsen principles. Hitler specifically mentioned the example of Soviet factories—but he was really thinking about the United States.[29]

In February the Führer named his friend Albert Speer to carry out this production miracle, as armaments minister of the Third Reich. Speer pledged that he would demonstrate to the German people that by converting their entire economy to all-out production of tanks, planes, and munitions, the Third Reich could still win the war. As armaments minister, Speer had the formal power to order which factories would produce what, and to move materials and workers to whatever industry he believed needed them—everything, in fact, that people in Washington wanted for an American production czar. He also had control over wages and prices, and the full resources of Goebbels's Propaganda Ministry to mobilize public opinion, as newsreels began to show factories turning out munitions in record numbers—just as they were doing in the United States.

What Speer lacked was Knudsen's secret weapon: America's prodigious industrial base built around free enterprise, which now was giving its full attention to war production. Speer was an architect by training. He knew nothing about how to lay out a factory or run an assembly line. Likewise, Germanic pride made many key industries resist the transition to American-style mass production. Tank and aircraft factory workers remained faithful to the traditions of quality craftsmanship, as did their managers, which ensured they never made enough. The German car industry, including the Opel factories the government had seized from General Motors, sat half-idle through the entire war.* And constant meddling and changes of priorities by the German military ensured that time and energy and materials were lost in a limitless bureaucratic maze.

Still, by stripping down every civilian factory and seizing every resource he could lay his hands on, and by grabbing every worker he could round up within the Nazi empire, Speer eventually got his production miracle. German production by 1944 surged by nearly half.[30] Yet Germany would still lose the war—and in the process Speer would reduce Europe to a barren wilderness.

Meanwhile, the smoke had cleared around Pearl Harbor. No fewer than eight modern battleships—*California, Arizona, Nevada, West Virginia, Tennessee, Pennsylvania, Maryland,* and *Oklahoma*—four destroyers, and two light cruisers were either sunk or too badly damaged to operate at sea. Pearl Harbor's docks, warehouses, and naval facilities had been bombed and left in flames. More than one hundred planes had been destroyed, and more than four thousand Americans were killed or wounded.

---

* The gigantic and ultramodern Volkswagen plant at Wolfsburg, for example, started the war with enough machine tools to produce 200,000 vehicles a year. Barely one-fifth of its capacity was ever used; one worker there recalled "there seemed to be no plans at all" what to do with the rest. Later, bombing by American Flying Fortresses and B-24s made the issue moot.

Someone would have to rebuild America's premier Pacific naval base, and get it ready for war on a scale no one had seen before. It was an ideal job for the Six Companies and Henry Kaiser. They had already had one sad reunion in January 1942 in San Francisco. Charlie Shea had finally succumbed to the cancer that had been killing him for years. Among the pallbearers were Kaiser, Felix Kahn, Harry Morrison, and Hoover Dam architect Frank Crowe. With Shea gone and buried, they threw themselves into rebuilding Pearl Harbor with a will.

Taking the lead was Shea's old firm, Pacific Bridge, which set to work repairing the bombed-out dry docks so that the *Tennessee, California,* and the other crippled giants could be towed in and repaired. The Japanese bombs had left the battleships wedged against each other in their concrete moorings like broken toys jammed in a drain. Pacific Bridge's teams joined with workers from Utah Construction to blast each concrete piling to pieces in order to get them out, while being careful not to inflict more damage on the stricken behemoths. Then more teams came in to weld on steel plate patches and make them seaworthy enough to float to safety.[31]

Pacific Bridge and Utah had the most taxing job, but Morris Knudsen had the most ghoulish. MK's engineers, cranes, and bulldozers had been hard at work for more than a year on a massive underground fuel facility for the Navy, gouged out of the side of the mountain overlooking Pearl. It was still unfinished when the Japanese bombers hit. Now one of its massive pits served as a mass grave for hundreds of those killed in the surprise attack.

Out of destruction and chaos came new order. Within two weeks new runways on Ford Island had been laid out. Docks were being built that would become home to a fleet of warships four times larger than the one destroyed on December 7 (including every battleship the Japanese thought they had sunk that day except two, *Arizona* and *Oklahoma*). Thousands of workmen labored round the clock pouring cement, tons of it, all across the harbor—almost half a million barrels' worth. As it happened, it was Kaiser cement, which Henry Kaiser had been stockpiling on Hawaii since the previous December. Now, it was vitally needed right where it had been stored.[32]

It was not there by accident. Three years before the Japanese attack,

Kaiser's partner Harry Morrison saw the Six Companies' next big opening in government contracts when in 1938 the Navy decided it was time to shore up its presence in the Pacific. It was adding new airfields and submarine bases at various outposts that later would ring with meaning for Americans: Wake Island, Midway, Guam, Cavita, Samoa, and Pearl Harbor's Ford Island.

The Navy knew someone good was going to have to build those airstrips and facilities, so it asked the biggest corporations it knew to submit bids. The Six Companies were the first. /

Morrison flew out to Washington from Boise to press their case. White haired and sunburnt in his Stetson and cowboy boots, he strode into the Navy building looking like a character from a John Ford western. The board was impressed with his presentation, but it was a consortium put together by Turner Construction of New York that finally won the contract worth $15 million.

Morrison shrugged off his disappointment. He knew it was a huge undertaking, and wondered if Turner Construction and its partners were really up to it. They would have to ship materials and heavy equipment thousands of miles to remote parts of the Pacific, then import thousands of laborers and construction crews to get the work started. Even with Felix Kahn's brother Albert supplying plans from his office in Detroit, the executives at Turner might be in over their heads. Eventually they were going to need him, and Henry Kaiser.

Sure enough, in early 1940—just half a year into the project—Congress decided to triple its size and scope. Worries about aggressive Japanese moves in the Pacific meant the work on Wake, Guam, and Samoa would get top priority, and Turner was crying uncle—their resources were stretched to the limit. The Navy called on the big man from Boise to help out.[33]

Morrison in turn divided up the work with his Six Companies partners. Steve Bechtel took over the work on Guam and Cavite in the Philippines; Morrison gave himself Midway and Wake. Kaiser had the easy part, supplying everyone's cement—although he had an enormous row with the Navy when he proposed shipping the tons of his cement around the Pacific not in bags but as bulk cargo. Navy people, with visions of tons of hardened concrete in the ship holds, were flabbergasted.

But Kaiser explained that it would not only be cheaper but meant transport ships could be loaded in one-fifth the time. The Navy still balked. So Kaiser silenced their objections by saying he would handle the shipping and assume the risks himself. And so in October 1940 the first shipments of cement began to arrive in Pearl Harbor, on their way to construction sites thousands of miles away in the western and central Pacific.[34]

On Christmas Day—the president had just given Bill Knudsen his new assignment as head of OPM, and the Arsenal of Democracy speech was still four days away—the first ship carrying Morrison's people appeared off Wake Island. It was loaded with two thousand tons of materials and machines, in addition to towing a four-thousand-square-foot barge laden with supplies and other equipment. In command was veteran MK engineer Dan Teeters, accompanied by his wife, Florence, who would be one of only three women on the island.

The island itself was not much more than a 2,600-acre strip of sand and coral, without a single hill or natural obstruction for Teeters's bulldozers. A cluster of huts and other buildings marked the detachment of Marines defending the tiny atoll. Yet everyone knew that in a shooting war, Wake would be of vital strategic significance. Twelve hundred miles southwest of Midway, and almost halfway from Hawaii to Manila, airfields on Wake could resupply the American garrison in the Philippines—while seaplanes and submarines could oversee the Japanese-occupied Marshalls. Teeters knew there was no time to waste, and he set his crew of eighty to work the next day.[35]

Six months later the number had grown to twelve hundred. By now they were joined by five hundred Marines under Major James Devereux. The work was already half-finished except for the submarine base. When Harry Morrison and his wife flew out in November, they found the place almost ready for operations. The only major job left for the airstrip was the construction of protective bunkers for the Marine planes. The Morrisons shook hands with Teeters and his wife, and greeted the workers, many of whom they knew from previous jobs. One of them was Joseph Crowe, son of Hoover Dam's designer, Frank Crowe. They talked about Crowe's prospects when he got back to Boise, and then had a sobering meeting with Major Devereux.[36]

War was almost certainly coming, he told Morrison, and Wake would be in the middle of it. The tiny island's prospects were slim if the Japanese attacked. The Navy was ordering the women to leave, but there would not be time to evacuate all the civilian workers. As Harry and Ann took off to return to Hawaii, he must have wondered if he would ever see Teeters and his men again.

Teeters, meanwhile, wasted no time. Since not a single Marine could be spared from his duties, every available construction worker had to help with the defense. Teeters's construction workers filled sandbags, redistributed and camouflaged Wake's supplies, and built bomb shelters and revetments. Teeters, a veteran of World War I, pulled together 185 volunteers to serve alongside the Marines. Devereux was in no position to refuse, and soon MK hard hats were taking their place around the five-inch guns and machine gun nests, waiting for the Japanese.[37]

They didn't have long to wait. On December 8, just hours after the attack on Pearl Harbor, Japanese bombers seemed to appear from nowhere, the sound of their engines drowned by the pounding surf until they were virtually on top of the island. The island's squadron of Marine fighters took off but lost the bombers in the clouds as death showered down on the tiny atoll. Eight of the Marine's twelve Grumman Wildcats were blown up, and two out of three pilots were killed or wounded. Dozens of MK's workers were also killed in the raid. Some of the survivors panicked and fled into the jungle. But most remained at their post, and stood shoulder to shoulder with the Marines through a second raid two days later, and when the first Japanese warships appeared on the horizon on December 11.[38]

It was a formidable force of three light cruisers and six destroyers, plus a contingent of transport with 450 soldiers loaded for an amphibious landing. Wake's chances for survival went from slim to none. Only two things stood between defeat and captivity. One was the Marines' four surviving Wildcat fighters. The other was the two batteries of five-inch guns, which Teeters's workers had reinforced with Henry Kaiser's cement.

As the Japanese troops tried to disembark, those twin batteries ripped into their escorting ships. Four shells hit the light cruiser *Yubari;* Platoon Sergeant Harry Bedell's Battery L blew the destroyer *Hayate* in

half with three salvos. Battery B pounded away at three Japanese destroyers, scoring direct hits on two of them.

Meanwhile, the Marine Wildcats had zeroed in on the Japanese light
cruiser *Kisaragi*. None of the young pilots had ever dropped a bomb
before, even in a practice run. With sheer courage and determination,
however, they scored the *Kisaragi* with perfect bull's-eyes. She was already aflame from a previous hit near her ammunition storage when
Lieutenant John Kinney pulled his bomb release lever and the
one-hundred-pounder hurtled down. It caught the *Kisaragi* amidships.
"A huge explosion engulfed the ship," Kinney later wrote, "and she
rapidly began to sink."[39] A cheer went up around Wake Island. They had
held out, against almost impossible odds. But could they hold out the
next time?

Miraculously, they did. The island was attacked every day after the
eleventh except one, while the MK workers dodged bombs and lived
on starvation rations. The four surviving Wildcats shrank to two, which
the Marine mechanics kept going by cannibalizing parts and trying out
bits from truck and bulldozer engines when the aviation equipment
ran out. All America followed the epic struggle on Wake on their radios;
President Roosevelt himself got daily bulletins. But on December 22,
the last Wildcat was gone.

The next day, Teeters, Kinney, and the others watched a new Japanese flotilla appear, much more powerful than the first. This time there
were four heavy cruisers and nearly two thousand Japanese soldiers—
plus two carriers, *Soryu* and *Hiryu,* flinging in their carrier planes before the final assault. Remarkably, the Marines managed to beat off the
Japanese who hit the beach on Wilkes. Captain Wesley Platt ordered his
ninety or so Marines to fix bayonets and charge an enemy who out-
numbered them five to one. Caught by complete surprise, the Japanese
panicked and fled into the surf. Platt's men killed almost all of them.[40]

On Wake itself, however, the Marines didn't have a chance. Pounded
by bombs and strafing planes, hammered by the cruisers' guns, they
were helpless to halt the Japanese advance. One of Teeters's workmen,
"Pop," had served in World War I as a lieutenant and had been a corporate executive until alcohol had cost him his marriage and position and
reduced him to menial jobs. Now he grabbed a bag of grenades and

waded into the surf. He tossed them into one Japanese landing craft and then another, until he ran out of bombs, and hightailed it back to safety. Workmen and Marines cheered, but Major Devereux knew they were doomed. He fired off an urgent radio message: "Enemy is on the Island. The issue is in doubt." A few hours later, he was told that the task force on its way to relieve Wake had been ordered back to Pearl. He tied a white rag to a mop handle and marched out to surrender what was left of his command. The battle for Wake was over.[41]

More construction workers than Marines had died in the fighting— forty-eight, versus forty-seven of Devereux's hard-pressed men. Two hundred and eight others would die in the brutal conditions of Japan's POW camps. Twenty or so were kept on Wake Island to work as slave labor for their captors. When it was clear the war was lost and Wake would have to be evacuated, the Japanese shot them all.

Dan Teeters would survive the war, despite leading a desperate escape attempt that led to his recapture and a savage beating. Florence Teeters mounted an unrelenting campaign in Washington to provide money and relief to the workers' families. Harry Morrison, Kaiser, and their fellow contractors pitched in $300,000.[42] The harrowing experience of the Wake Island workers would help to force one of the biggest changes in the Navy's way of conducting war—the creation of the Construction Battalions, or CBs, known to everyone else as the Seabees. From now on, the men who risked their lives building on the firing line would be in uniform, trained to fight and if necessary die facing the enemy.

The fall of Wake sealed the fate of the Philippines. The Japanese were now undisputed masters of the central Pacific. Yet the sacrifice at Wake had not been in vain. Even though they never sent the radio signal "Send Us More Japs" that rumor said they did, the Marines and Morrison's men had shown that Americans were ready to fight and die, even against steep odds.

They inspired a nation. They also sent Washington an urgent message.

Give the armed forces the right tools, and in the right numbers, and America just might win. That's what the Army's new head of logistics, General Brehon Somervell, was thinking about, too.

Under his boss, Undersecretary Robert Patterson, the Army had grown like a field of mushrooms. From 260,000 men in May 1940, it had expanded to more than a million, thanks to the Selective Service Act. The new U.S. Army had two armored divisions, whereas in 1939 it had none. In 1939 it had 1,500 planes. Thanks to Knudsen and his friends, it now had 16,000, and 22,000 pilots. Already, British and American war production was equaling that of the Axis powers combined.

With the coming of war, Somervell was now looking at an army that was going to expand from a projected one million in 1942 to seven million by the end of 1943. He also figured that the Army's supply of tanks, trucks, and planes would rise to 50 percent of its Victory Plan goals by the end of 1942. That meant America would be ready to go on the offensive. Until then, he told the War Production Board in one of its first meetings, the U.S. armed forces' job would be to keep the lines of communication open to our allies Britain and Russia.[43]

That made Kaiser's Liberty ship program more vital than ever.

CHAPTER TEN

SHIPS FOR LIBERTY

Moving a prefab deckhouse section, Richmond Shipyard No. 2, 1942. *Copyright 2012, Penton Media, 84595: 112SH*

> We see a greater America out here.
>
> *—Henry Kaiser*

"**THE FOUNDATION OF** all our hopes and schemes was the immense shipbuilding program of the United States."

Those were Winston Churchill's words, describing the situation at the start of 1942.[1] Merchant ships were no longer just the lifeline for Britain in its struggle against the Axis. They were now essential to America's ability to project its power across two oceans, the Atlantic and Pacific.

The coming of war meant big changes for the Liberty ship program, as well. How many ships were being made suddenly became a decisive factor in their chances of victory. It was American as well as British ships that were being taken out by German U-boats—more than 6.4 million tons' worth in the first half of 1942. The Germans' Operation

Drumbeat set up patrols of U-boats to catch merchant ships as they came out of every harbor on the East Coast, their victims framed against the coastal lights like silhouettes in a shooting gallery.[2]

With losses like this, Knudsen's and Admiral Land's estimate before Pearl Harbor of needing five million tons of shipping in 1942 and seven million for 1943 looked out of touch with reality.

Something had to be done to expand the program once again—even though every shipyard in America was going flat-out building war vessels. The pressure of events, however, was inexorable. During Churchill's visit to DC shortly after Pearl Harbor and just before Christmas 1941, the goalposts were moved yet again. The politicians agreed there would now have to be eight million tons built in 1942, and ten million in 1943.[3]

The powers that be brought in Admiral Howard Vickery, the Maritime Commission's head of construction. "Can you do it?" they asked.

Vickery was a large, intense man who was most comfortable with a pipe in his mouth. He looked over the figures. "If I can get to eight million tons in '42," he said, "ten will be no problem for '43."

It was an astonishing prediction. But like Bill Knudsen, Vickery understood that the real issue was not the numbers but the momentum. Once the yards got up to a certain pace of production, increasing it would be easy. As with a marathon runner, it was the pace that mattered.

Still, existing Liberty shipyards were slammed. New ones would have to be built, and Vickery knew whom to turn to for that. On March 3 he sent seven identical telegrams to Kaiser and the other heads of the Six Companies. He asked each of them to draw up a proposal for construction of a new yard that could start producing ships in 1942. It may have seemed an impossible task, but Vickery concluded, "The emergency demands all within your power to give your country ships."[4]

The first telegram he got back was at 11 P.M. that night, from Steve Bechtel. "We are studying the problem tonight," it read, "and will give you our sincere best judgment tomorrow." Steve put his younger brother Kenneth in charge of the task force and gave him twenty-four hours to plan out the yard and find a place to build it. On March 4, Ken showed his brother the results and Steve wired back to Washington. Nine days later the Bechtels had their contract.

The place they had found was in Marin County, on the other side of the Golden Gate Bridge from San Francisco, near Sausalito. It was a stretch of deserted land along the shore of Richardson Bay belonging to the Northwest Pacific Railroad. The railroad leased the land to the Bechtels, the Marin County Board agreed to the terms, and on March 28—little more than three weeks after Vickery's telegram—bulldozers broke ground.

"I'm betting on you fellows," Vickery told them. "I expect you to produce." They did. Even with the fierce competition for local labor from Richmond and their own Calship, the Bechtels managed to scrape up enough live bodies to put them to work in the new yard, dubbed Marinship. The marine architect described his supervisor staff as "an orchestra leader, a nightclub proprietor, and a cabinetmaker." Some of his draftsmen had never drawn a ship before. Many of the workers were disabled.[5] Still, with skilled hands on loan from Calship along with booms and equipment, and a crash seventy-hour training program for the rest, the Bechtel brothers were able to lay their first keel before the summer was out. Before 1942 was finished, Marinship would launch five ships just as promised—an astonishing feat even by Richmond standards.

All the same, if the United States was going to meet the desperate new goals, Henry Kaiser's yards were going to be at the center of the effort.

That suited Kaiser. The month before Pearl Harbor, he and his Todd partners had bought back the Richmond yards from the British. They would be producing for the American cause now. The arrival of war only sharpened his own appetite for work, and his two key lieutenants, his son Edgar and Clay Bedford, were working flat-out, seven-day-a-week schedules to hit the numbers.[6]

So were their workers. The historian Carlo D'Este's father worked the graveyard shift in the Richmond yards. He still remembers driving down at night to meet his father, with strings and strings of arc lights brightening up the sky like daylight while hundreds of workers milled around the unfinished hulks.[7] A British visitor, the radio commentator

Alistair Cooke, compared them to characters in a Disney cartoon, who "rush forth with welding guns and weld the parts into a ship as innocently as a child fits A into B on a nursery floor."

Cooke had seen normal shipyards in places like Philadelphia and the Mersey in his own country. He was a bit bemused at how clean and neat Kaiser's yard was. Everything was laid out with meticulous attention. "Sheets of steel are marked VK2 and MQ3, to indicate to a moron where they fit on a ship," since these were workers who had never built ships before. Cranes would swing overhead to gather a sheet, lay it down where drillers and fillers would break it up into the parts traced in outline in yellow chalk, then move it on into the lofts where the real work of assembling the ship was done.[8]

Inside the hull, the noise could be catastrophic to a newcomer. A woman who worked as a welder at Yard No. 1 remembered when the chippers would get under way and two shipfitters would start swinging sledgehammers at opposite sides of a steel bulkhead, "and you wonder if your ears can stand it." The sound "will seem to swell and engulf you like a treacherous wave in surf-bathing and you feel as if you are going under." Yet after a few days she became used to it and never gave it another thought—nor thought it was strange that she could sing popular songs at work at the top of her lungs without anyone hearing a sound.[9]

She grew to deal with it. So did the other welders, chippers, grinders, reamers, flangers, shipfitters, loftsmen, air-compressor operators, bolters, flanger-shrinkers, plate hangers, pneumatic drill and punch and shear operators, and riggers of cranes, machines, and planes—along with forty or so other trade workers who labored to get the plates assembled, the boilers erected and installed, and the ships ready for launching.[10] It was incredibly dangerous work. The same woman welder remembered having to jump three-foot gaps with a forty-foot drop below, welding torch in hand. She did it, but "my knees were a little shaky under the welding leathers."

Then there were the swinging scaffolds. Our lady welder never quite had the nerve to try, but others learned to ride up on one scaffold as it rose, then jump to another as it swung past on its way down, without a thought—even though a slight slip meant a neck-breaking plunge to the bottom of the hull. Working out on the far end of what would be the main deck was like standing atop a six-story building, with no re-straints or guardrails. There were electrical wires to trip on or to be electrocuted by; red-hot rivets to drop on a foot or 250-pound-per-square-inch metal presses in which to flatten an unwary hand or finger; plus the hazards every welder faces, of searing burns that leave arms and legs covered with scars.

All this for an average of sixty dollars a week.[11]

But the workers came. In 1942 the growth of the Richmond yards was explosive. In the summer of 1941, there were still only 4,000 em-ployees working there, most living in ramshackle shacks thrown up on the barren flats surrounding the yards. Pearl Harbor brought floods of new faces, many from as far away as New York and Boston. By the end of 1942, some 80,000 men and women were employed in the yards; a year later there were 100,000. The Portland yards trailed only slightly behind in numbers. At least 60,000 simply climbed into their cars and drove across the country. Many of them were destitute laborers from the Dust Bowl states, like characters from *The Grapes of Wrath*. When they arrived, they found an entire city being built by Kaiser and his Permanente Shipbuilding Company, complete with restaurants, movie theaters, schools, and hospitals. Eventually Henry Kaiser even began chartering a special train service to bring prospective workers to the Richmond site.[12]

It was a willing workforce, unionized by prior agreement with the Maritime Commission and the AFL, and backed by a production staff who blinked at nothing. All the same, when Admiral Vickery broke the news to Kaiser and his men that they now were expected to hit 105 days for completing a ship (60 on the ways, 45 for outfitting), their minds boggled. Work on Edgar Kaiser's first ship, *Star of Oregon*, was begun on May 19, 1941, and delivered on New Year's Eve: a total of 253 days. How would they ever reach the new totals? But forty-eight hours later, they were signed on.[13]

Kaiser's approach was to concentrate on pure production. It was a classic front-end philosophy. He set Clay Bedford on the case, whose teams were already building the new Richmond No. 2, while Edgar was building the brand-new yards on Vancouver Island.

Meanwhile, Edgar's team was learning rapidly, just as Land had predicted when he said American industry could cut the production time to just four and a half to six months. They were also learning that the faster they worked, the cheaper the cost. The *Meriwether Lewis* and the *William Clark* came down the slips in January and February 1942, and by the tenth ship, *Robert Fulton* in March, they were down to 154 days. Howard Vickery's goal was almost in sight.

Kaiser's men were also learning the importance of reorganizing the supply yard so that the seven hundred tons of shapes and materials, including 50,000 castings, were always on hand when crews were ready to install them, with no pause in the production. They were also discovering the importance of getting the subcontractors to deliver their goods on time, from the propeller shaft, two water-tube boilers, and two anchors, to winches, fans, lockers, compasses, chairs, antiaircraft guns, and the six onboard electric generators. And then there was the mammoth three-cylinder, reciprocating engine, standing two stories high and weighing 135 tons of dark gray, well-oiled steel.[14]

Next to procuring steel plate, the engine became Bedford and Kaiser's chief headache. Although it weighed 135 tons, the Liberty ship's engine had an output of only 2500 horsepower. It had long since been outperformed by modern diesel and turbine engines, the ones companies like GM were making for the Navy's subs and destroyers. It was a relic of a vanished maritime age. But the EC-2 reciprocating engine had one insuperable advantage that made it appealing to Land and Vickery. It could be built fast by a variety of companies and in a variety of conditions. Joshua Hendy Iron Works, of which Henry Kaiser was part owner and whose manager, Charlie Moore, reflected his flat-out, full-speed-ahead business attitude, became the main source for the Kaiser yards, and did it in record time and numbers.[15] Before 1942 was out, the Hendy plant was building thirty-five EC-2 engines a month, or one every twenty-one hours.

But the centerpiece of the Kaiser effort was Richmond's Yard No. 2.

In March 1941 it had been a long mudflat running along the Richmond channel, with a large marsh pond standing in the middle. The ink on Kaiser's contract with Admiral Vickery was barely dry, however, before a tiny clapboard building appeared on the edge of the pond. The building was the field engineer's office, thrown together in the driving rain even as Kaiser's crew were completing their survey of the land. Bedford had put McCoon in charge of construction again, and on April 22, McCoon's men dug a long drainage ditch to empty the pond. By mid-June they had sunk more than 40,000 piles, 12,000 for the twelve shipways to come and the rest for the massive outfitting docks and buildings where workers and subcontractors would complete the work on getting the hulls seaworthy.

McCoon brought in massive dredges to scour away 2.5 million cubic yards of mudflats in order to create a launching basin, where the completed hulls of Yard No. 2 would be shot out into the channel like bullets from a gun. Each shipway had a set of steel tracks on either side for the cranes that would do the heavy lifting, while huge steel plates were laid out between the shipways on top of a corduroy quilt of timbers laid end to end in the mud. These would provide solid, stable platforms on which the workers and technicians and welders and their supervisors could do their work around the ships—while a system of sliding roofs equipped with arc lights ensured they could work round the clock, in any weather.[16]

Meanwhile, McCoon dumped the silt on the marshy ground east of the basin, to create a base for sheds and materials storage. North of the shipways, the plate shop took shape, a huge gray steel-trussed building with a concrete floor for the four-ton steel plates that would become the hull subsections of No. 2's first Liberty ships.

When it was done, Richmond Yard No. 2 covered 185 acres with a dozen shipways, each 87 feet wide and 450 feet long—the same width as the shipways Bedford had built for Yard No. 1 but a good 25 feet longer. On September 17, the crews gathered to watch the laying of the first keels in shipways 3, 4, and 5. Henry Kaiser liked to have a little ceremony for events like this, even by remote control from Washington, so more than two thousand workers and managers had gathered for the laying. Richmond's mayor was there, as was the city's Chamber of Commerce president, P. N. Stanford. Todd Shipyard flew in Francis Gilbrick all the way from New York—although the dealings between Todd and Kaiser Permanente were about to undergo a radical shift.[17]

Three weeks after Pearl Harbor, on December 31, the first No. 2 Yard Liberty ship shot down the slips, the *James Otis*. On board was a Joshua Hendy reciprocal engine, the very first on a Liberty ship.

Richmond's efficient methods and frantic pace had slashed the assembly time of a Liberty ship down to 80 days. At Oregon, however,
Edgar Kaiser cut the time to 71, inspiring Washington columnist Drew
Pearson to dub him the nation's shipbuilding ace. But as German torpedoes sank more and more ships, that was still not fast enough.

On February 19, 1942, there was a tense conversation in the White
House bedroom, between the president and Vickery's boss, Admiral
Land. For once, FDR did not beat around the bush, and gave Land the
bad news. The truth was the Allies would now need 9 million tons of
new ships for 1942, not 8; and a staggering 15 million for 1943.[18]

Land was floored. Until now his entire reputation was based on
achieving amazing results with little or no preparation, thanks to men
like Kaiser, Bedford, and Moore. But now, precisely because they had
succeeded, the bar was being raised to what seemed an impossible level.

"I realize this is a terrible directive on my part," FDR wrote to Land
afterward, "but the great emergency left no options."

Land called Vickery, who was in the South looking for new shipbuilding sites. Vickery listened and said, "You know that's impossible."

"Yes," Land answered, "all I said was we would try."[19]

Meanwhile, the search for new sites had taken Vickery to Wilmington, to Panama City, to Savannah and New Orleans. But even if they
opened a half dozen new yards, both men knew another problem was
looming. Even with Joshua Hendy swinging into production, a growing bottleneck in engines and steel was threatening to shut the entire
program down. Looking at the numbers, a discouraged Stacy May
broke the news to Donald Nelson at the War Production Board. The
Liberty ship program would never hit its goals for March.[20]

At the same time, public pressure was growing. Criticism in the
newspapers and at the Capitol was flying thick and fast. Rumors circulated that even though the numbers had been reduced, the program
was in such chaos that they couldn't be met.

Land and Vickery were learning what Knudsen had discovered at
OPM. The ability to get amazingly quick results simply bred demands
for more results, and disappointment when the new ones weren't
achieved. And like Knudsen, Land and Vickery knew that labor problems, plus the shortage of steel, were at the heart of it.

As early as February 1942, Admiral Land had told Congress that strikes in 1941 had cost the Maritime Commission between seven and twelve ships—nearly 150,000 tons of shipping lost as surely as if it had been sunk by U-boats.[21] And things were getting worse. In 1942 the CIO and AFL would extend their perpetual battle for supremacy to the shipyards, where clashes over membership turf would divide the workforce and cause major headaches for management, Kaiser included.[22*]

Then there were the stories of unproductive workers, and absentee ones. Land said bluntly there was "too damn much loafing going on in the shipyards." Stories were told of managers finding marathon craps games in out-of-the-way corners of the unfinished hulls, and of people having full-time jobs in town and only showing up at the Richmond yard to collect a paycheck. Some said Kaiser's yards in particular were overstaffed, and that his "soft touch" with labor made him an easy mark with workers and organizers alike. A later Maritime Commission study found that Richmond No. 1 ranked number 33 of 41 shipyards in employee attendance.[23]

Kaiser hit back hard. "The talk about absenteeism has been grossly overdone," he bellowed to critics. "Let's talk about *presentism*. My hat is off to the 93 percent *faithful* in the Kaiser-operated shipyards....With hands and hearts they are fashioning complete victory as surely as if they were on the fighting front."[24]

Eventually Kaiser's record would silence his critics, because at Richmond Yard No. 2, Clay Bedford was changing how ships were made.

Under the traditional methods of shipbuilding, when a ship's hull was nearing completion and the deckhouses were being added, swarms of welders, electricians, cutters, pipe fitters, burners, and joiners moved in, out, and around the action to do their job—but also getting in each other's way. This meant the process of building a ship actually slowed down the closer it got to completion, as Kaiser's men were finding out.

---

* One of the ugliest would be in the Portland yards, where Edgar became a helpless spectator to the corruption in the AFL Boilermakers Local 72. Its president, Tom Ray, not only promoted racial strife and denied promotion to women, but had spent a quarter million dollars on parties for himself and his buddies. Ultimately the National Labor Relations Board had to strip Ray of his presidency and order a new election.

Edgar and Clay tried various ways to speed up the process. But they couldn't avoid the fact that the shipbuilding process required doing large numbers of tasks at once, rather than in sequence like Knudsen's auto assembly line.

Bedford decided there had to be a better way—and the place to start was the Liberty ship's mid and after deckhouses.

He talked his idea over with Norman Gindrat. Each deckhouse was made up of separate slabs of steel averaging twenty feet long each—the heaviest weighing 72 tons and the lightest 45 tons. Clay told him to create a prefabricating shop where workmen could weld these sections together and build the deckhouses off-site. Then he and Clay would find a way to move those assembled deckhouses and install them complete, onto the hull—like snapping the lid onto a box.[25]

What Gindrat came up with was a mammoth 480-foot-long steel-frame shed, with two 90-foot bays with three bridge cranes in each bay, and a 150-foot run out beyond the building where the slabs of steel would be set out—and a vertical clearance below the cranes of 40 feet. Work spaces for the various crafts for outfitting the deckhouses, from joining and pipe fitting to electrical and sheet metal shops, ran along the long sides of each bay.[26]

Once it was built, Bedford put Elmer Hann, a veteran shipbuilder Kaiser had recruited from Consolidated Steel in San Francisco, in charge and stood by to watch.

Plates and structural shapes went from the various suppliers direct to the warehouse, and then to the prefab center by flatcar or trailer. There three conveyor belts in each bay were set up to handle three deckhouses at a time. The belt was not a belt at all, but a three-foot-high concrete platform, on which were mounted trolley wheels at two-foot intervals—and on the wheels were the enormous mounted jigs carrying the deckhouse and pulled by a two-drum 10-horsepower hoist at the opposite end.

First the decks were laid out, made of thirty-six steel plates, and double-torched and match-marked to fit. Then the plates were set on an "upside down" jig on the conveyor belt, where they were welded together by two welding machines and a pack of Lincoln 300-amp welders.[27]

Then came the beams, stiffeners, and other shapes that were welded in place, each cut and bent to shape in large numbers ahead of time and stored in the "angle orchard." Then bridge cranes lifted each deckhouse and turned it right side up and onto a series of jigs, so that the bulkheads, boat decks, bridge decks, house tops—all cut, shaped, and machined ahead of time and stored in racks—as well as piping, plumbing, heating, and electrical wiring, could be installed, station by station, on the belt.[28]

By the time the deckhouse reached the end of the conveyor belt, it was complete in every detail, including temporary stiffeners and rigging for hoisting each deckhouse into place in the shipway. Then a retractor conveyor picked it up and jacked it up for a trailer. Each trailer was a Trailermobile weighing eighty-five tons, with thirty-two 10x15 tires. Then a Caterpillar DW10 tractor moved it to the ways, where four high gantry cranes lifted the finished deckhouse and slid it into place. Easier said than done, since coordinating all four cranes to lift at the same time took some planning and skill. But like everything else in the Kaiser yards, practice made perfect.

Bedford soon expanded this technique to include the engine room. All the one hundred sections of piping were prefab, which the pipe fitters worked together in a mock-up of the Liberty engine room, complete with a wooden dummy engine. Welders fastened down the flange at one end of each pipe with a complete weld, but the other ends were only spot-welded so that they could be disassembled, then refitted and welded into place in the actual ship.[29]

Assembly-line production had come to America's shipyards. By August the prefab yard had 2,500 workers, with 42 women welders and burners—and ships were ready that were 95 percent preassembled.[30] The time it took to launch a Liberty ship plummeted, while the man-hours required fell by almost half. The Kaiser yards had already found ways to reduce the time to build a ship from 220 days to 105. Now Clay Bedford was pointing the way to 50 days or less.

At Portland, applying those same preassemblies was transformational. Edgar Kaiser's tenth ship, *Robert Fulton,* had taken 154 days. In April the *Henry W. Longfellow* finished in 86 days, and in May the *James Whitcomb Riley* in 73. Edgar pushed his team still harder. In July, Hull No. 230, the *Thomas Bailey Aldrich,* got finished in just 43 days.[31]

Bedford was unwilling to let that record stand. In August 1942, Yard

No. 2 brought out a ship in just twenty-four days. Harold Vickery sent an ecstatic congratulatory telegram, but just as the battle of Guadalcanal was heating up on one side of the Pacific, the battle of the Kaiser shipyards was under way on the other side.

In September, Edgar one-upped Bedford. His assistant general manager, Albert Bauer, found ways to push through the preassembly envelope by increasing production per worker in every department: "More men and equipment are swung into the job," he explained. "We simply program the erection on a faster schedule."[32] On the twenty-third the *Joseph Teal* was finished in just ten days. The day before launching, Edgar called Clay Bedford down in Richmond, barely disguising his glee.

"Why don't you come up for the christening?" Edgar asked.

"Sorry," Clay replied. "I'm just too busy down here. Can't spare the time."

Edgar said, "Do you want me to call my father and have him order you to be here?"[33]

Clay blanched. He got the message and took the first train up to Portland. He knew there was another, even more important reason he had to be there.

The president of the United States was going to watch the christening.

Roosevelt arrived there after visiting the Seattle Boeing plant and the Bremerton Navy Yard, where five thousand ship workers heard him speak with a hand microphone from his open car. After Bremerton, Roosevelt was excited to see what wonders the Kaisers were performing at Portland. He was not disappointed.

He was greeted by Henry Kaiser himself—"a dynamo," FDR confessed later to his cousin Daisy Suckley.[34] He shook hands with the man of the hour, Edgar Kaiser, who smiled his father's smile of confidence. Clay Bedford was there, too, and got a handshake and a brief comment from the president. "I remember you from Grand Coulee Dam, when you were one of the men who showed me around there."[35]

Then the president toured the great yards. His car rolled past the plate storage area, the plate shop and assembly building, and then down to the pre-erection skids onto the ways, where the *Joseph Teal* was waiting.

Roosevelt's car was parked on a high ramp overlooking the christen-

ing ceremony. The president was mesmerized. As a former assistant
secretary of the Navy, he could remember the long, tedious process
involved in building the average ship, which Kaiser and his engineers
had now cut by almost 90 percent. Out of desolate marshland, they had
built, in little more than a year and a half, one of the country's most
dynamic and innovative industrial centers.

Fourteen thousand workers and six thousand onlookers watched as
Anna Boettiger tried three times to crack the champagne bottle on the
Teal's prow. Finally, on the third try, she succeeded, managing to shower
herself and the other dignitaries until "they were soaked to the skin,"
said onlooker Daisy Suckley—as the crowd cheered and cheered.

The president spoke. "I am very much inspired by what I have seen,"
he said, "and I wish that every man, woman, and child in these United
States could have been here to see the launching and realize its importance in winning the war."

Then it was Henry Kaiser's turn. "Here beside us is this great craft,"
he said, "only ten days from keel laying to launching; and in a few days
she will be on the ocean bearing cargo to our allies and our soldiers. It
is a miracle, no less—a miracle of God and of the genius of free American workmen."

Later, when the president's train pulled away and the goodbyes were
done, someone asked Kaiser how long the ten-day record would stand.

"I expect that record to go by the boards in the very near future," he
said.[36]

He was right. As Clay Bedford rode back to San Francisco, he was
already planning his next move.

Later that week the workers at Richmond No. 2 were getting off the
bus and picking up their copies of the shipyard newsletter, *Fore N Aft,*
when they found a flyer inside. "What's Oregon Got," it read, "That
We Haven't Got?"[37]

In the flyer Clay Bedford asked his crews to think of ways to regain
the record they had lost to the yards up in Portland. The flyer set the
Richmond crews of Yard No. 2, all three shifts, on fire. Bedford got back
more than 250 letters, each suggesting ways to speed up construction.

Bedford couldn't try them all. But he already had the dynamic key, which was prefabrication. All he had to do was speed up the process—*not* of putting together the ship itself, as Edgar was doing, but of pre-assembling the separate sections, so that they could be snapped together almost in sequence, like Lincoln Logs.

By now Bedford had the building of decks down to twenty-three separate preassemblies, which would then be lifted by crane into place and welded together. His engineers were now thinking they could manage to reduce that down to just seven.[38]

The superintendent of Yard No. 2 was J. M. McFarland. Bedford asked him point-blank: Did he think they could build a ship in just five days? McFarland charted out the process on paper and passed his calculations on to the production managers, who all agreed five days was achievable. Bedford was elated. There was only one worry. What would President Roosevelt think if the Richmond yards broke the record set by the *Joseph Teal,* the ship whose christening the president himself had supervised? Clay put the problem to Henry Kaiser, who put it to the president's assistant James Byrnes. Roosevelt was delighted. "Build it," was his response, "and if it can be built in *one* day, so much the better."[39]

On Saturday, November 7, 1942, the preassembled parts of the "five-day ship," Hull No. 440, were spread all over the yard. Masts, anchor chains, and deckhouses were stacked up in a confusing pile, ready to be taken down to Ship way No. 1, with more than half the ship's components already finished. The hull was laid out in five huge double-bottom chunks, the heaviest weighing 110 tons, while the deck units came in 250-ton chunks, with piping, hatches, portholes, radiators, and even washbasins and mirrors all preinstalled. On one side stood the trusty Joshua Hendy engine, all three stories of her. The whole thing looked like an abandoned machinery junkyard.

"Five days!" said one old-timer. "Hell, it'll take 'em five days to even find the keel."

A huge crowd gathered as midnight approached. Superintendent McFarland, Clay Bedford, and his two sons watched as at exactly 12:01 A.M. the keel was officially laid. Then people began to realize there was method to the madness. One by one the prefabricated pieces began to disappear in the hull shell. By the time the day shift arrived at 8 o'clock on Sunday, November 8, the ship already looked a week old.[40]

Sunday was a day to remember, even by Kaiser standards. Some seventeen banks of welding machines were hard at work, carrying out some 152,000 feet of weld line on ninety-three separate prefab sections, while chippers were hacking away at plate ends ten at a time. "It was one seething mass of shipfitters, welders, chippers," one worker remembered, "hose and cable a foot deep. . . . The biggest problem that first day," he added, "was persuading the guys in the rest of the yard not to wander down where all the action was."[41]

As the Sunday night shift arrived, the hull had taken shape and 1,450 tons of ship had been installed, including the 135-ton engine. "I'll be blind and deaf by next week," one worker laughed, "but it'll be worth it." By the end of the second day, November 9, the upper deck was done. Now other workers were arriving an hour early to watch the progress: McFarland had to send his men out to clear a path so that the next round of prefab pieces could get installed. Clay Bedford wired Kaiser back in Washington. Because of the thronging crowds, they were going to have to institute a ban on all workers not assigned to Hull No. 440 from coming down to Shipway No. 1.[42]

At the end of the third day, deckhouses, masts, and deck equipment were all in place. Excitement was building. This ship wouldn't be finished in five days, they were saying. It'd be done in four. Clay Bedford gave the go-ahead to McFarland to see if he could beat his own estimate.

November 11 saw teams of workmen completing the last installations, including final welding, electrical wiring, and painting. Elated and exhausted, Bedford and McFarland watched as the final pieces of their giant prefab puzzle slid into place. Neither man had slept much in the past seventy-two hours.

Then, at 3:27 P.M. on November 12, the *Robert E. Peary* was launched, just four days, fifteen hours, and twenty-six minutes after laying the keel. The wife of Jimmy Byrnes, Maude Byrnes, swung the champagne bottle, the crowd roared its approval, and Hull No. 440 entered history. Six minutes later the blocks for laying the keel for the next Liberty ship, Hull No. 443, were in place.[43]

Bedford got congratulatory telegrams from Henry Kaiser and from Jerry Land. "Every one of you should be proud of the ship which your sweat and energy built in record time," wrote the admiral. "Keep up the good work." But the one that meant the most came from Edgar Kaiser and the work crews up in Portland. Their congratulations came with a postscript: "Now if we cut your record in half, what will you do?"[44]

Bedford laughed. In fact, no one challenged his record then or later. It remained one of the supreme industrial feats of the war.

It took another three days of cleaning, refitting, and rewiring much of the electrical equipment before the *Robert E. Peary* was truly seaworthy and ready for delivery to the Maritime Commission, and in the end, the accelerated schedule proved too costly to reproduce again. Bedford was already warning Admiral Land that the pace Richmond was setting (Yard Nos. 1 and 2 launched no fewer than eighteen Liberty ships in November, an average of one every other day) couldn't be sustained because of looming shortages of equipment such as anchor chains, electrical cable, generator engines, and gauges and valves.[45] Critics claimed the whole thing had been a publicity stunt, and that all Bedford had done was take two months lining up the ship's parts and four days to slap it together—although that had been the point.[46] All the same, Bedford and the men and women of Richmond No. 2 had proved that the era of mass production had come to shipbuilding.

As for the *Robert E. Peary,* she showed no signs of being worse for wear by being assembled in just over 111 hours. She would log more than 42,000 miles in both the Pacific and Atlantic theaters of operation, and in May 1943 set a record of her own, loading 10,500 tons of cargo in just under 35 hours. She continued to be a cargo ship long after the war. It wasn't until June 1963 that the old ship finally headed for the breaker's yard in Baltimore.[47]

The ships were ready. What went in them, comes next.

CHAPTER ELEVEN

THE PRODUCTION EXPRESS

Artillery shells, Fisher Body Divison, General Motors. *General Motors LLC. Used with permission,*
GM Media Archives

> This is a hell of a congregation I'm pastor of.
> —*Donald Nelson, March 1942*

IF NEW DEAL progressives had thought Donald Nelson, the head of the
new War Production Board, would run the war their way, they were
wrong.

Nelson drove down daily from his suite at the Broadmoor Hotel on
Connecticut Avenue through Rock Creek to the WPB offices in the
Social Security Building. They had been Bill Knudsen's offices under
OPM. Nelson proved Knudsen's heir in more ways than one.

When he came to Washington from Sears and Roebuck in the summer of 1940, he was the mildest mannered of the dollar-a-year
men—the Clark Kent of OPM. Some, reflecting on his bland Mid-

western roots, compared him cruelly to Sinclair Lewis's George Babbitt.

When he was summoned to the White House in January 1942 to replace Bill Knudsen, however, he became the Washington media darling. Columnist Walter Lippmann hailed his hitherto-unnoticed talents. *Fortune* magazine was pleased that one man, *any* man, was at last in charge of the war production effort. So was *Time*—although Nelson might have noted its editors had once been enamored of the big Dane from Detroit, as well.[1]

Nelson also discovered the president had given him enormous powers compared to his predecessor. "We had authority to force a manufacturer to accept a contract," as he described it later, "and we occasionally employed it." Nelson could also requisition private property for war use, and he could order production of certain civilian goods halted.[2]

None of this bothered the New Dealers. Indeed, Nelson was something of a New Dealer himself. He had been a strong supporter of Roosevelt since 1932. As chairman of the wage committee for the textile industry during the National Recovery Act, Nelson was seen by Big Labor as a reliable friend of the workingman.[3]

Nelson came with another advantage for the White House: He had none of the independent stature of Bill Knudsen. He was a successful businessman but no titan of industry. Hopkins and others assumed he'd be good at taking orders. Unlike his predecessor, he would help them use conversion to a wartime economy as a tool for taking power away from businessmen and "the blind chances of an allegedly free competitive marketplace," and investing in "purposeful, detailed, and total economic planning by the national government"—even, as one later enthusiast put it, international government.[4]

Nelson disappointed them all. His regime turned out to be more like his predecessor's than anyone had supposed—which also suggested that Knudsen's approach had more merit than anyone supposed. Bill Harrison, ball-bearings magnate William Batt, who was OPM's deputy chief of industrial materials and was now vice chairman of WPB, John Lord O'Brian, Stacy May—even Knudsen's assistants ended up being his. Other dollar-a-year men like Montgomery Ward's Frank Folsom and GE's Charles E. Wilson soon joined them. "On this job we must get the maximum results from American industry," Nelson declared. "To do that we must have down here men who understand and can deal with industry's intricate structure and operation."[5]

The New Dealers' disappointment is still reflected in history textbooks that treat Nelson as a bumbling, rather ineffectual figure, lost in the corridors of Washington—or even a pawn of big business.[6] Nelson also caught heavy flak from the other side of Constitution Avenue, from the Munitions and Navy buildings. When he refused to give the Army and Navy *exactly* what they wanted, and exactly when they wanted it, they turned on him, as well. When Felix Frankfurter complained to Roosevelt that Nelson "was an utterly weak man incapable of exercising authority or making decisions," it was a judgment on which both War Department Republicans and New Deal Democrats were, for once, in agreement.[7]*

After a year in office, Donald Nelson was the most despised man in Washington.

Nelson knew there was nothing he could do about it. He continued to sit at his desk, pipe in mouth and pencil in hand, governing as best he could the thankless task Roosevelt had thrust upon him. No one seemed to notice that he was struggling to implement changes in the procurement system following the Truman investigating committee's devastating report on OPM, which found millions of dollars misspent through incompetence and fraud—not surprising when Knudsen and his people had no authority to examine how the money was being spent, only to draw up the contracts and count the results.[8] No one noticed that the numbers of strikes were easing, and that a concerted effort was under way to find housing for the thousands of defense workers crowding into places both large and small that were unable to handle them.

But the supreme thought governing his every action had governed Knudsen's, as well. Any sudden switch to centralized government con-

---

* So was Congress. At one point in 1943, there were no fewer than seven bills pending before Congress proposing ways to reorganize the War Production Board—and most of them started by getting rid of its director.

trol over war production, whether by New Dealers or the military, would spell the end of the American system that made the promise of prodigious production possible.

"As I understood my job," Nelson would write later, "it wasn't up to me to *tell* industry how to do its job; it was our function to *show* industry what had to be done and then to do everything in our power to enable industry to do it"—including stepping in if the marketplace couldn't deliver fast enough.[9]

"We are going to have to rely on our great mass production industries for the bulk of our increase under this war production," he told an audience of merchandising executives in his very first speech as director of WPB. He was referring to autos, textiles, chemicals, consumer durables, and metallurgies like iron and steel. "The only gauge we can apply to this process is: What method will most quickly give us the greatest volume of war production in this particular industry?" America was going to change the war, but the war wasn't going to change America.[10] Once they got Ford, General Electric, Westinghouse, and other companies going, the Axis wouldn't stand a chance. All America had to do was "step on the gas," as *Time* magazine put it that May.[11] And Donald Nelson saw his job as quietly, unobtrusively treading on the accelerator pedal.

Yet for the next year and a half, everywhere he went, and in every decision he made, he could make out the footprint of Bill Knudsen ahead of him.

Unlike Knudsen, Donald Nelson was no industrial production man. He was a chemical engineer, with a degree from the University of Missouri—a handy degree when later he had to look at priority claims for materials from the engineers and scientists running the Manhattan Project.[12]

In 1912, Sears and Roebuck, for almost a quarter century America's emporium for every product from sewing machines and tractors to overcoats and underwear, hired him to study the chemical composition of the textiles their suppliers were buying. Later they made him check the scientific descriptions of merchandise with what appeared in the catalogue copy. From that day until the day he became president, Sears never gave him a full-time contract.[13]

In the meantime Donald Nelson learned more about how nearly every one of the 135,000 products in the catalogue was made by some five thousand companies—from the sources of raw materials to costs and manufacturing methods—than he could have learned from a lifetime in the businesses themselves.

Sears had been a business of razor-thin margins, where lowering cost, even by a few pennies, was everything. Sears had taught Nelson how to get one manufacturer to convert to a line of products suddenly in high demand in the catalogue, like stoves or nylon stockings, and to drop all others. At times he would even act as purchasing agent for a Sears-run company, to make sure the brass or cotton or plate glass it needed to make the product came at a cheaper price.[14]

It was good training for running SPAB, and later the War Production Board. Nelson was conditioned to see the big picture behind the steadily rising mountain of data: how to coordinate the flow of materials from a myriad of sources to an equally complex network of suppliers and manufacturers, and then how to move the finished goods to the distributors on a nationwide scale so that ultimately they reached the customer on time—in this case, the Army and Navy and the Army Air Forces.* This also meant a myriad of toes to be stepped on, in trying to coordinate the intermeshing of an entire economy for one purpose, winning the war. But Nelson in his quiet way persisted, defying newspaper columnists, congressional investigators, outraged labor leaders, Army and Navy brass, and furious businessmen who thought they were being shortchanged or overburdened by Nelson's system—and sometimes both. As one of his own staff, and one of his fiercest critics, admitted, "The most striking thing about the whole war production program was not that there were so many controls but that all of them fell within the established patterns of industry."[15]

One of his first big battles was with organized labor. Walter Reuther and others hoped that Nelson's appearance on the scene would revive the idea of joint labor-management committees, to handle the war

---

* The Army Air Corps officially switched its name to Army Air Forces in June 1941.

conversion process and give unions a direct say in how the factories and production lines would be run. Nelson's dealings with the National Recovery Administration, however, made him wary of opening the door to the union way of doing things. "My experience," he once said, "was that whenever you set up a joint committee, industry and labor representatives get together to see how they can screw the public."[16] Instead, he insisted that WPB take as little or as much advice on production or conversion from separate industry committees and labor committees as it needed, and reserve for itself the final decision. As for the unions, they should keep their hands to themselves, and concentrate on getting workers work, pay, and adequate housing—in that order.

Another big battle was over antitrust.

Roosevelt's assistant attorney general Thurman Arnold was a crusader on the subject. He had fired off investigations into some of America's biggest corporations, from Standard Oil to DuPont and Alcoa, and firmly believed that without Justice's heavy supervising hand, America would never be safe from their anticompetitive collusions.

The new system devised by Knudsen and sustained by Nelson broke every one of Arnold's rules. Defense contracts were no longer based on competitive bids. There was no time. They were negotiated instead on a cost-plus basis, with the company negotiating the contract based on what the government would pay up front to get what it needed— planes, tanks, TNT, uniforms—instead of the company forgoing what it could to gain the contract in the first place.

In the mind of Thurman Arnold, this was a clear invitation to corruption. "The vast government spending for war production," Arnold thundered, had "created a great opportunity for conspiratorial agreements between businessmen."[17] He was also livid to see big-business executives serving as "dollar-a-year men" directing contracts toward their old industries, if not their old firms. General Arnold smelled a rat everywhere he sniffed. He started smoking them out in August 1940 by filing an antitrust action against no fewer than twenty-two major petroleum firms, for restraint of trade.

Donald Nelson, then coordinator of defense purchases for Knudsen, sensed disaster. The Army desperately needed gasoline, the Air Force special 100-octane aviation fuel. Everyone needed butyl petroleum for synthetic rubber and toluene for explosives. If executives in companies like Sun Oil, which was also building oil tankers for the Navy, had to devote their time fighting lawsuits and watching their backs with the Justice Department instead of focusing on production, America's rearmament would never get off the ground.

Knudsen agreed with Nelson. "The Production Express can't afford to be late," he said. Even Leon Henderson got the point, and had to explain to Arnold that national defense was a bigger priority than whether oil companies were forcing their filling stations to sell only their products (the main point of Arnold's suit).[18] Arnold, however, refused to yield. The lawsuit against the oil companies dragged on for a year and a half. Finally, in 1942 Nelson convinced Roosevelt that the standard antitrust rules would have to be bent if America was going to arm itself and keep a civilian economy going at the same time.

So Franklin Roosevelt, the bane of American business, issued an executive order suspending antitrust prosecution against companies deemed vital to defense production. Arnold and his allies fought back hard. But Roosevelt had an unexpected ally in the antitrust fight. The midterm elections in 1942 brought in a flood of Republicans, who sided with Nelson against the trust-busters. From 1943 on, Thurman Arnold troubled the defense buildup no more.[19] /

Nor was Nelson afraid to defend his dependence on the dollar-a-year men, whom he now appointed and controlled. Early on, the Truman Committee pushed hard to abolish them, or at least enforce a rule that "no person shall be employed in any position in which he will make decisions directly affecting the affairs of his own company"—which could mean Bill Batt could offer no advice on the manufacturing of vital ball bearings, even though his former company was one of their biggest producers, and no Goodyear executive on loan to the War Production Board could make decisions affecting the rubber industry.

Nelson said no. If such a rule were enforced in a draconian way, nothing could ever get done. "On this job we must get the maximum results from American industry," he patiently explained. "To do that we must have down here men who understand and can deal with industry's intricate structure and operation." He also pointed out that of the three hundred or so dollar-a-year men appointed since August 1940, more than 70 percent were technical engineers, production and operations managers, and heads of research divisions—not golf-playing board chairmen. As for making these men quit their jobs and become federal employees (another Truman idea), there was no way Washington could recruit top-caliber people with a meager civil service salary. These men would face daunting financial hardship if they went to Washington. The war effort's tap into business talent would slow to a drip.

In fact, what it would mean in practice is that only people of truly independent means could afford to serve. "And I don't think the Congress would like to limit the War Production Board to the ranks of the very wealthy," Nelson concluded, with a wry smile.[20]

Truman backed off. The dollar-a-year-man system remained in place for the rest of the war. In the end, even severe critics had to admit it largely worked. It provided not only expertise but opened an easy line of communication between the government issuing the orders and the businesses carrying them out. When a man such as GE's Charles Wilson weighed in with the electronics firms, they tended to sit up and listen. Bill Knudsen had pointed the way with his direct and intimate dealings with his friends in Detroit. Donald Nelson stuck to the Knudsen model to the end.

Of course, the ways of Washington sometimes baffled even the best business minds. The vice president of one New York bank applied for a post in the Office of Economic Warfare. He waited a long time in vain. Then one day the OEW's director showed up at the bank to ask its president if he knew any likely candidates for the very same job. The president mentioned his vice president, and the man was hired on the spot.

He moved to Washington and soon found himself inundated with the usual paperwork related to the OEW. A month or two passed, and a letter arrived forwarded from his old New York address. It was a rejection letter, regretfully turning him down for the very post he now occupied.

Now familiar with Washington bureaucracy, this came as no surprise to him. The surprise was he had signed the letter himself.[21]

In 1942—the year of Midway, Guadalcanal, and Operation Torch—
the production numbers began to hit, just as Knudsen had promised.

In 1941 the United States had made 3,964 tanks—more than twice
the number of the past three years. In 1942 it produced 24,754. In 1941
it produced 617,000 small arms and 97,000 machine guns. In 1942
the numbers swelled to 2.3 million and 663,000, respectively. Whereas
the previous year saw 318 B-17 and B-24 heavy bombers coming off the
assembly line, 1942 saw 2,618—along with 136,000 aircraft engines,
92,000 20mm antiaircraft guns (versus 2,042 in 1941), 20,000 75mm
guns, and 10 million rounds of small-arms ammunition. As for total
production of airplanes, it reached 47,873—just shy of the 50,000
Roosevelt had asked for just two years earlier, and which all the experts
had said was impossible.[22]

Before 1942 was out, the United States was producing more war
materiel than all three Axis powers—Germany, Italy, and Japan—
combined.[23]

In September the president got his own front-row view of what was
happening. Roosevelt's visit with Henry and Edgar Kaiser was part of
a nationwide tour of America's defense plants to see Nelson's "congre-
gation," in the WPB director's phrase, in action.

His first stop was on September 18, at the Chrysler Tank Arsenal.
K. T. Keller's and Eddie Hunt's experiment in making tanks the Detroit
way had grown into a full-blown operation. It was already producing
more than three thousand of the M3 Grants when in March 1942
Chrysler got the go-ahead to make one thousand of the new M4 tanks,
dubbed Shermans, a month.

Albert Kahn had given them another 500,000 square feet of factory
space to accommodate the new machine tools and parts, and expanded the test track where the big thirty-ton armored vehicles were
put through their paces. When Continental Motors' version of the
nine-cylinder Wright engine was called out for airplane production,
Chrysler engineers found a way to fasten together five of their own
200-horsepower six-cylinder car engines, then put an engine drive

gear at the end of each crankshaft, then mesh the gears with a single big one doing the work of pushing the drive shaft.[24]

When the Chrysler production version of the Sherman came off the assembly line on July 22, it was the first of 7,500 with the "multibank" engine. American tank commanders and gunners never liked the Chrysler multibank engine because its size left less space for ammunition and supplies. But in the Tunisian desert, the British outfitted their Eighth Army with them, and at least one British officer pronounced the M4A4 "the finest tank in the world."[25]

Keller also took Roosevelt to watch the graveyard shift engaged in gear cutting, and to watch an engine and transmission being installed in a Sherman. He also saw fifty of Chrysler's tanks running the test-track course—all business as usual at eleven o'clock at night.

Chrysler's success with the tank arsenal earned it its first Army-Navy "E" pennant for production excellence on August 10, 1942. The "E" award, too, had been Knudsen's idea, as a way to give manufacturers public recognition for the best war production achievements.[26] Another would be won by Fisher Body at its nearby plant in Flint, where production miracle worker Bud Goodman was making Shermans the GM way.

Goodman was only thirty-seven when he took over the Fisher Tank Arsenal. After quitting the University of Illinois when his father died, he had taken a job at Fisher as a metal finisher. He never looked back. Now in 1942 he was welding Shermans together with a new process that saved four-fifths of machining time, then bending them into shape using a 480-ton metal press. For the final assembly, huge thirty-ton jigs hoisted the tanks in the air and turned them around, as *Time* magazine said, "like ducks on a spit."[27]*

Roosevelt set off for nearby Ypsilanti, where he watched Ford engi-

---

* Chrysler's other major contribution was its reengineering and production of the 40mm Bofors antiaircraft gun. Chrysler's engineers got it into production in little more than half the time its Swedish creators required, and saved more time and money by broaching the gun barrel, instead of using the traditional rifling methods, cutting manufacturing time from three and a half hours to fifteen minutes. The Chrysler-made Bofors became standard armament on Navy ships, more than doubling the amount of antiaircraft coverage by 1943, and then doubling it again in 1944.

neers doing amazing things with B-24 bombers, inside the biggest in-
door plant in the world.* Then there was a stop at the Allis-Chalmers
plant in Milwaukee, which had been the scene of the bruising strike a
year and a half earlier, but where men and women were now turning
out aircraft engines by the hundreds. Nearby was the A. O. Smith factory, where Knudsen's friend Larry Smith had shown him the right
way to weld armor plate and where now the mighty iron pipe assembly
line was turning out hundreds, eventually thousands, of one-thousand-
and two-thousand-pound bombs to be dropped on Nazi Germany's
factories and cities.[28] /

Roosevelt also stopped in Minneapolis at the Federal Cartridge
Corporation, which was making .30- and .50-caliber machine gun
rounds, and noted the high number of women already doing jobs that
used to be considered fit only for men. Later the presidential train
pushed on to Texas, where Todd Shipbuilding was making Liberty ships
in Houston, Consolidated was erecting an enormous airplane plant in
Fort Worth, and, at Port Neches, B.F. Goodrich was helping to build a
synthetic rubber plant that government experts said would be producing up to 800,000 tons of butyl rubber by 1944. The actual number
would be closer to 1.4 million tons.

In fact, the 700,000 tons Port Neches produced in the first half of
that year was more rubber than the entire country was using in 1940.[29]

Roosevelt's tour of the West Coast included not only Kaiser's yards
but Boeing in Seattle and Douglas Aircraft in California. A former
plane designer for Glenn Martin, Donald Douglas had launched his
aircraft company in Los Angeles, from the rented back room of a barber
shop. He could remember the grim days of the thirties, when his company was the largest single supplier of aircraft to the U.S. military—in
batches of thirty or forty.[30]

Now Douglas had three factories going in Southern California, and
was introducing his new improved SBD-4 Dauntless dive-bomber,
which would wreak havoc on Japanese warships. The SBD-4 outclassed
the German Stuka and its Japanese counterpart in every respect, and
starting in October Douglas would produce more than three thousand

* For details, see Chapters 12–13.

for the Navy.[31] Plans were also under way to build new plants in Oklahoma City and outside Chicago at Orchard Place, to build the two
most famous military transports of the war: the C-47 Skytrain and the
four-thousand-mile-range C-54 Skymaster, which could carry American soldiers, paratroopers, and supplies from the skies over Normandy
to bases on the other side of the Himalayas.

Nearby in San Diego, Consolidated Aircraft's new president was
Kaiser's friend Tom Girdler, who was turning out B-24 bombers and
PBY flying boats using his modified mass-production techniques. In
Inglewood, North American was poised to replace Douglas as the
country's biggest plane maker as it turned out thousands of its
two-engined Mitchell bombers and launched a new single-engine
fighter, the P-51 Mustang, powered by those Rolls-Royce Merlin engines being made by Packard.[32]

Even more amazing, the coming of war forced an unprecedented
cooperation among these aviation competitors. Old rivals shared aero-
dynamic and engineering data, exchanged information on tooling and
equipment, and drew together a $250 million stockpile of parts and
materials under the management of the Aircraft War Production Council, to provide emergency help to anyone who needed it. Douglas
helped Consolidated build its B-24s at a plant in Tulsa, and helped Boeing build B-17s at its newest Long Beach plant. Lockheed did the same
for Boeing at its Vega plant in Burbank.[33]

Consolidated-Vultee may have been the first aircraft company to
hire women in its Downey plant,* and in 1943 the very first woman
engineer, but the Lockheed Vega plant would make them famous.
When *Life* magazine did a story on the Lockheed ladies, the picture of
a tall girl named Vera Lowe with her hair in a kerchief and a riveting
gun in her hand would catch the imagination of a nation as Rosie the
Riveter.

"I was impressed by the large proportion of women employed,"
Roosevelt would tell the country later, "doing skilled manual labor,
running machines.... Within less than a year from now, there will

---

* The managers rushed their start date a day early, to March 31, 1941, so no one
would think it was an April Fools Day joke.

probably be as many women as men working in our war production plants."[34]

He was nearly right. Six months after Pearl Harbor, barely 80,000 women worked in any defense industry. By the end of 1942, that number shot up to 3 million—and the War Manpower Commission warned they were going to need another 1.5 million as more and more men put on uniforms and went to war. By the fall of 1943, 36.5 percent of the workforce in the American aviation industry were women. They made up almost half the workforce in electrical equipment. There was no question that America could never have met its airplane production quotas after 1941 without them. For American airpower, they were truly the margin of victory.[35]

Roosevelt's final stop on his war plant tour was New Orleans, where he met the man who symbolized the vision, ingenuity, and sheer drive that made up the Production Express. He was Andrew Jackson Higgins, whom some dubbed the Henry Kaiser of the South.

A high school dropout with a decade-long history of odd jobs and failed businesses, Higgins had landed work with a New Orleans lumber export firm on the eve of World War I. After he set up his own firm a couple of years later, the need for a boat able to haul logs out of shallow waters around his stands of timber near Natchez, Mississippi, got him into the boat-making business. Out of it would come his most important invention, the Eureka, or Higgins, boat. Built to do thirty miles an hour even in water as shallow as one inch, all Higgins needed to do was to cut a ramp out of the front and suddenly he had the perfect machine for loading and unloading U.S. Marines on the beach—as Marine general Holland "Howlin' Mad" Smith realized when he first saw the Eureka boat in action.[36]

In 1940 and 1941, Andrew Jackson Higgins had a series of running battles with the Navy over the value of his boat, with Higgins and Smith pushing and the Navy's Bureau of Construction and Repair resisting. Once again, it was British orders that came to the rescue of an American manufacturer. On Sunday, December 7, 1941, Higgins was standing knee-deep in swamp water near New Orleans' Industrial

Canal surveying a site for a new factory to fill his British orders, when the car radio carried news about the attack on Pearl Harbor.[37]

At the time, landing craft ranked tenth on the Navy's priority list. The Navy's original plans for 1,189 landing craft grew to twice that number, and in April 1942 doubled again. They would need not just the Eureka but craft able to carry a medium tank onto the beach and into battle, and lightweight patrol torpedo, or PT, boats—for all of which Higgins had designs he had been pressing on the Navy for years, in vain.

Almost overnight Higgins went from persona non grata in the Navy Building to its production savior. By March 1942 he was employing more than three thousand workers filling orders for his ramp-equipped LCVPs, LCMs, and his ever-popular PT boats. On September 29, Roosevelt himself arrived to see what the fuss was all about.

Higgins and his four sons greeted the president at the siding, then offered him a ride in Roland Higgins's convertible. As they passed slowly through the six-hundred-foot assembly bay with workers in white overalls and hard hats gawking and nudging each other, Roosevelt got a front-row view of LCVPs arranged in four production lines, the hulls turned upside down as frames were made using jigs and templates. Next he saw the plywood and planking being applied, after which a crane with special canvas slings hoisted the boat upright as workers followed it down the line to complete whatever work was still needed.[38]

Then he saw the bay where workers swarmed around two rows of unfinished PT boats. Raised walkways let workers move from one production line to the other, giving them free access to every side of the vessels. At the end of the hour tour, Higgins assembled all his employees at the far end of the factory, where the Higgins Industries marching band played "Hail to the Chief" and "Anchors Aweigh." Roosevelt was in his element, smiling and keeping time by tapping his fingers on the side of the convertible. Then he was handed a sheet of music and lyrics, and followed silently along while the band played the composition of its popular trumpet player, a burly young man named Al Hirt. It was called "The Higgins Victory March."

When it was done, Higgins stood up on the car cushions and yelled, "All right, everybody! For the world's greatest man, three cheers!"[39]

Hip hip hooray! Hip hip hooray! Hip hip hooray! Roosevelt grinned and waved, workers clapped each other on the back and shook hands. Not much more than an hour after he had arrived, Roosevelt's train pulled away. Higgins returned to his office deeply satisfied. In a few months, he would be the biggest boatbuilder in America.

If Kaiser's Liberty ships were crucial to America's defensive phase of keeping the lines of supply and communication with the Allies open, Higgins's boats would be crucial in the next, offensive phase. As 1942 drew to a close all across the country shipyards, factories, and boatyards would be making thousands of landing craft with a profusion of confusing designations—LCIs, LCMs, LCPLs, LCTs, LCI (L)s, and LSTs. Twenty-one of them were in the Great Lakes and Midwest. Many, if not all, would be using Higgins designs.

In all, Higgins would design 92 percent of the vessels used by the U.S. Navy in World War II—although none of them would be big enough or important enough to warrant a christening. For July 1943 his New Orleans factory built more landing craft than all the other factories in America. Even Hitler got to know his name, and dubbed him "the new Noah." General Dwight Eisenhower simply called him "the man who won the war for us."[40]

Yet the general was wrong. It was the American economy—where immigrants like Knudsen and Elmer Hann and high school dropouts like Higgins and Kaiser could become the arsenal of democracy's most precious assets—that was shifting the balance of victory.

Donald Nelson knew this. He also knew what Knudsen had foreseen: that the key to winning this war of mass production was America's free enterprise industrial system. That meant keeping the drive for war production as *voluntary* as possible, so that the right incentives—which included the profit motive—found the right people to do the job. That also meant keeping the *civilian economy* as strong as possible, something that his critics in the War Department sometimes didn't seem to understand.

When they complained about the amount of newsprint being consumed for advertising and want-ad space, he pointed out that those ads might enable a defense worker to find an apartment or lead a military wife to a department store sale so she wouldn't have to spend as much on a new hat or a pair of shoes. When the Army pushed for funding only those synthetic rubber facilities that produced for military use, Nelson had to explain that without tires for autos, buses, and trucks, none of those defense workers would be getting to work. Likewise with gasoline and aluminum and other critical materials: Unless civilian producers, often the smaller businesses, could count on their share, the entire infrastructure on which the military counted for its planes, tanks, and machine guns would slow down and grind to a halt.[41]

Explaining elementary economics was never easy in Washington. Nelson had his work cut out for him. At one point a story circulated in the papers quoting a high Army official that the WPB's policy had created a shortage of 100-octane aviation fuel so severe that important overseas military operations had to be suspended. Nelson looked into it, and the story wasn't true.[42] But people continued to act as if it *were* true, and the presence of spot shortages of raw materials—a perennial problem in any war (and, it should be added, any economy with price controls)—was taken as evidence not of the extraordinary demand generated by war production, or of the market-distorting effects of the Office of Price Administration, but of extraordinary incompetence on the part of Donald M. Nelson.

Indeed, Nelson and his people did face shortages that were painful and sometimes seemed chronic. Aluminum was a perennial sore spot, because of its demand in the aviation industry in unprecedented numbers. In 1939 the United States had only one producer making some 327 million pounds a year. By 1941 the need for aluminum had all but doubled. Nelson's dollar-a-year man in charge, Alcoa's Arthur Bunker, was under siege from the press and Capitol Hill from almost the moment he arrived in Washington.

Yet in just a year Bunker was able to hit the numbers with the help of Jesse Jones's Defense Plant Corporation, which financed expanding facilities to meet the future need. By October 1943 the output had reached the point—2.25 *billion* pounds—that one WPB official was quoted as saying America had aluminum "coming out of our ears." By then American companies held 42 percent of the world's aluminum manufacturing capacity.[43]

Copper was a problem, too. In 1942 the shortage of this cheap but absolutely vital metal for making electrical wiring and brass for ammunition shells was so severe that the Army released 2,800 former copper miners from active duty to help. Then Nelson's men found a substitute: silver. Releasing it from vaults where it was being kept as a currency reserve, Nelson and the WPB made it an industrial metal—one that would eventually help to turn the tide in enriching uranium at Oak Ridge Laboratories for the Manhattan Project.[44]

The most serious shortage Nelson struggled with, however, was steel. Nothing seemed to help in getting on top of the situation. America's steel industry had taken a terrific pounding since the Great Depression. Annual production had slipped from 63 million metric tons in 1929, the year of the Wall Street crash, to barely 30 million. Under Knudsen at OPM and Nelson at SPAB, national output had jumped 5 million tons a year—but it wasn't nearly enough. A nation at war was going to need at least 80 million tons, and more.

On January 1, 1942, steel plate producers had a 4.5-million-ton backlog in unfilled orders.[45] There was an ongoing push to increase steel production by expanding and modernizing plants and pushing new technologies like the electric-arc melting furnace.[46] Even with the federal government and the Defense Plant Corporation paying more than half the bills, steel's production cycle was one of the slowest in heavy industry. Facilities going up in late 1941 wouldn't be ready to produce until 1943 or even 1944. Nelson tried collecting and reusing metal scrap, but the results were never enough.

As fall turned into winter, the shortage in shipbuilding was looking critical, especially on the West Coast, far away from the major suppliers. In the Midwest it was starting to slow tank and tank engine production, including at the Chrysler plant.[47] Machine tools, trucks and large landing craft, even vital new plant construction and expansion, might be next.

Then, seemingly out of nowhere, Henry Kaiser proved to be the hero of the hour.

CHAPTER TWELVE

STEEL MEN AND
CAST-IRON CHARLIE

Henry and Edgar Kaiser (second and third from left) with FDR at the Vancouver shipyards, September 1942. Clay Bedford stands behind Edgar. *UPI photo file*

The day of the West is at hand.

—Henry Kaiser

FOR DON NELSON, the steel shortage was an urgent but temporary worry.*

* The issue was finally put to rest when Nelson's assistant and investment banker Ferdinand Eberstadt devised the Controlled Materials Plan, which matched the supplies of critical raw materials like steel, copper, and aluminum directly to orders from the War and Navy departments.

For Kaiser and other industrialists on the West Coast, the steel shortage had been chronic for almost a decade. Steel giants like Bethlehem and Republic and Carnegie-Illinois were eastern or Midwest-based (Carnegie-Illinois was in Duquesne). There simply were no major steel mills west of the Rockies.

Even as he was laying down the first shipways in the marshes of Richmond, Henry Kaiser had decided to change that. On April 21, 1941, just as Lend-Lease was getting under way, he wangled an interview with the president himself and showed him plans for a $150 million steel production complex. He forcefully argued it could draw all the power it needed from the hydroelectric dams Kaiser and Six Companies had already built, so he could produce the kind of steel plate he and others needed for the Liberty ships.[1] Roosevelt liked his enthusiasm and pushed Kaiser on to a panel of government engineers who, in effect, told him he was crazy. He had no definite site; he had no financing; no plans for the plant's postwar use. A plant in Southern California, they argued, would also be vulnerable to possible Japanese attack or even sabotage. Above all, they cried, Kaiser knew nothing about producing steel.[2]

Henry Kaiser had never let that stop him before, and it did not stop him now. With his main energies still focused on Richmond and Portland, he continued to make phone calls and meet with Washington lobbyists, to get his dream realized—and to teach a lesson to the executives of Big Steel, who were hostile from the start. His biggest obstacle was still his old nemesis Bill Knudsen, but in mid-February 1942, Knudsen was gone. Facing a 4.2-million-ton steel shortfall just two months into the war, Donald Nelson and the WPB felt they had no choice but to approve.

The final hurdle was Jesse Jones. The crusty old Houston cotton broker didn't care much for Henry Kaiser, or his business methods. He knew Kaiser was already making, on a fee basis, between $60,000 and $110,000 for every Liberty ship he was building. Jones's Reconstruction Finance Corporation had already loaned him $28 million for a magnesium plant out in Utah, which was having huge problems getting started.[3] Now Kaiser was asking for *$100 million* to start up a steel plant in Southern California, more than 175 miles from the nearest iron source.

It was unprecedented; it was almost outrageous. But Jones eventually agreed to the loan, provided Kaiser move it fifty miles inland for security reasons (Kaiser wanted something closer to the coast, like Terminal Island) and that he secure the loan with the fees from his shipbuilding. Kaiser said yes—in part, as Jones later wrote, "because if he had not done so, probably 90 percent of [the Liberty ship fees] would have been taken from him in excess profit taxes."[4]

Still, it was a sweet deal that was finalized on March 19, 1942—two weeks after the internment of upward of 100,000 Japanese Americans on the West Coast calmed any remaining fears of possible sabotage. Kaiser's portion of the capitalization came to just under $100,000. All the rest, almost $111 million in the final tally, would come from the government. There was only one more condition, Donald Nelson said. The new mill would have to have a turbo-blower for the main blast furnace.

Kaiser said at once, "Why, that's no problem. We'll build our own." He and Nelson and the others shook hands, and then Kaiser and his lawyer Chad Calhoun ambled out into the hall. As they headed out of the Social Security Building, Kaiser turned to Calhoun as his characteristic grin faded.

"What's a turbo-blower?" he asked.

Calhoun couldn't believe his ears. He assumed Kaiser would know. "Well," he stammered, "it's probably a turbine and a blower,"—and left it at that.[5]

Kaiser's grin was back. "Then couldn't we build one at Joshua Hendy?"

So he wired his engine wizard Charlie Moore out in Sunnyvale, who wired back: "Regarding *turbine* blower, can build unit in three to four months."

That suited Kaiser. That was enough time, he figured, to get the plant built and ready to run—because he was determined to have that plant "blown in" before the end of the year.

The following day he called up his chief engineer George Havas. "George," Kaiser said, "you're going to build me a steel mill."

Havas, who like Kaiser had no experience in the business, asked, "What kind of steel mill?"

"Oh, just a small one," Kaiser reassured him, then added, "At least at first."[6] The only other question Havas had was where to build it. The location they finally chose was three miles west of Fontana, California, deep in the heart of the San Bernardino Valley.

It had three things going for it. The first was it was in the middle of nowhere, where land was cheap and space plentiful: "Think big," Kaiser liked to tell his men, "don't allow operations to be cramped." For a trifling sum, he was able to snap up two thousand acres of hog farms and orange and walnut groves. By the end of April 1942, ground had been broken and Havas's men were laying out the plant.[7]

The second was that Fontana sat close to the junction of three major railroads. That meant Kaiser could bring his iron ore and coal from Utah and then ship the finished plate up to the shipyards.

Third, labor in Fontana was cheap. People were desperate for a better job than picking oranges. The day the employment office opened, it was swamped with applications. In charge of the entire operation was Tom Price, an old Boulder Dam hand and the third man Kaiser ever hired. Price had been down in Panama, getting ready to launch still another Kaiser project in the Canal Zone, when he got the call from Kaiser. He was on the next flight out and, together with Havas and another rising Kaiser star, Gene Threfethen, ran the entire show.[8]

It was an enormous undertaking—but by now Kaiser people were used to that. Kaiser had to bring in workers from Morris Knudsen to lay down an additional seventy miles of rails to connect him to the main lines. There were no natural water sources, so Kaiser's men had to dig their own wells and devise a way to recycle every drop of the 160,000 gallons of water they would need to produce one ton of steel. The San Bernardino council was eager to get the plant, but worried about the soot and smoke drifting over their fair valley. So Kaiser had Price install a smokestack-scrubbing device on Fontana's chimneys, making it the most advanced antipollution technology in the country.[9]

Then Tom Girdler gave Kaiser vital Republic Steel engineering drawings for building the main sections of the plant, and also sent out some of his own people to help out. Hundreds of new technicians had to be brought in, men never seen on a Kaiser site before. There were experts in coke ovens, blast furnaces, open hearths, rolling mills, and conveyor belts, plus engineers to install the turbo-blower used to speed the heating of the blast furnaces to the necessary degrees Fahrenheit.

"Most of the men who were hired from other companies," Tom Price remembered, "came at the same salary they had been receiving." So why did they come? For some it was a matter of patriotism. For others it was curiosity, and the desire to be part of a steel mill that they knew would be like no other. "They were inspired by Kaiser," Price said simply, "and wanted to be part of his dream. . . . The men believed it, government officials believed it. It was a love child. How could it fail?"[10]

When it was done, Fontana had ninety coke ovens handling 1,720 tons of coal a day. In addition, Havas and Price installed a 1,200-ton blast furnace for smelting the raw ore into 438,000 tons of pig iron, which a giant conveyor system then carried to six massive 185-ton open hearths where the real work of making iron into steel was done. There Kaiser's turbo-blower played its part in getting the Fontana plant producing 472,000 tons of steel plate every year—almost 10 percent of America's capacity shortfall, and enough to supply shipyards up and down the West Coast.[11]

The scale of the achievement became clear when weighed against the WPB's other big steel plant venture, with U.S. Steel, in Geneva, Utah. Its builders had almost a year head start on Kaiser, yet Kaiser finished almost five months ahead of them. Geneva cost the government $220 million. Fontana came in at less than half that.

December 30, 1942, dawned bright and clear as Kaiser and his wife and son Henry Jr., and a dozen dignitaries from Washington and the San Bernardino County Council marched to a raised platform overlooking the vast complex. Almost eight thousand workers and onlookers had gathered, along with Kaiser's usual brass bands and fireworks.

At precisely 1:15 P.M., Henry Jr. asked his mother to throw the switch that would start the first "blow-in" of the famous turbo-blower of the main blast furnace—which Kaiser had named "Bess," after his wife.

Then Kaiser spoke. His voice was taut with emotion as he spoke of how brave men had come to California in the 1840s in search of gold, and in the process opened up half a continent. "Today, we take another, a baser metal and process it for the service of mankind." Then he said:

"The westward movement which began so long ago has not come to an end on the Pacific slope. It is poised now for the next great thrust. The day of the West is at hand."[12]

His partner Charlie Moore of Joshua Hendy put it slightly differently. "It's sort of a disease with us guys out here, building things this way and busting records," he told *Fortune* magazine. "Nothing can stop this area now. The West is on its way."[13]

Moore was right. Arming for total war was transforming the region, starting with California. The value of its manufactured goods tripled, to a figure three times the national average, from 1941 to 1945. The personal income of Californians doubled—even as millions of new immigrants poured into the state in what at least one historian has dubbed "the second gold rush." Much of the funding flowed from defense contracts. In 1940, Washington had spent roughly $1.5 billion in California. In 1945 it was $8.5 billion, almost all defense-related. But for every two dollars from the government, a third dollar—or roughly one-third of the cost of California's arming America for war—came from private banks and the businesses themselves.[14]

Meanwhile, the auto industry and Detroit were far ahead of them.

On February 10, 1942, a crowd of workers and managers had come together at the end of the assembly line at the River Rouge plant. A Ford V-8 came down the line, ready to be driven out of the factory. There was nothing unusual about that; what *was* unusual—and what had drawn the press and photographers—was that there was no car behind it. It was the last civilian production car at Ford. From now on, said the press, "the same assembly line that made Ford automobiles is now to be used for staff cars for Army officers"—as well as Navy service trucks, bomb service trucks, and, the most famous wartime vehicle of all, the jeep.

There was a little ceremony, even a speech. Then an army of technicians sprang into action. One by one they ripped out the machine tools and their fixtures, clearing the way for the new ones for trucks and military vehicles, which were stacked up in their packing cases outside.[15] The American auto industry, a business bigger than the economies of every country except Germany, Russia, and Great Britain, was moving to full-time war production.

The fact that the auto industry would wind up producing 20 percent of all U.S. munitions in the war was due ultimately to two men. The first was Bill Knudsen. It was he who first called on his friends, rivals, and colleagues to start making parts for airplanes back in October 1940, who had pulled together the Automotive Council for War Production three weeks after Pearl Harbor, and who called together more than eight hundred executives for its first meeting on January 24, 1942, to tell them the time had come to switch to full-time production—a meeting he was never able to attend because his job was no more.

The second was the man WPB's Don Nelson named to run the full-time conversion at that same meeting. He was Ernest Kanzler, whose success in overseeing the conversion Nelson later dubbed "nothing less than a miracle."[16]

In fact, miracles had little to do with it, or government dictates. Kanzler was a former Ford executive and a lawyer by training, an elegant man with cosmopolitan tastes and a pillar of Detroit's elite Grosse Pointe society. Kanzler was as much at home at the opera or the art museum as on the factory floor—or examining a car company balance sheet. Kanzler also knew the industry from inside and out, because after leaving Ford he had become head of Universal Credit Corporation, which handled the auto loan business for every major carmaker except GM. In the summer of 1942, no one was in a better position to know how to bring the diverse heads of the industry together for wartime production, win the support of the UAW and labor, and charm the skeptics in Washington than Ernest Kanzler.

He did it by letting the carmakers do it themselves. The Automotive Council for War Production had some two thousand members, but it was the big companies—Ford, GM, Chrsyler, Packard, Studebaker—who counted. Kanzler knew that once they were committed heart and mind to the fight, the subcontractors would follow. That was the secret to conversion, as Knudson had argued all along: the latent power of the subcontractors. Timken, a major axle manufacturer, was already making armor plate for Chrysler and Ford's tank arsenal, and trying out new innovations in its design. Houdaille Hershey, a parts supplier specializing in shock absorbers, was eliminating costly steps in manufacturing the .30-caliber machine gun—steps that the Army thought necessary but weren't. Soldiers found the aluminum handle broke easily; Houdaille Hershey found a sturdier substitute, which also saved on aluminum.[17] When Saginaw Steering Gear started making the Army's .50-caliber machine gun, engineer Bud Doerfner saw that the holes bored in the barrel for ventilation were elliptical. He told the Army that if they were round, he could drill three in a single operation instead of one. The Army tested it, and told him to go ahead. Soon Doerfner had a multi-spindle drill cutting ten at a time instead of three. In March 1942, Saginaw Steering Gear delivered 28,728 machine guns instead of the 2,000 they had first promised.

Bill Knudsen had foreseen it all. "I placed most of the business with big companies for the reason that there was a lot of engineering to be done on practically every job," he wrote later. "They were the only ones who had that kind of talent." But the subcontractors and "little business had an enormous part in the program," once full conversion got going.[18]

And conversion did roll as smoothly as Ernest Kanzler's tuxedo lapels. When civilian production halted at Plymouth's Lynch Road plant and the old machine tools were pulled out, the new ones were in place by the time the night shift arrived. At Buick, workers gathered to cheer as the last car came down the line. On its windscreen was a sign: "Until Total Victory We Dedicate Ourselves to the Objective 'When Better War Goods Are Built, Buick Workmen Will Build Them.'"

General Motors started up war production only twenty-nine days after ending the civilian line. In the end it would contribute 10 percent of all U.S. war production.[19] The others weren't far behind.

It was one of the great success stories of World War II. In 1939 the U.S. Army had barely 15,000 vehicles. In the spring of 1941, it was already looking to acquire a quarter million before Pearl Harbor raised everyone's calculations. Not counting tanks, by the end of 1942 the Army would be the customer for 800,000 vehicles of some 330 differ-

ent types. By 1945 the number would grow to 3.2 million—one vehicle for every 2.75 Americans in an Army uniform. Meantime the
Wehrmacht, the model of modern warfare in 1940, still relied on
horse-drawn transport. "When Hitler put his war on wheels," General
Brehon Somervell said at the end of the war, "he ran it straight down
our alley."[20]

In the end, American automakers would produce 50 percent of all
aircraft engines, 35 percent of aircraft propellers, 47 percent of all
machine guns, 87 percent of all aerial bombs, 80 percent of tanks and
tank parts, one-half the diesel engines for ships, submarines, and
other naval craft; not to mention 100 percent of U.S. Army trucks,
half-tracks, and other vehicles. They would go on to arm our allies as
well, from the 200,000 Studebaker trucks supplied to the Soviet Red
Army to the Bren gun carriers Ford built to British army specifications and shipped overseas for every army of the Dominion—13,893
of them.[21]

Kanzler saw to it that all this activity flowed through the coordinated effort of the Automotive Council for War Production—and the
other industry associations that brought together the different subcontractors and distributors. At the ACWP's head was Knudsen's friend
from Packard, Alvan Macauley, and he ran it according to Knudsen's
voluntarist model.[22] When a problem or a need came up, a committee
was formed. When it was solved, the committee dissolved. This allowed the auto industry to skirt a wave of steel shortages (another hit
in 1943) by forming a salvage committee, which pooled data on factory scrap and came up with tons of scrap metal and rubber waiting to
be recycled.

There were product committees, machine tool committees, labor
committees including labor representatives, methods committees
whose members met at each other's plants to see and discuss new ways
of saving time and labor.[23] There were advisory committees to the
Army Ordnance Department, the Army Air Forces, and after 1943 the
Armed Service Force. Everywhere there was volunteering of information, sharing of materials, pooling of resources and methods. The voluntarist model was so useful that soon aircraft manufacturers on the
West Coast copied it, and then on the East Coast; while the British sent

an industry research group to study how it achieved such prodigious results.

This was the industrial juggernaut Knudsen and Kanzler had set in motion. And of all the automakers turned munitions makers, Kanzler's former employer Ford, with its extensive network of thirty-four branch plants (including eighteen service parts distributors) and twenty-nine affiliated industries, would be among the most versatile.

Compared to Chrysler and GM and even Studebaker, it made only a small proportion of tanks and other vehicles produced during the war—fewer than 390,000 out of 2.66 million. But it would be famous for its aircraft engines and tank engines—nearly 27,000, most for the M4 Sherman. It would make aircraft parts, aircraft engine superchargers, aluminum, armor plate, magnesium, gun mounts, M7 antiaircraft gun directors (which required no fewer than 276 separate aluminum or die castings), and machine tools at its $117 million tool and die plant—probably the best in the entire car industry.[24]

In March 1942 the Army approached Ford about making gliders for its airborne forces (the first American parachute unit was created just eighteen months earlier, in October 1940). Ford found a place to mass-produce in northern Michigan at Iron Mountain, with a sawmill and woodworking plant. The Army gave the go-ahead on March 27 and conversion got started.[25]

In American landings on Sicily in 1943, Port Moresby in New Guinea, and finally in Normandy on June 6, 1944, in Operation Overlord, clouds of American glider troops led the way, and everywhere Ford-built gliders carried them and their equipment and supplies into battle. In 1942 less than 1 percent of all CG-4As were made by Ford. In 1943 that jumped to 36.6 percent. In 1944 it was 50 percent—and Ford's methods had cut the cost per unit by more than half, from $25,000 to $10,000.[26]

Ford also focused on specialized hard-to-make vehicles like British universal carriers, Navy cargo trucks, bomb service trucks, and of course the jeep, where plants at River Rouge, Dallas, and Louisville poured out 277,896 of them. Its plants at Chester, Pennsylvania, close by the Sun Company's yards, and Richmond, California, close by Kaiser's, would process and pack nearly everyone's tanks for shipment across the Atlantic and Pacific.*

All in all, the Ford Motor Company would produce more war materiel than the entire economy of Mussolini's Italy.[27] Yet from the start, Ford's wartime reputation boiled down to what one executive was doing at a place southeast of Ypsilanti called Willow Run.

It was a bright clear day in early January 1941 when a plane landed at San Diego Airport. A man with dark straw-blond hair and a square, determined jaw bounded down the stairway. He was Charles Sorensen—"Cast-Iron Charlie," Henry Ford's original wizard of mass production. Following close behind him was Dr. George Mead, Bill Knudsen's aeronautics man.

An elegant man in a three-piece suit walked forward to greet them. Reuben Fleet was one of the great aviation pioneers, founder of Consolidated Aircraft and its top executive for nearly twenty years. The trio briefly shook hands before they were joined by Edsel Ford and his sons Henry II and Benson, and a team of engineers from Ford.

The week before Christmas, Mead and Major Jimmy Doolittle had approached Sorensen and Edsel Ford. Can you help us build these planes? they asked. They showed them plans for a four-engined Army bomber called the B-24, which Consolidated's San Diego plant was turning out in less-than-stellar numbers. The Army was looking to add twelve hundred planes to the production total. They thought Ford could help.[28]

Sorensen said he'd have to check things out for himself—as he always did. Now, on January 8, the Ford team had arrived to inspect the Consolidated facilities and make a judgment call.

---

* Supplying the packing material was Dow Chemical Company, which had invented a clear plastic sheeting that sealed every tank, machine gun, and airplane part tight against moisture and dust. It was called Saran, and so Saran Wrap made its debut solving one of World War II's most difficult logistical problems.

Fleet made a gesture as if to say, "This way, gentlemen." He didn't realize that in less than twenty-four hours Cast-Iron Charlie would turn his world upside down.

Charles Sorensen was the other Danish immigrant who remade Detroit. He was born in Copenhagen not far from Knudsen's father's shop, in 1881. He immigrated to the United States years earlier than Knudsen, landing at the same immigrant station at Castle Garden. He also had the same fascination with machines and, growing up in Buffalo, knew Knudsen's mechanical alma mater, Keim Mills, well. As a boy Charlie Sorensen had even clambered over the Keim junk pile, pulling out discarded parts of bicycles and instinctively learning the principle of how interchangeable parts were laying the foundation for mass production.[29]

Sorensen was sixteen when he left home for Detroit, where he found work in Henry Ford's budding plant, starting as a shop floor hand. He was working at Highland Park the day machine tool wizard Walter Flanders explained to Ford how to position their machines on the factory floor in order to get the most out of them, and never forgot what he had learned. The pupil soon turned master. In no time Sorensen was showing Ford how to sequence the machining operations for his Model T's, and how to stamp rather than cut the sheet metal he needed.[30]

By the time Knudsen turned up with the rest of the Keim team in 1913, Sorensen was already one of the old boys, and a Henry Ford favorite. Sorensen's first glimpse of his fellow countryman came when Knudsen emerged from an assembly pit one day, his face smeared with oil and his customary grin.[31]

They were not destined to be friends. Sorensen had been "present at the creation," and the arrival of Knudsen—equally hardworking, quietly self-assertive, and gifted with production ideas of his own—disturbed the balance of power. Giants do not easily tolerate the presence of other giants, and in his autobiography Sorensen never lost an opportunity to poke fun at the rival Dane, or deprecate his accomplishments.*

---

* As for Knudsen, forty years later he could barely bring himself to mention Sorensen's name.

When Knudsen finally left for GM, Sorensen must have drawn a deep sigh of relief. His relief stopped short in 1927 when Knudsen completed his revolution at Chevrolet, and Ford's sales leadership fell into peril. Sorensen realized that production of the Model T, which he had spent two decades perfecting, would have to come to an end if Ford was to survive. He took his revenge by not only tearing out all the machine tools to make way for the Model A, but firing every engineer who had been part of creating the Model T, some of whom he had worked with for decades. It was a ruthless purge of the past to make way for the future.[32]

Sorensen never cared what others thought. One day someone sent him a postcard from Italy with a picture of Mussolini. It read, "M is to Italy what you are to Ford." Sorensen shrugged.[33] He wasn't at Ford to make friends, but to make cars. During his years at Ford, there were rumors of his punching out employees. Sorensen scoffed at the stories, then and later.[34] But the fact that the rumors persisted was a warning sign. The old employer who had said Sorensen was a wild man and Knudsen a mild man knew what he was talking about.

He and Bill Knudsen had barely spoken to each other for years when they met at the famous New Center meeting in October 1940. Sorensen had listened to Knudsen's speech, and looked over the plans Major Doolittle and others laid out, and agreed. Here was a good plan to get the auto industry involved in taking up the slack in warplane production. He had only one condition, he said, his jaw jutting in defiance and his hard blue eyes narrowing. Ford wasn't just going to make parts and engines for airplanes; it was going to make the entire plane.

Knudsen didn't think much of this idea. By now he understood the profound difference in the numbers of parts Sorensen was used to working with, versus a four-engined bomber like the B-24. A car demanded 15,000 parts; a B-24 almost *half a million,* plus 300,000 rivets in five hundred different sizes. The aviation industry had a completely different way of making dies for shaping parts—and airplane makers needed to be ready to change their engineering in order to keep up with a myriad of aeronautical variables, as well as those in combat.

Sorensen only shook his head. "It's the complete plane, or nothing." And when Cast-Iron Charlie got an idea into his brain, it was never going away until it was done.[35]

For two months nothing happened. Then came the meeting just before Christmas with Mead and Doolittle, and Sorensen felt vindicated. He arrived for the tour of Consolidated feeling something close to triumph. Before it was over, he was almost in despair.

Certainly the B-24 was a hard plane to fall in love with.

Hap Arnold had asked Reuben Fleet and his chief designer, Isaac "Mac" Laddon, back in January 1939 to give him a plane that would be everything the B-17 was *not*. It was to have a longer range, almost three thousand miles; a higher ceiling; and a bigger payload, 2,500 versus 2,000 pounds. Laddon saw at once this meant dramatically increasing the wing lift. Fortunately, he had just the thing he needed right in the Consolidated plant.

It was the creation of David Davis, a wealthy aviation fan who gave Douglas Aircraft its first $40,000 to build a plant and a plane to fly across the country. In 1938, however, Davis had gone broke. His own chance to recoup his fortunes was to sell the aviation industry on a special wing he had designed in his spare time, whose cross section resembled a teardrop. He told potential investors it would provide more aerodynamic lift than any airfoil ever made, but no one believed him until Reuben Fleet agreed to give him a chance. A team of professors from Cal Tech gave a Davis wing model a test in the Consolidated wind tunnel. They ran the test three times because no one could believe the final result. The Davis wing had a 102 percent efficiency rating, unheard of for the time.[36]

Mac Laddon tried it out on the Model 31 flying boat he was developing for the Navy—which later became the PBY Catalina. He also saw it as the solution to Arnold's specifications for the new XB-24, and on December 29, 1939, the plane took its maiden flight. In addition to the Davis wing, it had another innovation: the so-called wet wing fuel tank. Self-sealing fuel tanks at the time were still clumsy, heavy things, so the Consolidated engineers had sprayed the interior of the wing fuel tank with Duprene sealer, a DuPont product, which acted to prevent wing punctures from leaking or igniting a fire—or worse.[37]

As for the XB-24's engines Laddon wanted, for once Materiel Command did things right. It encouraged a competition between Buick and Chevrolet to see who could produce its Pratt and Whitney RB-1830 power plants faster, and at the lowest cost. It worked, and when the Army came to order 2,434 B-24s to be delivered in 1942, there were more than enough engines to get them in the air and flying.

"The B-24 has *guts*," said the Air Force's instruction manual for the plane. "It can take it and dish it out." Still, pilots found it was a tricky plane to handle. Fleet had added an extra three feet to the plane's fuselage, and when the French government ordered a shipment, they demanded a forward-firing turret, which Fleet retained for all his models. When loaded up with heavy .50-caliber machine guns, the turret proved a drag on the plane's performance. Someone who flew B-24s in nearly sixty missions, Lieutenant Colonel Jimmy Stewart, learned how the plane could suddenly lose altitude if your attention wandered from the controls. "You could never trim the son of a gun," another B-24 pilot remembered, "[you] had to horse it around constantly."[38] The constant pulling and pushing needed to keep the B-24 in the air made one pilot the arm-wrestling champion of his squadron.

By and large, American fliers and crews liked the B-17 better, and nobody ever made a movie about the B-24. The British, however, fastened quickly onto the plane, to which they gave its nickname: the Liberator. A B-24 Liberator became Winston Churchill's personal plane, and both Bomber and Coastal Command wanted them. It was that increase in British orders which forced Bill Knudsen's team to turn to Ford for help.

That clear January day in San Diego, Sorensen spent his time looking, listening, and jotting down notes. "I liked neither what I saw nor what I heard," he wrote later. If this was how aircraft companies worked, he thought, then the Air Force program was doomed.

"Inside the plant I watched men putting together wing sections and portions of the fuselage.... What I saw reminded me of nearly thirty-five years previously when we were making Model N Fords at the Piquette Avenue plant before Walter Flanders rearranged our machines," and got Ford going in assembly-line production. There was no orderly sequence or flow of materials, no sense of forward motion in the assembly process, no reliance on machined parts and machined parts only. "Here was a custom-made plane," Sorensen thought, "put together as a tailor would cut and fit a suit of clothes."[39]

Then he watched the final assembly take place outside, on a structural steel frame. Workers brought out the wings, tail, and fuselage as little by little the B-24 took shape. At the same time, the hot California sun expanded the aluminum metal so that parts that were made to fit inside the plant suddenly needed new custom adjustments before they came together. Sorensen shook his head. It was obvious that no B-24 ended up exactly like another; and obvious to everyone except the Consolidated people that any parts Ford made for the planes would almost certainly not fit once they were ready to put in place.

Fleet told him they intended to make 350 B-24s a year. Sorensen sensed at a glance that the facilities were woefully inadequate to hit that number. Yet no one wanted to stop to revamp or expand, for fear it would undercut existing production. Dr. Mead told him they preferred a little bit now, rather than none at the moment but lots later.

"All this was pretty discouraging, and I said so." Fleet and his engineers looked at each other, then posed the obvious question: So how would you do it?

"I don't know," Sorensen said, "but I'll have an answer for you tomorrow morning."[40]

All through dinner that night with Edsel and the Ford team, Sorensen kept running over the options in his mind. Comparing a Ford V-8 to a B-24 was like comparing a garage to a skyscraper, he knew, but the principles for assembling the one and the other were the same. "First break the plane's design down into essential units," he kept saying, "and make a separate production layout for each unit." Then you deliver each unit to its assigned place in the sequence until you have a finished plane. Finally you build a plant large enough to house the entire process—something much bigger than Consolidated's current plant.[41]

After dinner Sorensen went back to his room at the Coronado Hotel. He was too restless to sleep. Instead he sat down with his notes from the day's tour on one side, a pad of blank paper on the other, and rethought the entire problem.

He broke the bomber down on paper, section by section and subassembly by subassembly, and schemed out the production time of each based on his notes. As the hours ticked by, he added in the notes he had on Consolidated's labor force and average job performance, and the overhead costs. "I computed each unit operation, its timing, and required floor space as I saw them, and paper began to fly." Soon there were stacks of paper representing each unit piled up all around the room. In his mind he was back at the Piquette Avenue plant, sketching out Ford's assembly-line layout—and in his head he kept hearing Old Man Ford's words: "Unless you see a thing, you can't simplify it. And if you can't simplify it, it's a good sign you can't make it."[42]

By 4 A.M. Sorensen had the proper sequence down, and the production time allotted for each unit. Then he sat down once more and sketched out the floor plan of a plant that would produce B-24 bombers in this mass-production way: more bombers than anyone had reasonably imagined. Consolidated hoped for a bomber a day. Sorensen figured he could give them a bomber an hour. If Sorensen could get a dozen plants going at once, America was looking at close to three hundred brand-new bombers every twenty-four hours. "I was elated by the certainty that the Germans had neither the facilities nor the conception" to mass-produce planes in this way, Sorensen remembered.[43] It would turn the tide of airpower in the future.

And, he must have thought as the sun shone through the windows and he turned off the light, it would finally give him one up on Big Bill Knudsen.

At breakfast he showed Edsel Ford the sketches he had made. The son of the master of mass production was dazzled and urged him to go see the Consolidated people at once. Sorensen went to Reuben Fleet's office with his papers under his arm and Edsel's two sons in tow. Fleet was a former Army pilot who had founded Consolidated in 1923 with $15,000 of his own money and $25,000 borrowed from his sister.[44] Underneath his smooth executive exterior, he was an old fly-by-the-seat-of-your-pants man, and he was somewhat dazed by the scale of Sorensen's proposition. It's not clear if he really understood it all.

Fleet suggested maybe Ford would make the parts for wing sections, and offered a contract for one thousand sets of wings.

Sorensen's face became set. He repeated what he had said to Knudsen the previous October. "We'll make the complete plane," he said, "or nothing."[45]

Then Sorensen laid the full proposal out to Dr. Mead. If the Army Air Forces spent $200 million for the plant and equipment, he told him, Ford would do what no one, not even Knudsen, had imagined: build bombers with the speed and ease of building cars. Mead signed on at once; that left Fleet no choice but to go along. On February 25, 1941, Sorensen got his contract with Washington and Consolidated agreed to license the design for its heavy bombers. Ford was in the airplane business.

Back in Dearborn, the old man was fascinated. He immediately told Consolidated to fly out a B-24 for them to look over. He and Sorensen then had workmen take it apart piece by piece, rivet by rivet, so they could look at every component from propeller to tail, and then put it back together again.[46]

It was no small task. The B-24's 488,193 separate parts broke down into 30,000 components. Working side by side, Ford and Sorensen managed to work out the plane's preassembly into nine different departments, one for each section. Those were center wing section, two wings, two wing tips, nose and front pilot sections, then the nacelle and tail sections.[47] It was a little more complicated because the British order substituted a standard self-sealing tank for the Duprene-covered version. But things were beginning to come together and make sense in reality as well as on paper.

Then came thinking about the plant itself. Consolidated's plant had fifty-four separate workstations, which required an average of six hours for each unit to clear before it was ready to move on to the next station. Since Sorensen intended to cut the manpower hours from 140,000 to less than 100,000, a production flow chart based on six-hour intervals was useless. Instead he had architects draw up an imaginary cross section of a plant high enough to allow even the biggest sections to be stood on end if necessary (the tail assembly alone was as long as a city bus) with room for an overhead crane system; wide enough to allow an aisle between machines and the assembly line you could drive a car through; and long enough to more than double the number of subassembly stations (Consolidated had two sections for its fuselage, while

Ford would have thirty-three), all in order to speed up the manufacturing process.[48]

When they finished, the result impressed even Sorensen. It would be the single biggest factory in the world. The main assembly line of Consolidated's San Diego plant was three thousand feet long, or ten football fields. This one would be *one mile* long. Sorensen knew there was only one man in the world with the skill and vision to design such a plant. He placed a call to Albert Kahn's office, and overnight Kahn was working on the preliminary drawings.

That left the question of how to proceed. Even Sorensen knew he wasn't going to be able to start producing planes right away, no matter how sophisticated the plant facilities. There was too much to learn, and too many variables. He figured he would build the B-24s in three stages. First would come an "educational order" for making parts and dies. Then Ford would make all the parts for the B-24, which would then be assembled by the plane makers Consolidated and Douglas at new plants in Forth Worth, Texas, and Tulsa, Oklahoma.[49]

Finally, when Sorensen's team was really ready, Ford would embark on the third stage: manufacturing the complete plane from start to finish. Sorensen calculated that he could have the first "knockdown" versions of the B-24 shipped out to Tulsa and Fort Worth, one hundred per month, by May 20, 1942. The first finished Ford bombers would roll down the assembly line that September.

He had no doubt everything would come together as planned. "It can't be done" was a phrase that didn't exist in his vocabulary. In fact, old-timers could remember Cast-Iron Charlie firing men on the spot who dared to utter those words in his presence.[50]

The final word, however, belonged to the old man himself. Ford was impressed by Sorensen's preparations. But he couldn't disguise his skepticism. "By the time you get your first planes finished," he told his old protégé, "the war will be over."[51]

Henry Ford was wrong. Thanks to Sorensen, the U.S. Army Air Forces would get more B-24s than any other bomber. But even Ford could not have guessed what an avalanche of problems Sorensen's vision—his obsession almost—was about to bring down on his company's head.

CHAPTER THIRTEEN

AGONY AT WILLOW RUN

B-24s in assembly line at Willow Run. *From the Henry Ford Collection (P.833.77362.4/ THF91632)*

> "But, Mr. Sorensen, I don't know a thing about airplanes."
> "Who the hell does over there?"
> —*Exchange between Walter Wagner and Charlie Sorensen, December 1941*

IN MARCH 1941, Willow Run was a sleepy creek west of Detroit, surrounded by woods and farmland. Early on the morning of the twenty-eighth, its rustic tranquility was broken by the sound of bulldozers.

Construction workers began cutting down and uprooting trees and filling and leveling the land. In little more than a month, it would be transformed into the site of the biggest factory on earth. In 1939, Henry Ford had established a summer camp at Willow Run for inner-city youth. Now as he inspected the site and saw the huge piles of oak, maple, and elm logs stacking up from the land clearing, he said, "Let's build a sawmill and saw up the timber right here." The lumber the Ford sawmill generated would almost all go into housing for the workers who would soon be flocking to work at the Willow Run plant—some 50,000, it was estimated—once ground was broken on April 18.[1]

In the end, Sorensen never got his mile-long factory. Kahn's final design, however, did incorporate a mile-long assembly line housed in a giant L-shaped steel reinforced plant 3,200 feet long and 1,279 feet across at its widest point. Total factory area came to 3.5 million square feet covering 80 acres. (Once complete bombers were being built, it would grow to 4.7 million square feet.) Another 850 acres were set aside for a landing field with seven concrete fields where (it was hoped) in a little less than sixteen months Ford-built B-24s would be taking off around the clock, one every hour.[2]

Old Ford hand Harry Hanson had the staggering task of laying out the machinery and assembly stations in this vast space—"the most enormous room," *Time* magazine put it, "in the history of man." Technicians flew out from Detroit to San Diego seventy at a time, to learn all they could about the tools and dies and the sequence of operations and engineering skills needed to produce a fleet of bombers, while others chased down the aluminum, glass, steel, and bricks for the factory as well as the materials for making the planes themselves.[3]

Sorensen was learning this was a more complicated process than even he had imagined. The first thing he needed, he told Consolidated, was the blueprints for the plane. Consolidated had to inform him there weren't any—certainly not any complete set. Consolidated engineers largely made them up as they went along, modifying here and incorporating new elements and changes there, as field tests and new Army specifications came along.

"All right," Sorensen said, "we'll send out enough engineers and draftsmen to make a complete set."[4]

An entirely new Ford team took two freight car loads of drawings and plans from San Diego and redid the blueprints for everything, down to the tricycle landing gear (which the Ford people later completely redesigned). As for Consolidated, it began making changes of its own, including abandoning the old outdoor assembly process. Sorensen's man on the spot, Roscoe Smith, wrote, "There is considerable comment in circulation to the effect that Ford has gotten them off their fanny."[5]

When Smith flew back from San Diego to Detroit in late July, with his two hundred technicians and engineers in tow, he found at Willow Run the steel outlines of a factory, with bricklayers piling up the bricks—4.3 million of them—to build the walls. The last concrete floors were being poured. The site for the airport, which when Smith had left had been a sea of mud, was dry and level, with an elaborate sewer system. A special spur of the New York Central Railroad had been opened, for delivery of materials. A couple of weeks later, the first machine tools arrived.[6] On August 29 the U.S. Army Air Forces command approved the final changes Ford proposed to make on the bomber design. September 7 saw Roscoe Smith, whom Sorensen appointed to head the plant, bringing in his first workers to work the first punch presses. They were still a long way from making planes, but Smith was ready to start training his labor force. On November 15 the first limited production of plane parts began.[7]

Charlie Sorensen gazed out on his creation with impatience, but also satisfaction. Much had been accomplished. Things were on schedule—a schedule unaffected by the events at Pearl Harbor. By the end of December, Willow Run still didn't look like the industrial wonder he had planned. No part of the factory was done; the airfield was still a bare if vast empty plain. Most of his machine tools, including the huge Ingersoll mill he had ordered for drilling and milling the crucial wing sections, performing forty-two separate operations in thirty-five minutes, still hadn't arrived.[8] As for his workforce, they existed largely in his imagination.

Sorensen estimated he would need 60,000 workers once Willow

Run was up and running—although others thought the number might go as high as 100,000. No one, however, had a clear idea of where they would come from. Ypsilanti, a small, sleepy college town, couldn't provide anywhere near that number—and the whole idea of moving the plant outside Detroit was to avoid tapping into the already overstretched labor market in that city. No one had called the War Manpower Commission, which kept track of such things, to see if there were better labor pools closer to Ford satellite plants like Houston or Cleveland—one time when advice from Washington would have been helpful. Cast-Iron Charlie's attitude was, build the plant, and they will come.[9]

They did, but very slowly. Getting full production started was going to require 45,000 workers at a minimum. By April 7, 1942, there were only 9,000.[10] At the end of May, that had inched up to 15,000, including 1,800 women. Most had no place to live and were camped out in trailers and tents. Just training these newcomers to the laws of the assembly line took time and resources away from finishing the plant— and there were other interested visitors waiting in the wings. Walter Reuther of UAW and then CIO's Philip Murray came by for a chat. Murray asked how many workers Sorensen would finally have. Sorensen said he estimated 60,000. Murray's eyes lit up, thinking no doubt of all the new union members, and new union dues.

"Of course," Murray said casually, "we will take advantage of all our prerogatives," meaning for enforcing union maintenance. Sorensen watched him, sensing trouble ahead. He was right.[11]

Eventually the only place Sorensen was going to get his workers was from Detroit. But the roads to Ypsilanti were lousy and dirt paved: No one was going to be able to drive out unless something was done. So more construction time had to be diverted to building a multilane modern highway complete with concrete bridges and median strips.[12*]

Then there was the confusion over phasing in the plant layout. Sorensen's machines began to arrive, some 16,000 tools and 7,000 jigs. The Ingersoll milling machine for the central wing sections was meant to reduce the work done by thirty men at Consolidated to three, and

* Today it is U.S. Interstate 94.

the man-hours spent riveting from fifteen hundred to twenty-six. The problem was where to put it. The walls and roof were still not done. Installing and wiring up all the new tools didn't just require more workers, it meant more managers, as well—and Sorensen was short on both. *

He heard that one of his men, engine tooling expert Walter Wagner, had been offered the post of manager of the Ford plant in Houston, at three times his current salary. Sorensen called him over to the unfinished engine building and grabbed him by the lapel.

"Listen," he barked. "You belong to us. I'm going to take you over to the bomber plant and you're going to be a superintendent."

Wagner must have wondered if Sorensen was going to hit him. "But, Mr. Sorensen," he complained, "I don't know a thing about airplanes."

Sorensen responded, "Who the hell does over there?"[13]

It was a cry of frustration, as the unfinished walls of Willow Run began to close in. He made Wagner the assistant to Logan Miller, one of Mead Bricker's staff. Wagner was shocked the first time he entered the plant. It looked to him like an abandoned cave with workers and machines strewn about and huge gaps in the roof. How the place was supposed to make anything, let alone four-engined bombers, seemed anyone's guess.[14]

Finally Henry Ford turned to an old friend to help out. Charles Lindbergh had been one of the pillars of his America First Committee, and longtime advisor on matters aviational. In April he was asked to come to Willow Run as a consultant and help to pull things together from an aeronautical point of view. The plant would soon be scheduled to turn out its first knockdown B-24s—a goal that seemed nowhere in sight.

Lindbergh drove out to Willow Run on April 7, 1942. Starting at the unloading platforms where New Central's freight cars would pull into the building, he walked through all the various departments. The sheer size of the place was stupendous. It seemed to him "a sort of Grand Canyon of the mechanized world," with machine tools going full blast making parts in one corner while contractors were still erecting steel walls in another. Most of the machinery was not yet installed, and the concrete was still being poured for the final assembly floor. Yet Lindbergh felt certain the first bombers would be coming out even before construction was done (handmade Consolidated versions, not the full mass-produced ones). "Since this has been done to a large extent on theory," he added in his private diary, "we must expect many unforeseen problems."[15]

He was less impressed by the plane itself. He did an hour test flight with one of the B-24Cs Consolidated had sent out and "found the controls to be the stiffest and heaviest I have ever handled." He much preferred flying the B-17, and thought crews would, too. "I would certainly hate to be in a bomber of this type" if a couple of Messerschmitts caught up with it—which they would soon be doing, once the Willow Run B-24s made their way out to Europe.[16]

As for Charlie Sorensen, Lindbergh found him "a man of exceptionally strong character but with a number of weaknesses that often accompany strong character and obvious success." One was vanity. Another was a belief in his own ideas no matter how ill conceived, and a corresponding disbelief in what others, no matter how experienced, might say about it.

One of Sorensen's new obsessions, for example, was the idea of building a cargo plane with a one-thousand-foot wingspan. Air Force officials were appalled, and said so. Undeterred, Sorensen unveiled his plans to Lindbergh on the phone. Equally stunned, Lindbergh suggested starting with a five-hundred-foot wing instead. "You fellas are always blocking me, blocking me," Sorensen burst out, and hung up.[17]

Lindbergh also noted Sorensen's bullying ways. As they walked together through the plant, Lindbergh watched workers' eyes drop to their work, avoiding meeting Sorensen's terrifying stare. "No man wishes to cross him," he remarked sadly, "and no man can cross him and hold his job." It was no way to get at the truth of potential problems, or of how to correct them. The famed aviator summed it up this way: "His heart is so filled with the love of the machine that it has somewhat crowded out his love of the men who must run it."[18]

Still, Lindbergh could not deny the Ford man's ability: "He is certainly one of the men who has built this nation into what it is today." He also believed Sorensen's belief in Willow Run was correct. Once production was fully under way, "the output will be tremendous."[19]

When that would come about was, of course, the crucial question. That May the Ford team had to admit to Lindbergh they were at least a month behind schedule. Sorensen and Harry Bennett were at each other's throats, and Roscoe Smith found himself caught in the middle.

Bennett had his own ideas about where machines and men should be placed to speed things up, and began ordering certain equipment to be installed, which Smith ordered removed. There was an unholy row, and both Sorensen and Bennett stormed into Smith's office. Voices were raised, chairs were pushed back.

Suddenly Bennett lunged at Sorensen, who backed away, fists raised. Smith tried to step between the two men, and caught Bennett's punch on the jaw, sending him to the floor. When Smith tried to get up, Bennett knocked him down again.

Sorensen watched, then simply said, "Harry, I'm surprised at you," and walked out. Bennett called the old man to tell him his version of what happened. Henry Ford said, "Well, Harry, I think you hit the wrong fellow." When the story of the fistfight whirled around the Ford offices, everyone knew whom he meant.[20]

Roscoe Smith never set foot in Willow Run again.

Mead Bricker now took over the plant. No one envied him. A new battle developed, over tools and dies. The aircraft industry all made their molds, or dies, for parts from rubber and various soft metal alloys. Sorensen and the Ford people scoffed at this. It made exact measurements extremely difficult, especially since the dies were used over and over and lost their original firmness. Ford was going to use steel for their dies. After all, these would be mass-producing thousands of parts, and the expense involved, Sorensen's team felt, would be more than worth it.

Then they discovered that the steel dies damaged the delicate aluminum surfaces, forcing them to remake more and more parts. Now it was Consolidated's turn to gloat. Maybe you know about *mass* production, they warned, but we know about *quality* production. What was supposed to be a corporate partnership was becoming a bitter antagonism. "If the Consolidated men were carrying a chip on one shoulder," Lindbergh noted, the Ford men arrived with a chip on both.[21]

That was nothing, however, compared to the other problem with the steel dies. Two years after it had first flown, the B-24's design was constantly evolving. Changes demanded by Air Force command based on battlefield conditions, or new discoveries by Mac Laddon and his team on how to improve performance, forced modifications in how the plane was made, down to the tiniest subsection. Ford was learning that they barely had time to install their new expensive steel dies before they had to be junked. That meant not only new dies but changing the machine tools to fit them, and often a different jig to handle the altered part. That first year, the Air Force ordered 575 master changes alone—and all the while everyone was wondering where Ford's B-24s were.

It drove Sorensen to near fury. "We would agree on freezing a design, then be ready to go ahead," he remembered later. "Back from the fighting fronts would come complaints or suggestions regarding certain features, and the plane designers came through with alterations in design with no consideration for the production program."[22]

Of course, the Air Force's attitude was that learning from battlefield experience was what warplanes are all about. A change could make the difference between being shot down and coming home alive, or a safe versus a disastrous landing. When Sorensen complained, Hap Arnold said simply, "I'd feel as if I had blood in my hands if I ignored these boys' complaints." But for the people at Willow Run, it added to the feeling that they were trapped in a Sisyphean enterprise, with no way out. /

And by the spring of 1942, the public was noticing. Where were the mass-produced B-24s Ford had been promising for almost a year? Watching from the sidelines at North American's plant in Inglewood, Dutch Kindelberger scoffed, "You cannot expect a blacksmith to learn to make a watch overnight." He told the *New York Times* that in his opinion, far from speeding up the production of airplanes, getting the auto industry involved was slowing it down, especially (as at Willow Run) in the making of airframes. Pratt and Whitney's founder, Fred Rentschler, worried that the government had created "a Frankenstein's monster" by getting Ford and the car companies involved, which would end up hurting the aviation industry.[23]

The Office of War Information had to issue a statement reassuring the public over the delay. Investigators from the Truman Committee began sniffing around, wondering where all the government money was going when no planes were being made. Willow Run was becoming a public relations disaster for Ford, and a national joke. Wits in the newspapers changed the name from Willow Run to "Will It Run?"

On Monday, July 27, Lindbergh drove back out to Willow Run to meet Henry Ford, to see what he could do to help straighten out the growing mess. They drove together to the airfield where an Air Force bomber had landed to unload a passenger, an Air Force general. Lindbergh caught sight of him talking to Sorensen and Bennett and Edsel Ford in the development engineering department.

He was a tall man wearing an Air Force uniform, an older man with wide shoulders and a white mustache who spoke English with a Danish accent.

It was Bill Knudsen, now Lieutenant General Knudsen.[24] He was there in his new job as the War Department's head of production, and as Undersecretary Robert Patterson's troubleshooter to get Willow Run production off the ground. Indeed, Knudsen already had the answer.

The answer was field modification.

At first Knudsen had had trouble adjusting to his new Air Force uniform, and his new smaller office on the second floor of the Munitions Building. He had no formal staff or organization; the War Department's Materiel Command and its various Production Boards forged ahead without him. He learned he was there as a facilitator, as Stimson and Patterson's personal representative in charge of getting unstuck what the public and official Washington said was stuck: namely, wartime production at the factory level.

"You'll have no set schedule," Stimson told him. "Bottlenecks in production appear to be everywhere, so use your own judgment which ones to break first."[25] Knudsen would have a plane, and could go anywhere he wanted and see any data or reports he wished. On February 1, just three days after his appointment, he was off to the West Coast. He was starting a series of inspection trips that would last three years.

The former GM boss logged a quarter of a million miles, visiting twelve hundred factories as well as the jungles of New Guinea and the battle plains of Europe.[26]

The lieutenant general rank and the uniform were supposed to give him authority, especially with lieutenant colonels and brigadiers used to a more formal chain of command. But in the factories around the country, Bill Knudsen needed no title. He was *Knudsen* (he usually answered the phone that way, "This is Knudsen"), a living manufacturing legend, and his appearance on the factory floor was always a sensation.

He would spend an hour or two looking over blueprints and production schedules, with the nervous manager at his side, before heading for the factory floor. His black-ribbon pince-nez looked out of place with the khaki uniform, gold-bedecked cap, and three silver stars on each shoulder board. But behind those glasses were eyes that noticed every detail as he walked down every aisle, stopping at every machine and speaking to the men and women working them—sometimes taking over the controls to show them how to handle a tool more easily or safely.

Then he'd walk back to the manager and, pointing down the aisle, say, "Why don't you reverse the arrangement of the center of these three lines, so that the work will go down the first line, up the second, and down the third, instead of having to be carried back twice?" The manager would stare dumbfounded and tell an assistant to make a note.[27]

Then they would head for the parking lot. Knudsen would walk down the rows of employees' cars, pausing to point out a worn tire or a broken headlight, sometimes crawling under the car to trace an oil leak. "Get those fixed," he would tell the manager. "Defense workers always get priority on new tires or retreads. You don't want a blowout or a breakdown keeping an employee away from work." Knudsen never expected every car problem to get fixed. But he was sending a message to the higher-ups: Make sure all your workers get to work. Absenteeism could be as much a threat to the production schedule as a materials shortage or a labor strike.[28]

So it went, starting at eight o'clock, every day. Sometimes he visited

11 plants a day—350 those first six months—fixing labor shortages, material shortages, and bottlenecks large and small—"We're short on everything except bottlenecks," he quipped to his new friend and Forrestal aide Admiral Lewis Strauss.[29]* It was a demanding schedule for a man sixty-four years old with one kidney (the other had been taken out in an operation in 1938) and chronic high blood pressure. But Knudsen knew these were the final necessary steps to getting the weapons and munitions out of the factories and into battle.

All the while he never forgot his higher responsibilities. This was "the price that was being paid by families," he said, "who waited the return of their sons, their brothers, their fathers—yes, and their sisters."[30] To Knudsen they represented "the eternal forces of freedom"— what Hitler and the Axis were seeking to destroy. Every production delay took them one step further away from that moment of reunion— and further away from victory.

Including at Willow Run. During his days at OPM, Knudsen had followed the efforts of his old rival Charlie Sorensen with pain and misgiving. It seemed to undercut his whole working premise, that the auto industry could revolutionize aircraft production if done the right way—and seemed to prove that Sorensen's insistence on building planes, not parts, was the wrong way. Now in July he set out to Ypsilanti to see if he could unblock what was becoming a bottleneck of personalities, as well as production. In fact the answer was in his pocket.

He had mentioned it to Robert Patterson more than a year earlier, after the undersecretary had been grumbling about the failure of Glenn Martin's company to get its B-26 Marauder off the ground. What was the matter over there? Patterson wanted to know.

"Nothing's the matter," Knudsen said. "If your office, or the War Department, would quit making last-minute changes and leave the Martin people alone, they will make you planes that will fly."

Patterson was startled and barked, "What do you mean?"

"I think we should freeze the designs for a while so we can get some airplanes," Knudsen said. Trying to stay up to the minute on specifications at the factory end only meant being late on every plane and de-

* After the war, Strauss became chairman of the Atomic Energy Commission.

sign. "What I think we should do to keep abreast of things is build the airplanes first and add whatever improvements are necessary at some place especially equipped to do that."[31]

Patterson thought about it, and agreed. It marked the start of the Air Force's field modification program. In January 1942 the Materiel Division set up ten modification centers, the first of which was in Cheyenne, Wyoming. At first everyone thought the aircraft companies themselves would do the modifying at the centers, but Douglas, North American, and the rest already had their hands full. Airplane production was poised to more than double in 1942—from 19,000 to 47,000—and no one had people or materials to spare, even to modify their own planes.[32]

So the nation's airlines stepped up to fill the gap. American, Northwest, United, Southern, and Mid-Continental—all volunteered their personnel and materials to run the new modification centers. One of the very first was Mid-Continental Airlines, based in Minneapolis, which did the modifications that got Jimmy Doolittle's squadron of B-25s ready for their carrier flight on the way to bomb Tokyo in April 1942. By the time Knudsen came out to Ypsilanti in July, twelve centers were going, while the Army Air Forces' own Air Service Command was modifying five hundred planes a month to get them ready for overseas duty.[33]

Here clearly was the answer to Sorensen and the Air Force's problems. Let Willow Run build the bombers as is, ready to fly to modification centers where the field changes the generals wanted could be done bomber by bomber, instead of interrupting the flow of assembly-line production. And that meant complete bombers, *not* subassemblies or unfinished knockdowns. Knudsen noticed something else. The way Willow Run had been contracted and constructed was for building both finished planes and subassemblies such as wings and tail sections, which then had to be shipped someplace else. These two operations were running at cross-purposes, Knudsen realized, and needed to be brought together for a single purpose: making flyable B-24s from nose to tail.[34] That would also relieve Ford of some of the labor pressure, by letting them subcontract out subassemblies for delivery to Willow Run instead of the other way around.

The Air Force higher-ups got the message. Starting fall of 1942 Willow Run's operations finally became one. Everything flowed along four lines simultaneously, which converged to two, and then finally one at the end—2.3 million square feet later—which pointed out the doors to the blue sky and black tarmac beyond. A two-mile-long monorail conveyor carried the pieces of aluminum sheet metal, flashing under the glare of the plant's fluorescent lighting, to the separate assembly departments and thousands of machine tools and mechanical presses. A huge mechanized chain dragged each bomber through the four 60-foot bays of the assembly process, from the fuselage where the pilot's floor was set on a great merry-go-round of mechanisms that slowly turned as workers darted back and forth installing and riveting parts in place; through the center wing section with its massive Ingersoll mill which took the 56-foot chunk of aluminum lowered by crane and clamped, milled, drilled, reamed, bored, and then unclamped each section in one seven-cycle operation, before it moved on to the next bay.

There it met the outer wings as the plane now headed for final assembly. Station 1 brought the canopy and riveted it to the center wing. Station 2 brought bulkheads, bomb racks, and side panels of the bomb bay doors—sliding doors, not swinging doors like the Flying Fortress, for quicker opening and shutting. Then came the electric wiring and hydraulic system, plus the afterfuselage and tail sections. Finally workers put in the nose wheels, the B-24's four engines, and the trailing edges.[35]

Near the end, the bomber was pulled into one last room. When Charlie Sorensen had originally visited San Diego, he had been appalled to see technicians standing on stepladders to apply the spray paint to their planes. Now at Willow Run all spraying was done with miniature elevators raising and lowering painters over every square foot of the plane—even as the din and dust rose up from the work on the plane behind.

The very first completed Ford B-24 emerged into the sunlight on September 10, 1942. A week later President and Mrs. Roosevelt visited Willow Run and marveled at the size of the facilities and immensity of the achievement. Before the end of the month, Sorensen's team had completed 18. When 1942 ended, they had 56—a far cry from the

hundreds they had promised and the public had expected. But a turning point had been reached.

In January 1943, 31 Liberators were completed; in February—even
as one senator from Washington was telling the world, "Apparently
there has been practically no production to amount to anything"—there
were 74. March brought 104.[36] Willow Run was still not yet out of the
woods. There would be chronic labor problems: For every new worker
coming to Ypsilanti there was another who left, either for a better job
in Detroit or out of disgust with the still-inadequate housing or (if he
was male) because he had been drafted.

As Sorensen had foreseen, the unions also made constant trouble.
United Auto Workers Local 50, the "Bomber Local," spawned a series
of wildcat strikes that interrupted production. In July there was a
one-day foremen's strike over who would be allowed to use the plant's
telephone. Navy secretary Frank Knox personally arranged for Naval
Reserve lieutenant Henry Ford II to be released from active duty so he
could go back home to Ford and save the situation. The Army's Material Command got so worried at one point in September that it even
recommended the government take over the plant.[37]

Despite it all, Willow Run came through. By October B-24s were
coming off the line at the rate of three hundred a month. A new production schedule drawn up by Bill Knudsen in December shifted still
more subassembly work to outside plants, which relieved the labor
shortage and sped up final delivery. As 1944 dawned, Willow Run finally achieved Sorensen's vision of five hundred bombers a month, and
on March 3—the day before American bombers launched their first
daylight raid on Berlin—Don Nelson's assistant Charlie Wilson sent
Sorensen a congratulatory telegram:

"Our confidence in your company's ability to maintain a fine sustained production record has again been proven. . . . Our sincerest congratulations."[38]

Ford had turned a plane that used to cost two hundred thousand
man-hours to make into one that cost only eighteen thousand hours.
Willow Run built half of all the Liberators made during the war. But
it had been a bitter, exhausting journey. Nelson's telegram arrived just

as Sorensen was being forced out by his old mentor, Henry Ford himself, after nearly forty years of service. He never set foot in a Ford factory again. The constant tensions over Willow Run almost certainly
contributed to Henry Ford's son Edsel's health problems. He died in
March 1943. As for Alfred Kahn, Willow Run was his last project. He
died at his desk in 1942. The old man himself, Henry Ford, passed on
April 7, 1947.

Cast-Iron Charlie's one-man battle against the world kept him going
another quarter century, until his death in 1968.

As one bomber after another took off from Willow Run and banked
into the air, they headed south, where they flew into one of the arms
of Henry Kaiser's Six Companies octopus, Bechtel-McCone. Flush
from their Calship success, Steve Bechtel and partner John McCone
had won the contract from the Air Force in January 1943 to build its
biggest modification center yet, with some two million square feet of
factory space spread out over 285 acres near the Birmingham mu-
nicipal airport. The $15 million facility had been built without any
fee or profit.[39] But it would change airplane modification from a series of temporary fixes into a systematic manufacturing process.

Eighty-six percent of the people Bechtel and McCone hired to do
the modification had never worked with airplanes before. More than
half were women. But they carried out the immensely complicated and
time-consuming work of removing parts of planes that required modification or replacement—parts sometimes buried deep in the engine or
fuselage underneath a bewildering network of wires, hoses, or other
parts—and replacing or altering them according to Air Force Materiel
Command directives that, in the course of a single day, might cover a
wall of the supervisor's office. Some planes required as much as fifteen
to sixteen hundred hours of labor.[40]

Besides the Willow Run B-24s, others flew out from Consolidated's
own plant in San Diego, where Kaiser's friend Tom Girdler had moved
over from Vultee to replace Reuben Fleet. He and Harry Woodhead
had hurled the plane into full Ford-style production, beginning with
the C model and then the D, equipped with heavier armament and

supercharged engines and redesigned engine nacelles, and finally the E, the basic design as the Willow Run bombers.

But the most important of the B-24s that passed through Bechtel-McCone's Birmingham center were the Very Long Range Liberators, or VLRs, which would change the course of the war in the Atlantic and open the way for the Allied buildup in Europe.

Since September 1941 the British had been ordering B-24s through Lend-Lease in hopes the long-range bomber could close the so-called Atlantic Gap. This was the long, wide stretch southeast of Iceland that Atlantic convoys had to pass through but that no patrol plane could reach. The strategists in Washington and at Britain's Coastal Command called it the Atlantic Gap. Seamen had another name for it: the Black Pit. This was the great kill zone of the German U-boat wolf packs, and the graveyard of dozens of Liberty ships and their crews.

To everyone's surprise, out over the Atlantic the B-24's faults—its tough handling, its less-than-rugged airframe—faded to insignificance. Instead, its virtues—its long 2,850-mile range, its ability to carry a bigger load than the Flying Fortress, and its adaptability and versatility—stood out, especially on the B-24D, which the British dubbed the Mark III. Then Consolidated's engineers back in San Diego took a British suggestion and installed extra fuel tanks in one of the three bomb bays. At one stroke it doubled the range of maritime patrols guarding the approaches to Britain. Carrying almost three thousand gallons of fuel, the VLR could fly to the middle of the Atlantic and back from either Aldergrove or Iceland. Once the Bechtel-McCone people in Birmingham acclimated the plane to the near-Arctic conditions in the North Atlantic, suddenly the Atlantic Gap didn't look so large.

In fact, in the spring of 1943 the VLR Liberator slammed the Gap shut. In the first twenty days of March, the Germans sank ninety-seven Allied merchant ships—more than half a million tons. In the last ten days of March, Allied convoys lost exactly one ship, thanks to the VLR's vigilance. Then in April, British Coastal Command began flying the first of their "shuttle" patrols from Gander in Newfoundland to Reykjavik—clear across the Gap and well within the Liberator's range. In the seven patrols they ran that month, they spotted no fewer than ten submarines. Only failures in the depth-charge mechanisms saved the Germans from certain death. But as American crews in their own VLR squadron in Newfoundland, No. 6 Antisubmarine Squadron, soon learned, it wasn't necessary for the planes to actually sink U-boats. They just had to spot them and alert the convoy escorts, to hugely increase the odds in the Allies' favor.

For the rest of April 1943, the battle seesawed back and forth, as American escort carriers joined in the fight, as well. Then came the decisive turning point on May 4, when convoy ONS5 came under concentrated attack after it had been battered by gales off the southern tip of Greenland. For the next three days, ONS5 lost twelve merchantmen, but combined air and sea counterattacks sank six submarines and damaged several more. A few days later, another attack on a convoy cost the Germans one submarine for every ship sunk—unacceptable losses for the Germans, especially when one of the U-boat skippers lost was Peter Dönitz, younger son of the German navy's commander-in-chief. Attacks on the next four convoys cost the Germans six more boats, two of them killed by VLR Liberators. Every one of the Allied freighters got through unscathed.

A chastened Admiral Karl Dönitz did the dismal math. On May 24, 1943, he decided to call off his wolf packs. Germany had lost the battle for the Atlantic. Then and later, Dönitz put the blame squarely on the closing of the Atlantic Gap, and the B-24s. Later, Admiralty analysts calculated that every VLR Liberator patrol saved no less than six Allied ships. All in all, the Liberator squadrons would be credited with no fewer than seventy-two U-boat kills.[41]

Thanks to the B-24 and the men and women who made them, the way was fully clear for Kaiser's Liberty ships across the Atlantic. America was ready to turn its war production loose.

CHAPTER FOURTEEN

VICTORY IS OUR BUSINESS

Workers posing with 5000th Flying Fortress, signed by 35,000 Boeing employees, May 1944. *Copyright © Boeing*

> I don't think of the hope of reward as selfishness. Work is the prime mover of our economy, and the fuel that makes people work is profit.
>
> *—Tom Girdler*

NINETEEN HUNDRED FORTY-THREE was the year certain issues that had been lingering since Bill Knudsen first came to Washington got resolved once and for all. One was that Washington's long-simmering battle with Big Labor came to a boil. In April the leonine John L. Lewis, head of the United Mine Workers, decided it was time for his miners to get a raise. Their ranks were depleted by members who had left to join the armed services or for more lucrative and less dangerous work in war industries, while the rest worked longer. Unless they got another two dollars a day, Lewis thundered, they would go on strike. On April 28, 1943, strikes broke out in the Pittsburgh-area coalfields, and production came to a halt.

When Roosevelt got the news, he exploded. He ordered the army to take over the mines and prepared a radio broadcast for May 2 appealing directly to the miners to go back to work. He was being wheeled down to the Oval Office to make the broadcast when word came that Lewis had struck a deal to have the miners return to work in two days. Roosevelt gave the speech anyway.[1]

The Army never actually seized the mines, and no one at the White House had thought about how the Army would get the miners back to work if it did. "You can't run a coal mine with bayonets," Lewis said.[2] But the threat, plus the loss of prestige with the public, was enough to get the UMW back to work—back, that is, until June. On June 19 more than 60,000 coal miners dropped tools and went home.

This time the public reaction was overwhelming. Newspapers across the country denounced the strike as unpatriotic and vile. When Roosevelt threatened to strip the draft deferments from every mine worker, Lewis decided to halt the strike after three days, but the damage to organized labor was done. The Republican-dominated Congress passed the War Labor Disputes Act, ordering a thirty-day notice for all strikes and ending the secret ballot for union membership. On June 25, Roosevelt vetoed it. It took the Senate exactly eleven minutes to override him.[3]

As Knudsen had observed, labor trouble, far more than business foot-dragging or profiteering, had been the bane of war production. Work stoppages in 1943 alone cost 13.5 million man-days: almost triple the man-days lost in 1942. On December 27 a threatened railroad strike forced the Army to intervene for real. It seized control and ran the nation's rail system for more than three weeks before the strike ended.

But Big Labor had learned its lesson. It could no longer afford to be seen hindering the war effort; on the contrary, it wanted its workers to share in the credit for arming America in record time. So labor troubles eased slightly in 1944, with only 8.7 million man-days lost—just about enough to build six 35,000-ton battleships on 14,344 B-24s, but still not enough to make any appreciable difference in the burgeoning production numbers.[4]

Even so, a week before D-day, 70,000 workers were on strike at twenty-six plants in Detroit alone.[5]

A second turning point came in February, when Donald Nelson managed to fend off a concerted effort to replace him with the kind of all-powerful production czar he and Knudsen had resisted from the start.* Although Nelson did finally step down in July as an Office of War Mobilization came into being under Roosevelt's friend Supreme Court judge James Byrnes, the system he and Knudsen had devised for leaving defense production in the hands of business, not the government, remained—largely because everyone could now see how well it worked.

This was the other point of no return. In 1943 the numbers Knudsen and his colleagues had promised were taking on a life of their own. Production of Liberty ships was reaching 160 a month, while 18,434 Navy battleships, cruisers, carriers, subs, and destroyers poured out of America's shipyards—along with 16,000 landing craft. Heavy bombers soared from 2,618 in 1942 to 9,616—bombers that would soon be leveling Germany's cities and industrial heartland by day, while the RAF attacked them at night.

Tank production swelled to 29,495; small arms from 2.3 million in 1942 to almost 7 million; artillery shells from 693,000 to 800,000 tons; machine guns to 830,000; and airplanes of all kinds to 85,946—an air armada beyond anyone's wildest imaginings.[6] Imperial Japan and Nazi Germany, the symbols of modern military power just two years earlier,

---

* The driving force behind the effort was the Army, and their choice to replace him had been trusted old Bernard Baruch. Unlike in May 1940, this time Baruch was willing to get into harness—perhaps because he knew the really hard work had all been done.

were being drowned in the flood. In 1943, American war production was twice that of Germany and Japan combined.[7] Victory, which had seemed so elusive just ten months before, was now assured.

At the center of the effort, of course, were mammoth companies like General Electric. America's fourth-largest corporation in 1940 with some 30 million square feet of production space available in its thirty-four main plants scattered from Bridgeport, Connecticut, to Oakland, California, GE was a perfect illustration of Bill Knudsen's principle that the biggest companies are the biggest because they by and large get the best results.

The company got its first military contract on September 23, 1939, making mule-pack howitzers for the Army, and pushed on from there. In the first year of the war, GE spent $78 million of its own money expanding its facilities for military production; the federal government threw in another $120 million. GE would go on to make propulsion plants for warships, turbo-superchargers for airplanes, searchlights and military radios, radar sets and naval gun directors, and motors for operating the ramps of LSTs and Higgins boats. GE also came up with three hundred new types of electric lamps and manufactured 400,000 electrically heated flying suits, as well as designing a new torpedo for the Navy. It also provided the turbines for 10 of the Navy's carriers, 37 of its 43 cruisers, and 200 of its 364 destroyers. It even filled a contract for the Army for five thousand bazookas in thirty days, even though GE engineer Jim Power had to design the weapon himself in a marathon twenty-four-hour session, while four hundred workers labored around the clock to meet the deadline.[8]

Another major player was Knudsen's own company, General Motors. The biggest automaker company in the world had been slow getting into war production. As late as May 1941, chairman Alfred Sloan scoffed at the idea that war was coming—and Sloan insisted on keeping GM's overseas operations in Germany and Japan going far longer than even his close friends thought politically expedient.[9]

Yet when war came, GM shot from an almost standing start to converting almost 90 percent of its forty-one operating divisions to munitions production as war product sales shot from $406 million in 1941 to $3.5 billion in 1943. The automaking giant adopted a new slogan,

"Victory Is Our Business," and business turned out to be pretty good. It saw net sales of $13.4 billion, and a net profit of $673 million. These were slender numbers compared to peacetime, but still enough to make GM the emperor of wartime industry—making 10 percent of everything America produced to fight the Second World War.[10]

In 1943, GM was also building trucks and tanks for the Army, as well as Grumman fighter and torpedo planes for the Navy. The GM engineers at Eastern Aircraft learned from Ford's mistakes at Willow Run. By working closely with Grumman and by concentrating on subassemblies instead of entire planes, they produced 7,546 Avengers and 5,920 Wildcats before war's end. Another 200 GM-built Wildcats wound up flying with the Royal Navy.[11]

It was also General Motors who discovered that eight Liberty ships could carry the same number of two-and-a-half-ton trucks disassembled as one hundred could carry fully assembled. All you needed was a place to do the assembling: A few portable cranes, battery chargers, a couple of portable Quonset huts or even tents, a poured concrete floor, and a tractor and trailer or two worked fine. And with 40,000 employees, GM's Overseas Operations Division was perfectly poised to deliver and assemble whatever American forces needed, almost on the front line.

The first two temporary plants supported U.S. Army operations in Tunisia in 1942. Two more were set up in Heliopolis in Egypt for the Eighth Army. One was finally transferred to the southern terminus of the Burma Road. The other wound up repairing broken-down trucks in the jungle at Rangoon during the final push for the liberation of Burma.[12]

General Motors' most amazing war-front plant, however, took shape in Iran. Liberty ships landed parts for the plant to supply Russian forces at the northern end of the Persian Gulf. A one-track railroad then moved the parts to the factory site at Andimeshk. The first GM employees reached Andimeshk in March 1942, to find it a hellhole with typhus, dysentery, sand-fly fever, and a running temperature of 140 degrees Fahrenheit.

The first sixty men began assembling trucks out in the open, while the others worked to build a makeshift factory. Roving jackals raided the camp stores and kitchens at night. But by day the Andimeshk plant was soon turning out 2,500 military vehicles a month of all makes and types, with tool-working shops and a special oxygen-manufacturing unit for high-speed welding. For labor GM trained five thousand Iranians in the mass-production methods of Detroit, so that they could put together a complete truck in less than thirty minutes.

Once the trucks were tested and inspected, the General Motors men passed the keys to Russian drivers who took them over 800 miles of treacherous mountain roads to Tabriz and then across the border into the Soviet Union—each one heavily laden with Lend-Lease supplies. In July 1942 a second factory opened 185 miles south of Andimeshk at Khorramshahr.

It was not until June 30, 1943, that the Army finally took over the operation. By then the ultimate capitalist corporation, General Motors had delivered 20,380 trucks to the Red Army.[13]

There was, however, another, less epic side to the nation's war production machine. Bill Knudsen caught a glimpse of it in his Social Security Building office when a letter arrived from a retired railway worker in Reading, Pennsylvania.

This gentleman had an idea. He had figured out a way to recycle discarded boxcar wheels and suspensions, to convert them to wartime use. He already had the machine tools he needed, he said, in a warehouse near his home. There was no call for new steel or other priority materials. The wheels were deemed scrap. All he needed was a contract from the Army to get started.

Knudsen passed the letter on, first to Don Nelson at the Materials and Defense Contracts Division, then to the Army. The retired railway worker got his contract. In no time he had six men working for him, as they reground and refinished old boxcar wheels and got them ready for a new life with the United States Army.[14]

At nearly eighty, the man from Reading was the oldest defense contractor in World War II. But his wasn't the smallest business. That honor belonged to Clyde Walling of Cleveland, Ohio. Mr. Walling was president of a tool company that operated out of his two-car garage while he parked his car in the driveway to make room. By May 1941 he had an employee force of exactly three men.[15]

Subcontractors like Walling were the lifeblood of the American free enterprise system, as Bill Knudsen well knew. General Motors alone employed nearly 20,000 of them. Knudsen had aimed to make them the lifeblood of defense contracting, as well. They ranged in size from Clyde Walling's garage to major companies like Timken, which was also based in Cleveland but had branches in Detroit and other cities, and made everything from machine tools to axles, with a fair number of metal and steel products in between.

Turning the productive power of a Timken loose had been Knudsen's plan all along. For all the harping about how huge corporations snapped up the biggest contracts and made their fortunes during the war, it was the medium- to small-sized businesses that did much of the actual work—and made the arsenal of democracy work and grow.

Ma and Pa Harrington's "defense plant," for example, was a white clapboard farmhouse on a lonely crossroads near Rockford, Illinois. There they made machine tools for turning artillery shells and tank turrets, one thousand dollars a month's worth right in their living room, while the rest of the house doubled and tripled as home office, sales branch, and factory. Their twin sons worked with them. They had started the business in the middle of the Depression, by borrowing some money to build a machine shop. When Richard and Russell Harrington learned that their main tool was going to cost more than four thousand dollars, they made their own out of a junked lathe, an old washing machine motor, and an oil pump salvaged from a 1926 Chevrolet. Their mother's old washtub caught the oil that leaked from the bottom of the homemade tool.

When war came, the Harrington brothers pressed their father and mother into helping. Ma Harrington would run the lathes making parts for tank turrets and gun mounts before washing hands to make dinner. Pa Harrington, age sixty-eight, worked the grinder and would comment to visitors, "I have more fun than a kid in this place." The first visitors were inspectors from the Harringtons' various prime contractors, who simply could not believe parts of this quality were being turned out in the quaint house with its gambrel roof, dormer windows, and flower boxes under every windowsill.

Soon Harrington brothers had other visitors, like the War Production Board's local director and a reporter from *Time* magazine. "I don't think they knew what they were getting into when they started," the WPB man told the reporter, "but they had the nerve to make a success of it."[16]

That might have been the motto of every American business, large and small, in World War II. There was Frigidaire, enlisted to manufacture .30-caliber machine guns, and Rock-Ola, the Chicago jukebox maker that was drawn into a contract to make M1 carbines alongside Underwood the typewriter company, National Postal Meter, Quality Hardware, and IBM. On the upper end of the scale, there was Ex-Cello of Detroit, which made thread-grinding machines for turning the millions of screws for military hardware from airplanes to trucks and towed artillery; Okonite of New Jersey, which insulated thousands of miles of electrical wiring; and Missouri Valley Bridge and Iron and Chicgo B&I, which built hundreds of Land Ship Tanks at yards they created in Evansville, Indiana, the so-called prairie shipyards where ex-farmhands built LSTs to float down to the Mississippi and New Orleans for service overseas.[17] /

At the lower end, there was Frank Ix's mill, in Charlottesville, Virginia, which was making parachute cloth for every airborne division going into action from Burma to D-day; and R.M.R. of Madison, Wisconsin, which made batteries for walkie-talkie sets and, when the Army decided to raise the order from 100,000 to 400,000 cells a day, organized a committee to ring doorbells and recruit housewives and office clerks to meet the order. By the spring of 1945, R.M.R. had four thousand part-time employees making half a million cells a day.[18]

In between was another Wisconsin firm, Manitowoc Shipbuilding Company. It made small cargo vessels for the carrying trade on the Great Lakes when in mid-1942 Electric Boat of Groton came to them with a proposition. Let us use your yards and facilities and laborers, they said, and our engineers, foremen, and production managers will train them to make submarines. The Manitowoc men were startled but game to try. Before two years were out, twenty-eight Navy submarines would be launched from Manitowoc. They were powered by diesel engines being built for the Navy at a brand-new plant in Beloit, Wisconsin, by the weighing-scales company Fairbanks, Morse. The Manitowoc engineers also built huge pontoon docks to carry the finished subs through a series of shallow inland waterways, then down the Mississippi River to where the Navy took over in New Orleans. Halfway down they met Missouri Valley's LSTs going the same way.[19]

Bill Knudsen got to know many of these companies on his travels for Army production. When he wrote later that in those years he "saw America at its best," he meant precisely those companies with a few hundred to a couple of thousand employees who made the vital subassemblies, processed the raw materials, designed and made the tools and dies without which a Chrysler Tank Arsenal or Douglas Aircraft plant would have had to shut down. A myriad of others supplied the Kaiser shipyards, and the yards where battleships and submarines took shape in Chester, Pennsylvania; Camden, New Jersey; and Newport News, Virginia. They carried the spirit of free enterprise like a revitalizing force, with the power to meet the needs of total war without losing their identity or creativity or power of self-renewal.[20]

Lieutenant General Knudsen visited Eaton Manufacturing of Cleveland on his very first inspection trip, in February 1942. The company was filling orders for 8×8 axles for GM (1,000 axles a month), two-speed axles for Ford, Canada, and Chrysler, Canada (7,500 a month), 6×6 rear axles for Timken (1,200 a month), as well as axles for two manufacturers of the 40mm Bofors gun, Firestone and Koppers. Eaton and Timken were normally fierce rivals. Now the subcontracting web of defense work made them partners, and pooled their talents to get the Army on the move.[21]

In Elyria, Ohio, Knudsen visited General Industries, a company with twelve hundred employees, of whom only 20 percent were engaged in wartime work assembling M48 artillery fuses (this was in early 1942). With present and new orders, that was expected to jump to 50 percent—while the major parts for the fuses were themselves subcontracted. The rest of the company's work was on miscellaneous plastic products. Knudsen made a note that Army Ordnance had just approved three plastic parts to replace metal ones for a trench mortar fuse. Why not, he suggested, have those parts made here?[22]

The one thing Knudsen and the Army could *not* do, of course, was order General Industries or any other company to make the things they needed. The lines of Washington's control over the economy had been carefully drawn. It intervened to affect the *consumption* of civilian goods, some of which were rationed, such as meat and gasoline and coffee, and others made according to their place in the system of priorities. It also regulated wages and, to a more limited degree, prices.

Production, however, remained an entirely voluntary process. The War Production Board could and did order companies *not* to produce things: new cars, for instance, and refrigerators and other heavy durable goods. It never told anyone *what* to make. That was left to the imagination of American business.

This was how Bill Knudsen had designed things from the start, and it remained the pivot point of the entire wartime system. Everything made for the war effort was made by those who saw some advantage for themselves in doing so, and therefore they brought all their skills and tools and knowledge to bear on the task—both to help the country and to make some money. This drove the New Dealers crazy, but it was what Adam Smith had recognized a century and a half before as the cornerstone of capitalism, when he wrote, "It is not from the benevolence of the butcher, the brewer, or the baker, that we can expect our dinner, but from their regard to their own interest." The same was true when it came to making planes and ships and artillery shells in record numbers.

And Americans, by and large, accepted what might be termed the generosity of selfishness. "The public believes in the profit system," asserted J. B. Hartley, director of the National Association of Manufacturers, and "they do not believe in war" as a substitute.[23] This offended those who believed that war without self-sacrifice lacked a certain moral standing. What they couldn't change, however, was their reliance on a collaboration between businesses large and small forged years before by the free market, a system so complex and so constantly changing that no government agency could ever have devised a system to supervise—let alone plan out—the result.

When, for example, General Motors subcontractor Yellow Truck and Coach Company was under contract to the Timken–Detroit Axle Company, at the same time Timken was under contract to Yellow, because Yellow also made an essential component that Timken needed to make the axles it sent back to Yellow to make the wheel assemblies, which it then forwarded on to a General Motors plant to complete a military truck. When these interrelationships were multiplied by a thousand, and then ten thousand, it was hard to see how any top-down command system could have kept effective track of all the moving parts.[24]

Nor was it entirely a coincidence that no other wartime economy depended more on free enterprise incentives than America's, and that none produced more of everything in quality and quantity, both in military and civilian goods.

The process kicked off even before the war began in the spring of 1941, when a magazine such as *Business Week* began running stories on how to snag defense contracts by conversion to wartime production. It offered advice in answer to queries like "I would like to sell some shovels to the Army, but its purchases run to much larger quantities than I can handle," or "We have a canning plant which will probably be idle and could be used for war contracts. Can you tell us how to contact the proper parties?"[25] There was advice on where to write in order to get government loans to help with conversion: the RFC or the Defense Contracts Division of OPM. In addition, it said, the Army and Navy both made advances of up to 30 percent for prime contractors. *Business Week* also offered free advice on what materials to use as substitutes for those too hard to get for civilian production: plastic for aluminum film spools, say, or cast iron for brass bicycle locks. Human ingenuity could solve problems that government planning or rationing could not.

When war came, the scramble for defense contracts produced an extraordinary book published by the Research Institute of America, called *Your Business Goes to War*.[26] Page by page it told firms whom to contact for getting a government contract and how to draft one up. It explained where and how to get critical materials, how to work with the priority system, and how to deal with labor under the new wartime laws such as the rules concerning overtime. It offered several pages of suggestions on what products a company could offer to make. (See Appendix B)

If, for example, you made vacuum cleaners, there might be a place for you manufacturing gas-mask parts. A razor manufacturer might want to look into percussion primers for artillery shells; an office furniture company, into making bomb containers. A shoe company could make helmet linings; a maker of bottle caps and bottlers could turn out .50-caliber tripod mounts; while a lawn mower company might offer to machine shrapnel.[27]

Other companies have already done it, was the message. You can do it, too. "There is an alternative," its author added in the preface. "It is the shouted order, the broadcast ultimatum, the decision made by an unchallengeable Führer" in which "the executive becomes a clerk in the national warehouse." No one wanted that. But there was also another implicit message: Those companies who adapt to the new wartime conditions will survive and even thrive. Those who do not will not.

To that degree, wartime conditions reproduced important features of peacetime market conditions. The Army and Navy were like classic customers: demanding, even finicky, and reluctant to pay except for exceptional service. Contracts flowed to those who could produce at the most competitive rate—and after 1943 both services could force producers to renegotiate contracts if they thought the profits or costs excessive.[28] There were no favored state industries as in Nazi Germany or Japan. No state subsidy was on hand to save the incompetent or underperformer. But on the other hand, a raft of timely government loans could leapfrog a newcomer over his staid competitors. In wartime as in peacetime, entrepreneurs challenged the old established firms, as Henry Kaiser and a dozen others proved. The small and nimble rose up to compete with the large and slow-moving.

This rule didn't just apply to existing business. The war produced more than half a million *new* businesses, which became the hinge of change from the prewar to the postwar economy.[29]

There was, for example, Frank Hobbs and his partner George Comstock. Hobbs had grown up in California before moving to Portland, Oregon, to open his own Firestone tire dealership when he was barely out of his teens. Then, in the teeth of the Depression, Hobbs launched his own company to produce Masonite wallboard using superhard paint finishes as a substitute for more expensive tile. Soon he had perfected a process and substance he called Colotyle. It became a low-cost alternative to tile in kitchens and bathrooms up and down the West Coast. Henry Kaiser even used it for the heads in his Liberty ships.

The coming of war was for Hobbs just another business opportunity. In the spring of 1942, someone showed him the bulky, steel-ribbed shelters the Army was shipping out from Quonset, Rhode Island, for troops who would have to serve in the frozen wastes of Alaska. Hobbs was shocked. The huts were not only awkward and heavy to ship, but wasted that all-important critical wartime material, steel. He and his business partner George Comstock came up with the idea of a lightweight version made of hard-coated wood—a sturdy plywood igloo. Three weeks later they showed a model to the Army Corps of Engineers, Seattle District, who immediately ordered eighty-five more test huts. In no time Pacific Huts, with Hobbs as president and Comstock as vice president, had a contract for one thousand.[30]

What they needed now was a factory. They found it in a run-down industrial area just half a mile from Boeing's Seattle plant, at 6901 Fox Avenue South. They raised $100,000 from local bankers and in sixty days converted the old shipyard into an assembly line for making their huts. Five hundred employees built the sixteen-by-thirty-foot hut using Masonite, spruce or hemlock ribs, and plywood floors, complete with electrical wiring. Each was tall enough (nine feet at the center) for a man to stand in, and each could be assembled by five soldiers in eight hours.

Soon Hobbs's employees were turning out a completed hut every fifteen minutes and packing them up for shipment. In September 1943, Hobbs ran an ad in Seattle newspapers boasting of how his huts were two months ahead of schedule, thanks to employees' suggestions on how to boost production. The ads showed the names and faces of twenty-seven employees who had streamlined the process—each of whom also received a war bond as a reward.

Hobbs's Fox Avenue factory turned out more than 12,000 Pacific huts before the war ended. In Alaska thousands were left where they were erected when the Army withdrew. For four decades they stood forgotten and abandoned through snow, rain, and ice storms. Then in the 1990s the Pentagon sent out their Defense Environmental Restoration Program to survey the sites for demolition. They found that not only had Hobbs's huts weathered the decades better than the steel Quonsets, but most of them were intact and still livable.[31]

Ted Nelson had been an eleven-dollar-a-day welder in the Mare Island Navy Yard in 1940 doing standard welding chores, including the ten thousand upright studs on an average-sized naval vessel. It was a laborious process, in which Nelson had to melt the proper amount of flux before setting each stud. He retreated to his garage and experimented with a device that would perform both tasks at once. He called it his "rocket gun," and showed it to his amazed superiors. A fast welder working the old-fashioned way could do forty studs in an hour. Nelson's rocket gun did one thousand in the exact the same time.

Tom Nelson began selling versions of his rocket guns out of his garage to shipyards for $500 each. Then, with $95,000 he borrowed from Jesse Jones and the RFC, he created the Nelson Specialty Welding Equipment Corporation and built a plant in a cornfield near San Leandro. By war's end he was supplying his guns and other welding tools to more than one hundred shipyards up and down the West Coast, including the Kaiser yards at Richmond and Portland and the Bechtel-McCone yards at Calship.[32]

If businessmen like Hobbs and Nelson and Frank Ix and the managers of Manitowoc Shipbuilding were the living, beating heart of wartime production, its new workforce was the blood transfusion that kept it flowing and growing.

War production had triggered the greatest mass migration in American history.

At least 20 million Americans left their homes to find work in the new and old plants. At the end of the war, 15.3 million of them were living someplace other than where they were the day Pearl Harbor was bombed. As in the era of the covered wagons, Americans followed the call of opportunity—in this case opportunities created not by the birth of a nation but by the rebirth of American industry. If business profits rose during the war, labor's wages rose much more—an average of 70 percent.[33] It was either a very happy or very complacent worker who wouldn't get himself and his family on the road for wages like that.

At least seven million left America's farms, especially in the South.[34] Five and half million of those went to work in factories and cities; the rest went into the military. But instead of this being a disaster for the nation's ability to feed itself, farm payrolls fell by only a million.[35] Because if farmers were fewer on the ground, they were far from idle. They turned to mechanization and chemical fertilizers to make their acres more productive, so much so they also expanded pasturage for livestock by 22 percent. Some complained that Washington's restrictions on manufacture of machinery like tractors and harvesters made conversion that much harder. Some lamented that the big farms were devouring the small inefficient ones as well as the abandoned homesteads.[36]

But it was this concentration and mechanization that made it possible for American farmers to feed not only their own country better than it had been fed before the Depression, but their Allies, as well. By the time the war was over, they were ready to feed a devastated Europe for almost five years. After that, they would go on to feed the world.[37]

The biggest beneficiaries of the demographic shift from country to city were African Americans. Almost one million left the old states of the Confederacy for points north and west.[38] Another half million went into uniform.

Their passage into mainstream American life got an enormous boost on June 25, 1941, when Roosevelt issued an executive order calling for an end to employment discrimination based on race, color, or creed in the nation's growing defense industries. The idea came from A. Philip Randolph, head of the powerful railway porters' union, which he founded when no other union in the country would accept black railway workers. He had campaigned hard for the order with both the White House and Bill Knudsen as head of OPM.

Knudsen fully supported Randolph on desegregation. When the war effort truly hit its stride, he knew America's factories were going to need those additional black workers. But Knudsen still felt the best way to go about it was through "quiet work with the contractors and work-ers," as he put it, rather than executive fiat. Once employers realized that hiring black workers would work, they would come around.[39]

Randolph, however, was adamant. Recognizing the Negroes' equal right to work and serve in uniform, he wrote Knudsen, was partly what American democracy was all about. To Roosevelt he wrote a very dif-ferent letter. He was prepared, he told the president on May 29, to mobilize "from ten to fifty thousand Negroes to march on Washington in the interest of securing jobs . . . in national defense" as well as inte-gration in the armed forces.[40]

Roosevelt sensed a looming public relations disaster both for himself and for the Democratic Party, which was becoming increasingly suc-cessful in poaching black voters away from the Republicans, in spite of the Democrats' record supporting segregation in the Deep South. The president tried to get his wife, Eleanor, an acknowledged civil rights champion, Mayor Fiorello La Guardia, and others to talk Randolph out of the march. Nothing could move the black union leader. So finally, facing the prospect of a flood of black protesters flooding the National Mall and surrounding the Lincoln Memorial, Roosevelt backed down. He issued Executive Order 8802 six days before the march was sup-posed to start. Randolph graciously canceled the day of protest.

To Randolph and others, it was a historic moment—and a foretaste of the civil rights struggle that was to come. The order, however, had its limits. The armed forces remained segregated right up to the war's end. The committee FDR set up to oversee discrimination was likewise limited in its powers. Southern politicians closed it down as soon as the war ended. It's not clear whether Knudsen's approach might not have worked better.[41]

The results were certainly uneven. Henry Kaiser hired blacks in his shipyards, but few found jobs working on ships. Most did peripheral jobs, such as the road gang of blacks from Louisiana Clay Bedford em-ployed for paving roads around and through the Richmond complex.[42] Roy Grumman hired blacks and whites without discrimination, while Glenn Martin's Baltimore plant continued to be segregated. So was the Bethlehem-Fairfield shipyard. General Motors' Eastern Aircraft plant down the road, on the other hand, was not.

By and large, labor unions fought hard to keep the African Americans out. Even supposedly "progressive" CIO-affiliated unions like the Boilermakers made life miserable for blacks in workplaces like the Kaiser Richmond yards.[43] For some white workers, the presence of blacks in their midst, even in subordinate jobs, was jarring. Having them promoted could be infuriating. In Mobile a riot broke out at Moore Drydock when white workers learned African Americans were about to be upgraded as welders. In Beaumont, Texas, a riot left two dead before the state police and federal troops restored order.[44]

Still, hiring blacks to do "white men's work" signaled the emergence of a new American social compact where skill and content of character mattered more than skin color. It was no surprise that it drove up racial tensions in the South. But when you took a northern industrial city and combined a large influx of black workers with a larger influx of southern Appalachian whites who weren't used to dealing with blacks without the reassuring cushion of Jim Crow, then threw in some sweltering summer heat, you had a recipe for racial meltdown—as the people of Detroit found out.[45] /

There had been signs of trouble before that weekend of June 1943— the week before MacArthur launched his offensive to retake New Guinea in the South Pacific, and two weeks before the invasion of Sicily. In February 1942 a group of black families tried to move into a housing development for defense workers. They were met by a mob of three hundred whites armed with stones and clubs. The police moved in but fighting broke out between growing angry crowds of blacks and whites. Thirty people were injured, and over one hundred arrested.

Detroit's mayor tried to calm his city. "If we are one people," he declared, "the Negroes should go into the project."[46] They finally did, but only with the protection of state militiamen. What the police and mayor and state militia couldn't control broke loose the weekend of June 20 the next year.

Rumors that black teenagers had thrown a white man off a bridge on Belle Isle, the city park in the Detroit River, set off a murderous conflagration that tore through the city for two days. Roving gangs of whites, mostly teenagers, rampaged through the city killing blacks and setting cars and businesses on fire. Black gangs attacked whites. "There were about two hundred of us in cars," one sixteen-year-old white boy remembered. "We killed eight [blacks]. . . . I saw knives being stuck through their throats and heads being shot through. . . . It really was some riot."[47] Before federal troops poured onto the streets to restore order, 34 people were dead, 25 blacks and 9 whites. More than 670 were injured. Detroit, the original arsenal of democracy, was shrouded in national disgrace.

Another riot broke out in New York City in August. It killed seven and injured scores more. If winning the war was the issue that could pull America together, race was still the one that could pull it apart.

Executive Order 8802 had banned discrimination in defense employment based on race, color, religion, or creed—but not sex. Women were the one group *not* protected by Washington.* Yet they would gain the biggest foothold in the American workplace during the war.

At first companies and male workers had their doubts about hiring women, especially for industrial jobs. They had no understanding of machinery, went the argument. They'd be exhausted by any heavy duties, and they'd be a distraction to men on the job. Besides, no factories had women's washrooms.[48]

Almost from the start, however, employers began to reverse their thinking. As early as the spring of 1941, articles in magazines like *American Machinist* and *Business Week* told of women being trained to handle even the most complex machinery. Still, a photo of a class of trainees for a leading aviation company at about the same time shows not a single female—yet.[49]

All that was about to change. Bill Knudsen was present when the first twenty-five women went into the Consolidated-Vultee plant, on March 31, 1941. They were put to work in the electrical subassembly division, and started a day earlier than planned. The manager feared that if they had started the day their training was supposed to end, on April 1, everybody else would think it was an April Fools joke.[50]

---

* The exception was a ruling by the War Labor Board in September 1942 dictating equal pay for equal work in defense work.

Once the women set to work, however, the joke was on the males. The ladies of Vultee showed enormous skill at the subassemblies, running, threading, connecting, and checking electrical cables. Women had "lighter fingers," as Knudsen put it, that sometimes was as vital in manufacturing as the heavy lifting.[51]

North American was impressed enough that they began substituting women for men in their tubing department. Production jumped by 20 percent. Before long, everyone was hiring women for other departments, and they ran milling machines, drill presses, and complex cutout saws and worked in aircraft engine assembling. They could also squeeze into places men couldn't in airplane assemblies, such as the nose cone and tail section, to do spot welding or riveting or snapping in the electrical system.

By July 1944, 36 percent of all workers in prime defense contractors were female. And not just in aviation. In the end their numbers rose to nearly five million, doing every conceivable form of war work from making planes to building ships and tanks. In iron and steel companies, 22.3 percent of the workforce were women. At GM they were 30.7 percent of all hourly wage earners by the end of 1943, and in the Kaiser yards at Richmond they numbered 70 percent.[52]

The press and the nation elevated them to heroic status, as Rosie the Riveter. Norman Rockwell painted her for the May 29, 1943, cover of *The Saturday Evening Post* sitting at lunch in her overalls, with her riveting gun on her lap—and her foot mashing a copy of *Mein Kampf* into the dust. Lockheed launched a publicity campaign around "Rosie the Riveter, the Girl from Lockheed" when the photo of one their workers, tall, dark-haired Vera Lowe, appeared in *Life* magazine in goggles and wielding a riveting gun.[53] Artist J. Howard Miller thought he had found her archetype when he spotted a photo of a seventeen-year-old metal press worker at American Broach and Machine named Geraldine Huff. His poster for the Ad Council showing her wearing a polka-dot bandanna and flexing her muscle with the caption "We Can Do It!" turned her into a national icon.

But the attention directed at Rosie obscured the fact that millions more women *didn't* use a riveting gun, metal press, or welding torch. They cooked meals for defense plants, worked in defense contractors' offices as stenographers and bookkeepers and telephone operators, and did a hundred other jobs. Rockwell based his Rosie on May Doyle, a nineteen-year-old phone operator in a dentist's office in Arlington, Massachusetts. As for Miller's Rosie, Geraldine Huff, she quit American Broach after six months—to go study the violin. /

Women made gas masks for the Army, life rafts for the Navy and Coast Guard, and wove and stuffed parachutes for the Army Air Forces and airborne divisions. One of those parachute stuffers was a pretty brunette named Norma Jean Dougherty, who was barely seventeen and worked in an aircraft parts plant in Burbank, California, while her husband was in the Merchant Marine. In 1943 an Army newsreel team commanded by Captain Ronald Reagan spotted her and asked her to pose for some pictures. The photos of her in *Yank* magazine caused such a sensation that the Army used her as a model for several more shoots. After the war Norma Jean took her photos to a modeling agency and moved to Hollywood. There she dyed her hair blond and took a new name: Marilyn Monroe.[54]

For millions of other women, the discipline of the job was reward enough. New York writer Augusta Clawson found that out when she moved to California to work in Richmond Yard No. 1. The account of her days there, *The Shipyard Diary of a Woman Welder,* was the surprise bestseller of 1944 and gave many people, including other women, their first glimpse into the reality of Rosie the Riveter.

Clawson described signing up for training, and the advice given her by her "Job Counselor," also a woman, dressed in pink with gray hair and a youngish face. "Get gloves," Clawson was told, "you *have* to have them." The school was going to provide her helmet and goggles, but she had to buy her own welding leathers.[55]

"It gets plenty cold out there," the counselor also warned her, referring to the No. 1 shipways. "You can wear slacks and put coveralls over them; then you can take the coveralls off and you won't feel so dirty." And *don't* wear a watch: "the rays of the welding will magnetize its works."[56]

Training classes were under the stern eye of Mr. Dunn, who showed his ladies how to adjust the amperage and voltage of the welding machine and then turned them loose to practice for three to four hours at a stretch, with breaks for lectures on safety. At the end of her first day, Clawson barely had enough energy to eat an apple back in her hotel room before she fell asleep.

But she would grow used to it, just as she would grow used to rising at 5 A.M. every morning to catch the bus down to the Richmond yard and the ways. There she met her fellow laborers, both men and women, who came from every part of the country, and she described her pride when she had completed her first full week of work.

"Something has happened," she wrote, "I don't know quite what it is, but after work today I suddenly realized that I had no dread or fear any more in connection with this job."[57] When she had started, she had been terrified of heights. But now she felt comfortable climbing up a ladder high above the factory floor and stretching out on a board suspended between two uprights welded to overhead beams. "Imagine me," she wrote, "lying like suspended animation way above the floor ('scuse, I mean deck), resting comfortably and singing to myself."[58] Her fear of heights was gone, as was her lack of confidence about doing manual labor. It was a moment of emancipation as meaningful, perhaps, as any brought by the Nineteenth Amendment.

Written under the gaze of the wartime censor, Clawson's account of life in the ways was clearly positive. Katherine Archibald, a liberal sociologist, went to work in the Moore Dry Dock in Oakland hoping to find a nation united in the war effort. Instead she found a boiling cauldron of tensions. Men resented women, whites disdained blacks, old-settler African Americans resented the new "brothers," and the native Californians hated them all. Fights and brawls and slacking on the job were common. She also found the steady barrage of sex jokes demeaning and saw them as undermining "business-like relationships between men and women" on the job.[59]

The rough edge of life in the yards shocked and disillusioned Archibald. Later historians and feminists would be disappointed by the failure of women to achieve full equality of pay and promotion, and be disappointed by the fact that so many would quit their jobs after the war.

But most women who worked in the arsenal of democracy were not out for gender transformation. They were shamelessly conventional.

They would do their jobs, and appreciate the opportunity to earn some pay and serve their country. But the moment they looked forward to was the reunion with fathers and sons and brothers and husbands.

None would forget that moment when one of their co-workers would arrive in the morning with a crumpled telegram in their fist and tears in his or her eyes as they mumbled, "It's about my son . . ."[60] Most would appreciate the words of Katie Grant, who worked the graveyard shift for two years in the Richmond yards while her husband was in the Marines.

"I told Melvin later," she recalled years later, "that I helped to make the ship for him to come home in."[61]

CHAPTER FIFTEEN

THE MAN FROM FRISCO

Henry Kaiser cartoon from the *Phoenix Republic and Gazette*, circa 1943. *Courtesy of the Bancroft Library, University of California, Berkeley*

> You can't work as hard as I am getting production
> and pay any attention to personal relations.
> —*Henry Kaiser, June 22, 1943*

AS FOR HENRY Kaiser, he was sitting on top of the world.

The entrepreneur *Business Week* described as "the Man of Mystery" back in March 1941 was a mystery no longer. "He's terrific; he's colossal; he's completely unbelievable," gushed respected news commentator

Frazier Hunt in a CBS broadcast. "He's the master Doer of the world."[1]
Kaiser's bald head with its spectacles and irrepressible grin was plastered
across the covers of magazines and inside newspapers. Every other
month, it seemed, *Life* or *Time* or *Fortune* ran a featured story on the
Kaiser phenomenon; in January 1943, the *New York Times* called him
the Paul Bunyan of the age with his own three giant blue oxen in harness: Imagination, Organization, and Perspiration. A schoolteacher in
South Carolina asked her class if they knew which face launched a
thousand ships (referring to Helen of Troy in Christopher Marlowe's
Doctor Faustus). One boy's hand shot up. "Henry Kaiser," he said
proudly.[2]

In the spring of 1943, that larger-than-life reputation was about to
be turned loose on the U.S. Navy.

Under Navy undersecretary and Dillon, Read, investment banker
James Forrestal, the Navy was already embarked on the biggest shipbuilding program in history. From a force in 1939 still trapped in a
hemispheric defense mentality, it was now in effect a seven-ocean navy,
engaged in operations from Alaska and the Aleutians to Greenland, the
North and South Atlantic, and across the Pacific to the Indian Ocean
and Persian Gulf. The five biggest shipbuilding firms in the country
were filled with orders for battleships, cruisers, carriers, destroyers, and
destroyer escorts, while companies like Electric Boat in Groton were
building submarines in record numbers.

Events in the Pacific in 1942, however, had forced a major change in
thinking. The battles of Coral Sea and Midway had proved the value of
the aircraft carrier as the fleet's primary capital ship—even as battle
losses shrank that force from six to four. At the same time, both the
British and American fleets in the Atlantic saw the value of carriers for
convoy protection. From Atlantic to Pacific, the push was on for
carriers—not just the 34,800-ton monsters of the *Essex* class like *Yorktown* and *Intrepid,* but smaller carriers that could be built faster to fill
the gap.[3]

The result was the so-called *Independence* class of less than 15,000
tons, which could carry nine TBM Avenger torpedo planes and
twenty-four new Hellcat fighters, compared to the nearly one hundred
aircraft on a *Yorktown* or *Bunker Hill*. Likewise, Sun Shipbuilding and

Dry Dock in Chester, Pennsylvania, was converting old oil tankers into the 23,350-ton *Sagamon* class.[4]

Even this, however, was not enough. The Navy decided they would need something still smaller that could be built in one-quarter of the time of the *Independence* class—and since the yards were running out of hulls to convert, it would have to be designed from scratch.

In May 1942 the Navy posed their problem to the Maritime Commission's Admiral Land, who came up with what he thought was the perfect solution. Let Henry Kaiser do it.

It made sense. Kaiser was the reigning king of Liberty shipbuilding. By the start of 1943, he would cut the labor hours required for building a ship nearly in half, from 640,000 in March 1941 to 352,000. He had proven his engineers' ability to work from a completely new design. So why not turn him loose on escort carriers?[5]

Henry himself loved the idea. When Land wired him with the Navy's suggestion, he enthusiastically assented. Here was the company's chance to make ships that would not only supply the war, but fight it. It was also just the kind of production challenge his son Edgar would shine at. By March 1943, he said, Vancouver could switch all twelve ways over to aircraft carriers.[6] /

Kaiser turned to a design agent, George Sharp, to come up with the preliminary drawings. After consultations with both the Navy and the Maritime Commission, the proposed design met the construction specifications of both. Four hundred and ninety feet long and displacing 6,890 tons, it actually had a longer flight deck than the *Independence* carriers, although Seattle's conversion jobs were much bigger ships. There wasn't a single turbine or diesel engine available anywhere: They were all going to other warships. So Kaiser's designer opted for a five-cylinder reciprocating steam engine, which could deliver 5400 horsepower on each of its two propeller shafts.[7]

Simple, compact, easy to build—those were the hallmarks of the Kaiser shipbuilding philosophy and of his proposed new carrier. On June 2, 1942, he headed out to Washington to do the presentation to the Navy personally. All he needed was eighteen minutes, his lawyer Chad Calhoun had told Admiral Ernest King and the other Navy brass.

Kaiser delivered the proposal with his characteristic gusto, complete

with full-color drawings of the proposed ships and sheaves of engineering data. He summed things up by asking for a cost-plus contract
for one hundred CVEs, or escort carriers. He told King that six months
after the start of production, he'd have thirty ships ready to go to sea.[8]

Henry Kaiser stepped out of the room to await their decision. When
they called him back in, however, he was in for a shock. The Navy had
decided to turn him down. The vote was unanimous, sixteen to zero.

He and Calhoun left the Navy Building in stunned disbelief. The
Navy had explained that it felt the design was too flimsy to stand up to
enemy bombs and torpedoes. They also felt there were enough *Independence* and *Sagamon* class CVEs already on order. But there was also another reason they didn't mention.

The Navy wanted escort carriers, but they did not want Henry Kaiser.[9] His reputation as a showboat and prima donna had preceded him
and sunk his chances. The Navy wanted the focus to be on the ships,
not the shipbuilder. For once, Kaiser's ability to dominate the limelight
had proved a liability, not an asset.

A dejected Kaiser and Calhoun walked down the street in the heavy
Washington heat. Then Calhoun caught sight of a mutual friend, Mor-
decai Ezekiel. Ezekiel was also a Washington lawyer, and a friend of
President Roosevelt. As they exchanged greetings and shook hands,
Kaiser had an idea.

"Look here," he said, "the Navy has just turned down my proposal
to build them a series of small aircraft carriers."

Ezekiel expressed his condolences. "Mind if I have a look?" he
asked.[10]

They were standing on the sidewalk across from the Mall. Kaiser
suggested they stretch out the plans and data on the grass. Soon three
men in business suits were sitting on the lawn, surrounded by graphs
and drawings. Kaiser explained the strengths of the design. How the
flight deck was suited to quick operations; how the ship's turn radius
was amazingly tight ("practically a square corner" was Kaiser's phrase),
allowing it to outmaneuver those enemy bombs and torpedoes; and
how it could be built quickly without interfering with other shipyards.

Ezekiel was impressed. The president ought to see this, he told them.
"Can you keep yourselves available for a call later?" he asked. Kaiser

and Calhoun enthusiastically said yes. They returned to the Shoreham and waited. That evening, sure enough, the phone rang. It was Ezekiel. The three of them were to meet President Roosevelt at the White House in the morning.[11]

There Kaiser found not just the president but Admiral King and his aides, and Admiral Land. Roosevelt didn't just like the idea, he was now convinced Kaiser could do anything. With the president's intervention, the Navy relented and the contracts were signed. The one condition was that Land and the Maritime Commission, *not* the Navy, would supervise construction and the final design. That way the Navy had an out if the first of Kaiser's "baby flattops," as they would be called, came out of the slip and sank to the bottom of the ocean.

Their fears were misplaced. By March 1943, Edgar Kaiser had assembled a team ready for the most complex shipbuilding project Oregon Shipbuilding had ever undertaken.[12] As for Portland itself across the river, it was no longer the staid sawmill town Edgar first visited two years earlier. The Kaiser yards had brought in more than 100,000 workers and counting. Chartered trains brought people in from Texas, Oklahoma, and Louisiana, including thousands of African Americans. Every third person in town was a newcomer.[13]

Almost the rest of Oregon was emptied of workers, both men and women, who came looking for jobs in the Portland facility or Vancouver or Swan Island. One local employee was teenaged Patricia Cain Koehler, who signed up with a girlfriend to be electrician's helpers. After a couple of weeks' training, they graduated as journeymen electricians at $1.20 per hour.

"We celebrated by applying for jobs on the hookup crews, which worked aboard ships at the outfitting dock." Her first ship was one of the new baby flattops. "I was assigned to fire control. That meant guns! My leadman had never had a female working for him, and he was skeptical. [But] like a shadow, I followed his every move, anticipating what tool he needed next and handing it to him before he could ask. After a few days of this he relaxed and began teaching me the ropes . . . or rather the wires."

Working forty-five feet above the water, she had constant reminders of how dangerous the job could be. "Occasionally I looked down into

the swift current of the Columbia River and noticed small boats drag-
ging for a worker who had fallen in." Cain's own work wasn't without
mishap. Once she stumbled on a ladder clogged with rubber-hosed
welding leads and broke a toe. Another, more serious fall smashed an
elbow, and she "learned to work left-handed."[14]

The work progressed, but not at the pace Kaiser had confidently
predicted. He had hoped to deliver the first four by February 1943 and
have the rest done by the end of the year. The first delivery wasn't until
July. But Kaiser didn't care. On March 12, 1943, he had a special meeting at the White House and presented FDR with a glass-encased model
of the new aircraft carrier. Deeply pleased, Roosevelt agreed to have
Eleanor christen the very first baby flattop.[15]

On April 5 the First Lady smashed a bottle of champagne across the
bow of the USS *Alazon Bay*. Henry Kaiser's first aircraft carrier, with its
characteristic flat bow and stern, slid into the Columbia River. Micro-
phones carried Mrs. Roosevelt's remarks to the assembled throng. "The
president is greatly interested in this type of ship," she told them. "He
has sent Mr. Kaiser his very best wishes and hellos to the workmen."
The *Oregonian* reported she also said the Vancouver Kaiser yard was the
"neatest and tidiest I have ever seen, and everyone seemed busy at his
or her particular job."[16] She praised the dormitories of Hudson House,*
which the Kaiser people had erected for their workers, and the planned
community of Vanport City taking shape across the river. By May there
would be almost 19,000 people living in Vanport along with a 750-seat
theater, gyms and playgrounds, five new schools, a combined fire and
police station, and a 250-bed hospital—where the workers' bills were
paid, as with Richmond workers, by the health care package that took
its name from Kaiser's mining company: Kaiser Permanente. It was also
desegregated by law.[17]

Meanwhile, the Liberty ships were still coming down the Portland
slips as rapidly as before. The *B. F. Shaw*, the *Simon Bolivar, Louis Agassiz,
Gilbert Stuart, De Witt Clinton* (completed as the *Sevastapol* in tribute to
America's Soviet ally), and the *Richard Harding Davis:* seventeen in April

---

* Given its inhabitants, it was a tough place. Daily and nightly brawls earned the
hostel another name: Hoodlum House.

alone, or more than four a week (the last, Hull No. 671, would still be sailing in 1967). There was a story about a woman who had been asked to christen a Portland yard ship but arrived too late; it had already been launched. "Just keep standing there, ma'am," she was told, "there'll be another along in a minute."[18]

By now Kaiser's reputation was so big Hollywood got into the act. "Ahead of Him Success! Back of Him . . . A Woman!" That was the tagline for a movie Republic Pictures put together loosely based on Kaiser's career, called *The Man from Frisco*. Starring Michael O'Shea and Anne Shirley, it concerned a hard-charging engineer with some revolutionary ideas about shipbuilding. To call it a fictionalized portrayal would be criminal understatement.

> NOTHING'S IMPOSSIBLE for this red-headed tornado! He launched
> ships by the thousands . . . and had a love affair to go with each!

The growing legend of Henry Kaiser, however, left less and less space for the rest of the Six Companies. Kaiser had pulled away from his old partners. They hadn't joined him in his Fontana steel venture, and they played no part in his future plans. When Steve Bechtel wrote a note hoping they could meet and talk "just as we have in the good old days," Kaiser didn't answer.[19]

Kaiser was on his own, and on his way to the top. Franklin Roosevelt even began to wonder if the man from Frisco might be the perfect running mate in the presidential election in 1944.[20]

Yet just as the adulation reached its height, Henry Kaiser learned how easy it was for the bubble of media reputation to burst.

On the night of January 16, 1943, a Saturday, a new oil tanker, the *Schenectady*, was sitting peacefully at the outfitting dock at Kaiser's newest Portland yard, Swan Island. She was the first vessel built in that yard, and had just completed her seat trials when the entire crew was awakened by a terrible metallic bang. When they investigated, they found a massive crack had split across the deck and down both sides all the way to bottom shell plating. No one had a clue about what had happened.[21]

Then on February 12, the Liberty ship *Henry Wynkoop* split apart as she was being loaded in New York Harbor. At about the same time, two other Liberty ships cracked at sea. Then on March 29, another oil tanker, the *Esso Manhattan,* was leaving New York Harbor when it too suddenly broke in two. Her crew, thinking she had hit a mine, abandoned ship. It was only later that it was discovered that she was part of the same mysterious series of catastrophic failures.

Kaiser had been the nation's master shipbuilder. Overnight some wondered if he was also a careless one. The *Esso Manhattan* had been built by Sun Shipbuilding and Dry Dock, one of the country's biggest and most experienced yards; the *Wynkoop* by Delta. But the story the papers carried was about the Kaiser yard's *Schenectady.* Calls for investigation began. How much of our new 24 million tons of merchant shipping, critics were asking, was actually going to fall apart at sea thanks to Kaiser's slipshod methods?

"No one will deny that speed is needed in the construction and delivery of ships," the *Journal of Commerce* solemnly opined. "However, no matter how speedily a ship is delivered its worth is practically nil if its plates crack."[22]

The Maritime Commission also weighed in, with Admiral Vickery flying out to Portland in the middle of a snowstorm the day after the accident. Realizing the seriousness of the problem, he asked the civilian American Bureau of Shipping to appoint an independent subcommittee to investigate. What they found caused a sigh of relief—at least at first. The bureau's experts found that the accident was the result of "an accumulation of an abnormal amount of internal stress locked into the structure by the processes used in construction," including defective welding. They concluded "closer control of welding procedure . . . will prevent a recurrence of such major failures."[23]

Vickery made the changes. He canceled the use of automatic welding machines on main strength points, ordered crack arresters to be installed at key junctures in the ship's joints, and mandated design changes including separating the bulwarks from the top of the hull and bridging the gap with riveted stiffeners. The *Schenectady* was hauled out of the silt, repaired and refloated, and went on to a long, distinguished career as a tanker.[24]

Meanwhile, the Liberty ships kept cracking.

The public and Congress began to demand answers. Was it really poor welding, as the Bureau of Shipping claimed? Was it defects in the steel? the Truman Committee wanted to know. Or was it something else Kaiser was doing in his haste to build ships that was making them unsafe? And the headlines blared, ANOTHER SHIP FALLS APART.

Some suspected a whitewash of the politically popular Kaiser. John Green of the CIO's Industrial Union of Marine and Shipbuilding Workers angrily asked, "Has the Maritime Commission revealed all of the instances of Kaiser-built ships cracking up?"[25] Kaiser fired back that ships owned by the steel companies themselves had suffered the major cracks, and "we likewise have had some others, which have been minor ones." It was also pointed out that cracks were appearing on riveted ships, but the suspicions still fell on the welding—and on Kaiser.[26]

That July a special subcommittee of the House Committee on Merchant Marine and Fisheries weighed in, chaired by a freshman congressman from Washington State named Henry M. Jackson—"Scoop" to his friends. Jackson pointed out that only two out of more than a thousand Liberty ships had actually been lost, with no loss of life. Neither of the two, *Thomas Hooker* and *J.L.M. Curry,* had been built in Kaiser yards. The Truman Committee cleared Kaiser of any malfeasance and pronounced the Liberty ship "the truck horse of the fleet."[27] No one suggested stopping the building program, let alone halting Kaiser's own operations.

But rumors continued right to the end of the war, and afterward. With wartime censorship, who knew how many ships were lost the government *wasn't* telling us about?

In the winter of 1943–44, there were still more cracks, including several from Kaiser's Portland and Vancouver yards. One mariner said, "You could hear them crack like gunshots. And the cracks, once started, run like a woman's stocking."[28]

The fact was, no one knew exactly what was wrong, until many years later. The Bureau of Shipping's final word on the subject was published in 1947, when it became clear the problem wasn't Kaiser's welds but the steel they held together. The Bureau found that notches in certain welded ships tended to crack in the icy cold waters of the North Pacific and Arctic, due to rapid temperature change. The steel of the day suffered from a phenomenon known as "embrittlement," and was vulnerable to cracking under low-temperature, high-load conditions, and with constant rolling stress—like a rolling ship. And since so many of Kaiser's ships had served duty in the frigid North Atlantic and Pacific, they had been particularly vulnerable. One such ship, the Portland yard's *John P. Gaines,* had sunk in the North Atlantic with a loss of eleven hands in December 1942 before anyone knew anything about cracking.[29] Another fifteen sailors died when the *John W. Straub* broke apart in Arctic waters and went down in 1944.

Twenty-six deaths out of the tens of thousands of sailors who sailed in Liberty ships and out of the thousands who died in ships sunk by enemy submarines and aircraft and surface ships, 8 ships lost out of 2,744 made. Meanwhile, hundreds of other Libertys continued to sail, day in and day out, for two decades after the war.

Not a bad record for a ship that had been designed to be expendable from the start, and which had set off such a storm of controversy for two years.

Yet for Henry Kaiser himself, the cracking controversy was sobering. There was a price to be paid for being the most prominent businessman of the war. It made you the first to take the blame. He soon found this out when he ventured into the other boom industry of the war effort, aviation.

By 1942 annual American airplane production reached 47,873, fast approaching the 50,000 Roosevelt had laid down as a fantastic dream two years earlier. With Ford putting out B-24s at Willow Run and General Motors Grumman Wildcats and TBMs in Baltimore and Trenton, it was no surprise that Henry Kaiser would conclude that making airplanes was his inevitable destiny.

After all, it had been his dream when he first landed in Washington in the summer of 1940.[30] Then came the Liberty ship contract, and

Kaiser got distracted. But in 1941 he was thinking in that direction again, this time about cargo planes—airborne versions of the Liberty ship. All he needed was a partner who knew something about planes, and by September 1942—the same month the Maritime Commission announced the Liberty ship program had built 488 vessels in a single year—he thought he'd found him: Howard Hughes.

Hollywood tycoon and reclusive billionaire Howard Hughes would later become an American icon, a symbol of wealth gone wrong. But in 1942 he was a well-known private aviator and head of Hughes Tool Company, a California-based concern that had racked up a number of important defense contracts. The Navy Aeronautics Board's George Spangenberg, who met Hughes in early 1944, found him "a very competent engineer" with a wide-ranging knowledge of aeronautics as well as practical flying.[31] Like Kaiser, Hughes was a maverick, and like Kaiser, he was a man who dreamed big. And if Kaiser saw in Hughes an expert aviation industry insider whose brain he could pick while finding a project begging for joint investment, Hughes saw in Kaiser the man who could bankroll his most cherished project: building the biggest airplane in the world.

Boeing had shown the way with its four-engined bombers, first the B-17 and then the biggest and most complex of all, the B-29. Together with Consolidated's B-24, they ruled the skies of Asia and Europe as offensive weapons. Donald Douglas had made the big cargo plane a reality, first with his twin-engined C-47, the most ubiquitous airplane of the Second World War, and then his four-engined C-54 Skymaster, of which twelve hundred were made for the Army Air Forces and the Navy.[32]

Glenn Martin had carried the concept a step further with the JRM-3 Mars, a gigantic flying boat that could carry almost 100,000 pounds of cargo across the Atlantic Ocean—far above the reach of German U-boats. The Mars had its maiden flight on November 5, 1941, and seemed to be the last word on cargo-carrying megaplanes.*

Hughes, however, intended to outdo them all. He envisioned a plane with not four or even six but *eight* Pratt and Whitney R-4360 4000-horsepower engines and a wingspan of 320 feet—an entire foot-

---

* Two of them are still flying today.

ball field. Taking off from water like a seaplane, the Hercules (as he dubbed it) would carry one hundred tons of cargo, or 750 men or a Sherman tank, over a transoceanic distance at 20,000 feet—nothing less than a flying Liberty ship, in effect.

To Kaiser, the image was irresistible. There had been some talk at the War Production Board of giving him a contract to build the Martin plane, but he jumped instead at Hughes's plane. "These ships could land 500,000 fully equipped men in England in a single day," he enthused to *Time*. "The next day they could fly over again with 70,000 tons of fresh milk, beefsteaks, sugar and bombs."[33] He learned that General Hap Arnold had turned Hughes's superplane down flat—but then, Arnold had turned down Kaiser once as well. He heard aviation executives like Donald Douglas and Jack Northrop tell him the idea was insane—but then, traditional shipbuilders had said the same thing when he set out to build Liberty ships.* /

He declared that he and Hughes could have five thousand megaplanes in the air inside of two years, even though Consolidated's master of mass production, Harry Woodhead, warned him it couldn't be done in less than four.[34] And so, despite the misgivings of the aviation industry and the Air Force brass, the Defense Plant Corporation gave Kaiser and Hughes an $18 million contract to build three of their cargo planes under Hughes's direct supervision. There would be no fees; Kaiser and Hughes would be doing the entire thing for free. Kaiser was less than pleased. "Every builder knows," he protested, "that a non-profit contract is a loss."[35] But such was Kaiser's enthusiasm that he leaped at the chance to realize his dream of revolutionizing the aviation industry, just as he had almost everything else.[36]

Kaiser and his wife, Bess, met his new partner for dinner at the Shoreham Hotel in DC. The thin, taciturn Hughes walked in wearing sneakers and no necktie. He had a slinky blonde on his arm with long hair pulled down over one eye like Veronica Lake.

---

* At one meeting an Air Force officer warned Kaiser that Hughes's idea was untenable with existing technology. "You're talking as far ahead of the times as Leonardo da Vinci." Kaiser was puzzled. As he left with Calhoun, he asked his lawyer, "Have we talked to this da Vinci yet?"

"I think Mother Kaiser almost died," Kaiser's longtime secretary Edna Knuth remembered. "But that didn't bother Mr. Kaiser. He was talking business with Hughes and it was a big night for him. He didn't care about the blonde."[37]

Then reality began to intrude. Because aluminum and magnesium were in critical supply in 1942, the government had deemed that all new airplane prototypes be made from plywood. Hughes's first problem was finding enough wood for his massive project, and for the massive building in which to house it. In the end he settled on birch laminates, but the press preferred to think it was spruce so it could brand his plane the "Spruce Goose" (a name Hughes hated). But as Kaiser followed the plane's progress by phone calls and telegrams, he became more and more alarmed.[38]

Kaiser was obsessed with meeting deadlines. Hughes, on the other hand, was a perfectionist who considered deadlines imposed by others an intrusion into his own private vision. He was also prone to be inaccessible at critical times—a foretaste of the mysterious recluse of later years. Kaiser would show up at the plant in Culver City and learn that Hughes was missing. Then he would pace and fume while Hughes's aides hunted for their boss.[39]

By summer he was not only running out of patience but running out of time. He had to account to the War Production Board for the Spruce Goose delays, but Hughes was giving him almost no information. On August 27, 1943, the project's general manager called Donald Nelson out of his office. "We have a terribly chaotic situation out here," he warned. "It's going to blow right up in your face."[40]

Kaiser and Nelson were never mutual fans. Many felt Nelson had set the megaplane project up to fail: As journalist Eliot Janeway put it, he had told "Kaiser that, so to speak, he can have a ham sandwich if he can bake the bread, borrow the butter, and somehow steal the ham."[41] But for once they had a common foe, Hughes's unaccountable delays, and a common objective: to find out what the hell was going on.

In September the Navy's top aeronautics expert, George Spangenberg, was sent out to California with the head of the Civilian Aviation Board, Dr. Ed Warner, who had been Jimmy Doolittle's teacher at MIT. On the flight out, Spangenberg and Warner did hours of calculations of the plane's planned weight, fuel, and payload range—which became more sobering the longer they checked the figures.

Spangenberg had to admit he was "tremendously impressed" with the setup at Culver City. Hughes had figured out how to build everything from wood, including his factory—with the cap strips for the Spruce Goose's wing beams requiring no fewer than sixty-four laminations.[42] But he was furious that Hughes's engineers hadn't told their boss the aeronautical truth: while the plane's lift went up as the square of its linear dimensions, its weight went up as a *cube* of those dimensions. The "square-cube" law had doomed the project from the start, plywood or no plywood. The Spruce Goose might get off the ground but it would never fly—let alone across the Atlantic.

Spangenberg and Warner returned to Washington to write out their sixty-page grim report, and on February 11, 1944, Nelson canceled the Kaiser-Hughes contract.[43] After the war Kaiser put the blame squarely on his old nemesis Jesse Jones. Jones had said, he told a Senate committee investigating the Spruce Goose's cost overruns in 1947, that "there was no more able and reliable man" than Hughes and "if you go along with Hughes I want it understood that Hughes has the responsibility and you do not interfere with him."[44] Now Kaiser saw that had been a mistake. Jones's own view on being saddled with the Hughes debacle was never recorded.

On the Spruce Goose, Kaiser had learned his lesson and moved on. Hughes, however, refused to give up. He sank more than $11 million of his money into the plane's completion. It would fly a single maiden flight after the war, in November 1947, with Hughes himself at the wheel. Then it returned to its climate-controlled hangar, where it would remain until Hughes's death in 1976. Right to the end, Hughes kept on payroll a fifty-man team to fix and maintain his wonder plane in case the federal government, or Henry Kaiser, changed their minds.

Kaiser never did. But he was not done with airplanes by a long shot.

His opportunity to redeem himself came with Brewster Aviation. The Long Island company had a $275 million contract to make dive-bombers and one of the Navy's finest fighters, the Vought F4U Corsair. In February 1943 it produced exactly eight planes. Not one was a Corsair.

The problem was partly poor materials control, which created bottlenecks and slowed production. But the heart of the matter was management's battles with labor and the plant's UAW boss, Tom Di Lorenzo. Di Lorenzo was a hard-nosed union man who had fiercely opposed the no-strike pledge taken at the beginning of the war. "Our policy is not to win the war at any cost," he told the *Washington Post*, but "to win the war without sacrificing too many of [our] rights," including the right to strike. The latest strike, a bruising one, had come in August 1943—the same month Roosevelt and Churchill were meeting in Quebec to plan Operation Overlord. When the strike was over, Brewster president Fred Riebel decided it was time to quit. He was Brewster's fifth president in sixteen months.[45]

The Truman Committee felt it had to weigh in on this unacceptable interruption of production in a vital defense plant. It knew that Kaiser was on the board, so it presented him with a choice. Resign from the board, or take Brewster over. Kaiser was less than thrilled. "It's not an alluring prospect to take over what is reputed to be the worst situation in the country," he grumbled. But Undersecretary James Forrestal also intervened, asking Kaiser to take over as a personal favor. The Navy, he said, had to have those planes. So Kaiser agreed and handed the plant over to his younger son, Henry Jr. "Brewster will be back on schedule this month," he said.[46]

More than seven thousand Brewster workers and managers were on hand on Sunday, November 7, 1943, when Kaiser landed at La Guardia Airport. They wanted to hear how he was going to heal the labor wounds and turn their plant around. He wanted to fill them with the same enthusiasm and optimism about the war effort he was feeling, despite Howard Hughes. He strode to the microphone.

"I feel so cheerful I could sing to you," he announced. Then to the vast astonishment of his audience, he did.

> *"Oh, what a beautiful morning,*
> *Oh, what a beautiful day,*

> *I've got a beautiful feeling,*
> *Everything's going my way."*

"I can't sing," he told the newspapers afterward, "but . . . and seeing all those people there and the planes they helped to make, well, it gives you a feeling of confidence. That's why I couldn't help but to do my best in trying to sing."[47]

Kaiser decided the best way to get Brewster Aviation productive again was to work out a deal with its labor leaders. "You don't cure a patient by whipping him," he said. But some in Congress, like Representative Melvin J. Maas of Minnesota, thought he was going too far.

MAAS: Of course if you give [labor] all the candy he wants, he is for you, isn't he?

KAISER: That's not what I said. You are making a statement that I am giving them the candy: I am not. . . . I hope I am building morale. I build men. I hope I take those men that exist and build better men of them.

MAAS: That is a very nice platitude.

KAISER: They are not platitudes. Thank God they are not platitudes. . . . Do you know how many men I am employing under me? Three hundred thousand.

MAAS: I merely wanted to know. . . .

KAISER: Do you think I employ that many people by platitudes?

MAAS: I have just one or two questions and then I'm through, Mr. Kaiser.

KAISER: Thank God.[48]

Platitudes or not, Kaiser did get Brewster going again. The labor problems vanished and plane production rose. The youngest Kaiser got 60 planes out the door in January 1944, 74 in February, and 101 in March. When production reached 120 planes in April, the standard the Navy had demanded, Kaiser asked to hand over the factory to others.

For their seven months of work at Brewster, he, Henry Jr., and their operating team had worked for free, with no fee or remuneration.[49] He was ready to move on to his next big project, producing magnesium for the U.S. Air Forces.*

The war was moving on, as well. That February, Marines stormed Kwajalein Island in the Pacific, and then Eniwetok. American bombers clobbered the Marianas, only thirteen hundred miles from Tokyo, while others, including Willow Run B-24s, hit targets across Germany. Daylight bomber raids on Berlin were now normal, even as women made up 42 percent of the workforce building those bombers in West Coast aircraft plants.

As 1944 began, 70 percent of America's manufacturing was focused on wartime production. American factories were building a plane every five minutes, and producing 150 tons of steel every minute. Shipyards were launching eight aircraft carriers a month, including Kaiser's baby flattops, and fifty merchant ships a day.

Day and night, endless freight trains loaded with raw materials and finished war goods moved east and west to outfit a 12-million-strong American military and provide its British, Australian, Russian, and other allies almost $1 billion worth of aid a month—the equivalent of $50 billion in today's dollars. The effort required more than 142 million carloads—the most massive cargo lift in human history.† Yet, amazingly, while all this prodigious production was happening, more than half of America's businesses were still cranking out goods and services for the civilian sector, from shoes and lightbulbs to paint and restaurant supplies and newsprint for the funny papers—including some, like GE and DuPont, who were the biggest war contractors.

What war had revealed was not the power of American industry, but the inexhaustible resources of the world's biggest free-market economy.

Yet while the planes flew and the soldiers fought, and weapons poured out from America's plants, the man who had set it all in motion, Bill Knudsen, was dealing with his most difficult challenge yet.

---

* See Chapter 18.

† It was made possible by a logistical plan worked out for Knudsen by railroad executive Ralph Budd back in 1940, which prevented the kind of infrastructure collapse the same effort triggered during World War I.

CHAPTER SIXTEEN

SUPERBOMBER

A visibly strained Lieutenant General Bill Knudsen (left) and Secretary of War Robert Patterson meet Douglas MacArthur in New Guinea, August 1943. *Courtesy of the National Automotive History Collection, Detroit Public Library*

> There is in America a spirit that drives people to want to do different; they are just ornery enough that they will not stay where the rule was laid down. In that I believe you will find the greatest hope for America's future.
>
> —*William S. Knudsen*

ON AUGUST 17, 1943, a U.S. Army Air Force plane was making its way from Brisbane, Australia, to Port Moresby, New Guinea. It was Lieutenant General Bill Knudsen's longest trip yet as head of the Army war production effort, covering more than 9,000 miles from Washington and Los Angeles, to New Guinea, headquarters of General Douglas MacArthur's command.

Knudsen had no windows to catch a glance of the Pacific's azure waters as they began their descent to Port Moresby, and the incessant roar of the plane's four engines made conversation with his companion, Assistant War Secretary Bob Patterson, almost impossible. Flying in Air Force bombers had taken some getting used to. It meant lots of noise, no pressurization, and icy cold at cruising altitude even here in the steamy South Pacific. Knudsen had flown in his first when he was on the Defense Advisory Committee and made a field trip out to the airplane factories on the West Coast.[1] That was almost three years ago, he realized, when everyone wondered if America could produce a thousand airplanes, let alone fifty thousand. They had left those numbers far behind. Now, at Secretary Patterson's invitation, he was going to see how those planes and other weapons they were producing at such prodigious rates were being used on the battlefield.

As they touched down on the tarmac, the tropical jungle heat rose up to embrace them. Knudsen stripped off the coat he had been wearing and tucked it under his arm as General Douglas MacArthur and an array of generals and admirals stepped forward to greet their two distinguished visitors. Under MacArthur, Americans had just scored two significant victories, first at Buna and then in the battle of the Bismarck Sea, securing a foothold in Japanese-occupied New Guinea. The general gestured the way toward Government House, where he intended to explain to Patterson and Knudsen his plan for victory on the island, and then his strategy for the ultimate goal: the liberation of the Philippines.

In the crowd Knudsen picked out a familiar face. It was a long, rather cynical face that someone might have mistaken for that of film actor Humphrey Bogart, sitting atop a tall lean figure in an Air Force general's uniform. It was MacArthur's air chief and commander of the Fifth Air Force, General George Kenney. Knudsen had met him in Washington a year ago when he was still settling into being head of Army production and had to help Kenney get the planes, equipment, and spare parts he would need for his new South Pacific command.

George Kenney was tough, charismatic, outspoken. When MacArthur's chief of staff tried to protest how Kenney was handling his airplanes and crews, Kenney had grabbed a piece of paper and drew a pencil dot. "The blank area represents what I know about air matters," he growled. "The dot represents what *you* know."[2]

Kenney respected few men in or out of his profession, but one of them was Bill Knudsen. "His expertise in his field was unquestionable," he remembered after the war, and Kenney was drawn to Knudsen's simple, straightforward patriotism and wry sense of humor. Once Knudsen came out of a long Munitions Building meeting where no decision had been reached, shaking his head with a weary smile. Suddenly Knudsen said, "George, do you know what a conference is?"

Kenney said no.

"A conference is a gathering of guys that *singly* can do nothing and *together* decide nothing can be done." Knudsen also gave him his succinct translation of *status quo*. "That's Latin for what a hell of a fix we're in."[3]

Now Knudsen found himself standing next to Kenney. He glanced at his watch. It was nearly six o'clock. "If you can give me dinner," Knudsen whispered to Kenney, "I'd like to get away from all the brass hats and talk airplanes."

And so they did.

Their dinner lasted almost until one o'clock in the morning, and would have gone on longer if Kenney hadn't promised to get Knudsen back to MacArthur in time for a breakfast meeting.[4] As Knudsen recalled, "In our talk we practically took planes apart and put them back together"—just the kind of talk he loved.[5] They talked about the B-24 Liberator, which Kenney believed was the perfect bomber for long-range operations among the widely scattered islands between New Guinea and the New Hebrides, and North American's twin-engined B-25 Mitchell, which Kenney's engineering wizard Irving "Pappy" Gunn and North American field rep Jack Fox were transforming into a low-flying strafing machine—at one point even trying out a 75mm cannon in the nose.[6]

Knudsen in turn told him his impressions of the captured Japanese planes he had seen when he stopped in Brisbane, including the much-vaunted Japanese Zero. He had been less than impressed. The planes struck him as "standard construction, but generally lighter than ours"—and the products of a Japanese industrial base that was still stuck, like the German's, in a handcraft tradition.[7]

But mostly they talked about the twin-engined Lockheed P-38 fighter, which the British had nicknamed the Lightning and which had become the mainstay of Kenney's fighter force. "The Jap fliers give her wide berth," Kenney told him, and with her twin Allison turbocharged engines with sixteen hundred pounds of thrust supplying her speed (up to 414 miles per hour) and power, and allowing her to carry four .50-caliber guns, a 20mm cannon, and enough fuel to travel 475 miles, the Lightning was just the sort of long-range fighter needed over the big distances of the Pacific.[8]*

The Lightning had proved indispensable, but now the Army Air Forces had newer planes and designs than the Lightning, including the P-51 Mustang (Knudsen had seen a plant in Brisbane where the Australians would be making Mustang engines), and wanted to shift production away from the Lightning.[9]

Don't do it, Kenney and Whitehead pleaded. They took over an hour explaining how the P-38 was the ideal airplane for long hops over water and jungle, and how unlike in Europe if a pilot ran out of fuel and had to bail out, the enemy wouldn't just capture him but torture him to death. They fumed and stormed until "we finally ran out of both breath and argument," Kenney remembered.

Knudsen said nothing. Then, absolutely deadpan, he turned his face to Kenney and said in his biggest Danish accent, "George, I gather you like P-38s. Okay, we'll build them for you."[10]

Kenney laughed. That's what he and other Air Force people loved about Knudsen, his ability to cut through the red tape and fog of decision making and close in on the heart of the matter, and get it done. The P-38 would remain in production, and almost 10,000 would be

---

* At Lockheed's request, aviator hero Charles Lindbergh had flown out to Kenney's command to show his pilots a few tricks to extend that range even farther. On April 22, 1943, the Lightning performed her most spectacular exploit when a flight shot down the Betty bomber carrying Admiral Yamamoto, Japan's supreme naval commander and mastermind of the attack on Pearl Harbor.

made during the war. Together with Grumman's Hellcat, it would sweep the once-feared Zero from the skies and help to clear the way for the last stage of the war in the Pacific: the invasion and defeat of Japan.

Knudsen learned that was not going to be easy. What amazed him, touring aircraft plants on both coasts and the Midwest, was how confident everyone was that America was going to win, and win without effort. He feared it was beginning to affect production schedules, as both managers and workers were unwilling to work flat-out—in fact, people were feeling more and more free to take time off. The very success he and his colleagues had achieved, of making war production look simple and straightforward, had its downside. "In general, everyone patriotically supports the war," he told Don Nelson and his WPB colleagues back in July, "but too many are confident of an early and easy victory"—this, almost four months before the battle for Tarawa and almost a year before D-day.[11]

Kenney showed him the other, grimmer side of the war. The next day he personally flew Knudsen and Patterson over the Kokoda Trail, where American, Australian, and Japanese soldiers had been locked in a bitter struggle for months in the mountains and jungle, fighting typhus, malaria, and dysentery as well as one another. More than five thousand Allied soldiers had died fighting for the Kokoda Trail, and then in the capture of Buna. Knudsen sat expressionless as Kenney passed over an American military cemetery set high in the mountains, with over 425 white crosses gently winking in the sun.[12]

So many had died; so many more would die, whether it was in the mountains of New Guinea and Italy or on the beaches of Normandy and Iwo Jima. For Knudsen the goal was always to overwhelm the enemy with war materiel so that as few Americans as possible would have to die. "If the threat against them was with guns, he would meet it with more guns," his biographer wrote; "if with airplanes, he would meet it with more airplanes; if with bombs, he would meet it with more bombs."[13] Until now all his skill in organization, in forcing through production schedules and battling bottlenecks and delays, had been focused on that end.

It was beginning to affect his health. Photographs of him at Port

Moresby show Knudsen looking drawn and fatigued. At sixty-four the gentle giant would have to summon his last reserves of energy for the huge project ahead.

That arrived on his desk less than a month after he returned to Washington in September 1943. Its designers had conceived it as the ultimate weapon, the one they hoped would end the war almost by itself. Now they needed someone who could kick-start it into production.

The project was the B-29, and that someone was Bill Knudsen. It would make the P-38 program look like school recess—and at times even Knudsen would wonder if the biggest bomber ever created would ever get into the air.

The ball had started four years earlier with a midnight phone call at the Fountain Inn in Doylestown, Pennsylvania.

General Henry Arnold, the Air Corps' top general, and his wife were staying there on their way to West Point to visit their cadet son Hank. It was April 14, 1939. In Europe, Germany had just occupied Prague. Italy had invaded Albania. Dutch troops were being stationed on the German border, and in Rome they were conducting air raid drills. But across America, war still seemed very far away—until the phone call brought its reality home.

The phone rang and rang. Finally the Fountain's proprietor sleepily stumbled to the office in his bathrobe and picked up the receiver. The voice on the other end sounded agitated and urgent. There was also something familiar about the soft tenor voice and the Midwest twang.

"Is General Arnold there?" the voice said.

Yes, the inn's owner said. But it was late. Who was calling?

Moments later Arnold was awakened by an excited pounding on his hotel door. It was his host. Charles Lindbergh, the Lone Eagle and hero of the historic 1927 transatlantic flight, was on the phone, he explained. Lindbergh wanted to talk to the general at once. Arnold threw on a dressing gown and plunged downstairs. [14]

Lindbergh was America's most publicly recognized expert on airpower and had just returned to New York from a visit to Europe. It was vital they meet, he told Arnold over the phone, but he warned the general it wasn't safe to get together in New York. From the moment the *Aquitania* had docked, more than one hundred reporters and photographers had swarmed the gangway and followed Lindbergh everywhere. At every step Lindbergh took, he felt the glass of discarded camera flashbulbs cracking under his feet.[15]

Where could they meet?

"How about meeting my wife and me at West Point for lunch," Arnold said, "at the Thayer Hotel?"

The next day at noon, a late-model DeSoto pulled up in front of the crenellated stone entrance of the Thayer. The long, lanky form of Charles Lindbergh jumped out and dashed into the hotel dining room, with its splendid views of the Hudson River. Other guests and waiters gawped and tried to steal a peek of the world's most famous aviator, even though Arnold had arranged for a private dining room.[16]

Finally the two men decided they had to find a place where they could converse without drawing attention. They found it wandering over to the Academy baseball field, where Army was beating Syracuse. There in the relative anonymity of the bleachers, they watched the game and Lindbergh began to talk.

He talked of Nazi airpower. He spoke of row upon row of gleaming Luftwaffe fighters, of a regime training thousands of pilots and bombardiers, of factories producing hundreds of aircraft engines and bombs. He spoke of the might of a great industrial nation geared toward one end: the creation of an air force second to none.

Above all, Lindbergh talked about bombers. He told Arnold that Goering was building a long-range bomber force that would be able to range freely anywhere in Europe, one that could be used to dump unprecedented tons of bombs on any target but could also transport tons of men and materiel anywhere on the battlefield.[17]

War was coming, Lindbergh said. He was convinced of it. And Lindbergh told the head of the Army Air Corps that in his opinion Hitler already had the bombers he needed to destroy any city in Europe or Britain—and possibly even eventually reach the United States.

We now know Lindbergh's information wasn't entirely accurate. His hosts, Goering and General Milch, had put their best foot forward in their tour for Lindbergh, including flying planes from one aerodrome to the next ahead of Lindbergh's car to give the impression of a half dozen squadrons of Heinkels or Messerschmitts where there was only one. Nor were all his predictions correct. He told Arnold, for example, that he didn't think Germany had the planes and pilots for sustained air operations in 1940, which turned out to be tragically wrong.

Still, his picture was accurate enough, and scary enough, to alarm the Air Corps chief. Sitting there in the stands and surrounded by cheering cadets, Arnold realized he would have to drastically revise his plans for future aircraft, particularly offensive bombers.

The general had one last question. Would Lindbergh accept a commission in the Army Air Corps and agree to join Arnold's advisory committee for future military plane development? Lindbergh said yes. They shook hands and parted.[18]

Five days later the committee held its first meeting, at the Munitions Building. After listening to Lindbergh, it recommended the Air Corps develop an entirely new four-engine bomber, a longer-range bomber than the B-17—one that could even cross the Atlantic if need be, in case a German victory in Europe left the United States no margin for confronting the totalitarian menace.

The formal recommendation for such a superbomber came in June 1939.[19] That summer Hap Arnold and his staff turned to the two men they believed could conceive and create it: Claire Egtvedt and Ed Wells of Boeing Aircraft.

Egtvedt was a lean, spare Scandinavian, and ever since he saw Billy Mitchell use biplane bombers to sink two obsolete battleships, the USS *Virginia* and *New Jersey,* he had dreamed of creating a majestic plane that would sweep the skies and rain bombs on enemy targets at will—a true dreadnought of the air.[20] In the spring of 1931 he had found the engineer who could design it for him, twenty-eight-year-old Boise-born Ed Wells, who had been building his own cars since he was fifteen and had hoped to work with Bill Knudsen at Chevrolet or Henry Ford at Ford, but was forced to take a temporary job with Boeing because of the Depression.

Wells would spend the rest of his life running Boeing's Engineering Division. A whiz with a slide rule, pen, and draftsman's compass, he and

Egtvedt came up with a design for the U.S. Army in 1934 for a mono-plane bomber with an unprecedented four engines and a wingspan of 105 feet, and able to carry 45,000 pounds of gross weight and 10,000 pounds of bombs. They gave it enough range to patrol both coasts of the United States, as well as reach Hawaii and Alaska.

The Army called it the XB-17, but when Wells and Egtvedt unveiled the prototype on July 28, 1935, the local Seattle newspaper dubbed it "the Flying Fortress" and the nickname stuck. It would go on to be the mainstay of the Army Air Forces in World War II and pass into legend. All in all, 12,731 would be built. Laid wing tip to wing tip, that was enough Flying Fortresses to cover the distance from Washington, DC, to New York City.

That still lay in the future in the summer of 1939, however, when both Wells and Egtvedt were invited down to Wright Field for a chat. Waiting for them were General Arnold, Colonel Oliver Echols of Materiel Command, and Major Donald Putt, head of Materiel Command's experimental engineering division.

The Air Corps officers put the question straight. Could Boeing come up with an even bigger bomber than the Flying Fortress, one with almost double the bomb load capacity and with a range of say, four thousand to five thousand miles?

Egtvedt and Wells must have looked at each other. It was in fact a problem they had been contemplating almost from the day the B-17 was finished. After all, once you built one four-engine airplane, it was only a matter of pitting the power and lift of bigger engines against the drag of larger wings and fuselage.

Colonel Echols added there was one catch. The Air Corps would want no sacrifice of speed or defensive armament for this kind of su-perbomber.

Wells said, "Well, we can put in a lot of armament and cut down on performance, or we can keep performance up and stay out of range of fighter planes. Which do you prefer?"

Echols fixed him with a look, and said, "We've got to have both."[21]

Wells and Egtvedt had a lot to think about on their flight back to Seattle. This was going to require an entirely new concept than the one they had originally doodled up on their drafting boards. It would have to be a plane built around aeronautical principles no one had applied before—certainly one aerodynamically cleaner than any ever built before. /

Its projected bomb load capacity meant a plane almost *twice* the size of the Flying Fortress, closer to 60,000 pounds empty versus 30,000 for the Fort. It would have four engines, of course, but would need almost a thousand more horsepower per power plant, and a wing area of at least 1,700 square feet in order to get a fully loaded, seventy-ton plane into the air up to 30,000 feet—well beyond the reach of any fighter—and a pressurized cabin, so that the crew wouldn't pass out climbing to such high altitudes or suffer the bends coming back down.

And so Wells and his engineers worked at their drafting tables, so intensely that by the time the Army sent out a formal request for a larger four-engined bomber, on January 29, 1940, nearly every feature had been worked out at Boeing a year beforehand, only months after Lindbergh's secretive monologue in the bleachers at West Point.[22]

When Wells and his team were finished, there was no plane anywhere remotely like it. Wells had told his engineers to start from the bomb bay doors, knowing that their size, allowing for sufficient clearance to get bombs into the plane and then out again at 20,000 or even 30,000 feet, would dictate the shape of the rest of the plane—and those bomb bays would have to carry ten tons of ordnance, almost twice that of the B-17.

Boeing also knew that conventional bomb bay doors, which swung wide and open like the doors of a saloon, had become telltale visual invitations to fighter attack. A savvy fighter pilot knew that opening bomb bays meant a bomber had to slow down and hold course in order to hit its target. So Wells created a new, pneumatically driven bomb bay door that snapped open and shut in less than four seconds.[23]

From there Boeing engineers laid out the plane section by section. More than a thousand test drawings had to be thrown away for every one incorporated into the overall plan.

For their pressurized cabin, Wells and his team worked out a three-"bubble" system instead of trying to pressurize the entire plane—much less complicated and much safer, since sudden loss of pressure in one "bubble" wouldn't mean loss of pressure in the rest. The first bubble

was the cockpit area, where the pilot, co-pilot, engineer, and radio operator would sit. The second was in the midsection where the gunners
were, and the third was for the gunner in the rear. He would be effec-
tively locked in for the duration of the flight, sometimes for eighteen
hours—doomed to be the loneliest man in the Army Air Forces.[24]

The guns were a problem. Conventional turrets like those on a Flying Fortress or Liberator couldn't be pressurized, and areodynamics
expert George Schairer pointed out they would also add exterior drag
on a plane that could tolerate very little drag. So Schairer proposed
leaving them out altogether. After all, the B-29 was designed to fly
higher and faster than fighters could reach, anyway. Why worry about
protection against a theoretically nonexistent threat?

The Army thought about this. Then, a few days after Pearl Harbor,
General Kenneth B. Wolfe, the man who would eventually head the
B-29 program, sent his assistant Jake Harmon out from Wright Field
along with tech chief Roger Williams. They read Wells and Schairer the
riot act. There not only would be gun turrets on the B-29, he told
them, but retractable ones, both below and above the fuselage. The
Boeing men retorted that this would make pressurizing the interior
cabin impossible. They explained the unacceptable drag and other
technical problems that would arise. Harmon was sympathetic but adamant.

"The general will bust us both to second lieutenants," he told Wells,
if he and Williams didn't come back with a pledge from Seattle to install those gun turrets.[25]

There was some silence in the room. Then Roger Williams happened to mention something he had seen demonstrated at Wright
Field by the General Electric Company, an electronic device for aiming
and firing the machine guns of fast-flying aircraft: the first onboard
airplane computer.

GE's little machine was like the fire-control systems that had been
on Navy warships for years—but they were bulkier and slower and far
less precise than a fighter pilot would need. This one could not only
aim every gun on a warplane but fire them as well, while correcting
errors in direction and angle of deflection simultaneously. Its "brain"
was a tiny black box connected to a motor called a selsyn, which was

able to compute in fractions of a second the speed and direction of an incoming plane, including variables like wind speed and exterior temperature, then could either aim weapons for firing separately at a fighter making a sweeping pass, or have the guns all converge on a single "aiming point"—all at the touch of a button.[26]

Wells made a call to General Electric, and working with Sperry Gyroscope, Boeing and GE were able to create a remote fire-control system for the superbomber—the first "smart" automated weapons system and ancestor of today's precision-guided munitions and "smart bombs."

That left what to do about the wings. The B-29 would be twice the size of the B-17, but had to have the same drag in order to get the high-altitude performance the Army was demanding. Aerodynamics expert Schairer designed the wing with sleek narrow lines and new lighter metals for the engine nacelles and supercharger system for the Wright 2200-horsepower R-3350 engines. But it was still not enough.

The result was Fowler flaps, developed by aviation engineer Harlan Fowler. They were in effect airfoil spoilers that—unlike most flaps—didn't just hinge down from the wing. Boeing built them so that they actually slid out from inside the wing and then rotated down, creating a visible slot between the flaps and the wings. The device actually increased the wing area by 20 percent, in addition to increasing the wing's lift. More wing area, noted George Schairer with satisfaction, also meant more range and a bigger load capacity—not just more bombs but more armored protection for the crews.

Flaps like those on the B-29 are now standard for big jet propulsion planes. But in 1941 they were a breathtaking revolution, one that expanded the envelope of the standard four-engine bomber. Together with a heavy aluminum beam called the spar chord inserted through the heart of each wing, it enabled Boeing to guarantee that this plane would carry a high wing loading of sixty-nine pounds per square foot.[27]

Impossible, exploded the Air Corps engineers. No plane could sustain flight under that kind of wing load. They dragged Wells, Schairer, and their boss, Wellwood Beall, out to Wright Field in March to show them the error of their ways by running the numbers on a hypothetical airplane called "Design X." Wells patiently explained why they thought a real B-29 would do better than Design X. The Army engineers listened, and backed off. The Boeing men returned to Seattle.[28]

On May 17, 1941, Boeing's president got a letter placing a provisional order for 250 B-29s, with a production goal of 25 B-29s per month by February 1943. Ten million dollars would be advanced for development, with $3.5 million for expanded plant facilities.[29] The XB-29 was now the YB-29, and its first three prototypes would be the templates for a warplane whose orders would rapidly expand when war came in December.

Considering that Boeing was already working flat-out to produce its B-17s, the fact that the first prototype rolled onto the runway in early August 1942 was a considerable achievement. It was a stunning sight. Ninety-nine feet long and weighing fifty-eight tons fully loaded, it had a 141-foot wingspan—almost half a football field. Balanced on its tricycle landing gear, its long olive-drab fuselage stood nearly 30 feet high. A B-17 sitting on the ground was only 19 feet high. Yet somehow the YB-29's four Wright Cyclone R-3350 engines would give this gargantuan beast a cruising speed of 357 miles per hour—70 miles an hour faster than the Flying Fortress—and a ceiling of 31,000 feet—plus an unheard-of range of 5,330 miles, enough to go from San Francisco to New York and back in one trip.

Two more prototypes were finished by September. Still, Boeing had warned the Army that it would take at least two hundred hours of engine tests before any of them were ready for flight. Almost nine hundred different engineering changes had been made by September 9, 1942, when the engines were revved up for the first time and the plane was given its first taxi test.[30] On the fifteenth, the engines got still more tests and the plane was put through a series of "hops" fifteen feet off the runway, to test the landing gear.

Then on September 21, 1942, Boeing's test pilot Eddie Allen climbed into the cockpit of XB-29 41-002 and at 3:40 P.M. was airborne. One hour and fifteen minutes later, the plane flashed over the field, flared out, and dropped her Fowler flaps, then her wheels touched down with a screech. Allen climbed out and was surrounded by a crowd of engineers, designers, and mechanics. "Well, she flew," he said, and broke into a broad smile.[31]

By that date, some 1,664 Superfortresses were on the order book. Designing and building the prototype had been the easy part. Manufacturing them would be another matter.

First problem was where. Boeing plants were slammed building B-17s, a production program that had spilled over to Vega and Douglas. Those two firms, Boeing's erstwhile competitors, would produce the so-called BVD Flying Fortresses, more than eleven hundred of them.[32] The only solution seemed to be for Boeing and its subcontractors to set up entirely new production plants to build the B-29 airframes—which also meant training an entirely new workforce—while other aircraft companies and *their* subcontractors handled the parts and equipment needed for final assembly. To top it all, everything would have to be done under the veil of official secrecy.

No government agency, not even the War Production Board, was prepared to handle this sort of challenge. So in the end, five principal companies—Boeing, North American, Bell Aircraft, Wright Aeronautics, and GM's Fisher Body—got together with the Army Air Forces to work out a comprehensive production plan.

They agreed Boeing would build most of the B-29s at a brand-new plant out in Wichita, Kansas. It would produce twenty-five B-29s a month by May 1943, they decided—not bad for a facility that didn't yet exist. North American would in turn convert its B-25 facility in Kansas City to make B-29s, and Bell would build a plant in Marietta, Georgia, to make still more. Meanwhile, Wright would churn out the R-3350 engines the planes would need as fast as they could at their main plant in Paterson, New Jersey, and General Motors would dedicate a new Fisher Body plant in Cleveland to producing the last B-29s needed to fill the Army's order.

Even this arrangement didn't last long. It was soon decided to let North American continue to make B-25s in Kansas City and take up the B-29s at a new plant in Omaha. Fisher Body never did make entire B-29s, although they supplied the bulk of wing assemblies and engine nacelles for Wichita, Marietta, and Omaha—as well as for a fourth principal assembly plant in Renton, outside Seattle.[33] The production of R–3350s ended up being farmed out, as well, with new plants coming on line in 1943 at Woodbridge, New Jersey, and outside Chicago.

All in all, the B-29 was turning out to be the most massive project in the history of aeronautics. It was also, in the words of historian Tom Collison, "the most *organizational* airplane ever built."[34] American business had never before been asked to undertake an industrial project of this size or cost or complexity. Even the Manhattan Project turned out to be cheaper. Boeing and its partners set up a Liaison Committee to supervise the entire effort, which included representatives of the biggest of Boeing's one hundred major subcontractors: Chrysler, Goodyear, Hudson Motors, McDonnell of St. Louis, and Republic Aviation. Major government agencies agreed to stay away. Production and development of the B-29 was left to American business and the Army. In the process, a new working relationship would be forged that would last long after World War II.

And at the center of the entire project were four principal plants in four different cities: Wichita, Marietta, Renton, and Omaha. All four would produce B-29s for Boeing in staggering numbers; all would end up employing tens of thousands of men as well as women; and all would transform the economy of their localities.

But the first, and most important, was Wichita.

"One continuous landing field." That was one newspaper's description of Kansas in 1942, and Wichita in particular. Fog was rare in Wichita, and the winters were mild and clear. Boeing already owned a plant there, producing civilian aircraft under the name of Stearman. Two other Wichita companies, Cessna and Beech, had been making small Army and Navy trainers and "puddle jumpers" for the past twenty years.[35]

Altogether the three companies employed some fifteen hundred workers. When Wichita's city fathers found out that the new Boeing plant would employ ten times that number, they realized an economic tornado was about to hit their city. Sixty years later, it would still be making its impact felt as Wichita changed from a rather sleepy former cow town into a major industrial center.

Even as construction of the Wichita plant got started, Boeing production managers realized they were facing a massive problem: No one, not even Ford at Willow Run, had come up with an assembly-line layout that could handle the gargantuan size and staggering complexity of the Superfortress, with 40,540 different parts and a *million* rivets. The solution Boeing came up with was something not even Sorensen or Knudsen or the other denizens of mass production had ever contemplated. Boeing production engineer Oliver West had developed it with his counterparts at Douglas and Lockheed for building the BVD Flying Fortress, and dubbed it "multi-lining." /

This replaced the classic one assembly line with six, all funneling together around three short final assembly lines at the threshold of the plant's main doors. The workers on one line worked on the nose and forward fuselage sections; those in the second, on the center section and bomb bays; those in the third, on the tail section; and so on, with the center wing, engine nacelle, and the outboard and leading edge wing, including the all-important Fowler flaps, all getting their separate assembly lines, while pushcarts and forklifts and conveyor belts kept the parts flowing to each separate line.[36]

The plan was to keep all the B-29's preassembly sections as small as possible until the final stage, when cranes hoisted each section into place in the giant final assembly bay, where four B-29s took shape at a time. In the final assembly, workers clambered around and through the fuselages and under the wings, bolting wings together with the whir and thud of a hundred rivet guns, stringing and fixing miles of electrical wiring and control systems, attaching the sixteen-foot props to the engines, and then lowering the landing gear before rolling the gleaming aluminum airplane out of the door to ready it for flight test.

The multi-assembly-line method marked yet another revolution in American manufacturing. First tried at Wichita, it became standard at all the Superfortress plants. Compared to Willow Run, with its long, winding L-shaped construction, a B-29 plant could be built as a square or rectangle: a huge cost saving both for Boeing and the government. And it meant parts didn't have to travel as far on the plant floor, a saving of time and man-hours impossible to achieve at a plant like Willow Run. It also required fewer workstations than the standard auto single assembly line, and had the flexibility to introduce new engineering modifications almost as part of the flow of production, instead of forcing everything to come to a halt while changes were made.[37]

That turned out to be important, because no airplane ever required more modifications, both on and off line, than the B-29. It was not only the most expensive machine ever produced, but the most complex. From nose to tail, a B-29 consisted of more than 40,000 different parts—compared to a measly 25,000 for a B-24 Liberator. Building one also required Boeing production managers to keep track of fourteen hundred subcontractors, both large (like GE and Bendix, who made the automated gun turrets, and DuPont, who made the Plexiglas observation blisters) and small, who were responsible for everything from the letters of the gauges on the instrument panels to machine tools for pressing and cutting the aluminum for the wings. A single subcontractor slowdown could throw production schedules into a tailspin, while nearly every inspection, every preassembly test and check, turned up another glitch, another problem in a part that perhaps had never been made before, which had to be engineered out before production proceeded. The engines alone required over nine hundred separate engineering changes from the time the first prototype rolled out until the first flight.

So it was no real surprise that while the first B-29s were ordered in May 1941, and Wichita was up and ready to start making them in August 1942, it was almost a year after that before the first plane came off the assembly line.

In between came one engineering problem after another. As one wag put it, the B-29 turned out to have "more bugs than the Entomology Department at the Smithsonian Museum."

Allen's first successful flight, on September 21, was followed by another in the same plane by the Army Air Forces' Colonel Putt, on the twenty-second. Then on the thirtieth, more tests had to be suspended for engine issues. These were ironed out and tests resumed and then an engine inexplicably failed on prototype 41-002. November 1942 brought more tests on the superchargers and power plants.

On December 26 an engine quit just thirty minutes into the flight. The plane landed and two engines were replaced. On December 29 still another engine quit, and engineers and mechanics realized they would be spending the rest of the old year pulling R-3350 engines apart to figure out what was going wrong.

The next day, Ed Wells watched as Eddie Allen took the third prototype, 41-003, aloft. Everything seemed fine until he reached three thousand feet, when the No. 4 engine suddenly burst into flame. Allen made several efforts to put out the flames with the engine's built-in extinguishers, but it kept reigniting. Allen had to land with a smoke-filled cockpit, and the ground crew finally got the fire under control.[38]

Allen was undeterred. He was convinced the plane was a magnificent piece of flying machinery, regardless of the problems, and Ed Wells believed him. Allen had told the Air Force brass it might take four to five months before the prototype was fully ready. So on January 18, 1943, he got set to take the second prototype up again, this time for a three-hour flight that would expose any new glitches with the power plants' cooling and performance, including a flight test with only two engines.

The fully crewed flight was supposed to take three hours. It lasted barely seventeen minutes. At five thousand feet, a fire started in Engine No. 1. By feathering the prop, closing the cowl flaps, and working the extinguishers, Allen's engineer managed to put it out. Five minutes later, at 2,400 feet, Allen radioed the tower. The fire wasn't serious, he said, and no need for crash equipment but he needed clearance for immediate landing.

It was twelve-fifteen. Ed Wells was at a staff meeting with Boeing president Philip Johnson when the phone rang in the outer office. Ed stepped out to answer it. When he came back to the meeting, his face was ashen.

"Eddie's coming in," he said, "and his wing is on fire."[39]

Everyone rushed out to see. Sure enough, as Allen and the XB-29 made their final approach over Seattle's commercial district, the men on the ground could see the plane trailing a thick black plume of smoke and leaving a trail of flaming bits of metal.

The men in the control tower heard Allen come back on the radio. His voice was calm but urgent.

"Have fire equipment ready. Am coming in with wing on fire."

The horrified men of Boeing watched the radio operator bail out only to hit some high-tension wires, as did one of the props. They caught a final glimpse of the flame-engorged cockpit as Allen banked the B-29 left, desperately trying to ditch in an open marshy field on the edge of Boeing field. Instead, the plane kept banking left toward the Frye Packing Plant on Airport Way.[40]

A group of Army recruits had been driving on the same road to attend a boxing match at Seattle's Civic Auditorium when they saw the plane hit the plant's fifth floor and vanish in a ball of flame. They stopped their truck and dashed into the burning building. Corporal Kenneth J. Christner found a phone on the ground-floor office and called both the fire and police departments. The others rushed to the top floor and rescued the employees still alive there, some of whom were on fire. Private Sam Davis had his eyebrows burned away carrying four of them to safety.[41]

Eddie Allen and the rest of his aircrew had died instantly, while nineteen were killed inside the Frye building. One firefighter lost his life fighting the blaze. Without Corporal Cristner and his men, the death toll would have been worse. Yet none of them, nor the Seattle police or fire authorities, knew what kind of plane had crashed. The B-29's existence was still officially a secret, and newspaper reports detailing the tragedy simply said that the plane had been "a four-engine bomber." Seattle citizens assumed it was an errant B-17 that had taken America's most famous test pilot to his death.[42]

Hap Arnold and those who read the news in Washington, of course, knew better—and knew it was an unimaginable setback for the B-29. No one understood the B-29 and its myriad intricacies better than Allen. He had virtually co-engineered the three prototypes, including the plane's temperamental engine, the R-3350. Many were ready to blame Curtiss-Wright's creation. But the crash investigation showed the fire had started out on the wing, not the engine. Instrument tubing running through the wing's leading edge had caught fire from the exhaust system, burning a hole that in turn ignited the petrol tank—and turned the XB-29 into a giant flaming Molotov cocktail. What was miraculous was that all three prototypes hadn't blown up before.[43]

For engineers at Boeing, it meant an agonizing return to the drawing board. For Ed Wells, it meant personal heartbreak—and possibly the end of the line for his magnificent superbomber. More than twenty months after the first plane was ordered and hundreds of millions of dollars spent, Wells still hadn't come up with a B-29 ready for safe flying. Already the word from Washington was that officials wanted to stop the program before any more money was wasted—and any more lives lost. The Truman Committee decided the B-29's engines were defective and substandard, and no more money should be spent. The president himself hinted perhaps it was time to pull the plug on the Superfortress.

Then Big Bill Knudsen came to the plane's rescue.

CHAPTER SEVENTEEN

THE BATTLE OF KANSAS

Warming up the Pratt & Whitney R-3350 on a B-29. Note the technicians with fire extinguishers. *Copyright © Boeing*

> This country seems able to do more by accident
> than any other country can do on purpose.
> —*Employee at Bechtel-McCone B-29 modification*
> *plant, Birmingham, Alabama, 1943*

IT WAS FITTING. He had begun his role as America's armorer by dealing with airplanes. He was going to finish with them—finish with the biggest ever.

First, however, he had some help.

The plane's progenitor, Hap Arnold, was the first to step in. The B-29 was his baby, from that first conversation with Lindbergh in the

West Point bleachers to one meeting after another with Marshall and Lovett cajoling the War Department into spending still more millions while other generals argued the money would be better used for proven bombers like the B-24 and the Flying Fortress. Arnold realized the Allen crash meant doom to the entire program unless he acted fast.

"We cannot, will not stop," he told subordinates. Instead he worked up a proposal for assigning the first finished B-29s to the China-Burma-India theater (or CBI), to show American support for Chinese president Chiang Kai-shek. Arnold made his pitch at the Trident Conference in front of Roosevelt and Churchill, and won their approval. Arnold also promised that once the bugs were worked out, B-29s would be ready for deployment no later than January 1944. The Army Air Forces' superbomber at last had an operational destination, but Arnold had made a promise he had no way of knowing he could keep.[1]

Because the bugs showed no sign of letting up. On April 15 the very first B-29 rolled off the assembly line at Wichita, but no one dared to take it up in the air. Instead, on May 23 Jake Harmon took up the original prototype once again, only to discover that during a maintenance check someone had inadvertently reversed the aileron control cables, so raising the flaps up actually dropped them down, and vice versa. Harmon had to make an emergency landing after nearly crashing the plane.[2]

Yet Harmon was still adamant in his faith in the B-29. "A hell of a good plane," he kept telling people, even after stepping away from his near-fatal crash, "just a tremendous plane." And it was Harmon who finally figured out how to pull the B-29 program back from oblivion.[3]

He and General Wolfe sat down together and worked it out. Hap Arnold would be put in personal charge of every aspect of the B-29, from the assembly line to modification centers to the recruitment and training of crews and mechanics. The entire operation would be branded a War Department Special Project, meaning no funding or other changes could be made without prior approval of the Joint Chiefs and the secretary. The industry's Liaison Committee could then address all engineering and production problems without outside interference, while the planes themselves would be organized as a separate independent bombardment wing. Each would have four combat groups of fifty bombers each. A fifth wing would serve as an operational training unit to funnel replacements to the other groups overseas.

Every overhanging branch of standard chain of command, every piece of government agency and military red tape, would be cut away. From now on, everyone riveting or engineering a B-29, fixing a B-29, or flying a B-29 would be working for the head of the Air Force himself.

Harmon and Wolfe typed up their plan as a memo. At the bottom they left room for a signature, and typed under it: "H. H. Arnold, Commanding, U.S. Air Forces."

They went down the hall and gave it to Arnold. The general read it. He said without expression, "Why doesn't someone else do something for me once in a while?" Wolfe handed him a pen, Arnold signed the memo, and the B-29 Special Project was born.[4]

Hap Arnold also lifted the veil of secrecy that had been draped over the project since its inception. This meant the bomber had to have a name. Boeing wanted "Superfortress"—a salute to its most famous venture. Others pushed for "Annihilator." Arnold didn't particularly care; he had other things to worry about besides the B-29 naming contest, like what bomber groups to send to Europe, and how to keep Kenney and his Fifth Air Force supplied in the Southwest Pacific. He decided Boeing's name would do.[5]

That still left the issue of how to get enough B-29s produced to make a difference in the war—and keep Arnold's promise to have them in China by next year. That's when Arnold called on Bill Knudsen.

He had always had his doubts about Knudsen. Although Arnold speaks highly of Knudsen in his memoirs, in the scramble before the war he saw him only as an oversold production man, someone who was full of great speeches but knew nothing about airplanes.[6] The big Dane didn't even know what an engine nacelle was.* But if anyone could understand the complex problems facing the manufacturing end of the B-29 program, it would be Knudsen. He had flown out to Seattle soon after Allen's death. He had met with Egtvedt and Wells and seen their glum faces and sensed the loss of confidence although not conviction

---

* Just for the record, the nacelle is the metal sheath holding and enclosing the engine.

at Boeing. "The Boeing Company never did lose faith in their baby," Knudsen wrote later, but they "almost gave up hope following that crash." Some five months later, there still wasn't a combat B-29 available, "and the bugs had not begun to be ironed out of the ships that were flyable."[7]

That would be Knudsen's job: to get the bugs out, and the planes in the air and into action. So in the late autumn of 1943, Knudsen stepped in to win what would be remembered forever in Air Force circles as the Battle of Kansas.

As the name suggests, the main battleground was the B-29 plant in Wichita. When Knudsen paid his first visit, it was hard at first glance to see what the problem was. Some 26,000 people were now working in the Boeing facilities, which included 86 million cubic square feet of plant space, offices, warehouses, and hangars, and covered 185 acres—almost half the size of the National Mall.[8] Schools, day-care centers, theaters, shopping malls, and some six thousand brand-new homes—most of them paid for by the Federal Housing Administration—surrounded the site, with fifty-four buses moving workers into work every day. Mobile cafeterias rolled through the plant to minimize time off for lunch.

"The Great Boeing Kitchen" dispensed hot food, along with soup, coffee or tea, and buns, all for only twenty-eight cents. "This beats any meal I ever had anywhere," one young man said. A foreman said the rolling cafeteria meant "my men don't gripe about their wives as they used to"—and kept their minds focused on their jobs.[9]

Knudsen found at Wichita a workforce that was entirely new to manufacturing work and trained entirely by Boeing—and made up of almost 40 percent women. It was a workforce as skilled and dedicated as any in the country. They literally worked longer than the day is long: three shifts of ten hours each, with every other weekend off and time and a half for every hour beyond forty hours a week.

Still, absenteeism was low, worker morale high, and the production numbers were impressive. The planes were apparently getting built, but somehow they weren't getting to the Air Force. Knudsen thought this was odd, because when he arrived he had noticed rows of B-29s on the airfield. Why weren't they on their way? he asked. The manager had to point out that because of the rubber shortage, all the planes had wooden tail wheels and couldn't be flown.

When Knudsen walked closer to one row of sixteen B-29s, he noticed something even odder.

None of them had engines.

Slowly the truth came out. In order to make their production quotas, managers were counting planes as complete even when all their parts hadn't been installed, whether it was tail wheels or even engines. A manager shamefacedly explained that from time to time an engine would be taken off the assembly line and put into one of the "gliders" on the field. Otherwise, the planes were useless.

Knudsen shook his head. There was going to be a new rule, he said. No more B-29s could be turned out of the shop without engines. In fact, "we ruled that an airplane wasn't really an airplane," Knudsen said later, "until it was flown and accepted by the Air Force."[10]

The Battle of Kansas had begun.

From Wichita, Knudsen headed for Marietta. No facility was more of a sore point to the Army than the Bell plant there. Army generals all but accused Bell executives of deliberate sabotage. If Wichita was at least making airplanes, however incomplete, at the cost of $44 million Marietta was making none.

Knudsen saw at once what the problem was. The Bell executives, headquartered two thousand miles away in Buffalo, had gotten in over their heads. They had wildly underestimated how long it would take to get a four-million-square-foot plant built out in the middle of Cobb County in rural Georgia, and how long it would take to train a workforce of 40,000 rural Southerners to work on a complex assembly line like the B-29's—when Cobb County's entire population was only 35,000. People who were being trained to press aluminum sheets into wings and ailerons first had to be shown what aluminum looked like.[11]

Bell nonetheless had promised to have the plant producing planes by September 1942. But by the end of June that year, the building was still only 3 percent complete. My March 1943 the building was nearly finished, but only three thousand men were at work—most of them engineers brought down from Buffalo—making tools for plants elsewhere. Worker morale was low and pay worse. In June 1943, five hundred workers simply walked out and never came back.

When, in July, the air-conditioning finally came on in the enormous Plant No. 6—it looked "like something from another and larger planet," one Atlanta reporter said—Marietta had yet to make a complete plane.[12]

Knudsen decided a change was needed at the top. He brought in Colonel Carl Cover, a former vice president for Douglas, to be in charge.[13] As time went on and the facilities were finished, it turned out Bell's training program was one of the best in the industry. School-teachers, salesmen, clerks, hairdressers, bank tellers, and housewives became skilled aviation workers, learning to cut aluminum sheets, lay out electric cable, or buck and rivet for ten hours at a stretch.

One of those wielding a riveting gun when Knudsen visited was a widow who lived in a tiny trailer outside Atlanta. She had been at the gates of the Marietta factory the day it opened, and remained there working the 8 A.M.-to-4:45 P.M. shift every day until the war ended.

She wasn't just any widow. Helen Dortch Longstreet was the widow of Confederate general James Longstreet, whom she had married when she was thirty-four and he was seventy-six. She was eighty when she started work at Bell. Every day she drove in to work in her Nash coupe in her black sweater and slacks and black visored cap, a cigarette dangling from her lips. The noise and vicious kick of the riveting gun bothered her not at all. "I was head of the class in riveting school," she liked to tell people. "In fact, I was the only one in it." Her foreman could tell Knudsen Mrs. Longstreet was never late and never missed a day of work.[14]

Over time, Mrs. Longstreet and Colonel Cover almost made Marietta the most efficient B-29 plant of them all. In November the first plane came out the factory doors. General Wolfe confessed to the Bell people, "I didn't think you could do it."

By the fall of 1944, its 28,000 workers had made producing B-29s so routine that Bell was able to renegotiate its contract at a lower cost-per-plane basis, and even Cover's tragic death in a plane crash did nothing to break the factory's stride.[15] By the time the war ended, the Bell-Marietta airplane factory, once a symbol of government inefficiency and corporate waste, had become a symbol of the New South. Its new general manager became so popular he was nominated for governor in 1946, and the plant remained a pillar of the Sun Belt industrial resurgence down to the 1990s.*

At Omaha, Knudsen found the situation a little better. Martin Aircraft had broken ground there in the spring of 1941, with a line of bulldozers and Euclid tractors, each with a Stars and Stripes flying from its rearview mirror. The plant had been built to supply the Army with B-26 Marauders, but production was phased out in July 1943 to shift to the B-29. When Knudsen first visited, the new jigs and dies were still showing up—at a cost to the Army of some $90 million.[16]

But Knudsen liked the two Martin managers, Hartson and Willey, the latter a shrewd, thickset Englishman who had transferred from Martin's Baltimore plant to oversee the new operations. In the end, however, the Omaha plant—like Boeing's at Renton—would become a final assembly center for B-29 parts made elsewhere, a rendezvous point for so many of the companies and corporations that had made the arsenal of democracy.[17]

From Chrysler came nose sections, nacelles, leading edges, and center wing flaps, shipping by rail from Detroit. From Goodyear in Akron came the all-important bomb-bay fuselage sections, sections so large that they took up the full height of the factory building in Akron. To make room, the massive concrete foundations that Goodyear engineers used to neutralize vibrations for jigs used for making wings for Martin B-26s had to be broken up with a one-ton wrecking ball and dragged away.[18]

Meanwhile, Hudson Motors—which had designed one of the first weapons whose program Knudsen had overseen, the 20mm Oerlikon antiaircraft gun—supplied fuselage waste sections and tail gun turrets. J. I. Case, the tractor company, made outer wing panels, wing tips, and ailerons, and Bendix Corporation supplied the dorsal and belly turrets.[19]

That still left the problem of the engines—and here even Knudsen found himself facing near-certain defeat.

---

* As for Helen Dortch Longstreet, in 1950 she ran for governor herself on a platform of desegregation and ending Jim Crow. She did not win.

The country's second-biggest aircraft engine firm, Curtiss-Wright, had designed the R-3350 as far back as 1935 as the ultimate piston engine. On the drawing board, its eighteen cylinders could deliver no less than two thousand horsepower with less than half the weight of other engines. As Wright engineers liked to put it, it was as powerful as the average train locomotive but weighed as much as the average locomotive wheel.[20] But there had been a host of problems. Its eighteen cylinders sat in radial fashion like spokes on a wheel, or rather two wheels of nine each, packed close to each other. Preventing overheating, including inside the exhaust system, proved almost impossible—as Eddie Allen had found at the cost of his life. Overheating problems in the reduction gears and exhaust system seemed destined to keep the engine from ever reaching production—that is, until Pearl Harbor.

In 1942 the Army suddenly set huge hopes on the R-3350, especially for its new Boeing superbomber. Millions of dollars poured into Wright Aeronautical to expand its plant in Woodridge, New Jersey, and Chrysler's Dodge division agreed to mass-produce the engine at a completely new plant on South Cicero Street on Chicago's West Side. It quickly eclipsed Willow Run as the largest manufacturing plant in the world, with some four million square feet. It was so huge that when Bill Knudsen paid a visit in late 1943, he almost forwent his usual personal walk-through. "I had quite a time trying to visualize that acreage filled with machine tools and people."[21]

Because the plant was still largely empty. The Wright engineers were having so many problems with the motors they were building that the Dodge people saw no point in opening up full production. The problems weren't just engineering ones. The R-3350 required more than nine thousand separate machine cutting tools to make. It was the most complex piece of machinery ever mass-produced in the United States, but it had to be made by one of the country's most inexperienced workforces.[22] Most of the three thousand employees at Woodridge had never worked in a factory before. They were completely unprepared for the scale and complexity of the R-3350, as were their supervisors. And when Wright instituted an intensive training program on the engine, some employees learned enough to quit and get higher-paying jobs at aircraft plants elsewhere. No wonder three of the inspection supervisors in the Woodridge crankcase and housing departments wound up leaving for psychiatric treatment.[23]

For Knudsen, too, it was a depressing experience. "It was rather tough for me," he confessed later, "a production man, to face these manufacturers at a time when all the engines they would have in their plants would be for that day's production," with no other inventory on hand "and no shipping data for the next supply." As he paced the vast half-empty bays of the Chicago facility and saw workers sullenly standing, sleeping, and shooting craps in the dark corners of the Woodridge plant, he must have wondered if finally, with the R-3350, he had chosen an assignment too tough even for him.[24]

Still, Knudsen crossed his fingers and stayed hopeful. He knew there were powerful companies behind the engine project—he had arranged for GM's Fisher Body to start building the B-29's enormous engine nacelles—and that the key to making the operation more efficient was not just better handling of employees, but better use of subcontractors. Starting in September 1943, Wright-Woodridge and Dodge-Chicago began exchanging those parts each was producing more efficiently, in order to speed up output. A bevy of new subcontractors were found. They included Studebaker; American Radiator in Elyria, Ohio; U.S. Radiator of Geneva, New York; Bohn Aluminum; and Dow Chemical. Chrysler assigned workers from plants in Detroit and Kokomo to make R-3350 parts, while Wright turned to its satellite plants in Ohio and New Jersey to do the same.[25]

All in all, the B-29 engine program turned Curtiss-Wright into the second-biggest prime military contractor in the country, right after General Motors.* Morale at Woodridge gradually improved, as the Air Force and Knudsen insisted on raising workers' pay, especially those working in the hot and dangerous foundry section, and tying pay bonuses to production quotas. Workers came alive to the fact that the

---

* With the B-29, their reputation was on the line. In 1943, the Truman committee unearthed evidence that the company had sold some defective engines to the Air Force, and falsified inspection reports. Senior Curtiss-Wright executives had to resign, and one Army general went to jail. The incident was notorious enough that Arthur Miller made it the basis of his play *All My Song*.

machines they were building were going to have a massive impact on the future of the war.

One twenty-year-old woman from Georgia told a reporter how her Air Force boyfriend had been killed in action, and how working at Woodridge made her feel she was helping to make sure other boys didn't die the same way. "We've got to stick to our jobs to get these engines out," one Bronx woman declared, "so we can get those B-29s across the water where they can knock hell out of the Japs."[26]

Knudsen agreed, and was ready for the next stage. In December— just as Dwight Eisenhower was named Supreme Commander of Allied forces in Europe and after the Marines suffered three thousand killed and wounded taking the island of Tarawa—General Wolfe flew off to China to build the first airfields for the B-29, and Knudsen took over the entire program.[27]

Meanwhile, Hap Arnold had had a visitor.

It was General Leslie Groves from the Army Corps of Engineers, who had spent the last year working with a team of the country's most distinguished scientists and engineers from DuPont, Union Carbide, Allis-Chalmers, Tennessee Eastman, and other corporations, on what he could only describe to Arnold as a superweapon—one that could win the war.* To deliver it, they were going to need a superplane, he said, a plane big and fast enough to carry it into action.

"In calling on him at this time," Grove remembered after the war, "I was of course assuming that our work would be successful"—since they still had not extracted an ounce of enriched uranium, and the first test of a bomb was more than six months away.[28] Still, the chief worry was whether Arnold's superbomber would be ready in time. Neither Boeing's B-17 nor Consolidated's B-24 would be up to the job. Groves warned they might have to consider using a British plane, the Avro Lancaster, instead.

Arnold shook his head. An American plane was going to carry that bomb, he said, and he would have the B-29 ready. What he would work out with Groves over the next year was modifying the size and shape of the bomb to fit into the Superfortress's bomb bay compart-

---

* It was, of course, the atomic bomb.

ment, while the Air Force and Boeing engineers would figure out the rest.[29]

The Manhattan Project (so called for its early location at Columbia University and other sites around Manhattan) had engaged the nation's brightest minds and biggest corporations in a $2 billion venture—one that an American economy fully engaged in war production could find the time, energy, and resources for. It was, in historian Paul Johnson's words, a truly "capitalist bomb." Now the biggest industrial program in the nation's history, to build the most destructive weapon ever conceived, was converging with the second biggest, the race for a plane beyond anyone's dreams. As America's factories, shipyards, offices, and plants were still getting war production into high gear, light began to dawn on a new horizon.

The Age of the Superpower.

Yet as the winter of 1943–44 wore on, Knudsen's headaches with B-29 production were getting worse, not better.

As director of the program, he tried to keep the all-important Liaison Committee meetings down to one a month, with each company sending one or two representatives out to Wichita or Marietta or Renton to hash out problems and offer advice on solutions.[30] Even apart from the engines, the problems were still multiplying. More and more planes were now in the air, and each test flight, it seemed, raised new issues.

One of the trickiest was adjusting the airframe to the pressurized cabin compartments. DuPont had developed special Plexiglas observation blisters to fit into the fuselage. Unfortunately, they had a nasty habit of blowing out when the pressure outside the plane changed too drastically. On one test at 30,000 feet, all the B-29's crew were at their stations wearing their parachutes, and one of the side-gunners was examining his sights, when the blister popped.

"It was like an elephant kicking me in the pants, sir," he related to Knudsen. The boy was sent flying through the aperture, along with his guns, his equipment, and just about everything that wasn't strapped down.

"So what did you do?" Knudsen had to know.

"Well, sir," the boy answered, "I found myself up there without any airplane and just pulled my cord." Knudsen ordered the blister problems solved.[31]

Since almost every feature of the plane was new, everything needed multiple tests, both on the ground and in the air. At the Bechtel-McCone modification center in Birmingham, enough "mandated changes" arrived every week to paper the side of the main office wall. Even then the bugs didn't go away. When the Birmingham people finished work on one Superfortress, the pilot pushed the button activating the intercom and the bomb bay door opened instead.[32]

Outside the center one day, an Air Force officer counted no fewer than thirty B-29s waiting on the tarmac. "If the Old Man could see that," the man said nervously, referring to Hap Arnold, "Christ, he'd just go through the roof."[33]

Arnold didn't, but he was getting nervous. He had promises to keep—and as the January deadline approached, Knudsen had to tell him it couldn't be met. They changed it to March. Arnold went to Wichita to see for himself, and his patience ran out. By now he had Leslie Groves and the Manhattan Project people looking over his shoulder, and wondering. He told Knudsen he had to have that first batch of B-29s in the air by April 15. No excuses.

The Battle of Kansas entered its climax. Six hundred Boeing specialists flew out to Wichita and spent the next four weeks working out every problem on the spot. Since there was no place to put the planes as they overloaded the assembly line's final stages, workers had to work outside.

Huge 114-foot wings were rolled out onto the field, while cranes lifted the four 2,000-pound engines out of the crates in which they had been shipped from the Chrysler plant in Chicago. Then came the massive four-bladed propellers, twelve feet in diameter, shipped from a company in Dayton, Ohio, that before the war had been making refrigerators.[34] Finally, there were thousands of gallons of paint stowed under canvas, waiting for the final overcoating—three hundred pounds of paint for the plane's underwings alone.

Wichita's supposedly wonderful weather turned nasty. With freezing

winds blowing off the plains, including the occasional drenching snow
shower, they labored to install parts, even entire engines, by hand. This
involved disconnecting every electrical and fuel circuit and then—
while fingers froze—detaching and lifting a defective R-3350 and
then, with a hoist and groups of technicians and engineers, sliding in its
replacement. Bolts and hoses and lines were reconnected, all in the
frigid open air, and then the endless tests began, one after another, as
Wichita workers gathered around in the gathering frigid darkness and
watched.

This time, *maybe this time,* everything would work out, they thought.
Maybe they could go home to their families instead of spending the
night lifting out and reinstalling yet another engine from the factory.

The days and weeks passed. Boeing had to scrounge around and find
electrically heated flight suits for their workers. Meals at home didn't
get eaten and grew cold, like the workers. In spite of the freezing temperatures, the Witchita managers sweated. What if they couldn't meet
the deadline?

They weren't alone. Knudsen was so worried about the engines out
of New Jersey that he insisted the results from Paterson and Woodbridge be phoned directly to him every day. Sitting in his Pentagon
office, he would grab the ringing phone at nine o'clock sharp to hear
the daily count. The reports started with four engines a day. Then they
grew to five a day, and then seven a day until suddenly they fell back to
four again. "It gave me the jitters," Knudsen said later.[35]

Then the numbers started to turn around.

They started with Wichita. In November 1943 the plant had managed to produce just 17 planes. In December, Knudsen got that number
up to 31—while Marietta completed 3. Then in January Wichita
reached 46 Superfortresses, and 51 in March. By May all four plants
were producing finished planes, with Wichita hitting 65 a month—unheard of before Knudsen stepped in. By September total production of
B-29s was in the triple digits.[36]

Meanwhile, Wright-Woodridge was still struggling. "Bad planning,
bad supervision," was how Knudsen expressed his frustration in mid-
1944 in a report for Secretary Patterson, "rate of rework runs at 50 to
60 percent."[37] But engine production at Chrysler-Dodge was going so

well that in August Arnold's people began calling for a scale-back in numbers. Workers were putting out at a rate of 11,000 R-3350s a year. The Air Force's biggest worry now was where to store all the extra motors.[38]

Meanwhile, by stopping work on all other planes and with 5,200 workers at the Birmingham facility scrambling flat-out, Bechtel and McCone whittled the usual modification schedule down to just nine weeks—nearly half the time it took to build the plane from scratch. In spite of the crazy schedule and the ramshackle conditions, Knudsen was able to deliver his two hundred B-29s in five months. An exhausted Knudsen and his weary team had won the Battle of Kansas, but just barely.[39]

Perhaps the most dramatic success story, however, had been the Dodge Chicago plant. There had been no organizational flow charts, no elaborate management plans. Managers, executives, inspectors, foremen, and workers had simply tackled the problems as they came up and solved them. Everything had been done on a "making do" basis, and it had worked.

The result, Knudsen had to admit, had been "outstanding." He was inclined to agree with the Bechtel-McCone employee who said, "This country seems to be able to do more by accident than any other country can do on purpose." Certainly the production system Knudsen had devised for arming America had raised itself to an entirely new level of coordination and complexity, one that paralleled what was going on at the uranium plants in Oak Ridge, Tennessee, and presaged what would happen when Americans wanted to reach for the moon.

Yet the fiery trials of the B-29 had just started.

CHAPTER EIGHTEEN

FIRE THIS TIME

A B-29 emerges from the far doors of the Wichita plant, circa 1944. *Copyright © Boeing*

You're going to deliver the biggest firecracker the
Japanese have ever seen.
—*General Curtis E. LeMay to B-29 crews,*
March 9, 1945

You and your workers helped immensely to
shorten the war and save thousands of American
lives.
—*Captain G. E. Dawson, Chemical Warfare*
Service, U.S. Army, to Henry Kaiser,
August 29, 1945

BANKING A SHARP left, Colonel Jake Harmon landed the first B-29 on Indian soil at Chakulia outside Calcutta on April 4, 1944. The runway consisted of thousands of tightly packed stones, which rumbled under his skidding tires until the huge plane finally skidded to a halt. Thanks to Bill Knudsen, Harmon now had a plane. Thanks to Henry Kaiser, in a few months he and other B-29 pilots would soon have the tools of victory in their grasp, from a Kaiser project Knudsen himself had pronounced a "lemon."

Out of the Battle of Kansas had emerged the first operational squadron of B-29s, the 58th Bomb Wing, made up of three groups, with Harmon in charge. It had been a mind-boggling epic trip from Salina, with refueling stopovers in New York, Newfoundland, Marrakech, Cairo, and finally Karachi before the final twelve-hundred-mile leg to Calcutta. As Harmon stepped on the runway, the heat and humidity rose up to envelop him like a stifling blanket even as a hot wind blew clouds of dust that stung the eyes and choked the throat. He knew that spelled trouble for the mission his boss, Hap Arnold, had laid out for the world's most complex airplane.[1]

The B-29 did not deal with heat very well. Given the fact that its engines suffered from chronic overheating, no mechanic or engineer or pilot could be very surprised. The planes that followed Harmon watched their performance plummet the farther east they went. One crashed at Marrakech, a total loss; another crashed at Cairo. Then five more went down, two complete wrecks on the Karachi runway. The rest still en route had to be grounded while engineers grappled once more with the overheating engines. By April 15 only thirty-two B-29s out of two hundred had arrived in the theater of war.[2]

In the 120-degree heat, no B-29 engine behaved like it did in the States. Cylinder-head temperature gauges started in the red zone and stayed there the whole way. "I'd tell my flight engineer to keep his mouth shut about how hot they were running," a pilot with the 58th Group, Jack Ladd, remembered. "I said I didn't want to know."[3] The heat caused other problems. The Plexiglas blisters designed by Bendix cracked as they expanded, then they would contract and explode as planes labored to fly over the Himalayas to their final destination in China—while carburetors froze up at the same time.

They still had unreliable engines and a chronic lack of spare parts and supplies—but on April 26 the B-29 passed one crucial test. A plane flown by Major Charles Hansen had its first encounter with the Japanese, when they ran into a flight of Kawasaki Ki-43 Oscars passing over the India–Burma frontier at 16,000 feet. The Japanese followed the plane for a long time, as if they couldn't believe their eyes at the size of the plane and its speed at that altitude. When they finally attacked, Hansen and his crew shot down one and came through only slightly damaged after the Japanese tried twelve separate passes. Although the electrical system of the top turrets had shorted out, rendering the guns useless, there was no question left. This was a plane ready for battle.[4]

In June 1944, Operation Matterhorn was launched, involving a series of attacks on Japanese bases in China, Thailand, and Singapore. On the fifteenth there was even a trial run on Japan itself, with a raid on the steel-producing town of Kyushu that did little damage but proved the planes could operate over Japanese airspace.

All they needed was a way to close the distance a bit. So simultaneously with Matterhorn, the Navy launched into the central Pacific the biggest and most powerful naval armada ever seen, with fifteen carriers, fifteen battleships, twenty-one cruisers, and sixty-eight destroyers—plus hundreds of fighter and torpedo planes and thousands of amphibious craft, including the ubiquitous Higgins boat. It was not only the most powerful, but so new most vessels were less than two years old. Only five of the cruisers were prewar built; all but nineteen of the destroyers had launched since 1942—as had fourteen of the fifteen carriers.[5] The force was the culmination of not just a new, modern U.S. Navy, but also the productive forces of American industry and shipbuilding Knudsen and his colleagues had let loose in the tide of war.

The Marianas campaign was focused on capturing a handful of islands. Thousands of Americans would die taking the largest: Guam, Tinian, and Saipan. Yet all the fierce fighting that summer, all the death and destruction, took place in order to provide the Superfortress with the island bases it would need to reach Japan. American technology was now driving military strategy, rather than the other way around.

The assault on Saipan began on June 15. Even with the battle still raging on the beaches, Navy engineers and Construction Battalions were ferrying in to start laying out the island's airfield. A month later the battle was still going on. Even though the Seabees were under constant enemy fire, work on the runway never stopped.

Saipan's Isley Field would be the headquarters of the new B-29 force, the 21st Bomber Command. The first Superfortress, *Joltin' Josie*, fresh from Wichita, arrived on October 12. Soon Saipan would be home to the eighty planes and 20,000 men of the 21st's 73rd Wing, and Guam would be ready for the next wing in December. Tinian, they figured, would be set by February or March 1945.[6] It was time to carry the war to Japan.

Yet the initial results were disappointing. The officers of 21st Command tried the same old approach of hitting specific targets day and night. The results were dismal. The B-29s flew seven missions, dropping 1,550 tons of bombs. Not even 2 percent hit within a one-thousand-foot radius of the target. Of 350 sorties versus the aircraft engine factory at Musashino near Tokyo, only 34 hits were achieved on the plant itself.[7]

And the mechanical problems just kept coming. Overheating and blown cylinders, defective valve push rods, busted valve springs, defective fuel pumps, and faulty fuel transfer systems—they kept more than half of the planes from hitting the primary targets, and caused three-quarters of the aborts.

The other big problem was the December weather, and the gales from the jet stream over Japan, sometimes up to 230 miles per hour. Planes downwind were passing over the target at 500 miles per hour. Bombardiers and radio operators barely had time to recognize the target on their newfangled radar scope with its black screen and flashing yellow lights (something else to adjust to), when it would be gone.

After the first wave of B-29 raids, the Japanese were able to breathe easier. Their empire in the Pacific was collapsing, island by island. The American armada in the Marianas had virtually finished the Japanese naval air arm, the proud corps of sailors and pilots who had bombed Pearl Harbor, as a fighting force. But the Japanese homeland remained safe. So many B-29 bombs fell into Tokyo Bay that people joked the

Americans were trying to starve Japan into submission by killing all the fish.[8]

Then the jokes died.

On January 19, 1945, there arrived at Guam a soft-spoken, pipe-smoking, cigar-chomping major general named Curtis LeMay, an Ohio country boy with an engineering degree from Ohio State and a reputation as the mastermind of daylight bombing in Europe, to take charge. LeMay decided training on how to fly the B-29 in battlefield conditions had to be the top priority, over bombing of Japan.

The number of planes for each mission would be reduced, and time was spent honing skills in pattern bombing, navigation, gunnery, and cruise control to gain mastery of fuel economy. As the sleek silver planes swarmed and swooped over the blue water to attack their practice targets, LeMay held one conference after another with his commanders, chomping on a cigar or his corncob pipe.

Finally, at the start of February, LeMay judged his men and planes ready. He launched 21st Bomber Command in sixteen sorties against primary targets in Japan. Afterward reconnaissance planes flew high over the bombed areas, snapping pictures. The photos revealed that in fourteen of the sixteen raids, not one target had been destroyed, despite dropping five thousand tons of ordnance. Losses remained high. Twenty-nine B-29s had been lost to enemy fire—and twenty-one had crashed due to mechanical failure.

LeMay's crews were sore, and more discouraged than ever. LeMay didn't care. "I'm not here to make friends," he liked to say, "but win a war." But how to do that was still eluding him.

Then in March he had it.

It was a drizzly afternoon when LeMay's adjutant Colonel Edward "Pinky" Smith wandered into the Tinian war room. At first Smith thought the place was empty, but then he realized LeMay was there, sitting in the darkness and gazing at the big map on the wall. He had been there a long time.

Sitting and thinking was something LeMay often did at his desk, which was almost always clear of papers. "The general does less work than any man in the Army," one of his aides said. But another added, "But he *thinks* more than any man I have ever known." LeMay was averaging four hours of sleep a night, and when he wasn't out on the landing strip or reading reports, his officers could find him at his desk, staring into space—or writing letters to the wives and children of his killed and lost crewmen.[9]

In any case, the sight of a silent, meditative LeMay didn't surprise Smith. He was turning to leave the general alone with his thoughts when LeMay suddenly spoke.

"No, Pinky, don't go away. I want to talk to you. There's something I've been thinking about—a new way of hitting them." Smith sat down. For the next few minutes, LeMay laid out his plan, almost to the last detail, with occasional forays to point at the map.

As Smith listened to LeMay's monologue, it seemed to him "almost unbelievable." Later he admitted it made his flesh creep. But as he listened, his airman's instinct told him LeMay's plan might work, for all its terrible awesomeness. It also told him LeMay *knew* it would work.[10]

In part because he had a silent partner in Henry Kaiser.

Even after building ships, aircraft carriers, airplanes, and steel, one industrial dream had eluded "the man from Frisco": processing magnesium.

That seems a strange addition to Kaiser's wish list. But magnesium had become the new miracle metal of the modern aircraft industry. Lighter than aluminum and far more plentiful, magnesium was harder and more capable of bearing precise tooling than steel. When the British learned in the summer of 1940 that the Germans were using the metal in massive quantities for Luftwaffe parts and airframes, they immediately contacted the United States for help.

That December it was Bill Knudsen who first learned about the vital importance of magnesium from Churchill himself. The British thought they might be able to produce 27,000 tons by 1942, if the Americans were willing to make up the difference.

"Your figures are wrong," Knudsen had told the prime minister. "You will not produce more than half that amount because you haven't the facilities, and you will not have them"—certainly not in time. Given magnesium's new importance (it didn't even appear on the Army's critical materials list in 1940), the United States was going to have to produce enough for both its own aircraft industry and that of its Lend-Lease ally, he decided—close to 12 million pounds of magnesium per year.[11]

That had triggered a crash program for magnesium production, in the shadow of the Blitz. The one American company capable of mass-producing magnesium in that tight time frame was Dow Chemical, the biggest chemical company in the country. Its founder, Herbert Dow, had been obsessed by the light white metal. Back during the First World War when the commodity's price kept falling, Dow had been convinced magnesium would be the building material of the future. Even though there were no customers, Dow had kept his plant in Midland, Michigan, making it, even after he retired.[12]

Now, anticipating the wartime need even before the federal government did, Dow had built a brand-new plant in Freeport, Texas, at its own expense, ready to extract millions of pounds of magnesium from seawater. But Dow's method was its own, a virtual monopoly—a nasty word in New Deal Washington. So late in 1940, Henry Kaiser had waded into the competition, determined to find a method of extracting magnesium that would break Dow's monopoly *and* give him a lucrative government contract.[13]

He found what he was looking for in an odd little Austrian scientist named Dr. Fritz Hansgirg. Hansgirg's method was more like the one the Germans were using, a carbothermic reduction process that turned brucite clay into magnesium oxide, heated it up with carbon to burn off the oxygen, then cooled it with natural gas. Harry Davis, Kaiser's man at Kaiser Permanente Cement, checked out Hansgirg and declared the idea good, at least in theory. With the Davis report in hand and his lawyer Chad Calhoun pushing from behind, Kaiser managed to squeeze a $9.2 million loan from his arch-nemesis, Jesse Jones, in the spring of 1941, to build a plant next to his cement factory in Manteca, California, deep in the San Jose Valley. Kaiser was fully launched in the magnesium business, with Dr. Hansgirg as his technical advisor.[14]

It was a disaster almost from the moment they broke ground on the facility. Hansgirg proved to be a cantankerous, unreliable character contemptuous of American business methods and—even more alarming—with more-than-casual ties to the Nazi government.* Nine days after Pearl Harbor, the FBI scooped him up as a security risk and threw him in jail. Kaiser was undeterred, and kept at the Hansgirg process even though it failed to produce much magnesium and was turning positively dangerous. /

In August 1941 a fire in a retort furnace killed three Manteca workers; a few weeks later another accident killed two more. By March 1942 the head of the War Production Board's Magnesium and Aluminum Division dubbed the entire experiment a failure, and lamented the amount of money lost thanks to Kaiser's "too rapid push attitude without much thought or study." He noted that the usually ebullient Kaiser looked down in the dumps, surveying the meager production numbers month after month. *Time* magazine had to pronounce the Manteca venture a "flop so far," as Henry Luce wondered if this was one miracle even his hero couldn't pull off.[15] Even Bill Knudsen, no fan of Kaiser, felt free to weigh in, pronouncing Kaiser's magnesium venture a "lemon."

But what Henry Kaiser lacked in patience, he made up for in persistence. Over the course of 1942, as Kaiser's people hammered away at the problems with the Hansgirg method one by one, they also began building three other magnesium-producing facilities using other methods, including Dow's seawater method. At the government's request, that company had generously offered to donate its formula and technical specifications to a number of other companies, including Kaiser's Permanente.[16]

By early 1943, *Time* was able to report: "After many a delay, Henry J. Kaiser's $6 million Permanente Magnesium plant is finally over the hump." Finished ingots began to pour out of the four facilities and into factories and plants around the West Coast for making light airframes, bomb casings, and magnesium flare shells. Kaiser was still losing money. But later that year, Kaiser engineers, working with the Army's Chemical Warfare Service, found another use for Kaiser magnesium that would alter the course of the war.

---

* Hansgirg's son was chief psychologist for the Wehrmacht.

They called it "goop." It was a mixture of powdered magnesium, a magnesium distillate, and asphalt. Permanente chemists began making it to sweep up all the finely powdered magnesium dust floating through the plant—a highly flammable not to mention explosive hazard. Then they wondered if it wouldn't have a wartime application.[17] Both the Germans and British had developed incendiary bombs and used them with telling effect on both cities and industrial targets. The American Air Force was doing the same. But this "goop," the Kaiser people pointed out, didn't just burn like fire but stuck like glue. Once it started a fire, it would be nearly impossible to put it out.

The Chemical Warfare people discovered this when they tried the goop out in the middle of the Utah desert, at the Army's Dugway Proving Ground. There they built a complete replica of a Japanese village—just the kind of place where parts of planes and tanks were being assembled in Japan's highly dispersed war industries. New York architect Antonin Raymond, who had lived for years in Japan, designed at Dugway a five-block site complete with industrial and residential buildings. There were even soldiers playing Japanese air raid wardens and firemen, who tried to put out the fires that the dropped goop spread—all in vain.[18]

The Army was very impressed. It immediately ordered Kaiser to halt magnesium ingot production. Now everything coming out of his Manteca plant would be in the form of goop—while DuPont and Standard Oil chemists worked out how to make it safe for manufacture. That suited Kaiser, since making goop took one-fourth the time, and at 18.3 cents per pound proved profitable enough to recoup his losses and repay his loans. Even better, "this is our real opportunity," he crowed, "to be of service to the war effort"—and final victory over Japan.

In little more than a year, Kaiser Permanente had turned out 410,000 tons of goop—all of it to be stuffed into ten-pound cylinders together with proximity fuses and dubbed the M-74 incendiary bomb.[19] And by the end of 1944, almost all of *those* were headed in one direction: westward across the Pacific to the Marianas and the waiting arms of Curtis LeMay, who would use them to transform his B-29 strategy.

He first tried out the goop incendiaries on December 18, 1944, in a raid on Japanese-occupied Hankow in China. The first trial run on Japan came on February 25. It proved a bust.[20] Even though Japan's densely packed wooden houses should have burned like tinder, the bombing results had been largely ineffectual. That was the problem LeMay had been hashing out in his mind, on that rainy afternoon in March. And it was there that he realized in a flash the problem wasn't the plane, or the M-74 that was being dropped. It was the *height* at which they were being dropped. If you expected to create genuine mayhem, you had to get in closer.

Until now, no B-29 had ever attacked below 20,000 feet. LeMay decided every single one of his planes would attack at less than half that altitude, at between 5,000 and 8,000 feet.[21] It was a revolutionary concept—as was its combustible corollary. Instead of carrying a mixture of bombs and incendiaries, as the British did for their attacks on German cities, LeMay's crews would carry nothing *but* incendiaries. A front line of pathfinders would drop several tons of bombs and flares from about 25,000 feet in order to mark targets and get things started. Then the real fireworks would come in at a fraction of that level, all at once and without warning.

LeMay also decided daylight raids were a waste of time and planes. The attackers would come at night, not in formation but singly: each B-29 using its radar scope to hunt out a place where its ordnance load would do the most damage.

Even more shocking, LeMay decided they would go in unarmed. Unlike the B-29s, Japan's night fighter force had insufficient radar to track and catch individual bombers flying in irregular patterns. By the time the Japanese figured out what was happening, LeMay figured, his B-29s would be safe and gone. So, taking a page out of General Kenney's book, he ripped out all the Superfortress's precious gun turrets except the one in the rear and got rid of the co-pilot and bombardier. As Kenney had discovered, there was no need for a bombardier at that low level. It also created room for still more M-74s.[22]

LeMay's plan wasn't just to reduce certain targets or cities to smoldering rubble, as British and American bombers were doing to Germany. It was to burn out the heart and soul of an entire nation. The goal was to save American lives by the thousands by taking away lives by tens or even hundreds of thousands—and above all to prevent the need for a long, protracted invasion of Japan by the ruthless application of a single instrument: the B-29 Superfortress.

That was the plan. "Probably the greatest one-man military decision ever made," as someone later put it.[23] LeMay had thrown away the proverbial book. But he had also finally come up with a strategy to match the awesome new weapons at his disposal. When the planes arrived over Tokyo, he calculated, twenty-five tons of incendiaries would be raining down on every square mile of the city.[24]

When LeMay outlined his plan to his commanding officers, some of them called it plain murder. They weren't thinking of Japanese civilians, but American B-29 crews coming in exposed and almost unarmed at that low level. "Sitting ducks," they told each other with a shake of their heads, "we'll be sitting ducks."

LeMay thought differently. The few night fighters the B-29s couldn't beat off with their remaining guns, they could evade with superior speed. He also felt confident that the B-29 with its magnificent airframe could absorb whatever battle damage it did incur, and still get back to base.

The first low-level raid was set for March 9, 1945. Meanwhile, Douglas MacArthur had raised the American flag over Corregidor as the liberation of the Philippines entered its final stages. Other American soldiers were getting ready to land on Okinawa, in preparation for the invasion of the Japanese homeland. Experts had told the secretary of war that the invasion would last through most of 1946 and cost upwards of a million U.S. casualties.[25] LeMay had one goal: to make that invasion unnecessary.

That afternoon when the word went out to the aircrews, "You will come over the target at an altitude of five thousand feet," there were gasps of surprise and shock. But in the 504th, its colonel, Glen Martin, heard the initial shouts of "Crazy" and "This is nuts" turn into "a roar of surprise and enthusiasm," as he put it, once his crews realized the scope of the entire plan.[26]

Some 334 B-29s lumbered into the air and made the fifteen-hundred-mile flight to Japan, arriving just after night had settled over an unsuspecting Tokyo. The effect was terrifying. In LeMay's words, "It was as though Tokyo had dropped through the floor of the world and into the mouth of hell."[27] Two thousand tons of incendiaries rained down on the city from every direction, burning out sixteen square miles of the city and destroying more than a quarter million buildings. Some 83,000 people died in the conflagration that set entire blocks alight and boiled away the water in Tokyo's canals. LeMay's planes returned with their underwings and bomb bay doors blackened by the smoke and soot. Crews could smell roasting human flesh below, which lingered in their planes until they landed back at base.

It was the single most destructive air raid in history—and set an apocalyptic scale for what was to come.

News of the raid reached Bill Knudsen many thousands of miles away, in Dayton, Ohio, at the Air Force's Wright-Patterson Field. It had been the home of the Wright brothers' first airplane factory. It was now Bill Knudsen's office, and his last.

With the Battle of Kansas won and the B-29 in action, there was still a lot left for him to do. The Air Force had learned that the key to airpower was logistics: how to keep all those thousands of planes in the air gassed, armed, and ready—and headed in the right direction. So in September 1944, he had been put in charge of the new Air Technical Service Command, or ATSC, the Army Air Forces' logistical and air services.

As for airplane production, the numbers were hitting almost unimaginable heights. For 1944 it included 93,000 airplanes—almost *double* the number Roosevelt had proposed in 1940 and which everyone had pronounced impossible. In addition, America was producing a quarter of a million aircraft engines, three-quarters of a million machine guns for the Army, four and a half million rifles and small arms, and 17,500 tanks.[28]

Yet that was almost half the number produced in 1943, and deliberately so. The fact was the problem now was not how to speed up or even maintain production, but how to slow it down as the war's end approached. Back in July 1943, the New Deal critics had finally gotten their wish. A new centralized agency was set up with a single czar to oversee both war production and manpower mobilization. The czar was Roosevelt confidant and Supreme Court justice James Byrnes, and as head of the new War Mobilization Board he had so many sweeping powers, some called him the Assistant President.[29]

Yet from his first day in office until the end of the war, he spent most of his time trying to *de*mobilize the war effort and get American business back on track for an orderly transition to a peacetime economy. Production of civilian products had resumed in August 1944—a sure sign that Washington felt it was safe to begin to wind down mobilization. "Reconversion" became the catchphrase of the day.[30]

Such was the power of the production monster Knudsen had unleashed and American business had created. Certainly as far as Knudsen was concerned, he felt his job was done. He was worn out, his health strained to the breaking point. His daughter Martha remembered him sitting at home with tears streaming down his face as the radio announcer told of German cities he once knew—Hamburg, Lübeck, Cologne—reduced to rubble by the bombers he helped build. After six months at Dayton and less than a month after V-E Day, Knudsen formally resigned from the Army, on June 1, 1945. The day before, Hap Arnold had pinned the oak leaf cluster to the Distinguished Service Medal Knudsen had been awarded the previous May, "for exceptionally meritorious and distinguished services in the performance of duties of great responsibility." Bob Patterson told the press he calculated just by being there Knudsen had single-handedly "raised America's war production totals by 10 percent."[31]

As Knudsen saluted and shook hands and set off from Dayton to rejoin his family in Detroit at last, the problem of how to finish the war had passed into other hands. It was no longer a matter of mass production. It was a matter of applying the awesome new technologies industry had developed, in the right places and in the right way.

Here Knudsen had made one final contribution.

On June 11—just ten days after Knudsen stepped down—a flight of specially modified B-29s began arriving at Tinian. The planes had been built at the Glenn Martin plant in Omaha—the plant Knudsen had turned around with the help of a pair of hard-driving managers. These B-29s were different from the others, with slightly wider bomb bay

doors and a modified cockpit with extra room for technicians and special instruments. None of the Omaha workers had known why, and
even the top managers knew only that they were part of a special project dubbed Silverplate.

Silverplate's commanding officer was a thin Air Force colonel with
wavy hair and dark eyebrows. Paul W. Tibbets had been operations officer of the 97th Bombardment Group in North Africa and Europe,
and commanded the first flight of B-17s to arrive in Europe. Then he
had switched to B-29s, where he proved so adept at handling the tough,
temperamental machines that Hap Arnold had pulled him from combat and set him to work training other pilots. There was probably no
one in the entire Air Force who knew as much about the B-29 as Tibbets—and certainly no one as qualified for as nerve-racking an assignment as Silverplate.[32]

After months of special training in the Utah desert, and two months
in Cuba teaching his crews about long over-sea flights, Tibbets was assembling his men and planes at Tinian for their final preparation. Whatever their mission would be—and Tibbetts had only been told that it
would very probably end the war—he had decided that the B-29 with
which he would lead the Omaha pack (serial number B-29-45MO
44-86292) would be spray-painted with the name of his mother, who
had encouraged him against his father's will to enter the Air Force.

She lived in Miami, and her name was Enola Gay.

For the rest of the summer, B-29s dropped tons of Henry Kaiser's
magnesium goop and burned out the heart of industrial Japan. Tokyo,
Nagoya, Kobe, Osaka, Yokohama, Kawasaki, Toyama: all vanished in a
blistering cloud of fire. LeMay's six hundred B-29s roamed the Japanese islands almost at will. They took to dropping leaflets on Japanese
cities before a raid, urging the population to evacuate before they
were incinerated.[33]

It wasn't until May that LeMay was told about the atomic bomb, and
the imminent arrival of Colonel Tibbetts's 509 Composite Group.
LeMay had no control over what they were doing, and he didn't like
the setup at all. He certainly didn't like the attitude of Tibbetts and his

specially trained crews. "They were the Second Coming of Christ," or so they seemed to think, he grumbled later.[34] LeMay did convince Leslie Groves that the best way to deliver the bomb was with a single B-29; that way, he said, it would be less likely to attract Japanese attention until it was too late.[35] But LeMay was also not convinced that the bomb was really necessary. His strategy alone would force Japan to surrender in time, he believed, and his arguments were persuasive enough that his boss, Hap Arnold, was the only senior military or civilian leader to oppose dropping the atomic bomb.

But the truth was that by August, LeMay was running out of targets. Two of the last, the cities of Hiroshima and Nagasaki, were chosen for the final act—the one that all hoped and prayed would compel Japanese surrender. On August 1 assembly of the bomb parts unloaded from the cruiser USS *Indianapolis* began, and on the fifth, LeMay watched as it was stowed on Tibbetts's B-29, the name *Enola Gay* flashing jauntily in the tropical sun.

LeMay couldn't believe it. The five-ton device was so heavy it couldn't be loaded the usual way. "The only way to load the bomb was to put it into a hole in the ground, taxi the airplane over the top of the bomb, then jack it up into the plane."[36] No one had flown with a 10,000-pound bomb before. But Claire Egtvedt and Ed Wells's Superfortress could handle 20,000 pounds with ease, and so the next day at 2:45 A.M. *Enola Gay,* together with two other B-29s carrying cameras and monitoring instruments, rumbled down the Tinian runway and pulled themselves up into the air and away into the darkness.

A eight o'clock Tibbetts dropped his single thirteen-kiloton uranium atomic bomb on Hiroshima, killing 50,000 people almost instantly. Two days later another Omaha-built B-29, *Bock's Car* (serial number B-29-40MO 44-279297), dropped the Hiroshima bomb's plutonium cousin on Nagasaki, killing another 36,000. The Japanese government, fearful that there might be more such superweapons, surrendered on August 15.

The war was over.

For hundreds of thousands of American soldiers, and almost certainly millions of Japanese, it meant being spared death in a prolonged invasion and land campaign to take the islands. To Ed Wells, the B-29's designer, the news came with a sense of vindication, if not triumph. The plane over which he and the rest of Boeing had labored for almost five years, and which had faced cancellation more than once, had finally come through. Wells himself had spent most of March and April 1945 on Guam with a group of Boeing engineers.

They had arrived days after the first historic raid on Tokyo. Pilots and crews described with awe how thermals erupting from the burning city threw their planes into violent spins, rolls, and Immelmann turns, but the Superfortress had been unfazed. "I've flown a lot of Boeing Flying Fortresses," one pilot told him, "and always thought they were fine planes. But the B-29 beats 'em all."[37]

But for the future, the bombs dropped on Hiroshima and Nagasaki revealed something else.

Buried deep within the arsenal of democracy, beyond the piles of tires and oil drums and the stacks of steel and bags of concrete; the endless ranks of trucks, jeeps, artillery pieces, and tanks; the harbors full of ships and submarines and aircraft carriers; the skies filled with fighters and bombers; and underneath the piles of charts and graphs and sheets of statistics, was hidden a suicide note. No one consciously put it there. It had simply turned up, unbidden. A power had been unleashed that, if mishandled, could destroy modern industrial civilization itself. Yet it was also a power that, if properly harnessed, could transform the nature of that civilization for the better.

This posed a dilemma, which Bill Knudsen summed up simply and succinctly. "Progress is only made when fear is overcome by curiosity," he said. "If you are curious enough, you will not have any fear."[38]

Some might think that judgment too optimistic. But as of today, the suicide note remains unsigned.

CONCLUSION

RECKONING

Workers at the Glenn Martin plant in Omaha, Nebraska, where *Enola Gay* was built. *Lockheed Martin Corporation*

America is the only country that is constantly
being reborn.

—*William S. Knudsen*

THE WAR WAS OVER.

All at once work in the Richmond shipyards stopped. Factories everywhere that had been making tanks, landing craft, rubber boats, and artillery shells sat silent. At Grumman aircraft factory in Bethpage, New York, thousands of workers had been turning out Navy fighters and torpedo planes at four plants at once. Now the vast empty buildings that had once been coursing with frantic activity had a strange, eerie quality. "It was like coming to work on Sunday," one worker remembered.[1]

Bill Knudsen was in Germany when he got the news of Japan's surrender. After resigning his commission from the Army on June 1, he had returned to Detroit, where there had been a big parade with floats and bands and American GIs marching down Woodward Avenue. General Marshall and Undersecretary of War Robert Patterson were there on the dais, paying tribute to the man who had built the U.S. armed services into the greatest military machine in history. The mayor gave him a key to the city. When Knudsen spoke, he said simply, "Good night, my friends, and God bless you all."[2]

Following Japan's surrender, Bob Patterson, the War Department's original tough guy, penned Knudsen a heartfelt letter from his new air-conditioned office at the Pentagon. "To me you are the great American," he wrote. "You have never done anything for yourself, only for your country. You have never spared yourself."[3]

Nor was Knudsen sparing himself now. Only two days after he came home to his family, Alfred Sloan asked him to go to Europe to see what was left of GM's shattered plants after Allied bombers and Russian looters finished with them. Knudsen was able to speak to his family in Denmark for the first time in seven years, and had lunch with the Danish king. When he had last been there, Hitler had been lording it over Europe, and America had been totally unprepared for the conflagration about to engulf the world. So now, as news of final victory came, Knudsen must have had a moment to think about what he and his colleagues had done.

From the moment Knudsen kicked off the armament program in July 1940 until August 1945, the United States had produced $183 billion in arms. Aircraft and ships together accounted for half that total.

In those five years, America's shipyards had launched 141 aircraft carriers, eight battleships, 807 cruisers, destroyers, and destroyer escorts, 203 submarines, and, thanks to Henry Kaiser and his colleagues, almost 52 million tons of merchant shipping. Its factories turned out 88,410 tanks and self-propelled guns, 257,000 artillery pieces, 2.4 million trucks, 2.6 million machine guns—and 41 *billion* rounds of ammunition.

As for aircraft, the United States had produced 324,750, averaging 170 a day since 1942. That was more than the Soviet Union and Great Britain combined, although the U.S. supplied enough raw materials to enable those two allies to be the number two and number three airplane producers in World War II, respectively.[4] For the U.S. had not only armed its own troops, marines, and sailors, it had armed its allies as well—some $50 billion worth through Lend-Lease. When Stalin, Roosevelt, and Churchill first met at Tehran in 1943, and Stalin raised his glass in a toast "to American production, without which this war would have been lost," it was a stunning tribute from the leader of world Communism to the forces of American capitalism.

Yet America had done all this while remaining the least mobilized of the Second World War combatants. The smallest percentage of the male population entered the armed forces. Compared to the Soviet Union or Great Britain, more women remained at home rather than going to work—more than 60 percent. And the United States converted the least of all its economic output to the war effort, just over 47 percent in 1944 compared to almost 60 percent for Britain and more for Germany and the Soviet Union, only to outproduce everyone else put together, including Japan.[5]

Yet the output of consumer goods was larger every war year than it had been in 1939, despite the restrictions and rationing. In 1945 Americans ate more meat, bought more shoes and gasoline, and used more electricity than they had before Hitler invaded France. The dream of an economy vibrant enough to produce both guns and butter had been realized thanks to American business.[6]

By contrast, the supreme war effort had left Europe in ruins, and not just from Allied bombing. Albert Speer's reign as Nazi production czar had boosted arms production as he had promised, almost doubling output. But it came at the cost of turning Germany and much of the rest of Europe into a vast slave labor camp, employing some 17 million unwilling foreign workers—including inmates at places like Auschwitz and Treblinka—while devouring every last shred of normal economic life.[7] Britain's mobilization had consumed one-quarter of its national wealth; Russia's would have been impossible without America's Lend-Lease aid, which fed and clothed civilians and soldiers alike—and which gave Britons one out of every four meals they ate during the war.

No one had foreseen this, except Bill Knudsen. He had sensed from the beginning that Washington didn't have to command or ride herd over the American economy to achieve new heights of production, even after a decade of depression. All you had to do was put in the orders, finance the plant expansion, then stand back and let things happen. And they did, in prodigious amounts.

Total economic production in the United States had doubled;* wages rose by 70 percent. American workers were twice as productive as their German counterparts, and four times more productive than the Japanese. Later critics would point out that those numbers were no different before the war than they had been during it.[8] But that was the point. What made America productive wasn't the war or government dictates or a supreme sense of national urgency. It was the miracle of mass production, which, once turned loose, could overcome any obstacle or difficulty.

That included what happened next.

Starting in 1946 nearly 10 million men and women in uniform would be coming home, eager to return to normal life, including a house and a job. They would be returning to an American economy—even after a year and a half of gradual reconversion—still geared around producing tanks and planes, not clapboard houses and refrigerators. And the unions whose record of cooperation had been less than stel-

---

* It had not come without a human cost. The number of workers, male and female, who were killed or injured in the U.S. industries in 1942–43 exceeded the number of Americans killed or wounded in uniform, by a factor of twenty to one.

And not just workers. One hundred and eighty-nine senior GM officials died on the job during those five years of intense mobilization and activity. The obituary pages of *American Machinist* in those years show the names of one corporate executive after another who "died unexpectedly of a heart attack" or was cut down "after a brief illness."

lar in the war years were poised to resume their battle with private management—in the case of the auto industry, demanding postwar pay raises from Ford and GM as high as 30 percent.

How could America afford it? Now accustomed to anticipating and paying for everything that happened, Washington became worried again. A report released by Senator James Mead of New York predicted massive unemployment and inflation in the war's aftermath, as America's fighting men would be returning to empty factories and empty store shelves. "There should be no mincing of words" with the American people, the new head of the Office of War Mobilization and Reconversion, John Snyder, warned President Truman. The end of war production would mean the end of prosperity, and lead to eight million unemployed by the spring of 1946. Economist Leo Cherne thought that number wildly optimistic. It would be closer to 19 million, he asserted.[9] And Professor Paul Samuelson, later the dean of American economists, warned that unless the government took immediate action, "there would be ushered in the greatest period of unemployment and industrial dislocation which any economy has faced"—one that would equal the Great Depression.[10]

Others were not so sure. One was Knudsen's old boss Alfred Sloan. As he told the American Manufacturing Association in New Jersey back in June 1944, he foresaw a postwar world filled not with gloom and the pinched faces of the unemployed, but with a bright new explosion of American growth as the workers who had been saving away their paychecks now turned those savings loose.

"Out of this situation that I speak of, this tremendous aggregation of purchasing power, the tremendous demand for goods," Sloan predicted a very different future. "If American industry stepped forward and planned boldly and dramatically with courage, and expanded its operations, expanded its capacity, to take care of this post-war demand," then the result would be a huge jump in national income and rise in standard of living far greater than anything Americans had experienced before.[11] The dream of the future he and Knudsen had offered at the 1939 World's Fair would be realized within his lifetime.

Sloan was right, the doomsayers wrong. There was a brief hiccup in the last half of 1945 and early 1946, as national output dropped and unemployment rose to 3.9 percent. As price controls were lifted, inflation rose by 20 percent.

Then things smoothed out. Private capital investment, which had gone flat and even turned down during the war, tripled from $10.6 billion in 1945 to $30.6 billion in 1946 and never looked back. Companies began to turn to the capital and bond markets to raise funds for their postwar ventures. Stock prices surged, and by 1947 shares had gained value by 92 percent. As one economist has put it, "As the war ended, real prosperity returned almost overnight."[12]

It also turned out that for every returning veteran, there were three jobs waiting. The vast majority of women who had gone to work in the aircraft plants and steel mills set aside their welding tools and union membership and went home. Inflation eased, and factories that had converted to wartime use learned how to convert back to civilian production even faster. Companies like Frigidaire, Allis-Chalmers, and Walter Kidde quickly found their feet again in the new consumer-driven market. When the first Ford and Dodge and Chevrolet cars in four years rolled off the Detroit assembly lines, the buyers lined up to buy.

The gross domestic product of the United States in 1947 stood at $231 billion—roughly what it was in 1945. It rose to $258 billion in 1948, paused there for 1949, and then went from $285 billion in 1950 to $398 billion in 1955. In the two decades after 1948, GNP grew at an average annual rate of 4 percent. It was, as historian Michael Barone notes, "the most awesome economic growth ever seen in human history."[13]

It was a growth helped by a government debt much lower than it should have been, thanks to tax increases during the war, when everyone's incomes were rising. Federal tax receipts, which had been $5 billion in 1940, jumped to $49 billion the year of Hiroshima. This was followed in 1946 by a tax cut—imposed on a reluctant president by Congress, led by a coalition of Republicans and conservative Democrats—that pumped still more private investment into the reviving economy. Growth came on so fast that it could withstand the renewal of war in Korea in 1950 without missing a beat—and sustain a massive Pentagon budget all through the Cold War. Guns and butter had come to stay.

While the new U.S. military establishment built by American industry during the war guarded the free world, the new postwar American economy saw no limits to its growth. By 1960 the United States dominated the globe economically and strategically as no nation had ever done, before or since. A political scientist at Yale University, William T. R. Fox, coined a word to describe it: "superpower."[14]

And the man who had pulled the trigger on it all never lived to see it.

Bill Knudsen had come back from Europe exhausted but still willing to assume new duties at General Motors. But Alfred Sloan drew the line. "No, Bill, I'm sorry," he said, "you know the corporation's retirement policy." At age sixty-five, executives automatically became inactive.[15] Knudsen retired back to his house at 1501 Balmoral Drive. He worked with an automotive writer, Norman Beasley, on his memoirs, which were published as a somewhat rambling biography in 1947.

But his health had been broken by his unstinting service during the war. His granddaughter remembered visiting him and seeing a frail shadow of the big, boisterous grandfather her family had known before the war. In 1947 the American Legion hosted a dinner in his honor, but Knudsen was too ill to attend. On April 27, 1948—seven years and eleven months after President Franklin Roosevelt read the headlines about the collapse of France and picked up the phone—the world learned that the man everyone called Big Bill Knudsen had had a cerebral hemorrhage and died in his Detroit home.

"All of us," Knudsen wrote before his death, "have a duty to perform in this world."[16] Knudsen had performed his, with spectacular results. But already by his death the memory of what he had done was being erased, like a bronze monument being eaten away by acid rain.

Those who had been disappointed about being left out of the major decisions about the economy during the war—New Dealers and others—took their revenge by seizing control of the historical message. Business had had nothing to do with the miracle of war production, went the narrative. In fact, there was no miracle at all; it was the vast resources and extended reach of the federal government all along. As

Bruce Catton, editor of *American Heritage* magazine, wrote in his memoirs of his years as public relations officer at the War Production Board, big business constantly got in the way by demanding it be well paid for its services and refusing to embrace a new social contract combining government, business, and labor—an American version of socialism, one in which "labor moved up to partnership with owner-ship in the great U.S. industries" and government respected "its right and duty . . .to disregard the last vestiges of property rights in a time of crisis.[17]

Catton's version of the war years in Washington, which cast big busi-ness as the great obstructionist villain, joined up with the narrative put together by acolytes of economist John Maynard Keynes. Far from demonstrating that government intervention failed to revive the Amer-ican economy during the New Deal years, they argued that war mobi-lization proved the opposite. Roosevelt in the thirties simply hadn't spent enough, they claimed. Three hundred billion dollars of deficit spending for the war completed the job the New Deal's $50 billion couldn't. The implications were profound. Keynesians asserted, in war-time *or* peacetime, all you had to do to generate economic growth was increase demand through growing the federal budget or by running government deficits, or both. From 1940 to 1945, business and industry had simply been the lucky recipients of federal largesse. In peacetime, the poor, disadvantaged, and elderly would be next to receive the bless-ings of big government deficit spending. "Our mixed economy," wrote economist Paul Samuelson—the same man who predicted economic depression at war's end—"has a great future before it."[18]

Knudsen had forced Washington to give up the illusion of M–Day—of government effortlessly mobilizing an economy of war with the throw of a fiscal switch. Now the illusion returned, disguised as a Keynesian miracle rather than a mass production one.

Even before the war was over, Keynes's disciples occupied key posts in the Office of Price Administration, the Commerce Department, the Bureau of the Budget, and Treasury. When Keynes appeared at the in-ternational economic conference at Bretton Woods in 1944, the dele-gates sang, "For he's a jolly good fellow."[19] Knudsen and the businessmen who had made production possible were already forgotten. Samuelson's

Keynesian account of World War II in his best-selling textbook, *Economics,* completed the process of amnesia.

But then, the people Knudsen had recruited early into the war effort, the roll-up-the-sleeves men who had built their companies up from the ground and had spent their lives learning to make more things better and cheaper, were also disappearing. Henry Ford died a year before the big Dane, in April 1947. Bill Jeffers, the railroad man who built the synthetic rubber industry from nothing, went the way of all flesh in 1953. Andrew Jackson Higgins, the landing-craft wizard had died the year before, as did Alvan Macauley of Packard, whom Knudsen had called when he needed someone to build Rolls-Royce Merlin engines.

Kaufman T. Keller, whom Knudsen had also called that summer of 1940, quit as president of Chrysler in 1950. That year the unions and the big auto and steel makers, acting under the watchful eye of President Truman, cut a deal that allowed union wages and fringe benefits— in 1943 Congress had exempted health and pension concessions from federal taxation—to steadily rise in exchange for those companies knowing what their labor costs would look like, year to year. Keller stayed on the board of the company until 1956. His death followed a decade later.

Tom Girdler, Kaiser's steelmaking mentor who had turned Consolidated Aircraft into a mass-production giant, died in 1965. Felix Kahn was struck down by a heart attack in 1958—as it happened at the Shoreham Hotel in Washington, where his old Six Companies partner had headquartered the Kaiser war effort.

As for Knudsen's old rival Charlie Sorensen, he stayed as tough and ornery as ever. When Henry Ford II took over his father's company in December 1943 and failed to offer Sorensen any part in senior management, Cast-Iron Charlie abruptly quit. He switched to Willys-Overland, the makers of the jeep, and supervised their conversion to peacetime production, including turning out more versions of the most famous Army vehicle of World War II.

Sorensen went through more than one clash with the Willys board, but managed to hang on until 1950. Then he retired and took off for the Caribbean, where he sailed his beloved yacht, *White Cloud,* and nursed his many resentments.

Three years later Willys was sold to the other giant of the war years, Henry Kaiser.

Kaiser was one of the last of the old breed, and the most complicated.

He had anticipated the postwar boom by four years. "We have only a glimpse of what the future holds," he told an audience in September 1942, echoing Alfred Sloan's words at the World's Fair three years earlier. "A pent-up consumer demand will be released, seeking satisfaction in every artifice and device we know how to make."[20]

When the war ended, Kaiser plunged out in every direction. He struggled hard to keep the Richmond and Portland yards open. In August 1946, Richmond No. 3 was still employing 3,500 workers. But in October the Maritime Commission officially wrapped up operations in both yards. A tearful Kaiser told his workers and managers of his "deep regret" at having to shut down what had become the most famous shipyards of the war.[21] But in his own mind, he had already moved on.

He expanded his steel and magnesium operations, and started up Kaiser Aluminum in 1946, turning a $5 million profit his first year of operation. His experience with building homes for shipyard workers drew him to the possibility of postwar home building. He recruited designer Norman Bel Geddes—the same designer who had built GM's Futurama for the 1939 World's Fair—to create a prefabricated three-room steel frame house for only $1,300. He launched Kaiser Community Homes, Inc., which built miles of sprawling suburban homes across places like Panorama City, California—the ancestor of the tract housing development.

In the postwar glow, it was easy to forget the shortcomings of the Kaiser empire. After all, there had been the Hughes debacle, the cracked Liberty Ships, and the ubiquitous but cheaply made and under-armored baby flattop carriers that the sailors who sailed them called "Kaiser coffins" and "one-torpedo ships."[22] What finally pulled the public up short, however, was his disastrous venture into the Detroit auto industry.

Just as he had humbled Big Steel and Big Aluminum, so Henry Kaiser figured he could teach Ford, GM, and Chrysler something about how to make cars. He had all the elements of the Kaiser success formula. There was the teaming up with Willys-Overland's knowledgeable boss, Joseph Frazer; the sweetheart deal with the United Auto Workers, including health benefits for all workers; a plant that he could boast was the largest in the world—nothing less than Charlie Sorensen's Willow Run, which he had bought from Ford for $12 million. Then there was the Kaiser public relations machine, splashing raves across the pages of *Time* and *Life;* and an award-winning automobile design, the "Henry J."

The one thing missing was generous government funding. Kaiser learned that selling to the American public was more difficult than selling to the federal government. He had to rely instead on private investors and the Bank of America, and soon found himself fatally undercapitalized. He planned to build the Henry J. for less than four hundred dollars—something his car allies told him was an impossibility.[23] No one bought his cars, so Kaiser opened plants in Argentina and Brazil, hoping to attract Latin American buyers. In desperation he reconverted Willow Run into an aircraft factory, to make transoceanic cargo planes—reviving the old Hughes dream.

Nothing worked. A discouraged Henry Kaiser had to sell his entire operation in 1958. It had been a spectacular disaster. Although he went on to launch successful construction ventures in California and Hawaii, his new adopted home, and Kaiser Aluminum remained a powerful industrial enterprise, his reputation as America's entrepreneurial wizard was permanently tarnished.

Still, the master builder now in his sixties remained as tough and tireless as ever. Associate Tim Yee recalled doing a full day's work in Honolulu, then catching a red-eye back to the mainland with the old man, which meant discussing business all night and a normal workday on arrival. Clay Bedford's brother Tim recalled a whirlwind trip to Brazil to find investors for Kaiser-Frazer, which involved an all-night flight from Oakland and deplaning in a hot, sticky early-morning Rio de Janeiro. There was no time to change or visit the hotel. Instead, he and Kaiser trooped off to a series of meetings with Brazilian notables through lunch, drinks, and cigars until late afternoon. Kaiser decided

Bedford needed to go over some of the figures they had presented that morning, but also insisted he accompany Kaiser and the Brazilians on a tour of Rio nightclubs.

Sometime after midnight Bedford got back to the hotel and re-worked the numbers. At 5 A.M. he threw himself into bed. Two hours later the phone rang. It was Kaiser, who had spent the night partying with his hosts. "Where are the figures?" he wanted to know. He and Bedford scanned them over breakfast, then headed back to a second round with the Brazilians. Henry Kaiser did the presentation himself. "It was dynamite," Tim Bedford had to admit, "he was just incredible."[24]

By 1966 the man who used to rise regularly at 4:30 A.M. and hit the telephone to associates around the world finally began to flag. Building Hawaii Kai on Honolulu Island was his last great construction project. At the insistence of his second wife, Ale, he had slimmed down to 225 pounds for his eighty-fourth birthday. But the old drive was gone; more and more time during the day was spent in bed. What revived him were visits by those who had been his allies during the war years, like his son Edgar and Clay Bedford. Sensing this, the faithful Alonzo Ordway sent him a letter, dated February 6, 1967.

It concerned the day they jumped off the train, at the start of the great adventure.

> You probably recall that it was 46 years ago this month when you and I walked into the general offices of the Division of Highways [in Redding].... Now their headquarters is in a large multi-story building just opposite the Capitol and covers about a block. Possibly you recall that the receptionist the first time we called (who was also the switchboard operator) told us her feet were cold, so we went out and bought an electric heater for her, which of course paid for itself many times over in our later business....
>
> I would like to visit you someday for a few hours at your convenience so that I can see your pet project and enjoy smell-ing dirt with you. I would only plan to be there for part of the day....[25]

Ordway never got the chance. In late August of 1967, at age eighty-five, an increasingly bedridden Henry Kaiser slipped into a coma and died on August 24. Ordway would be a pallbearer at the funeral.

Already the era of American industrial exuberance that character-ized the arsenal of democracy was fading. Thanks to two decades of concessions to unions, Kaiser's steel and aluminum companies were about to suffer from the same problems as the rest of industrial Amer-ica: high costs and low productivity plus cutthroat overseas competi-tion—ironically, from Japan and Germany, where Kaiser Engineers had helped to install new efficient steel- and ship-making facilities after the war. The same fate was about to befall Detroit, the heartland of the arsenal of democracy. From Fontana to Pittsburgh, manufacturing America was in headlong retreat. The term "smokestack industry" would soon become a term of derision, even abuse, as it conjured up images of pollution, drab company housing, and dead-end blue-collar jobs.

Yet no man had tried to do more for his own employees than Henry Kaiser, and no firm left a more important legacy for the future of pri-vately funded health care for workers than Kaiser Permanente. And no one gave America's push for victory in World War II a sunnier, more optimistic face than the bald man with the glasses and the big grin.

It was the same optimism that had animated Bill Knudsen: the sense that America carried the seeds of its own renewal, the capacity to over-come failure and disaster and push forward. Even on his deathbed, his grandson Henry F. Kaiser remembers, he always spoke about the future, not the past.

After Kaiser's death someone remembered his encounter with a dis-couraged workman at a work site ruined by a passing storm. Every-thing, including the big earth-moving equipment, was submerged in a sea of mud.

"What are we going to do?" the worker moaned. "Just look at this mud."

"What mud?" Kaiser said. "I see only that big sun shining down. It's going to turn that mud into solid ground."

See the sun. Smell the dirt.

ACKNOWLEDGMENTS

THIS BOOK IS a special salute to the millions of Americans who worked in the factories, shipyards, mines, farms, plants, and offices to make victory in World War II possible—and to those who spoke to me about their service and sacrifice during those years. We all owe a permanent debt of gratitude to them.

Writing this book was an amazing experience. So many wonderful people shared their time, thoughts, and labor to make it happen, and I'm pleased to have the opportunity to thank as many of them as I can.

I start with the American Enterprise Institute, where I served as a visiting scholar from September 2010 to May 2012. AEI's former president Chris DeMuth was enthusiastic about the project from the start, saw its rich possibilities, and offered invaluable advice at every stage. AEI's current president, Arthur Brooks, warmly extended every resource AEI had to offer, as did its executive vice president, David Gerson. Henry Olsen, director of the National Research Initiative, made sure support for the book was there at critical times, and helped me enormously in understanding the book's lessons for the present.

The list of AEI colleagues who helped in my research is staggeringly long, but certain names stand out: Joe Antos, Michael Auslin, Claude Barfield, Michael Barone, Kevin Hassett, Bob Helms, Marvin Kosters, Michael Novak, and Alex Pollock, as well as Tom Donnelly and Gary Schmitt of AEI's Center for Defense Studies. Véronique Rodman encouraged me to think creatively about the book's many audiences, as did John Cusey of AEI's Government Relations Office. And a very special thanks goes to my research assistant Keriann Hopkins, who tirelessly helped with the research and then correcting the typescript and galleys, and tracked down books, images, and photo permissions with riveting diligence. Thanks also to interns Joey McCoy and Harrison Dietzmann for their help along the way.

One of the first people I spoke to about this project was my friend Roger Hertog, a champion and advocate of all my work. Paul Johnson and Steve Forbes helped to shape many of the book's major themes, as did Dan Senor and the Discovery Institute's George Gilder. And every historian venturing into the arena of industrial mobilization during World War II owes an enormous debt to Alan Gropman of the National Defense University, Professor Mark Harrison of the University of Warwick, and Professor Richard Overy, author of *How the Allies Won.* Without their prior work, this project would not have been possible.

Grateful thanks also go to the staff of the National Automotive History Collection at the Detroit Public Library and the Henry J. Kaiser Papers at the University of California, Berkeley's Bancroft Library; the Library of Congress; the Henry Ford Collection; the National Archives at College Park, Maryland; the libraries at Georgetown University and George Washington University; the New York Public Library; the Navy Historical Center at the Washington Shipyards; and the U.S. Army Center of Military History at Fort McNair, particularly its former chief archivist Frank Shirer; as well as the friendly people who run the Rosie the Riveter Trust at the Home Front National Park in Richmond, California.

The Cosmos Club Library, and librarian Karen Mark, helped with the earliest stages of my research. Staff past and present from the Grumman History Center at Bethpage, New York, answered many important questions, while the resources for studying the history of American business at the Hagley Library and Archives in Wilmington, Delaware, are matched only by the helpfulness of the staff and the beauty and comfort of its surroundings.

The libraries at the University of Virginia in Charlottesville, especially the Brown Science and Engineering Library, were indispensable to the project from start to finish, as were the efforts of librarians Philip McEldowney and Warner Granade in making my work as painless and trouble free as possible.

I also want to thank the many people who agreed to sit down for interviews about parents and grandparents who were central to the book. They included Fred Eberstadt, Peter and Clay Bedford Junior, Richard Girdler, and Judith Knudsen Christie. Ms. Christie also kindly gave me permission to read the unpublished oral history interview of her aunt and Bill Knudsen's daughter, Martha Knudsen. Warren Kidder, author of *Willow Run: Colossus of American Industry,* offered interesting insights about working with Henry Kaiser in the postwar years. And many years ago the late John J. McCloy generously took time to answer my questions about working with the legendary Colonel Henry L. Stimson at the War Department.

Automotive scholar Mike Davis kindly took time to read the first chapter of the book, while Bob Brown, editor of *Magnesium Monthly Review,* not only read chapters but provided help with everything from documenting Henry Kaiser's magnesium ventures to finding me a B-29 pilot's manual. My friend Jeb Nadaner, formerly of the Department of Defense and now at Lockheed Martin, carefully followed the book's progress and offered suggestions and insights that all helped to make it a better book.

Tom Veblen's friendship, support, and sage counsel decisively charted the book's course, and he kindly read an early draft of the manuscript. Linda Veblen's hospitality and her reminiscences of her father's service as a B-25 pilot in Italy also helped to understand the real meaning of the arsenal of democracy. My editor at the *New York Post,* Bob McManus, saw the significance of the project and passed along materials to help.

Other friends offered advice, encouragement, read early chapters, or generally put me on to the right research trail. They include (again, in alphabetical order) Captain Joseph Callo, USN (ret.); James Capua; Mike Du Pont; my former *Commentary* editor, Neal Kozodoy; my brother-in-law Captain Keith Krapels, USN; John W. Miller; Chet Nagle; Mark J Reed; Ivor Tiefenbrun; and Kevin Weir. Arlene Anns generously opened her private collection of materials relating to *American Machinist* magazine during the war years, and Philip Anns, ex-Hellcat pilot and Royal Navy (ret.), provided special inspiration and expert help. Friend and neighbor Len Wolowicz helped me to solve the problem of why Liberty ships developed cracks, and answered innumerable questions about the wartime steel industry.

So many scholars helped with individual chapters or problems both literary and archival, I can't list them all, but certain ones deserve special mention: Max Boot, Carlo D'Este, Victor Davis Hanson, Tim Kane, Richard Langworth, Andrew Roberts, Alex Rose, and Mark Wilson of the University of North Carolina–Charlotte.

My editor at Random House, Jonathan Jao, not only read and edited early drafts with an expert eye, but inadvertently contributed to the book's birth in 2009 by asking me what I *really* wanted to write about after *Gandhi & Churchill*. My agents Glen Hartley and Lynn Chu relished the project from the start almost as much as I did. My parents, Arthur and Barbara Herman, read chapters, sent research materials, and reminisced about life in home front America in ways that helped to make the book more authentic.

My most important debt however, is to my wife, Beth. She understood the importance of this book almost from the moment I started working on it, and put up with the piles of books, diagrams, and back issues of *American Machinist, Business Week,* and *Fortune* that threatened to devour our house. She read early drafts of chapters, and I couldn't have completed *Freedom's Forge* without her. She has stuck with me through thick and thin.

That is why the book is lovingly dedicated to her.

APPENDIX A

GROWING THE ARSENAL OF DEMOCRACY, 1940–1945

Total U.S. Munitions Spending

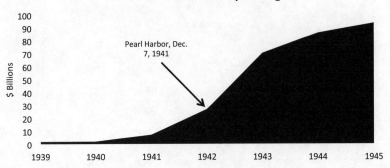

Rate of Increase in U.S. Munitions Spending

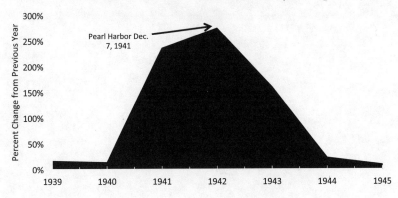

Source: "Bicentennial Edition: Historical Statistics of the United States, Colonial Times to 1970," U.S. Department of Commerce & USGovernmentSpending.com

APPENDIX B

JOINING THE ARSENAL OF DEMOCRACY

The following is an excerpt from *Your Business Goes to War* by Leo Cherne (Boston: Houghton Mifflin, 1942, pp. 50–53).

Typical Facility Conversions

Lists of typical conversions should be taken only as guides. Whether or not your plant can be converted to turn out a specific military product is an engineering problem which requires an engineering answer based on the size, facilities, and the other productive resources of your business. Each plant must be surveyed individually before it can be decided whether conversion to war output is possible. The following list of conversions which have already been carried out is suggestive.

Peacetime Products	War Products
Adding machines	Automatic pistols
Agricultural implements	Artillery shell
	Combat wagons and gun carriages
Automatic lead pencils	Ammunition components
Automobile accessories	Shell, 37m/m
Automobile bodies	Airplane parts
Automobile cranks, brakes, rods, etc.	Fuze, P.D., M52
Automobile engines and motor cars	Airplane type combat tank engines
Automobile loading devices	M.C. mounts
Automobile steering gears	Machine guns

Automobiles	Artillery projectiles—shell
	Cartridge cases 75m/m
Automotive specialties	Bullet cores
Batteries, sparkplugs, radio parts, roller skates	Fuze, B.C., M58
Boats and lighters	Pontoon bridges
Bottle caps, bottlers, dairy and packers' machine closures, cork insulation	Mounts, tripod, cal. .50
Bottle coolers and dispensers	Mine anti-tank, metal parts
Box toes	Scabbards
Buses and trolleys	Machining, 75m/m H.E. shell
Business machines and appliances	Artillery shell
Canners' machinery	Ammunition boxes
Canning and cooking apparatus	Fuze, P.D., M51 (metal parts)
Cans and food containers	Gas-mask canisters
Cash registers and business machines	Bomb fuzes
Casters, wheels, and furniture hardware	Fuze, P.D., M56
Clamps, magneto couplings, etc.	Fuze, anti-tank mine
Coin-operated vending machines and ice-cream freezers	Shell, R.F., H.E. 40m/m
Commercial steel castings	Tripods for anti-aircraft guns
Conveyors, excavators, stokers, chain belts	Mounts T2, 90m/m
Cooling systems and equipment	Helmets
Cork and glass products	Shell, 3″ M42B2
Cotton mill machines (looms)	Shot, S.A.P., 37m/m, M74
Cranks, ball	Casing, burster, M6
Die casting (non-ferrous)	Booster, M22
Drop forgings	Machining, artillery shell
Electric cleaners, clothes washers, etc.	Mounts, tripod, M.G., cal. .50
Electric elevators	Recoil mechanisms for 3″ A.A. guns

Electric equipment	Cartridge cases, 105m/m howitzer
Electric fans, dryers, heaters, motors	Flares, A.C., parts, M26
Electric refrigerators	Airplane parts
Electric storage batteries	Fuze, P.D., M48 (metal parts)
Electric utility outdoor equipment	Shell, 75m/m, M48 (M)
Electric welded pipe	Demolition bombs and torpedo parts
Enameled steel stamping, specialties and signs	Anti-tank mine
Fabricated basic-steel products	Armor-piercing projectiles
Fabricated piping and air-conditioning equipment	Bomb bodies
Fire sprinklers and alarms	Artillery ammunition components
Fireworks and toys	Signals, A.C.
Flexible shafts, electric household appliances, electric shavers, etc.	Fuze, percussion, no. 253
Gas-stove burners, valves and lighters	Fuze, percussion, M31 (metal parts)
Glass moulds	Burster, M7 for bomb
Hardware	Cartridge cases, 37m/m
Heating and cooling systems	Sighting devices, cal. .30 rifles
Household appliances	Fuze, T.S.R., M54
Jewelry	Fuze, B.D., M58
Lawn mowers	Machining shrapnel
Linoleum and floor coverings	Machining, 75m/m artillery shell
Locomotive type boilers	Track shoe links on tanks
Matches	Aircraft cartridge signals
Metal fabricators and enameling	Shell, 105m/m
	Case cartridge, 105 howitzer
Metal household specialties	Anti-tank mines, H.E.
Milling and drilling machines, precision lathes, dial indicators and gauges	Gauges
Mimeograph brand products	Fuze, B.D., M58

Mining machinery	Light combat tanks
Motor cars	Light combat tanks
Motor cooling equipment	Airplane landing wheels
Office furniture	Bomb containers
Oil well and drillers' supplies	Machining 155m/m shell
Pipe fittings and valves	Hand grenades
Pipe organs	Saddle frames
Plumbing and sanitary fixtures	Machining artillery shell
Portable machinery, agricultural implements, hydraulic presses, sawmill machines	81m/m machine mounts
Postal meters	Bomb mechanisms
Precision instruments	Navigation compasses
Printing presses	Gun—howitzer parts. Recoil mechanisms for 155 m/m howitzers
Pullman cars	Forgings for 105m/m howitzer
Pumps and woodworking machinery	Machining artillery shell
Pumps, meters, valves	Fuze, percussion no. 253, 20m/m
Radio-phonographs	Bomb fuzes and parts
Radio vibrators, antennae	Fuze, bomb, M103
Rail and wire products	Artillery shell
Railroad cars	Artillery shell forgings
Railroad locomotives	Machining 155m/m shell
Railway signals	Machining artillery shell
Razors	Primers, percussion, M23A1
Rolled copper plate	Metal components for ammunition
Rolled steel products	3″ anti-aircraft gun forgings
Roller skates, wheels, keys, etc.	Metal parts for boosters
Sash doors and blinds	Cartridge cases, 37m/m, M17
Screens-steel sash, dies, pulleys	Fuze, P.D., M52
Screw-machine products, milling machines and hair-clipping machines	Projectiles, ball, 20m/m

Sheet-metal novelties	Links, for 20m/m gun M1
Shoe and harness machines	Shot, A.P., 20m/m
Shoes, men's	Helmet linings
Silk ribbons (also silk goods)	Silk, parachute, pyrotechnics
Springs and metal stampings	Gas-mask parts
Steel-lead containers	Ammunition adapters and boosters
Steel products	Forgings, 75m/m H.E. shell
Steel vaults	Shell, 105m/m (M)
Stoves, sheet-metal products, etc.	Metallic belt links
Textile machines	Mounts, tripod
Textile trimmings, etc.	Ammunition belts
Tools, dies, jigs, fixtures, gauges, and special machines	Gauges, manufacturing 37m/m guns
Vacuum cleaners	Gas-mask parts
Valves, cocks	Shell, 20m/m H.E. (metal parts)
Washing and ironing machines	Anti-tank mine H.E., M1
Watches	Mechanical time fuzes
Watch bracelets	Booster, M22
Wheelbarrows and road scrapers	Ammunition carts for machine guns

The major key to your ability to produce on munitions is your machine tool equipment. If you have machine tools which are scarce, your chances of getting into war production should be good. Following is a list of the machine tools most needed for work on war prime and subcontracts:

Horizontal boring machines	4″ bar and up
Vertical boring machines	54″ and up
Radial drills	15″ column and up
Jig borers	All sizes
Gear-grinding machines	All sizes
Thread-grinding machines	All sizes
Hobbing machines	All sizes
Engine lathes	36″ and up
Turret lathes	Chucking Type and 2½″ bar and up

Multiple spindle automatic screw machines	3″ bar and up
Milling machines (vertical or horizontal)	No. 2 and up
Thread–milling machines	All sizes
Planers	72″ and up
Die sinkers	All sizes
Reciprocating table surface grinders grinding periphery of solid wheel	For work 12″ wide by 12″ high and up
Cylindrical grinding machines (est.)	24″ work dia. and up
Planer type milling machines	For work 48″ wide by 48″ high and up
Vertical shapers (not slotters)	All sizes
Gear shapers, plane (Int.)	54″ and up

NOTES

PROLOGUE

1. Marc Bloch, *Strange Defeat* (New York: Norton, 1968), 40–43.
2. John Lukacs, *The Duel: The Eighty-Day Struggle Between Churchill and Hitler* (New York: Ticknor and Fields, 1990), 64.
3. C-9x, May 13, 1940, in Warren Kimball, ed., *Churchill and Roosevelt: The Complete Correspondence,* Vol. 1 (Princeton, NJ: Princeton University Press), 37.
4. Kimball, *Churchill and Roosevelt,* Vol. 1, 37.
5. William Langer and S. Everett Gleason, *The Undeclared War, 1940–1941* (New York: Harper and Brothers, 1953), 198, 200.
6. Report of the Special Committee on Investigation of the Munitions Industry, U.S. Congress, Senate, 74th Congress, Second Session, February 24, 1936, 3–13.
7. Francis Walton, *The Miracle of World War II: How American Industry Made Victory Possible* (New York: Macmillan, 1956).
8. Duncan Ballantine, *U.S. Naval Logistics in the Second World War* (Princeton, NJ: Princeton University Press, 1947), 29.
9. W. F. Craven and J. L. Cate, *The Army Air Forces in World War II,* Vol. 1 (Washington, DC: Office of Air Force History, 1955), 104.
10. A.J.P. Taylor, *The Origins of the Second World War* (Greenwich, CT: Fawcett, 1966), 185.

11. Quoted in Frank Friedel, *Franklin D. Roosevelt: A Rendezvous with Destiny* (Boston: Little, Brown, 1990), 311.

12. Craven and Cate, *Army Air Forces in World War II,* Vol. 1, 104.

13. *Life,* November 30, 1942, 124.

14. Richard Holl, *From the Boardroom to the War Room: America's Corporate Liberals and FDR's Preparedness Program* (Rochester, NY: Rochester University Press, 2005), 41.

15. Holl, *From the Boardroom,* 78.

16. David Reynolds, *From Munich to Pearl Harbor* (Chicago: Dee Publishing, 2001), 70.

17. Forrest Pogue, *George C. Marshall,* Vol. 2 (London: MacGibbon and Kee, 1964), 17.

18. Norman Beasley, *Knudsen: A Biography* (New York: McGraw-Hill, 1947), 228.

19. Stanley Weintraub, *Eisenhower, MacArthur, Marshall: Three Generals Who Saved the Country* (New York: Simon and Schuster, 2007), 106.

20. Beasley, *Knudsen,* 229.

21. Walter Millis, *Arms and Men: A Study in American Military History* (New York: Putnam, 1956), 270.

22. John Morton Blum, *From the Morgenthau Diaries,* Vol. 2 (Boston: Houghton Mifflin, 1965); Beasely, *Knudsen,* 229–30.

23. Kimball, *Churchill and Roosevelt,* Vol. 1, 40.

24. Bernard Baruch, *Baruch: The Public Years* (New York: Henry Holt, 1957), 273.

25. Holl, *From the Boardroom,* 46; R. Elberton Smith, *The Army and Economic Mobilization* (Washington, DC: Center of Military History, 1991), 37–38.

26. Beasley, *Knudsen,* 230.

27. *The Goebbels Diaries 1939–1941* (New York: Putnam, 1982), entry for June 14, 1941, 414.

CHAPTER ONE: The Gentle Giant

1. Beasley, *Knudsen,* 1.

2. Beasley, *Knudsen,* 1.

3. Christy Borth, *Masters of Mass Production* (Indianapolis: Bobbs-Merrill, 1945), 60.

4. *American National Biography* (hereafter cited as *ANB*) (New York: Oxford University Press, 1999), Vol. 12, 843.

5. Beasley, *Knudsen,* 2.

6. Beasley, *Knudsen,* 3–4.

7. Borth, *Masters of Mass Production,* 40.

8. Detroit Public Library: Knudsen Collection, Part 4, Box 1: Keim Mills, May 1, 1940.

9. *ANB,* 843.

10. Beasley, *Knudsen,* 28.

11. James Fink, "William Signius Knudsen," in George May, ed., *The Automotive Industry 1920–1980* (New York: Facts on File, 1989).

12. David Hounshell, *From the American System to Mass Production 1800–1932* (Baltimore: Johns Hopkins University Press, 1984), 221–22.

13. Hounshell, *American System,* 223; Charles Sorensen, *My Forty Years with Ford* (New York: Norton, 1956), 45.

14. Hounshell, *American System,* 230–31.

15. Beasley, *Knudsen,* 41.

16. Beasley, *Knudsen,* 42,

17. Beasley, *Knudsen,* 52–53.

18. Beasley, *Knudsen,* 59–60; Hounshell, *American System,* 264.

19. Knudsen, "How the Chevrolet Company Applies Its Own Slogan to Production," *Industrial Management* 76 (August 1927), 65–68.

20. Allan Nevins, *Ford: Expansion and Challenge, 1915–1933* (New York: Scribner, 1954–63), 255.

21. Beasley, *Knudsen,* 54.

22. Borth, *Masters of Mass Production.*

23. Beasley, *Knudsen,* 56.

24. *ANB,* 843.

25. Nevins, *Ford: Expansion and Challenge.*

26. Beasley, *Knudsen,* 62–63.

27. Beasley, *Knudsen,* 94.

28. Beasley, *Knudsen,* 107.

29. Beasley, *Knudsen,* 109.

30. Malcolm Bingay, *Detroit Is My Own Home Town* (Indianapolis: Bobbs-Merrill, 1946), 50.

31. Alfred P. Sloan, *Adventures of a White-Collar Man* (New York: Doubleday, 1941), 8.

32. Alfred P. Sloan, *My Years with General Motors* (New York: Doubleday, 1964).

33. Walter Chrysler, *Life of an American Workman* (New York: Dodd and Mead, 1950), 143.

34. Lawrence Gustin, *Billy Durant: Creator of General Motors* (Grand Rapids, MI: Eerdmans, 1973), 91.

35. Gustin, *Durant,* 115–16, 185–89.

36. Sloan, *My Years with General Motors,* 27.

37. Gustin, *Durant,* 208.

38. Sloan, *My Years with General Motors.*

39. Sloan, *Adventures,* 134.

40. See "Organization Study," in Alfred D. Chandler Jr., *Strategy and Structure* (Cambridge, MA: MIT Press, 1962), 133–42.

41. David Farber, *Sloan Rules: Alfred Sloan and the Triumph of General Motors* (Chicago: University of Chicago Press, 2002), 50.

42. Beasley, *Knudsen*, 113; Sloan, *Adventures*, 138.

43. *Life*, March 31, 1941, 107.

44. Sloan, *Adventures*, 140.

45. *Life*, March 31, 1941, 107.

46. Arthur Kuhn, *GM Passes Ford, 1918–1938* (University Park: Pennsylvania State University Press, 1986), 112–13.

47. Beasley, *Knudsen*, 115.

48. *Life*, March 31, 1941.

49. J. Smith, *Reminiscences*, quoted in Nevins, *Ford: Expansion and Challenge*, 16.

50. Beasley, *Knudsen*, 119.

51. "How the Chevrolet Company Applies Its Own Slogan to Production," *Industrial Management* 76 (August 1927), 65–68.

52. Beasley, *Knudsen*.

53. Kuhn, *GM Passes Ford;* Beasley, *Knudsen*, 128.

54. Beasley, *Knudsen*, 132.

55. Hounshell, *American System*, 264–65.

56. Memo by Alfred Sloan, July 29, 1925, quoted in Hounshell, *American System*, 263.

57. Richard Crabb, *Birth of a Giant: The Men and Incidents That Gave America the Motor Car* (Philadelphia: Chilton, 1970), 398.

58. "How the Chevrolet Company," 66.

59. Hounshell, *American System*, 266.

60. Kuhn, *GM Passes Ford;* Hounshell, *American System*, 266.

61. Beasley, *Knudsen*, 139.

62. Crabb, *Birth of a Giant*, 404–6.

63. See Beasley, *Knudsen*, 219–21.

64. *Detroit News*, May 3, 1937, quoted in Beasley, *Knudsen*, 177.

CHAPTER TWO: The Master Builder

1. Mark Foster, *Henry J. Kaiser: Builder of the American West* (Austin: University of Texas Press, 1989), 9.

2. Kaiser Papers, Bancroft Library, University of California, Berkeley: *Los Angeles Evening Express*, December 13, 1948.

3. John Gunther, *Inside U.S.A.* (New York: Harper and Brothers, 1947), 65.

4. Foster, *Kaiser*, 13.

5. Foster, *Kaiser*, 16.

6. Kaiser Papers: "Notes for Speech to Kaiser-Frazer Dealers, Willow Run, January 10, 1949," Carton 61, Folder 7.

7. Kaiser Papers: "Facts about Henry J. Kaiser," pamphlet (Oakland: Kaiser Co., September 19, 1946).

8. Beasley, *Knudsen*, 29.

9. Gary Giddins, *Bing Crosby: A Pocketful of Dreams—The Early Years, 1903–1940* (New York: Little, Brown, 2001), 36, 39.

10. Kaiser Papers: "Notes for Speech to Kaiser-Frazer Dealers."

11. Foster, *Kaiser,* 22.

12. Foster, *Kaiser,* 23.

13. Kaiser Papers: "50 Year Book," n.p., n.d., Carton 295.

14. John B. Rae, *The Road and Car in American Life* (Cambridge, MA: MIT Press, 1971).

15. Quoted in Stephen Adams, *Mr. Kaiser Goes to Washington: The Rise of a Government Entrepreneur* (Chapel Hill: University of North Carolina Press, 1997), 17.

16. Foster, *Kaiser,* 29.

17. Kaiser Papers: Questions and Answers about Henry J. Kaiser, p. 48.

18. Albert Heiner, *Henry J. Kaiser: Western Colossus* (San Francisco: Halo Books, 1991), 21–22.

19. Heiner, *Kaiser,* 22.

20. Kaiser Papers; Clay Bedford interview, quoted in Heiner, *Kaiser,* 41.

21. Foster, *Kaiser,* 32.

22. Author's interview with Peter Bedford, October 17, 2010.

23. Quoted in Heiner, *Kaiser,* 47.

24. Heiner, *Kaiser,* 29.

25. Kaiser Papers: Alonzo Ordway to Neal Fellom, January 31, 1967, Carton 257.

26. Quoted in Adams, *Mr. Kaiser Goes to Washington,* 2.

27. Joseph Stevens, *Hoover Dam: An American Adventure* (Norman: University of Oklahoma Press, 1988), 4–5, 48.

28. Reis interview, quoted in Heiner, *Kaiser,* 48.

29. Stevens, *Hoover Dam,* 42.

30. "Earthmovers I," *Fortune,* August 1943, 104–5.

31. Stevens, *Hoover Dam,* 40–41.

32. "Earthmovers I," 145.

33. Donald E. Wolf, *Big Dams and Other Dreams: The Six Companies Story* (Norman: University of Oklahoma Press, 1996), 29.

34. Stevens, *Hoover Dam,* 79.

35. "Earthmovers I," 211–14.

36. Interior Papers: Ickes to Kaiser, March 23, 1936, quoted in Foster, *Kaiser,* 60.

37. Stevens, *Hoover Dam,* 245.

38. Stevens, *Hoover Dam,* 246–48.

39. Foster, *Kaiser,* 64.

40. Quoted in Adams, *Mr. Kaiser Goes to Washington,* 41.

41. Friedel, *Franklin D. Roosevelt,* 295.

CHAPTER THREE: The World of Tomorrow

1. James Mauro, *Twilight at the World of Tomorrow* (New York: Ballantine Books, 2010), 217–18.

2. David Gelernter, *1939: The Lost World of the Fair* (New York: Free Press, 1995), 37.

3. Gelernter, *1939,* 19–20.

4. Beasley, *Knudsen,* 222–23.

5. David Halberstam, *The Reckoning* (New York: Morrow, 1986), 378.

6. *Life,* May 31, 1941, 119.

7. Beasley, *Knudsen,* 197.

8. Douglas Haskell, "To-morrow and the World's Fair," *Architectural Record,* August 1940.

9. Sloan, *Adventures,* 206.

10. Gelernter, *1939.*

11. Mauro, *Twilight,* 172.

12. Geoffrey Hellman, "Design for Living–III," *New Yorker,* February 22, 1941, 29–31.

13. Mauro, *Twilight,* 177.

14. Gelernter, *1939,* 24–25.

15. Sloan, *Adventures,* 207–8.

16. Beasley, *Knudsen,* 202.

17. Knudsen Papers, Subseries A: Box 4, correspondence 13–16.

18. Mauro, *Twilight,* 291.

CHAPTER FOUR: Getting Started

1. Beasley, *Knudsen,* 234.

2. Russell Buhite and David Levy, *FDR's Fireside Chats* (Norman: University of Oklahoma Press, 1992), May 26, 1940, 159; Beasley, *Knudsen,* 231.

3. Interview with Martha Knudsen McKenney, quoted in M.W.R. Davis, *Detroit's Wartime Industry: Arsenal of Democracy* (Charleston, SC: Arcadia Publishing, 2007), 8.

4. Farber, *Sloan Rules,* 205.

5. Albert Blum, "Birth and Death of the M-Day Plan," in Harold Stein, ed., *American Civil-Military Decisions: A Book of Case Studies* (Tuscaloosa: University of Alabama Press, 1963), 77.

6. Beasley, *Knudsen,* 235.

7. Thomas Fleming, *The New Dealers' War: F.D.R. and the War within World War II* (New York: Basic Books, 2001), 161.

8. Robert Sherwood, *Roosevelt and Hopkins: An Intimate Biography* (New York: Harper and Brothers, 1948), 160.

9. Beasley, *Knudsen,* 237.

10. *New York Times,* May 28, 1940.

11. Beasley, *Knudsen,* 238.

12. Beasley, *Knudsen,* 238.

13. Richard Overy, *Why the Allies Won* (New York: Norton, 1995), 190.

14. Walton, *Miracle of World War II,* 41.

15. See chart in Alan L. Gropman, *The Big "L": American Logistics in World War II,* "Industrial Mobilization," 75.

16. Walton, *Miracle of World War II,* 25.

17. Burnham Finney, *Arsenal of Democracy: How Industry Builds Our Defense* (New York: Whittlesey House, 1941), 142–43.

18. John Paxton, "Myth vs. Reality: The Question of Mass Production in WWII," *Economic and Business Journal: Inquiries and Perspectives* (Vol. 1., No. 1, October 2008), 91–93; Mark Harrison, "Resource Mobilization for World War II, the USA, UK, USSR, and Germany, 1938–45," *Economic History Review,* Vol. 41, No. 2 (1988), 184.

19. *The Secret Diary of Harold L. Ickes,* Vol. 3 (New York: Simon and Schuster, 1953), 393.

20. *Secret Diary,* Vol. 3, entry for June 2, 1940, 194–95.

21. Thomas Fleming, *The New Dealers' War,* 85–86.

22. *Secret Diary,* Vol. 3, entry for June 30, 1940, 223.

23. Dwight Tuttle, *Harry L. Hopkins and Anglo-American-Soviet Relations 1941–45* (New York: Garland, 1983), 41–42.

24. Baruch, *Memoirs,* Vol. 2, 283.

25. Jesse Jones, *Fifty Billion Dollars* (New York: Macmillan, 1950), 66.

26. Jones, *Fifty Billion Dollars,* 271–75; Bascom Timmons, *Jesse H. Jones: The Man and the Statesman* (New York: Holt, 1956), 295.

27. Timmons, *Jones,* 296.

28. Gropman, *The Big "L,"* 12–13.

29. Holl, *From the Boardroom,* 72.

30. Gropman, *The Big "L,"* 12.

31. Harrison, "Mobilization for World War II," 9–10.

32. Beasley, *Knudsen,* 90.

33. Borth, *Masters of Mass Production,* 49.

34. David Lloyd George, *War Memoirs,* Vol. 2 (Boston: Little Brown, 1934), 1831.

35. Beasley, *Knudsen,* 245–46.

36. Harry C. Thomson and Lida Mayo, *The Ordnance Department: Procurement and Supply* (Washington, DC: Center of Military History, 1960, 2003), 45–46.

37. Robert G. Albion, *Forrestal and the Navy* (New York: Columbia University Press, 1962), 44–47.

38. *Time,* June 12, 1940, 18–19.

39. Knudsen Papers: Speech to General Motors Key City Club, September 1937.

40. Finney, *Arsenal of Democracy,* 27–28.

41. Beasley, *Knudsen,* 247.

42. *Time,* June 17, 1940, 17.

43. Henry Stimson, *Diary,* entry for October 4, 1940, 18.

44. Holl, *From the Boardrooom,* 53.

45. Minutes of the Advisory Commission-Council on National Defense (Washington, DC: Government Printing Office, 1946), 1–2.

46. Beasley, *Knudsen,* 254; Smith, *The Army and Economic Mobilization,* 130.

47. Beasley, *Knudsen,* 254–55.

48. Stimson, *Diary,* July 25, 1940, 36; August 14, 1940, 87.

49. Stimson, *Diary,* May 1941.

50. Quoted in Farber, *Sloan Rules,* 225.

51. Beasley, *Knudsen,* 295.

CHAPTER FIVE: Call to Arms

1. Alistair Cooke, *The American Home Front* (New York: Atlantic Monthly Press, 2006), 246.

2. John B. Rae, *Climb to Greatness: The American Aircraft Industry, 1920–1960* (Cambridge, MA: MIT Press, 1968), 104.

3. Edward Stettinius Jr., *Lend-Lease: Weapon for Victory* (New York: Macmillan, 1944), 14.

4. James Winchester, ed., *American Military Aircraft: A Century of Innovation* (New York: Metro Books), 282–83.

5. Stettinius, *Lend-Lease,* 23; Finney, *Arsenal of Democracy,* 56–57.

6. Richard Thruelson, *The Grumman Story* (New York: Praeger, 1976), 112.

7. Walton, *Miracle of World War II,* 419.

8. Cooke, *American Home Front,* 247.

9. Stettinius, *Lend-Lease,* 23.

10. Rae, *Climb to Greatness,* 103.

11. Kenneth Clark, *The Other Half: A Self-Portrait* (New York: Harper and Row, 1977), 17.

12. Stettinius, *Lend-Lease,* 25.

13. Stettinius, *Lend-Lease,* 26.

14. Stettinius, *Lend-Lease,* 28.

15. Smith, *The Army and Economic Mobilization,* 130–31.

16. *Industrial Mobilization for War* (History of the War Production Board and Predecessor Agencies, 1940–45) (Washington, DC: Government Printing Office, 1947), Vol. 1, 42.

17. Burns Memo, June 13, 1940, G-4/31733, and Smith, *The Army and Economic Mobilization,* 130.

18. *Industrial Mobilization,* Vol. 1, 41.

19. Beasley, *Knudsen,* 248.

20. Jacob Vander Meulen, *Building the B-29* (Washington, DC: Smithsonian Institution Press, 1995), 13.

21. Stimson, *Diary,* August 2, 1940, 55.

22. Beasley, *Knudsen,* 249.

23. Beasley, *Knudsen,* 250.

24. Walton, *Miracle of World War II,* 129.

25. John Colville, *On the Fringes of Power: 10 Downing Street Diaries, 1939–October 1941* (London: Hodder and Stoughton, 1985), 225–26.

26. Stimson, *Diary,* July 23, 1940, 29.

27. Stettinius, *Lend-Lease,* 48.

28. Craven and Cate, Vol. 6, *Men and Planes,* 399.

29. Langer and Gleason, *The Undeclared War,* 183.

30. *Industrial Mobilization,* Vol. 1, 51.

31. Stimson, *Diary,* July 25, 1940, 36.

32. *Fortune,* April 1941, 40.

33. Borth, *Masters of Mass Production,* 63.

34. Donald Nelson, *Arsenal of Democracy* (New York: Harcourt, Brace, 1946), 123; Beasley, *Knudsen,* 283.

35. Borth, *Masters of Mass Production.*

36. Minutes, AC-CND, August 9, 1940, 57; Stettinius, *Lend-Lease,* 54.

37. Borth, *Masters of Mass Production,* 65.

38. Borth, *Masters of Mass Production,* 65.

39. Borth, *Masters of Mass Production,* 194.

40. Eliot Janeway, *Struggle for Survival* (New Haven, CT: Yale University Press, 1951), 169.

41. Michael Green and James Brown, *M4 Sherman at War* (Minneapolis: Zenith Books, 2007), 20.

42. Beasley, *Knudsen,* 329.

43. Beasley, *Knudsen,* 330.

44. *Life,* March 31, 1941.

45. Green and Brown, *Sherman at War,* 20.

46. Stettinius, *Lend-Lease,* 55.

47. Beasley, *Knudsen,* 264.

48. Beasley, *Knudsen,* 264; Sorensen, *Forty Years with Ford,* 275.

49. Sorensen, *Forty Years with Ford,* 275–76.

50. Robert Higgs, *Depression, War, and Cold War: Studies in Political Economy* (Oxford, UK: Oxford University Press, 2006), 39–40.

51. Beasley, *Knudsen,* 265.

52. James Ward, *The Fall of the Packard Motor Company* (Palo Alto, CA: Stanford University Press, 1995, 15.

53. Ward, *Packard,* 15.

54. Walton, *Miracle of World War II,* 89.

55. Nelson, *Arsenal of Democracy,* 81.

56. Ward, *Packard,* 44–45.

57. Nelson, *Arsenal of Democracy,* 226–27.

58. David Fisher, *A Race on the Edge of Time* (New York: McGraw-Hill, 1988), 268.

CHAPTER SIX: Arsenal of Democracy

1. Knudsen Papers: Speech to Army Ordnance Association, October 8, 1940; *Time,* October 21, 1940, 23.
2. Quoted in Heiner, *Kaiser,* 61.
3. Borth, *Masters of Mass Production,* 115.
4. Adams, *Mr. Kaiser,* 74–75; *Secret Diary of Harold Ickes,* Vol. 2.
5. Adams, *Mr. Kaiser,* 79.
6. Adams, *Mr. Kaiser,* 8.
7. Knudsen Papers: Speech to Los Angeles Chamber of Commerce, August 22, 1940.
8. Kaiser Papers: Calhoun to Kaiser, July 22, 1940, Carton 127, Folder 11.
9. Jonathan Utley, *Going to War with Japan 1937–1941* (Knoxville: University of Tennessee Press, 1985), 121–22.
10. Borth, *Masters of Mass Production,* 68.
11. NDAC Minutes, 29.
12. Borth, *Masters of Mass Production,* 166–67.
13. Thomson and Mayo, *Ordnance Department,* 130–31.
14. Nelson, *Arsenal of Democracy,* 213.
15. Beasley, *Knudsen.*
16. Stimson, *Diary,* September 16, 1940, 170.
17. Beasley, *Knudsen,* 274.
18. Borth, *Masters of Mass Production,* 69.
19. Beasley, *Knudsen,* 286; Borth, *Masters of Mass Production,* 70–71.
20. Borth, *Masters of Mass Production,* 70.
21. Borth, *Masters of Mass Production,* 70–71.
22. *Time,* November 4, 1940, 71.
23. Alan Clive, *State of War: Michigan in World War II* (Ann Arbor: University of Michigan Press, 1976), 34–36.
24. Stimson, *Diary,* October 16, 1940, 57.
25. Craven and Cate, Vol. 6 *Men and Planes,* 322.
26. *The Nation,* November 1940.
27. Craven and Cate, *Men and Planes,* 323.
28. Beasley, *Knudsen,* 287.
29. Knudsen Papers: memo of November 18, 1940.
30. John Morton Blum, *V Was for Victory: Politics and American Culture During World War II* (New York: Mariner Books, 1976), 123.
31. Beasley, *Knudsen,* 259.
32. Vander Meulen, *Building the B-29,* 28.
33. Sloan, *Confessions,* 134.
34. Quoted in Farber, *Sloan Rules,* 185.
35. *Life,* March 1941, 116.
36. Quoted in Langer and Gleason, *The Undeclared War,* 180.
37. Janeway, *Struggle for Survival,* 16.

38. *The Secret Diary of Harold L. Ickes,* Vol. 3, entry of December 21, 1940, 391.

39. Beasley, *Knudsen,* 270–71.

40. Stimson, *Diary,* December 19, 1940, 46.

41. Heiner, *Kaiser,* 117.

42. Frederic L. Quirk, *Kaiser's Richmond Yards* (National Park Services: Historic American Engineering Record, 2004), 9–10.

43. Foster, *Kaiser,* 71–72.

44. *Life,* March 31, 1941.

45. Stimson, *Diary,* Vol. 32, December 3, 1940, 10.

46. Stimson, *Diary,* December 3, 1940, 11.

47. Langer and Gleason, *The Undeclared War,* 228–29; *From the Morgenthau Diaries,* Vol. 2, 202–3.

48. Langer and Gleason, *The Undeclared War,* 229.

49. *From the Morgenthau Diaries,* Vol. 2, 208–9.

50. Lynne Olson, *Citizens of London* (New York: Random House, 2010), 3.

51. Stimson, *Diary,* December 20, 1940, 40.

52. Stimson, *Diary,* December 21, 1940, 51.

53. Knudsen Papers: NAM Speech.

54. Buhite and Levy, *FDR's Fireside Chats,* 171–73.

55. Robert Sherwood, *Roosevelt and Hopkins* (New York: Harper, 1948), 226; Jesse H. Jones and Carl Pforzheimer, *Fifty Billion Dollars* (New York: Macmillan, 1951).

56. Finney, *Arsenal of Democracy,* 14–15.

CHAPTER SEVEN: Ships, Strikes, and the Big Book

1. Foster, *Kaiser,* 71.

2. Heiner, *Kaiser,* 120.

3. Harry Thayer, *Management of the Hanford Engineer Works in World War II* (New York: American Society of Civil Engineers Press, 1996), 95.

4. Historic American Engineering Record (HAER) No. CA-326, "Kaiser's Richmond Shipyards," 48–50.

5. Interview with Peter Bedford, October 12, 2010.

6. Hannay Testimony, U.S. House of Representatives, Production in Shipbuilding Yards, Hearing Part Four, June 30, 1943, 1000–1.

7. Hannay Testimony, 1015.

8. Cooke, *Home Front,* 170.

9. Kaiser Papers: Oregon Shipbuilding, Carton 9, Folder 19.

10. Foster, *Kaiser,* 32–33.

11. Kaiser Papers: "Quotes from Henry Kaiser's Speeches," n.d, Carton 294.

12. Foster, *Kaiser,* 75.

13. John Bunker, *Liberty Ships: The Ugly Ducklings of World War II* (Annapolis, MD: Naval Institute Press, 1972), 13.

14. Foster, *Kaiser,* 75.

15. Charles H. Coleman, *Shipbuilding Activities of the NDAC and OPM,* Report 18, Policy Analysis and Records, WPB (Washington, DC: Government Printing Office, 1945) 10–14.
16. Lane, *Ships for Victory,* 52–53.
17. Lane, *Ships for Victory,* 73.
18. Lane, *Ships for Victory,* 77.
19. Lane, *Ships for Victory,* 84.
20. Lane, *Ships for Victory,* 85.
21. HAER, 56.
22. Lane, *Ships for Victory,* 59.
23. Beasley, *Knudsen,* 303.
24. Nelson, *Arsenal of Democracy,* 132.
25. Jim Lacey, *Keep from All Thoughtful Men* (Annapolis, MD: Naval Institute Press, 2011), 30.
26. Langer and Gleason, *Undeclared War,* 436.
27. Nelson, *Arsenal of Democracy,* 133.
28. Steve Fraser, *Labor Will Rule: Sidney Hillman and the Rise of American Labor* (New York: Free Press, 1993).
29. Max Kampelman, *The Communist Party vs. the CIO* (New York: Arno, 1971), 25–26.
30. Borth, *Masters of Mass Production,* 251–52.
31. Beasley, *Knudsen,* 305.
32. Knudsen Papers: National Press Club, March 19, 1941.
33. Stimson, *Diary,* March 7, 1941.
34. Stimson, *Diary,* March 7, 1941.
35. Beasley, *Knudsen,* 326.
36. Beasley, *Knudsen,* 313.
37. *Fortune,* April 1941.
38. Nelson, *Arsenal of Democracy.*
39. Beasley, *Knudsen,* 306.
40. Kampelman, *Communist Party vs. the CIO,* 26.
41. Ian Kershaw, *Fateful Choices: Ten Decisions That Changed the World, 1940–1941* (New York: Penguin Books, 2007), 241.

CHAPTER EIGHT: Countdown
1. *Business Week,* May 24, 1941, 15.
2. *Fortune,* April 1941, 48.
3. Walton, *Miracle of World War II,* 265.
4. Nelson, *Arsenal of Democracy,* 152.
5. Knudsen Papers: Speech to Los Angeles Chamber of Commerce, August 22, 1940.
6. Beasley, *Knudsen,* 305.
7. Finney, *Arsenal of Democracy,* 47–49.

8. Walton, *Miracle of World War II*, 216–17.

9. Finney, *Arsenal of Democracy*, 54–55.

10. Wayne Broehl, *Precision Valley: The Machine Tool Companies of Springfield, Vermont* (Englewood Cliffs, NJ: Prentice-Hall, 1959), 132–33.

11. Knudsen Papers: Memo Henry Stimson to Jesse Jones, January 25, 1941.

12. Beasley, *Knudsen*, 303.

13. Borth, *Masters of Mass Production*, 123.

14. James Schwartz, *Frederick V. Geier, 1893–1981* (Cincinnati: Cincinnati Museum Center, 2002), www.libraries.uc.edu.

15. Schwartz, *Geier*.

16. Schwartz, *Geier*.

17. *American Machinist*, May 14, 1941, 452d.

18. Beasley, *Knudsen*, 315.

19. Walton, *Miracle of World War II*, 220.

20. Schwartz, *Geier*.

21. *American Machinist*, June 25, 1941, 622c.

22. *Fortune*, April 1941, 36.

23. *Fortune*, April 1941, 52.

24. Stimson, *Diary*, May 29, 1941.

25. Buhite and Levy, *FDR's Fireside Chats*.

26. Beasley, *Knudsen*, 317.

27. *Strikes in American Industry* (National Association of Manufacturers, 1942), 15.

28. James Gaston, *Planning the American Air War* (Washington, DC: National Defense University Press, 1982), 44–45.

29. Gaston, *Planning the American Air War*, 43.

30. Gaston, *Planning the American Air War*, 43.

31. Nelson, *Arsenal of Democracy*, 152–53.

32. Beasley, *Knudsen*, 324.

33. *Industrial Mobilization*, Vol. 1, 115.

34. Brinkley, *Washington Goes to War*, 68–69.

35. Gropman, *The Big "L,"* 58.

36. Perret, *Days of Sadness*, 257–58.

37. William Baumol, Robert Litan, and Carl Schramm, *Good Capitalism, Bad Capitalism, and the Economics of Growth and Prosperity* (New Haven, CT: Yale University Press, 2007).

38. Bruce Catton, *War Lords of Washington* (New York: Harcourt, Brace, 1948), 8–9.

CHAPTER NINE: Going All Out

1. Stimson, *Diary*, Dec 7, 1941; Henry Stimson and McGeorge Bundy, *On Active Service in Peace and War* (New York: Harper and Brothers, 1948), 390–91.

2. "Ultimate Requirements Study Estimate of Army Ground Forces," reprinted in Charles Kirkpatrick, *An Unknown Future and a Doubtful Present: Writing the Victory Plan* (Washington, DC: Center for Military History, U.S. Army, 2010), 129.

3. Beasley, *Knudsen,* 242.

4. Beasley, *Knudsen,* 330.

5. State of the Union Address, January 6, 1942, the American Presidency Project (www.presidency.ucsb.edu).

6. Beasley, *Knudsen,* 337.

7. Beasley, *Knudsen,* 336–37.

8. Nelson, *Arsenal,* 121–22.

9. Charles Sorensen, *Forty Years with Ford,* 287; Craven and Cate, *Men and Planes,* Vol. 6, 334.

10. Beasley, *Knudsen,* 321.

11. *Washington Post,* December 23, 1941.

12. Perret, *Days of Sadness,* 185.

13. *Time,* January 19, 1942, 10.

14. *Business Week,* January 17, 1942, 18.

15. *American Machinist,* June 25, 1941, 655d.

16. Doris Kearns Goodwin, *No Ordinary Time: Franklin and Eleanor Roosevelt: The Home Front in World War II* (New York: Simon and Schuster, 1994), 314.

17. Fleming, *New Dealers' War,* 98–99.

18. Clive, *State of War,* 35–66.

19. Knudsen Papers; letter Eleanor Roosevelt to WSK, January 13, 1942.

20. Beasley, *Knudsen,* 341.

21. Beasley, *Knudsen,* 342. For another version of events, see Catton, *War Lords of Washington,* 71.

22. "Address of the President," December 9, 1941 (http://docs.fdrlibrary .marist.edu.).

23. Jones, *Fifty Billion Dollars,* 272.

24. Timmons, *Jesse H. Jones,* 314.

25. Jones, *Fifty Billion Dollars,* 273.

26. Press Statement, January 15, 1942, quoted in Keith Eller, *Mobilizing America,* 236.

27. Beasley, *Knudsen,* 346.

28. Walton, *Miracle of World War II,* 551.

29. Overy, *Why the Allies Won,* 203.

30. Adam Tooz, *Wages of Destruction: The Making and Breaking of the Nazi Economy* (New York: Penguin Books, 2008), 553–54.

31. David Woodbury, *Builders for Battle: How the Pacific Naval Air Bases Were Constructed* (New York: Dutton, 1946), 55.

32. Kaiser Papers: Pearl Harbor Dry Dock 6 (1941–42), Carton 9.

33. Woodbury, *Builders for Battle,* 59–67.

34. Foster, *Kaiser,* 166.

35. Wolf, *Big Dams,* 134; Ronald Spector, *Eagle Against the Sun: The American War with Japan* (New York: Free Press, 1985), 101.

36. Wolf, *Big Dams,* 135.

37. James Devereux, *The Story of Wake Island* (New York: Grosset and Dunlap, 1974), 42–45.

38. Devereux, *Story of Wake Island,* 58–65.

39. John F. Kinney, *Wake Island Pilot: A World War II Memoir* (Washington, DC: Potomac Books, 1995), 66.

40. Spector, *Eagle Against the Sun,* 103–5.

41. Devereux, *Story of Wake Island,* 152–53.

42. Wolf, *Big Dams,* 142.

43. Minutes, War Production Board, February 10, 1942, 11.

CHAPTER TEN: Ships for Liberty

1. Winston Churchill, *The Second World War.* Vol. 5: *Closing the Ring* (New York: Bantam, 1962).

2. Michael Gannon, *Operation Drumbeat* (New York: Harper and Row, 1990).

3. Lane, *Ships for Victory,* 139.

4. Lane, *Ships for Victory,* 142.

5. Wolf, *Big Dams,* 105.

6. E.g., Kaiser Papers: telegram Clay Bedford to Carl Lynge, Office of Production Management, December 24, 1941.

7. Carlo D'Este interview, February 25, 2011.

8. Cooke, *The American Home Front,* 161.

9. Angela Clawson, *Shipyard Diary of a Woman Welder* (New York: Penguin Books, 1944), 59.

10. Kaiser Papers: J. N. Bowman, "Job Descriptions, Kaiser Shipyards, Richmond, California," Carton 1.

11. Clawson, *Shipyard Diary,* 64.

12. Foster, *Kaiser,* 72–73.

13. Lane, *Ships for Victory,* 140.

14. *Fortune,* July 1943, 121.

15. *Fortune,* July 1943.

16. HAER, 58–59.

17. Kaiser Papers: Kramer, "The Story of the Richmond Shipyards," 14–15.

18. Lane, *Ships for Victory,* 144.

19. U.S. House of Representatives, Appropriations Committee, Higgins Contracts, Executive Hearings, Part 3, 252–53.

20. Lane, *Ships for Victory,* 145.

21. Lane, *Ships for Victory,* 298.

22. HAER, 162–63.

23. Foster, *Kaiser,* 299, n. 42.

24. Foster, *Kaiser,* 82.

25. HAER, 62.

26. "How Kaiser Builds Liberty Ships," *American Machinist,* November 12, 1942, 1299–1306.

27. "How Kaiser Builds,"1303.

28. "How Kaiser Builds," 1302–6.

29. HAER, 101–2.

30. Kramer, "Richmond Shipyards," 23–25.

31. Bunker, *Liberty Ships,* 12.

32. Quoted in Heiner, *Kaiser,* 129.

33. Heiner, *Kaiser,* 128.

34. Davis, *FDR: The War President,* 616.

35. Kaiser Papers: Clay Bedford folder.

36. Heiner, *Kaiser,* 129.

37. Kaiser Papers: "Hull No 440 . . . and Why," *Fore N Aft,* November 12, 1942.

38. HAER, 60.

39. Heiner, *Kaiser,* 130.

40. Heiner, *Kaiser,* 130.

41. Heiner, *Kaiser,* 131.

42. Kaiser Papers: Clay Bedford to Henry Kaiser, November 9, 1942, Crate 25, File 26.

43. "Hull No 440 . . . and Why."

44. Heiner, *Kaiser,* 131.

45. Kaiser Papers: OPM.

46. Foster, *Kaiser,* 84.

47. Sawyer and Mitchell, *The Liberty Ships,* 132.

CHAPTER ELEVEN: The Production Express

1. *Time,* January 19, 1942, 11–12.

2. Nelson, *Arsenal of Democracy* 208.

3. Cabell Phillips, *The 1940s: Decade of Triumph and Trouble* (New York: Macmillan, 1975), 144.

4. Davis, *FDR: The War President.*

5. Quoted in Catton, *War Lords,* 117.

6. E.g., Brinkley, *Washington Goes to War,* 69–70; Blum, *V Was for Victory,* 121–22.

7. Brinkley, *Washington Goes to War,* 71.

8. Fleming, *New Dealers' War,* 101–2.

9. Nelson, *Arsenal of Democracy,* 208.

10. Quoted in Catton, *War Lords,* 112–13.

11. Perret, *Days of Sadness,* 258.

12. Nelson, *Arsenal of Democracy*, 60.
13. Nelson, *Arsenal*, 60.
14. Davis, *FDR: The War President*, 400.
15. Catton, *War Lords*, 121.
16. Catton, *War Lords*.
17. Quoted in Blum, *V Was for Victory*, 133.
18. Nelson, *Arsenal of Democracy*, 99.
19. Blum, *V Was for Victory*, 134–35.
20. Catton, *War Lords*, 117–18.
21. Brinkley, *Washington Goes to War*, 112.
22. Gropman, *The Big "L,"* 82–91; Beasley, *Knudsen*, 381.
23. Harrison, "Resource Mobilization for World War II," 184.
24. Charles Hyde, *Riding the Roller Coaster: A History of the Chrysler Corporation* (Detroit: Wayne State University Press, 2003), 137.
25. Green and Brown, *M4 Sherman at War*, 30–32.
26. Beasley, *Knudsen*, 355–56.
27. *Time*, March 23, 1942, 12.
28. Walton, *Miracle of World War II*, 397.
29. Walton, *Miracle of World War II*, 48.
30. Rae, *Climb to Greatness*, 9, 67.
31. Bill Yenne, *The American Aircraft Factory in World War II* (Minneapolis: Zenith Press, 2010), 80.
32. Yenne, *Aircraft Factory*, 86.
33. Rae, *Climb to Greatness*, 145.
34. Buhite and Levy, *FDR's Fireside Chats*, 243.
35. Walton, *Miracle of World War II*, 380–83; Gropman, *The Big "L,"* 78–79.
36. Jerry Strahan, *Andrew Jackson Higgins and the Boats That Won World War II* (Baton Rouge: Louisiana State University Press, 1994), 11–12; Holland M. Smith, *Coral and Brass* (1948; Washington, DC: U.S. Marine Corps, 1991), 90–91.
37. Strahan, *Higgins*, 93–94.
38. Strahan, *Higgins*, 143–44.
39. Strahan, *Higgins*, 144.
40. *Life*, August 1943.
41. Nelson, *Arsenal of Democracy*, 361.
42. Nelson, *Arsenal of Democracy*, 362.
43. Nelson, *Arsenal of Democracy*, 354; Walton, *Miracle of World War II*, 541; Gropman, *The Big "L,"* 69.
44. Minutes, War Production Board, 54–56; Nelson, *Arsenal of Democracy*, 353–58.
45. Walton, *Miracle of World War II*, 419; Nelson, *Arsenal of Democracy*, 355.
46. Walton, *Miracle of World War II*, 420.
47. Hyde, *Roller Coaster*, 137.

CHAPTER TWELVE: Steel Men and Cast-Iron Charlie

1. *Time,* April 28, 1941, 77–78.
2. Foster, *Kaiser,* 302.
3. Jones, *Fifty Billion Dollars,* 331–32.
4. Jones, *Fifty Billion Dollars,* 333.
5. Heiner, *Kaiser,* 173.
6. Foster, *Kaiser,* 95.
7. Heiner, *Kaiser,* 172.
8. Heiner, *Kaiser,* 174.
9. Wolf, *Big Dams,* 181.
10. Quoted in Heiner, *Kaiser,* 174.
11. Walton, *Miracle of World War II,* 421.
12. Heiner, *Kaiser,* 175–76.
13. *Fortune,* October 1943, 122.
14. Gerald D. Nash, *World War II and the West* (Lincoln: University of Nebraska Press), 4–5.
15. Allan Nevins, *Ford: Decline and Rebirth* (New York: Scribner, 1963), 199.
16. Nelson, *Arsenal of Democracy,* 277.
17. Janeway, *Struggle for Survival,* 195.
18. Beasley, *Knudsen,* 260.
19. Davis, *Detroit's Wartime Industry,* 45.
20. Quoted in Finney, *Arsenal of Democracy.*
21. Walton, *Miracle of World War II,* 237; Clive, *State of War,* 22.
22. Nelson, *Arsenal of Democracy,* 228–29.
23. Walton, *Miracle of World War II,* 237.
24. Nevins, *Ford: Decline and Rebirth,* 203–4.
25. Nevins, *Ford: Decline and Rebirth,* 207.
26. Nevins, *Ford: Decline and Rebirth,* 208.
27. Overy, *How the Allies Won,* 195.
28. Sorensen, *Forty Years with Ford,* 279.
29. Sorensen, *Forty Years with Ford,* 59–61.
30. Hounshell, *American System,* 224–25.
31. Sorensen, *Forty Years with Ford,* 127.
32. Hounshell, *American System.*
33. Jasper Guinon to Charles Sorensen, March 8, 1925, quoted Hounshell, *American System,* 292.
34. Sorensen, *Forty Years with Ford,* 8.
35. Nevins, *Ford: Decline and Rebirth.*
36. See Martin Bowman, *Combat Legend: B-24 Liberator* (Shrewsbury, UK: Airlife Publishing, 2003).
37. Stephen Ambrose, *The Wild Blue: The Men and Boys Who Flew the B-24s over Germany* (New York: Simon and Schuster, 2001), 21–23, 79–80.

38. Starr Smith, Steve Gansen, and Walter Cronkite, *Jimmy Stewart, Bomber Pilot* (Minneapolis: Zenith Press, 2005).

39. Sorensen, *Forty Years with Ford,* 280.

40. Sorensen, *Forty Years with Ford,* 281.

41. Sorensen, *Forty Years with Ford,* 281.

42. Sorensen, *Forty Years with Ford,* 281–82.

43. Sorensen, *Forty Years with Ford,* 282–83.

44. Rae, *Climb to Greatness,* 12.

45. Sorensen, *Forty Years with Ford,* 284.

46. Walton, *Miracle of World War II,* 307.

47. Walton, *Miracle of World War II,* 308–9.

48. Nevins, *Ford: Decline and Rebirth,* 189.

49. Sorensen, *Forty Years with Ford,* 286.

50. Nevins, *Ford: Decline and Rebirth.*

51. Sorensen, *Forty Years with Ford,* 279.

CHAPTER THIRTEEN: Agony at Willow Run

1. *Time,* March 1942.

2. Nevins, *Ford: Decline and Rebirth,* 189.

3. Nevins, *Ford: Decline and Rebirth,* 189.

4. Sorensen, *Forty Years with Ford,* 284–85.

5. Nevins, *Ford: Decline and Rebirth,* 190.

6. Nevins, *Ford: Decline and Rebirth,* 192.

7. Sorensen, *Forty Years with Ford,* 286.

8. Timothy J. O'Callaghan, *Ford in Service to America: Mass Production During the Two World Wars* (Jefferson, NC: McFarland, 2009), 60–61.

9. O'Callaghan, *Ford in Service to America,* 72–73.

10. Charles A. Lindbergh, *The Wartime Journals of Charles A. Lindbergh* (New York: Harcourt Brace Jovanovich, 1975), April 7, 1942, 615–16.

11. Sorensen, *Forty Years with Ford,* 291.

12. Davis, *Detroit at War,* 84.

13. Nevins, *Ford: Decline and Rebirth,* 210.

14. Nevins, *Ford: Decline and Rebirth,* 210–11.

15. Lindbergh, *Wartime Journals,* April 7, 1942, 616.

16. Lindbergh, *Wartime Journals,* 613.

17. Nevins, *Ford: Decine and Rebirth,* 217.

18. Lindbergh, *Wartime Journals,* May 8, 1942, 637.

19. Lindbergh, *Wartime Journals,* 638.

20. Nevins, *Ford: Decline and Rebirth,* 213.

21. Lindbergh, *Wartime Journals,* May 15, 1942, 644.

22. Sorensen, *Forty Years with Ford,* 298.

23. Craven and Cate, Vol. 6, *Men and Planes,* 328–29.

24. Lindbergh, *Wartime Journals,* July 27, 1942, 682.

25. Beasley, *Knudsen,* 351.

26. Borth, *Masters of Mass Production,* 91–92.

27. Borth, *Masters of Mass Production,* 91.

28. Beasley, *Knudsen,* 351.

29. Lewis Strauss, *Men and Decisions* (New York: Popular Library, 1963), 143.

30. Beasley, *Knudsen,* 347.

31. Beasley, *Knudsen,* 288.

32. Craven and Cate, Vol. 6, *Men and Planes,* 335–36.

33. Craven and Cate, Vol. 6, *Men and Planes,* 336.

34. Walton, *Miracle of World War II,* 312.

35. Walton, *Miracle of World War II,* 310–11.

36. Nevins, *Ford: Decline and Rebirth,* 218.

37. Craven and Cate, Vol. 6, *Men and Planes,* 329.

38. Nevins, *Ford: Decline and Rebirth,* 223.

39. Rae, *Climb to Greatness,* 148–49; Wolf, *Big Dams,* 158–59.

40. Craven and Cate, Vol. 6, *Men and Planes,* 337.

41. Martin Middlebrook, *Convoy* (New York: William Morrow, 1976), 50–52; Dan van der Vat, *The Atlantic Campaign: World War II's Great Struggle at Sea* (New York: Harper and Row, 1988), 304–6, 326.

CHAPTER FOURTEEN: Victory Is Our Business

1. Sherwood, *Roosevelt and Hopkins,* 727.

2. Quoted in John Ohly, *Industrialists in Olive Drab: The Emergency Operation of Private Industry During World War II* (Washington, DC: Center of Military History, U.S. Army, 2000), 58.

3. H. G. Nicholas, ed., *Washington Dispatches, 1941–1945: Weekly Political Reports from the British Embassy* (Chicago: University of Chicago Press, 1981), 209.

4. Phillips, *The 1940s,* 169.

5. *American Machinist,* July 6, 1944, 16–17.

6. Gropman, *The Big "L,"* 86–91.

7. Harrison, "Resource Mobilization for World War II," 184.

8. Walton, *Miracle of World War II,* 401–3.

9. Farber, *Sloan Rules,* 232–33.

10. General Motors Annual Report 1945, 9; Farber, *Sloan Rules,* 233.

11. General Motors Corp., *A History of Eastern Aircraft Division* (n.p., 1944).

12. Walton, *Miracle of World War II,* 448.

13. *Fortune,* November 1943, 150–54; Walton, *Miracle of World War II,* 448–50.

14. *American Machinist,* December 10, 1941, 1430.

15. *Business Week,* May 10, 1941, 17.

16. *Time,* November 16, 1942, 21.

17. Barbara Forgy Schock, "The Prairie Shipyard," www.thezephyr.com.

18. Walton, *Miracle of World War II*, 469.

19. Roger Franklin, *The Defender: The Story of General Dynamics* (New York: Harper and Row, 1986), 92–93.

20. Beasley, *Knudsen*, 357.

21. Knudsen Papers: 1942 tour notes, quoted in Beasley, *Knudsen*, 360.

22. Knudsen Papers: 1942 tour notes, quoted in Beasley, *Knudsen*, 360–61.

23. Hagley Museum, National Association of Manufacturing Collection; J. A. Hartley, "The Public's View of War and Profits," NAM pamphlet, May 1942, 3.

24. Walton, *Miracle of World War II*, 537.

25. *Business Week,* March 15, 1941, 38–42.

26. Leo Cherne, *Your Business Goes to War* (Boston: Houghton Mifflin, 1942).

27. Cherne, *Your Business Goes to War,* 50–53.

28. Robert Connery, *The Navy and Industrial Mobilization in World War II* (Princeton, NJ: Princeton University Press, 1951), 271–75.

29. Walton, *Miracle of World War II*, 555.

30. *Time,* March 23, 1943.

31. National Archives, Image No. 80 G349504, reprinted on Hobbs and Pacific Hut site, historylink.com.

32. Walton, *Miracle of World War II*, 555.

33. Blum, *V Was for Victory*.

34. Michael Barone, *Our Country: The Shaping of America from Roosevelt to Reagan* (New York: Free Press, 1990), 154; Harold Vatter, *The U.S. Economy in World War II* (New York: Columbia University Press, 1985), 51.

35. Vatter, *U.S. Economy,* 54–55.

36. Donald L. Losman, Irene Kyriakopoulos, and J. Dawson Ahalt, "Economics of America's World War II Mobilization," in Gropman, *The Big "L,"* 188.

37. See Gregory Fossedal, *Our Finest Hour: Will Clayton, the Marshall Plan, and the Triumph of Democracy* (Stamford, CT: Hoover Institution Press, 1993), 124–26.

38. Barone, *Our Country,* 154.

39. Goodwin, *No Ordinary Time,* 249.

40. Quoted in Blum, *V Was for Victory,* 186.

41. Barone, *Our Country,* 160.

42. Clay Bedford Jr., interview, October 13, 2010.

43. HAER, Richmond Shipyard No. 3, 163.

44. Blum, *V Was for Victory,* 191.

45. Clive, *State of War,* 171–73.

46. Blum, *V Was for Victory,* 201.

47. Quoted in Blum, *V Was for Victory,* 203.

48. Walton, *Miracle of World War II*, 374.

49. *American Machinist*, June 11, 1941, 51–52; *Business Week*, March 15, 1941, 76.

50. Walton, *Miracle of World War II*, 380.

51. Beasley, *Knudsen*, 354.

52. Walton, *Miracle of World War II*; HAER, 159.

53. *Life*, June 5, 1944, 74–79.

54. Emily Yellin, *Our Mothers' War: American Women at Home and at the Front During World War II* (New York: Free Press, 2007).

55. Clawson, *Shipyard Diary*, 5–6.

56. Clawson, *Shipyard Diary*, 6.

57. Clawson, *Shipyard Diary*, 89.

58. Clawson, *Shipyard Diary*, 91–92.

59. Roger Lotchin, *The Bad City in the Good War* (Bloomington: Indiana University Press, 2003), 139.

60. Effie Walling interview, in Lotchin, *The Bad City*, 80.

61. Katie Grant, "Wartime Memories," Rosie the Riveter Trust, www .rosietheriveter.org/memory.htm.

CHAPTER FIFTEEN: The Man from Frisco

1. Foster, *Kaiser*, 117.

2. Kaiser Papers: Nellie Bent to Kaiser, June 29, 1943, Carton 18.

3. Lane, *Ships for Victory*, 612.

4. Lane, *Ships for Victory*, 612; *United States Naval Vessels* (Division of Naval Intelligence, 1946; Schiffer, 1996) 47–48.

5. Lane, *Ships for Victory*, 610.

6. Heiner, *Kaiser*, 145.

7. Lane, *Ships for Victory*, 611.

8. Heiner, *Kaiser*, 145.

9. Lane, *Ships for Victory*, 612–13.

10. Heiner, *Kaiser*, 175.

11. Heiner, *Kaiser*, 146.

12. Lane, *Ships for Victory*, 613.

13. Carl Abbott, *Greater Portland: Urban Life and Landscape in the Pacfic Northwest* (Philadelphia: University of Pennsylvania Press, 2001), 43.

14. See *Oregon Historical Quarterly* 91, Fall 1990, quoted in Abbott, *Greater Portland*, 44–45.

15. Lane, *Ships for Victory*; Heiner, *Kaiser*, 146.

16. *New York Times*, April 3, 1943.

17. Foster, *Kaiser*, 76–77.

18. Sawyer and Mitchell, *Liberty Ships*, 114–15.

19. Kaiser Papers: Stephen D. Bechtel to Kaiser, August 17, 1942, Carton 13.

20. Foster, *Kaiser*, 120–22.

21. Lane, *Ships for Victory,* 544–45.

22. *Journal of Commerce,* February 1, 1943, 18.

23. Lane, *Ships for Victory,* 547–48.

24. Heiner, *Kaiser,* 128.

25. U.S. Senate, Truman Committee hearings, Part 18, March 25, 1943/7350.

26. *Washington Post,* March 26, 1943.

27. Lane, *Ships for Victory,* 553.

28. Lane, *Ships for Victory,* 554.

29. Lane, *Ships for Victory,* 55.

30. Adams, *Mr. Kaiser Goes to Washington,* 72.

31. George Spangenberg, oral history interview, 1990, www .georgespangenberg.com, Oral History as PDF File, 75.

32. Winchester, ed., *U.S. Military Aircraft,* 136–37.

33. *Time,* July 27, 1942, 71.

34. Heiner, *Kaiser,* 157.

35. Kaiser Papers: handwritten draft of testimony on Hughes case, 7.

36. Foster, *Kaiser,* 182–83.

37. Heiner, *Kaiser,* 159.

38. Kaiser Papers: Kaiser statement on Howard Hughes, 7, Carton 127, Folder 35.

39. Foster, *Kaiser,* 183.

40. WPB Papers, Ed Bern to Donald Nelson, August 30, 1943, quoted in Foster, *Kaiser,* 184.

41. *Fortune,* September 1942, 184.

42. Spangenberg oral history interview, 76.

43. Kaiser Papers: Contract cancellation, Carton 127, Folder 12.

44. Kaiser Papers: Kaiser statement on Hughes, 7, Carton 127, Folder 35.

45. *Time,* October 18, 1943, 77.

46. *Time,* October 18, 1943, 77.

47. Heiner, *Kaiser,* 161.

48. Heiner, *Kaiser,* 163–64.

49. Heiner, *Kaiser,* 165.

CHAPTER SIXTEEN: Superbomber

1. Beasley, *Knudsen,* 274.

2. Quoted in Spector, *Eagle Against the Sun,* 227.

3. George C. Kenney, *General Kenney Reports: A Personal History of the Pacific War* (1949; Washington, DC: U.S. Air Force, 1997), 14.

4. Kenney, *General Kenney Reports,* 285.

5. Beasley, *Knudsen,* 378.

6. Spector, *Eagle Against the Sun,* 227–28.

7. Knudsen Papers: Log of Pacific Trip, entry for August 26, 1943.

8. Knudsen Papers: Conversation with Lieutenant General Kenney and Major General Whitehead, September 15, 1943.

9. Knudsen Papers: Log of Pacific Trip, entry for September 1, 1943.

10. Kenney, *General Kenney Reports,* 286.

11. Minutes, War Production Board: July 27, 1943 meeting, 264.

12. Knudsen Papers: Log of Pacific Trip, August 28, 1943.

13. Beasley, *Knudsen,* 247.

14. H. H. Arnold, *Global Mission* (New York: Harper and Row, 1949), 188.

15. Lindbergh, *War Journals,* 183.

16. Lindbergh, *War Journals,* 183; Arnold, *Global Mission,* 188.

17. Arnold, *Global Mission,* 189.

18. Arnold, *Global Mission,* 189.

19. Geoffrey Perret, *Winged Victory: The Army Air Forces in World War II* (New York: Random House, 1993), 37.

20. Harold Mansfield, *Vision: A Saga of the Sky* (New York: Duell, Sloan and Pearce, 1956), 158.

21. Mary Wells Geer, *Boeing's Ed Wells* (Seattle: University of Washington Press, 1992), 93–94.

22. Geer, *Boeing's Ed Wells,* 94.

23. Gene Gurney, *Journey of the Giants* (New York: Coward-McCann, 1961), 23.

24. Gurney, *Journey,* 24.

25. Geer, *Boeing's Ed Wells,* 96–97.

26. Walton, *Miracle of World War II,* 404–5.

27. Vander Meulen, *Building the B-29,* 16–17; Walton, *Miracle of World War II,* 352.

28. Walton, *Miracle of World War II,* 353.

29. Vander Meulen, *Building the B-29,* 17.

30. Walton, *Miracle of World War II,* 353; Geer, *Boeing's Ed Wells,* 98.

31. Gurney, *Journey,* 29.

32. Yenne, *American Aircraft Factory,* 64.

33. Vander Meulen, *Building the B-29,* 31.

34. Tom Collison, *The Superfortress Is Born* (New York: Duell, Sloan and Pearce, 1945).

35. Vander Meulen, *Building the B-29,* 37.

36. Vander Meulen, *Building the B-29,* 51.

37. Vander Meulen, *Building the B-29,* 53.

38. Robert Mann, *The B-29 Superfortress Chronology, 1934–1960* (Jefferson, NC: McFarland, 2009), 27.

39. Geer, *Boeing's Ed Wells,* 99.

40. Steve Birdsall, *Saga of the Superfortress* (New York: Doubleday, 1980), 14.

41. Gurney, *Journey,* 40–41.

42. Gurney, *Journey,* 42.

43. Graham White, *Allied Aircraft Piston Engines,* 368–69.

CHAPTER SEVENTEEN: The Battle of Kansas

1. Arnold, *Global Mission,* 478–79.
2. Birdsall, *Saga,* 16.
3. Mann, *Superfortress Chronology,* 28.
4. Birdsall, *Saga,* 16.
5. Vander Meulen, *Building the B-29,* 32.
6. Perret, *Winged Victory,* 38.
7. Beasley, *Knudsen,* 366.
8. Vander Meulen, *Building the B-29,* 38.
9. Vander Meulen, *Building the B-29,* 41.
10. Beasley, *Knudsen,* 370.
11. Vander Meulen, *Building the B-29,* 76.
12. Vander Meulen, *Building the B-29,* 78.
13. Beasley, *Knudsen,* 367.
14. *Life,* December 27, 1943, 37.
15. Vander Meulen, *Building the B-29,* 84–85; Beasley, *Knudsen,* 367.
16. Vander Meulen, *Building the B-29,* 70.
17. Beasley, *Knudsen,* 368.
18. *Goodyear Aircraft Corporation* (New York: 1945), 17.
19. Vander Meulen, *Building the B-29,* 31.
20. White, *Allied Aircraft Piston Engines,* 256–59; Vander Meulen, *Building the B-29,* 86–87.
21. Beasley, *Knudsen,* 370–71.
22. Vander Meulen, *Building the B-29,* 88, 92.
23. Vander Meulen, *Building the B-29,* 92.
24. Beasley, *Knudsen,* 371.
25. Beasley, *Knudsen,* 368; Vander Meulen, *Building the B-29,* 94.
26. Vander Meulen, *Building the B-29,* 94.
27. Beasley, *Knudsen,* 366.
28. Leslie Groves, *Now It Can Be Told: The Story of the Manhattan Project* (1962; New York: Da Capo Press, 1975), 253–54.
29. According to Groves, this was in the spring of 1944. *Now It Can Be Told,* 254.
30. Beasley, *Knudsen,* 366.
31. Beasley, *Knudsen,* 368.
32. Walton, *Miracle of World War II,* 252.
33. Vander Meulen, *Building the B-29,* 35.
34. Walton, *Miracle of World War II,* 362–63.
35. Beasley, *Knudsen,* 371.
36. See chart in Vander Meulen, *Building the B-29,* 54.
37. Quoted in Vander Meulen, *Building the B-29,* 96.
38. Vander Meulen, *Building the B-29,* 96, 98.
39. Beasley, *Knudsen,* 371.

CHAPTER EIGHTEEN: Fire This Time

1. Gurney, *Journey,* 67.
2. Birdsall, *Saga,* 43.
3. Birdsall, *Saga,* 44.
4. Gurney, *Journey,* 72.
5. Barrett Tillman, *Clash of the Carriers: The True Story of the Marianas Turkey Shoot of World War II* (New York: New American Library, 2005) 16–17.
6. Gurney, *Journey,* 160.
7. General Curtis LeMay, *Superfortress: The Story of the B-29 and American Air Power* (New York: McGraw-Hill, 1988), 103–5; Birdsall, *Saga,* 163–64.
8. G. E. Patrick Murray, *Bomber Mission* (New York: Barnes and Noble, 2006), 16.
9. Gurney, *Journey,* 210.
10. Gurney, *Journey,* 211.
11. Beasley, *Knudsen,* 352–53.
12. Don Whitehead, *The Dow Story: The History of the Dow Chemical Company* (New York: McGraw-Hill, 1968), 85–86, 90.
13. Actually, Kaiser's interest dated back further than that, to January 1940, when Permanente Metals spent $25,000 to research the metal. Adams, *Mr. Kaiser Goes to Washington,* 65.
14. Foster, *Kaiser,* 197.
15. Adams, *Mr. Kaiser Goes to Washington,* 112–13.
16. Whitehead, *The Dow Story,* 169–70.
17. Heiner, *Kaiser,* 112.
18. LeMay, *Superfortress,* 121–22.
19. Kaiser Papers: "Speech by Captain G.E. Dawson, Chemical Warfare Service," Carton 180; Heiner, *Kaiser,* 112–13.
20. LeMay, *Superfortress,* 91.
21. LeMay, *Superfortress,* 121.
22. Murray, *Bomber Missions,* 16.
23. Gurney, *Journey,* 210.
24. LeMay, *Superfortress,* 123.
25. Stimson, "On Active Service," 619.
26. Birdsall, *Saga,* 182.
27. LeMay, *Superfortress,* 123.
28. Beasley, *Knudsen,* 381.
29. *Mobilization: World War II and the U.S. Army,* 21.
30. See Herman Somers, *Presidential Agency: OWMR, the Office of War Mobilization and Reconversion* (Cambridge, MA: Harvard University Press, 1955).
31. Quoted in Beasley, *Knudsen,* 381.
32. Richard Rhodes, *The Making of the Atomic Bomb* (New York: Touchstone, 1986), 583.

33. Birdsall, *Saga,* 263–64.

34. LeMay, *Superfortress,* 151.

35. Groves, *Now It Can Be Told,* 260–61.

36. LeMay, *Superfortress,* 150.

37. Geer, *Boeing's Ed Wells,* 105.

38. Beasley, *Knudsen,* 387.

CONCLUSION: Reckoning

1. Thruelson, *The Grumman Story,* 220.

2. Knudsen Papers: June 1, 1945; Beasley, *Knudsen,* 380.

3. Eiler, *Mobilizing America,* 444.

4. Gropman, *The Big "L,"* 81–92.

5. Harrison, "Resource Mobilization for World War II," 184.

6. Gropman, *The Big "L."*

7. Adam Tooze, *Wages of Destruction* (New York: Viking, 2006), 648–52.

8. Paul Koistinen, "Warfare and Power Relations in America," 102–3.

9. Cooke, *The American Home Front,* 300–1; Brinkley, *Washington Goes to War,* 279; Cherne, *The Rest of Your Life* (New York: Doubleday, 1944).

10. Quoted in Robert Sobel, *The Worldly Economists* (New York: Free Press, 1980), 101–2.

11. Farber, *Sloan Rules,* 236.

12. Robert Higgs, "Wartime Prosperity? A Reassessment of the U.S. Economy in the 1940s," in *Depression, War, and Cold War* (New York: Oxford University Press, 2006), 74–75, 108.

13. Barone, *Our Country,* 197.

14. Fred Kaplan, *Wizards of Armageddon* (New York: Simon and Schuster, 1983), 22.

15. Beasley, *Knudsen,* 381.

16. Beasley, *Knudsen,* 389.

17. Catton, *War Lords of Washington,* 310, 122.

18. Quoted in Mark Skousen, *The Big Three in Economics: Adam Smith, Karl Marx, and John Maynard Keynes* (London: M. E. Sharpe, 2007), 168.

19. Liaquat Ahamed, *Lords of Finance: The Bankers Who Broke the World* (New York: Penguin Books, 2009), 494–95.

20. *Oakland Tribune,* September 30, 1942.

21. Foster, *Kaiser,* 139.

22. Evan Thomas, *Sea of Thunder* (New York: Simon and Schuster, 2006), 246.

23. See Richard Langworth, *Kaiser-Frazer: Last Assault on Detroit* (New York: Automobile Quarterly Press, 1975).

24. Tim Bedford interview, 1984, quoted in Foster, *Kaiser,* 241.

25. Kaiser Papers: A. B. Ordway to H. Kaiser, June 14, 1966, quoted in Heiner, *Kaiser,* 188.

SELECT BIBLIOGRAPHY

PRIMARY SOURCES

Henry Kaiser Papers, Bancroft Library, University of California, Berkeley.

Henry L. Stimson, Diary (microfilm), Manuscripts and Archives, Yale University Library, New Haven, CT.

Knudsen Papers, National Automotive History Collection, Detroit Public Library.

National Association of Manufacturers Collection, Hagley Business History Museum, Wilmington, Delaware.

War Production Board Records, National Archives, Washington, DC.

Report of the Special Committee on Investigation of the Munitions Industry, U.S. Senate, 74th Congress, Second Session, February 24, 1936.

Appropriations Committee, U.S. House of Representatives, 78th Congress, First Session, Higgins Contracts, Executive Hearings, Part 3.

Special Committee Investigating the National Defense Program, U.S. Senate, 80th Congress, First Session, Part 40, July–August 1947.

AMERICAN MACHINIST
May 14, 1941
June 11, 1941
June 25, 1941
December 10, 1941
November 12, 1942
July 6, 1944

BUSINESS WEEK
December 9, 1940
March 15, 1941
May 10, 1941
May 24, 1941
January 17, 1942

DETROIT NEWS
May 3, 1937
May 28, 1940

FORTUNE
April 1941
July 1943
August 1943

LIFE
March 31, 1941
November 30, 1942
June 5, 1944

THE NATION
November 1940

TIME

June 12, 1940

June 17, 1940

April 28, 1941

November 4, 1941

January 19, 1942

July 27, 1942

November 16, 1942

VITAL SPEECHES OF THE DAY

April 1, 1941

WASHINGTON POST

May 14, 1940

December 23, 1941

Personal interview with Clay Bedford Jr., October 17, 2009.

Personal interview with Peter Bedford, November 3, 2009.

Personal interview with Frederick Eberstadt, May 11, 2010.

Personal interview with Judith Knudsen Christie, November 2011.

Army and Navy Journal. *United States at War: December 7, 1942–
    December 7, 1943*. Washington, DC: Army and Navy Journal, 1943.

Arnold, H. H. *Global Mission*. New York: Harper and Brothers, 1949.

Automotive Council for War Production. *Freedom's Arsenal: The Story
    of the Automotive Council for War Production*. Detroit: Automotive
    Manufacturers' Association, 1950.

Baruch, Bernard. *Baruch: The Public Years*. New York: Henry Holt, 1957.

Beasley, Norman. *Knudsen: A Biography*. New York: McGraw-Hill,
    1947.

Bingay, Malcolm. *Detroit Is My Home Town*. Indianapolis: Bobbs-
    Merrill, 1946.

Bloch, Mark. *Strange Defeat*. New York: Norton, 1968.

Blum, John Morton. *From the Morgenthau Diaries*. Vol. 2: *The Years of
    Urgency*. New York: Houghton Mifflin, 1965.

Borth, Christy. *Masters of Mass Production*. Indianapolis: Bobbs–Merrill, 1945.

Buhite, Russell, and David Levy, eds. *FDR's Fireside Chats*. Norman: University of Oklahoma Press, 1992.

Catton, Bruce. *War Lords of Washington*. New York: Harcourt, Brace, 1948.

Cherne, Leo. *Your Business Goes to War*. Boston: Houghton Mifflin, 1942.

Chrysler, Walter. *Life of an American Workman*. New York: Dodd and Mead, 1950.

Churchill, Winston. *The Second World War*. Vol. 5: *Closing the Ring*. New York: Bantam, 1962.

Clawson, Angela. *Shipyard Diary of a Woman Welder*. New York: Penguin Books, 1944.

Coleman, Charles H. *Shipbuilding Activities of the NDAC and OPM, Report 18, Policy Analysis and Records, War Production Board*. Washington, DC: Government Printing Office, 1945.

Colville, John. *The Fringes of Power: 10 Downing Street Diaries*. Vol. 1: *1939–October 1941*. London: Hodder and Stoughton, 1985.

Cooke, Alistair. *The American Home Front 1941–1942*. New York: Atlantic Monthly Press, 2006.

Devereux, James. *The Story of Wake Island*. New York: Grosset and Dunlap, 1974.

Finney, Burnham. *Arsenal of Democracy: How Industry Builds Our Defense*. New York: McGraw-Hill, 1941.

General Motors Corporation. *General Motors Annual Report, 1945*.

———. *A History of Eastern Aircraft Division*. Linden, NJ: Eastern Aircraft, 1944.

Grant, Katie. "Wartime Memoirs," Rosie the Riveter Trust, www.rosietheriveter.org/memory.htm.

Groves, Leslie. *Now It Can Be Told: The Story of the Manhattan Project*. New York: Da Capo Press, 1975.

Gunther, John. *Inside U.S.A.* New York: Harper and Brothers, 1947.

Hartley, J. A. "The Public's View of War and Profits." National Association of Manufacturers, May 1942.

Ickes, Harold. *The Secret Diary of Harold Ickes, 1939–1941*. Vol 3. New York: Simon and Schuster, 1954.

Janeway, Eliot. *The Struggle for Survival: A Chronicle of Economic Mobilization In World War II.* New Haven, CT: Yale University Press, 1951.

Jones, Jesse H. *Fifty Billion Dollars: My Thirteen Years with the RFC, 1932–1945.* New York: Macmillan, 1951.

Kenney, George C. *General Kenney Reports: A Personal History of the Pacific War.* Washington, DC: U.S. Air Force, 1997.

Kimball, Warren, ed. *Churchill and Roosevelt: The Complete Correspondence.* Princeton, NJ: Princeton University Press, 1984.

Kinney, John. *Wake Island Pilot: A World War II Memoir.* Washington, DC: Potomac Books, 1995.

Knudsen, William. "How the Chevrolet Company Applies Its Own Slogan to Production," *Industrial Management* 76 (August 1927).

LeMay, Curtis. *Superfortress: The Story of the B-29 and American Air Power.* New York: McGraw-Hill, 1988.

Lindbergh, Charles. *The Wartime Journals of Charles A. Lindbergh.* New York: Harcourt Brace Jovanovich, 1970.

Lloyd George, David. *War Memoirs.* Boston: Little, Brown, 1934.

National Defense Advisory Commission. *Minutes of the Advisory Commission to the Council of National Defense: June 12, 1940 to October 22, 1941.* Washington, DC: Government Printing Office, 1946.

Nelson, Donald. *Arsenal of Democracy: The Story of American War Production.* New York: Harcourt, Brace, 1946.

Nichols, H. G., ed. *Washington Dispatches 1943–1945: Weekly Political Reports from the British Embassy.* Chicago: University of Chicago Press, 1981.

Office of Production Management. *Minutes of the Council of the Office of Production Management: December 21, 1940, to January 14, 1942.* Washington, DC: Government Printing Office, 1946.

Sloan, Alfred P. Jr. *Adventures of a White-Collar Man.* New York: Doubleday, 1941.

———. *My Years with General Motors.* New York: Doubleday, 1964.

———. "Organization Study." In Alfred D. Chandler, ed., *Strategy and Structure: Chapters in the History of American Industrial Enterprise.* Cambridge, MA: MIT Press, 1962.

Smith, Holland M. *Coal and Brass*. Washington, DC: U.S. Marine
    Corps, 1991.

Sorensen, Charles. *My Forty Years with Ford*. New York: Norton,
    1956.

Spangenberg, George. "Oral History Interview," 1990, www
    .georgespangenberg.com/gasoralhistory.pdf.

Stettinius, Edward. *Lend-Lease: Weapon for Victory*. New York:
    Macmillan, 1944.

Stimson, Henry, and McGeorge Bundy. *On Active Service in Peace and
    War*. New York: Harper and Brothers, 1948.

Strauss, Lewis. *Men and Decisions*. New York: Popular Library, 1963.

Taylor, Fred, ed. *The Goebbels Diaries 1939–1941*. New York: Putnam,
    1982.

U.S. Civilian Production Administration. *Industrial Mobilization for War:
    History of the War Production Board and Predecessor Agencies, 1940–
    1945*. Vol. 1: *Program and Administration*. Washington, DC:
    Government Printing Office, 1947.

U.S. Navy, Division of Naval Intelligence. *United States Naval Vessels
    [1946]*. Atglen, PA: Shiffer Military History, 1996.

War Production Board. *Minutes of the War Production Board: January 20,
    1942, to October 9, 1945*. Washington, DC: Government Printing
    Office, 1946.

SECONDARY SOURCES

Abbott, Carl. *Greater Portland: Urban Life and Landscape in the Pacific
    Northwest*. Philadelphia: University of Pennsylvania Press, 2001.

Adams, Stephen. *Mr. Kaiser Goes to Washington: The Rise of a
    Government Entrepreneur*. Chapel Hill: University of North Carolina
    Press, 1997.

Albion, Robert G. *Forrestal and the Navy*. New York: Columbia
    University Press, 1962.

Ambrose, Stephen. *The Wild Blue: The Men and Boys Who Flew the
    B-24s over Germany*. New York: Simon and Schuster, 2001.

American National Biography. Oxford: Oxford University Press, 1999.

Ballantine, Duncan. *U.S. Naval Logistics in the Second World War*.
    Princeton, NJ: Princeton University Press, 1947.

Barone, Michael. *Our Country: The Shaping of America from Roosevelt to Reagan*. New York: Free Press, 1990.

Baumol, William, Robert Litan, and Carl Schramm. *Good Capitalism, Bad Capitalism, and the Economics of Growth and Prosperity*. New Haven, CT: Yale University Press, 2007.

Birdsall, Steve. *Saga of the Superfortress*. New York: Doubleday, 1980.

Blum, Alfred. "Birth and Death of the M-Day Plan." In Harold Stein, ed., *American Civil-Military Decisions: A Book of Case Studies*. Tuscaloosa, AL: University of Alabama Press, 1963.

————. *V Was for Victory: Politics and American Culture During World War II*. New York: Harcourt Brace Jovanovich, 1976.

Bowman, Martin. *Combat Legend: B-24 Liberator*. Shrewsbury, UK: Airlife Publishing, 2003.

Brinkley, David. *Washington Goes to War*. New York: Knopf, 1988.

Broehl, Wayne. *Precision Valley: The Machine Tool Companies of Springfield, Vermont*. Englewood Cliffs, NJ: Prentice-Hall, 1959.

Bunker, John. *Liberty Ships: The Ugly Ducklings of World War II*. Annapolis, MD: Naval Institute Press, 1972.

Clive, Alan. *State of War: Michigan in World War II*. Anne Arbor: University of Michigan Press, 1976.

Collison, Tom. *The Superfortress Is Born*. New York: Duell, Sloan and Pearce, 1945.

Connery, Robert. *The Navy and the Industrial Mobilization in World War II*. Princeton, NJ: Princeton University Press, 1951.

Crabb, Richard. *Birth of a Giant: The Men and Incidents That Gave America the Motor Car*. Philadelphia: Chilton, 1970.

Craven, W. F., and J. L. Cate. *The Army Air Forces in World War II*. Vol. 1. Washington, DC: Office of Air Force History, 1955.

Davis, Kenneth. *FDR: The War President, 1940–1943: A History*. New York: Random House, 2000.

Davis, M.W.R. *Detroit's Wartime Industry: Arsenal of Democracy*. Mount Pleasant, SC: Arcadia Publishing, 2007.

Eiler, Keith. *Mobilizing America: Robert Patterson and the War Effort, 1942–45*. Ithaca, NY: Cornell University Press, 1997.

Farber, David. *Sloan Rules: Alfred Sloan and the Triumph of General Motors*. Chicago: University of Chicago Press, 2002.

Fink, James, "William Signius Knudsen." In George May, ed., *The Automotive Industry 1920–1980*. New York: Facts on File, 1989.

Fisher, David. *A Race on the Edge of Time: Radar—The Decisive Weapon of World War II*. New York: McGraw-Hill, 1988.

Fleming, Thomas. *The New Dealers' War*. New York: Basic Books, 2001.

Fossedal, Gregory. *Our Finest Hour: Will Clayton, the Marshall Plan, and the Triumph of Democracy*. Stanford, CA: Hoover Institution Press, 1993.

Foster, Mark. *Henry J. Kaiser: Builder of the American West*. Austin: University of Texas Press, 1989.

Franklin, Roger. *The Defender: The Story of General Dynamics*. New York: Harper and Row, 1986.

Fraser, Steve. *Labor Will Rule: Sidney Hillman and the Rise of American Labor*. New York: Free Press, 1991.

Friedel, Frank. *Franklin D. Roosevelt: A Rendezvous with Destiny*. Boston: Little, Brown, 1990.

Gannon, Michael. *Operation Drumbeat*. New York: Harper and Row, 1990.

Gaston, James. *Planning the American Air War*. Washington, DC: National Defense University Press, 1982.

Geer, Mary Wells. *Boeing's Ed Wells*. Seattle: University of Washington Press, 1992.

Giddins, Gary. *Bing Crosby: A Pocketful of Dreams—The Early Years, 1903–1940*. Boston: Little, Brown, 2001.

Goodwin, Doris Kearns. *No Ordinary Time: Franklin and Eleanor Roosevelt: The Home Front in World War II*. New York: Simon and Schuster, 1994.

Green, Michael, and James Brown. *M4 Sherman at War*. Minneapolis: Zenith Books, 2007.

Gropman, Alan. "Industrial Mobilization." In Alan Gropman, ed., *The Big "L": American Logistics in World War II*. Washington, DC: Government Printing Office, 1997.

Gurney, Gene. *Journey of the Giants*. New York: Coward-McCann, 1961.

Gustin, Lawrence. *Billy Durant: Creator of General Motors*. Grand Rapids, MI: Eerdmans, 1973.

Harrison, Mark. "Resource Mobilization for World War II: The USA, UK, USSR, and Germany, 1938–1945." *Economic History Review* 41:2, 1988.

Heiner, Albert. *Henry J. Kaiser: Western Colossus.* San Francisco: Halo Books, 1991.

Hemphill, W. Edwin, ed. *Pursuits of War: The People of Charlottesville and Albemarle County, Virginia, in the Second World War.* Charlottesville, VA: Albemarle County Historical Society, 1948.

Higgs, Robert. *Depression, War, and Cold War: Studies in Political Economy.* Oxford: Oxford University Press, 2006.

Holl, Richard. *From the Boardroom to the War Room: America's Corporate Liberals and FDR's Preparedness Program.* Rochester, NY: Rochester University Press, 2005.

Holley, Irwin Burton. *Buying Aircraft: Materiel Procurement for the Army Air Forces.* Washington, DC: Office of the Chief of Military History, 1964.

Hounshell, David. *From the American System to Mass Production, 1800–1932.* Baltimore: Johns Hopkins University Press, 1984.

Hyde, Charles. *Riding the Roller Coaster: A History of the Chrysler Corporation.* Detroit: Wayne State University Press, 2003.

Kampelman, Max. *The Communist Party vs. the CIO.* New York: Arno Press, 1971.

Kaplan, Fred. *Wizards of Armageddon.* New York: Simon and Schuster, 1983.

Kenney, David. *Minnesota Goes to War.* St. Paul, MN: Minnesota Historical Society Press, 2005.

Kershaw, Ian. *Fateful Choices: Ten Decisions That Changed the World, 1940–1941.* New York: Penguin Press, 2007.

Kuhn, Arthur. *GM Passes Ford, 1918–1938.* University Park: Pennsylvania State University Press, 1986.

Kirkpatrick, Charles. *An Unknown Future and a Doubtful Present: Writing the Victory Plan.* Washington, DC: Center for Military History, U.S. Army, 2010.

Koistinen, Paul. "Warfare and Power Relations in America." In James Titus, ed., *The Home Front and War in the Twentieth Century: The American Experience in Comparative Perspective: Proceedings of the Tenth*

Air Force Academy Military History Symposium. Washington, DC: Office of Air Force History, 1984.

Lacey, Jim. *Keep from All Thoughtful Men: How U.S. Economists Won World War II*. Annapolis, MD: Naval Institute Press, 2011.

Lane, Frederick C. *Ships for Victory: A History of Shipbuilding Under the U.S. Maritime Commission*. Baltimore: Johns Hopkins University Press, 1951.

Langer, William, and S. Everett Gleason. *The Undeclared War, 1940–1941*. New York: Harper and Brothers, 1953.

Langworth, Richard. *Kaiser-Frazer: The Last Onslaught on Detroit*. Detroit: Automobile Quarterly Press, 1975.

Leighton, Richard, and Robert Coakley. *Global Logistics and Strategy 1940–1943*. Washington, DC: Center of Military History, 1995.

———. *Global Logistics and Strategy 1943–1945*. Washington, DC: Center of Military History, 1968.

Livesay, Harold. *American Made: Shapers of the American Economy*. 2nd edition. New York: Pearson/Longmans, 2007.

Lotchin, Roger. *The Bad City in the Good War*. Bloomington, IN: Indiana University Press, 2003.

Lukacs, John. *The Duel: The Eighty-Day Struggle Between Churchill and Hitler*. New York: Ticknor and Fields, 1990.

Mann, Robert. *The B-29 Superfortress Chronology, 1934–1960*. Jefferson, NC: McFarland, 2009.

Mansfield, Harold. *Vision: A Saga of the Sky*. New York: Duell, Sloan and Pearce, 1956.

Middlebrook, Martin. *Convoy*. New York: William Morrow, 1976.

Millis, Walter. *Arms and Men: A Study in American Military History*. New York: Putnam, 1956.

Murray, G. E. Patrick. *Bomber Missions*. New York: Barnes and Noble, 2006.

Nash, Gerald. *World War II and the West*. Lincoln: University of Nebraska Press, 1990.

Nevins, Allan. *Ford: Expansion and Challenge, 1915–1933*. New York: Scribner, 1954.

———. *Ford: Decline and Rebirth, 1933–1962*. New York: Scribner, 1963.

Novick, David, Melvin Anshen, and W. C. Truppner. *Wartime Production Controls*. New York: Columbia University Press, 1949.

O'Callaghan, Timothy. *Ford in Service to America*. Jefferson, NC: McFarland, 2009.

Ohly, John. *Industrialists in Olive Drab: The Emergency Operation of Private Industries During World War II*. Washington, DC: Center of Military History, U.S. Army, 2000.

Perret, Geoffrey. *Days of Sadness, Years of Triumph: The American People 1939–1945*. New York: Coward, McCann, and Geoghegan, 1973.

———. *Winged Victory: The Army Air Force in World War II*. New York: Random House, 1993.

Phillips, Cabell. *The 1940s: Decade of Triumph and Turmoil*. New York: Macmillan, 1975.

Pogue, Forrest. *George C. Marshall*. Vol. 2: *Ordeal and Hope, 1939–1942*. London: MacGibbon and Kee, 1964.

Quivik, Frederick. *Kaiser's Richmond Yards*. National Park Service: Historic American Engineering Record, 2004.

Rae, John B. *Climb to Greatness: The American Aircraft Industry, 1920–1960*. Cambridge, MA: MIT Press, 1968.

———. *The Road and Car in American Life*. Cambridge, MA: MIT Press, 1971.

Reynolds, Tom. *From Munich to Pearl Harbor: Roosevelt's America and the Origins of the Second World War*. Chicago: Dee Publishing, 2001.

Rhodes, Richard. *The Making of the Atomic Bomb*. New York: Touchstone, 1986.

Sawyer, L.A., and W. H. Mitchell. *The Liberty Ships*. Newton Abbot, UK: David and Charles, 1970.

Schock, Barbara Forgy. "The Prairie Shipyard." www.thezephyr.com.

Schwartz, James. *Frederick V. Geier, 1893–1981*. Cincinnati: Cincinnati Museum Center, 2002.

Skousen, Mark. *The Big Three in Economics: Adam Smith, Karl Marx, and John Maynard Keynes*. London: M. E. Sharpe, 2007.

Smith, R. Elberton. *The Army and Economic Mobilization*. Washington, DC: Center of Military History, 1991.

Smith, Starr, Steve Ganson, and Walter Cronkite. *Jimmy Stewart, Bomber Pilot*. Minneapolis: Zenith Press, 2005.

Sobel, Robert. *The Worldly Economists*. New York: Free Press, 1980.

Somers, Herman. *Presidential Agency: OWMR, the Office of War Mobilization and Reconversion*. Cambridge, MA: Harvard University Press, 1950.

Spector, Ronald. *Eagle Against the Sun: The American War with Japan*. New York: Free Press, 1985.

Stevens, Joseph. *Hoover Dam: An American Adventure*. Norman: University of Oklahoma Press, 1988.

Strahan, Jerry. *Andrew Jackson Higgins and the Boats That Won World War II*. Baton Rouge: Louisiana State University Press, 1994.

Taylor, A.J.P. *The Origins of the Second World War*. Greenwich, CT: Fawcett, 1966.

Thayer, Harry. *Management of the Hanford Engineering Works in World War II*. New York: American Society of Civil Engineers Press, 1996.

Thomas, Evan. *Sea of Thunder*. New York: Simon and Schuster, 2006.

Thomson, Harry, and Lida Mayo. *The Ordnance Department: Procurement and Supply*. Washington, DC: Center of Military History, 1960.

Thruelson, Richard. *The Grumman Story*. New York: Praeger, 1976.

Tillman, Barrett. *Clash of the Carriers: The True Story of the Marianas Turkey Shoot of World War II*. New York: New American Library, 2005.

Timmons, Bascom. *Jesse H. Jones: The Man and the Statesman*. New York: Holt, 1956.

Tooz, Adam. *Wages of Destruction: The Making and Breaking of the Nazi Economy*. New York: Penguin Books, 2008.

Utley, Jonathan. *Going to War with Japan 1937–1941*. Knoxville: University of Tennessee Press, 1985.

Vander Meulen, Jacob. *Building the B-29*. Washington, DC: Smithsonian Museum Press, 1995.

Van der Vat, Dan. *The Atlantic Campaign: World War II's Great Struggle at Sea*. New York: Harper and Row, 1988.

Vatter, Harold. *The U.S. Economy in World War II*. New York: Columbia University Press, 1985.

Walton, Francis. *The Miracle of World War II: How American Industry Made Victory Possible*. New York: Macmillan, 1956.

Ward, James. *The Fall of the Packard Motor Company*. Stanford, CA: Stanford University Press, 1995.

White, Graham. *Allied Aircraft Piston Engines of World War II*. Warrendale, PA: Society of Automotive Engineers, 1995.

Whitehead, Don. *The Dow Story: The History of the Dow Chemical Company*. New York: McGraw-Hill, 1968.

Winchester, James, ed. *American Military Aircraft: A Century of Innovation*. New York: Metro Books, 2005.

Wolf, Donald F. *Big Dams and Big Dreams: The Six Companies Story*. Norman: University of Oklahoma Press, 1996.

Woodbury, David. *Builders for Battle: How the Pacific Naval Air Bases Were Constructed*. New York: E. P. Dutton, 1946.

Yellin, Emily. *Our Mothers' War: American Women at Home and at the Front During World War II*. New York: Free Press, 2004.

Yenne, Bill. *The American Aircraft Factory in World War II*. Minneapolis: Zenith Press, 2010.

INDEX

NOTE: Italicized page numbers refer to picture captions.
FDR refers to Franklin Delano Roosevelt.

ABOUT THE AUTHOR

ARTHUR HERMAN earned his PhD in history at the Johns Hopkins University and is currently a visiting scholar at the American Enterprise Institute. He is the *New York Times* bestselling author of *How the Scots Invented the Modern World,* a Pulitzer Prize finalist for *Gandhi & Churchill,* and a regular columnist for the *New York Post.* He lives in Charlottesville, Virginia, with his wife, Beth, who is a painter and an author of children's books.

ABOUT THE TYPE

This book was set in Bembo, a typeface based on an old-style Roman face that was used for Cardinal Bembo's tract *De Aetna* in 1495. Bembo was cut by Francisco Griffo in the early sixteenth century. The Lanston Monotype Machine Company of Philadelphia brought the well-proportioned letter forms of Bembo to the United States in the 1930s.